Jewish Autonomy
in a Slave Society

THE EARLY MODERN AMERICAS

Peter C. Mancall, Series Editor

Volumes in the series explore neglected aspects of
early modern history in the western hemisphere.
Interdisciplinary in character, and with a special
emphasis on the Atlantic World from 1450 to 1850,
the series is published in partnership with the
USC-Huntington Early Modern Studies Institute.

Jewish Autonomy in a Slave Society

Suriname in the Atlantic World,

1651–1825

Aviva Ben-Ur

PENN

UNIVERSITY OF PENNSYLVANIA PRESS

PHILADELPHIA

Published by
University of Pennsylvania Press
Philadelphia, Pennsylvania 19104-4112
www.upenn.edu/pennpress

Printed in the United States of America
on acid-free paper
1 3 5 7 9 10 8 6 4 2

Library of Congress Cataloging-in-Publication Data

Names: Ben-Ur, Aviva, author.
Title: Jewish Autonomy in a Slave Society : Suriname in the Atlantic world,
   1651–1825 / Aviva Ben-Ur.
Other titles: Early modern Americas.
Description: Philadelphia : University of Pennsylvania Press, [2020] | Series: Early
   modern Americas | Includes bibliographical references and index.
Identifiers: LCCN 2019044559 | ISBN 9780812252118 (hardcover)
Subjects: LCSH: Jews—Suriname—History. | Slavery—Suriname. |
   Suriname—History—To 1814. | Suriname—Ethnic relations.
Classification: LCC F2431.J4 B455 | DDC 988.3/004924—dc23
LC record available at https://lccn.loc.gov/2019044559

CONTENTS

Jews, Slavery, and Suriname
in the Atlantic World

Since Candide first beheld him in 1759, the "negroe stretched upon the ground" has become paradigmatic of the brutality of Suriname's slave regime. This "poor man," whose right hand was severed during a sugar mill accident, and whose left leg was amputated by his master in retribution for absconding, remains nameless in the novella. But neither his identity nor even the basic facts about colonial Suriname were of any significance in the satirical *Candide*, for Voltaire, born in 1694 as François-Marie Arouet, inserted the slave encounter as an afterthought, as a camouflaged jibe directed at his swindling Dutch publisher Johannes van Duren. The man's last name in garbled form became that of the "cunning" Surinamese slave owner, Vanderdendur, a pseudonym meant to evoke the French expression *dent dure*, or "scathingly critical." Voltaire never even visited Suriname. He was apparently unaware that the lingua franca of slaves was Sranan Tongo, rather than Dutch, that most unfree people in the colony practiced Afro-Creole spiritual traditions, instead of Christianity, and that runaways were punished with the severance of an Achilles tendon, not with the removal of an entire limb. Nor did he seem to mind that ships to Suriname sailed and arrived from North America and the Dutch Republic, not Buenos Aires, Venice, or Bordeaux, or that to reach Suriname from another land one passed through rainforest, rather than desert. Not even the name of the capital city, Paramaribo, was of concern to Voltaire—he misidentified it reductively as the "town of Surinam."[1]

In a parallel way, much of what is commonly known about Jews in hemispheric American slave societies—particularly their association with the Atlantic slave trade and slave ownership—also materialized from an

intention to defame rather than to anchor knowledge in credible sources
and analysis. *The Secret Relationship Between Blacks and Jews*, published
anonymously by the "Historical Research Department" of the Nation of
Islam in 1991, contends that Jews played a disproportionate role in the African slave trade. It sparked a national debate about history, epistemology of
the past, and particularly the (perceived) social and economic relationships
between U.S. Jews and African Americans in the twentieth century, the
modern-day preoccupation that provided the impetus for the book's creation. The volume's assignment as required reading in college courses
sparked public discourse that typically disintegrated into diatribes identifying Jews as the utmost oppressors of blacks or into the shopworn apologia
that Jews, because of their own experience of persecution in Christian
Europe, were benevolent masters or ardent Civil Rights activists who participated in the liberation movement beyond their proportion in the larger
white population.[2]

In the ensuing quarter of a century, even the archivally driven works
stimulated by the controversy remained straitjacketed within a binary that
framed Jews as either persecutors or protectors of enslaved Africans and their
descendants.[3] Eli Faber's *Jews, Slaves, and the Slave Trade: Setting the Record
Straight* (1998) was the first to empirically refute the conclusion that Jews
dominated the slave trade as financiers and merchants.[4] Jonathan Schorsch
followed in 2004 with his *Jews and Blacks in the Early Modern World*, an
erudite history of ideas, experiences, and legislation, which argues that Atlantic and Mediterranean Jews of European origin did not differ from the majority of white Christians among whom they lived in terms of attitudes and
behavior toward people of African origin.[5] Schorsch prepared the ground
for his opus with a biting journal article, published in 2000, lambasting
twentieth-century Jewish historians for their apologetic stance toward Jewish
involvement in medieval and early modern slaveholding.[6] Even scholars who
refuted the representation of Jews as especially cruel slave owners transmitted
an implicit indictment against their modern-day descendants. Wieke Vink,
who provided a refreshing analysis of Surinamese Jews as "Creole," commented in the pre-publication version of her dissertation (2008) that the
image of the persecuted Jew in contemporary historiography "in an era of
continued violence in Palestine . . . is increasingly problematic; but also in a
Surinamese historical context . . . largely untenable."[7]

For the history of Suriname, though, these findings are either inconse-
quential or axiomatic. Does it really matter whether or not Jews (or any

other ethnic group) were at the forefront of the slave trade? Can we even ask if Jews were "mild" or "harsh" slave owners so many decades after scholars definitively disproved the cultural determinism of Frank Tannenbaum, who argued in 1946: "better a slave in the Catholic Iberian colonies than in the Protestant British Caribbean or U.S. South"?[8] Was it really possible for Jews, or anyone for that matter, to exist in a slave society while remaining largely impervious to its brutality, or to conduct themselves according to the dictates of post-slavery interpretations of the Hebrew Bible, treating their human possessions as chattel in name only?[9] It is not only the richness of the archives that provides a clear answer, a resounding "no." It is the very nature of slave society itself. Slave societies, as students of ancient Roman history have also observed, have always produced an inevitable mixture of populations.[10] And it is this very mingling that hurls history and its actors into exceptionally unanticipated directions.

* * *

Jewish Autonomy in a Slave Society explores the unforeseen social consequences of living in a Dutch colony characterized by both extreme coercion and unprecedented autonomy. Suriname was centered on the "Wild Coast" or "Guiana," a vast area that stretched from Venezuela to Brazil. Roughly the size of the State of Georgia in the United States of America, Suriname borders the Atlantic Ocean to its north and is bounded by French Guiana to the east, English-speaking Guyana to the west, and Portuguese-speaking Brazil to the south. The northern coast of South America was a region where the English, French, and Dutch had traded since the late sixteenth century. Suriname was first colonized in 1651 under the proprietary rule of Francis Willoughby of Parham (1614–66). It passed virtually without bloodshed from English to Dutch hands in 1667 when a Dutch naval squadron attacked. Amid frequent warfare, only two colonies on the continent's northern coast remained Dutch for a prolonged time: Berbice, which prevailed from 1627 through 1796, in present-day Guyana, and Suriname, which remained a Dutch colony for most of the three centuries leading up to its independence in 1975.

In early modernity, Suriname was one of two major Caribbean possessions under Dutch rule, the other being Curaçao, an island at a distance of 1,028 miles (1,654 kilometers) from Suriname's capital city of Paramaribo. Both had fallen under Dutch sovereignty during the so-called "Dutch moment in Atlantic history," a period spanning the first eight decades of the seventeenth century and characterized by imperial ambition, "large-scale deployment of troops and warships, and rapid colonial expansion and contraction."[11] After the loss in the seventeenth century of Brazil and New Netherland, a territory that extended from Albany, New York, to Delaware, the Dutch Atlantic had constricted to several fortresses along the coast of West Africa, the Guianas, and six Caribbean islands.[12] While Curaçao served as a major commercial entrepôt, and produced crops solely for local consumption, Suriname was largely agrarian, its economy heavily based on the export of sugar, coffee, and cacao. Throughout the eighteenth century, the crops Suriname sold to the Dutch metropole were "more voluminous and valuable" than the harvests collectively produced by the three other Dutch colonies of the Guianas, Berbice, Demerara, and Essequibo.[13]

This tropical produce was cultivated, harvested, and processed by multi-ethnic and multilingual people, most of whom originated in the vast region extending some 2,200 miles between the Gold Coast (roughly coinciding with modern-day Ghana), the Slave Coast (coinciding with the coastal regions of present-day Togo, Benin, and western Nigeria), and Loango-Angola (between the Congo River and what is today Cameroon).[14] Forcibly transported from West Africa to the Americas through the Atlantic slave trade, this labor force comprised upwards of 90 percent of Suriname's population by the late eighteenth century.[15] Sugar is the main explanation. It was a labor-intensive crop that relied on a huge workforce—three times as many laborers per acre as tobacco cultivation—and required extensive labor division and specialization, including ground preparation, weeding, harvesting, transporting cane to the mills, boiling, grinding, and curing the juice.[16] It is thus unsurprising that enslaved people constituted at least 80 percent of the population of most Caribbean sugar colonies, regardless of the imperial jurisdiction under which they were governed.[17]

The extreme brutality executed against Suriname's enslaved population, as historians now universally agree, was a function not of the ethnicity or religion of slave owners, nor of Dutch rule, but rather of sugar production itself. The cultivation, boiling, and milling of the sweet cane, together with the colony's extensive water management system, which involved the digging, maintenance, and repair of polders, translated into a harsh disciplinary regime and ceaseless, mortal toil that so often incited the enslaved to flight or rebellion.[18] Although exports of coffee, cacao, cotton, and hardwood became increasingly significant to the Surinamese economy over time, sugar remained the main export product throughout the period of slavery, with the exception of the seventy-year interval preceding 1820, during which time it was still a significant product.[19]

Suriname was a slave society par excellence. In "societies with slaves," such as those of the U.S. North, slavery was not the mainstay of the economy and that institution did not influence every economic, social, and cultural niche.[20] By contrast, a slave society, as defined by most scholars, was a society whose economy was largely dependent on slave labor. If this labor force were to have been suddenly freed or removed, the entire economy would have collapsed. In slave societies, at least one-third of the population was held in bondage for an extended period of time and slavery fundamentally defined local economies, societies, and cultures.[21] With upwards of 90 percent of its population in chains by the late eighteenth century, Suriname was a colony "overqualified" for the slave society label. As Michel-Rolph Trouillot notes with only slight exaggeration, the people who lived in such societies, "free or not, lived there because there were slaves."[22]

The Jewish presence in Suriname was closely interrelated with the colony's slave regime. A diasporic people with roots in the ancient Middle East, Jews had lived in Christian Europe since the fourth century CE, with few exceptions, as the continent's only religious nonconformists. Their non-European origins, however, did not fundamentally compromise their racial belonging as whites in the Atlantic World. Whether in seventeenth-century Brazil, the Caribbean, or North America, the whiteness of Jews was never legally questioned by local colonial administrations.[23] So long as they maintained their status as whites, their privilege to be free was also unquestioned. By the 1730s, at least 70 of some 200 plantations that lined the Suriname River were in Jewish hands.[24] Eager to retain and increase the white population, colonial authorities extended to Jews a territorial and communal autonomy unparalleled in the Jewish diaspora of the time. The confidence and insistence with which Jews continually and largely successfully negotiated the safeguarding and expansion of the favors and exceptions they enjoyed over the course of a century and a half speak to the critical role of Jews in the colony both as whites and as planters.

The term "autonomy," derived from the ancient Greek roots meaning "self" and "law," was unknown to early modern peoples.[25] Rather, Jews in Suriname referred to the edicts that established their partial self-rule in the colony as "privileges" (*privilegios* in Portuguese and Spanish; *privilegiën* in Dutch; *privilèges* in French) and their consequent communal ordinances as *ascamot*, the Portuguese-inflected Hebrew word for "agreements." The body of privileges, a direct outgrowth of Dutch policy vis-à-vis Jews in its former colonies in Brazil and in the seventeenth century in what are today French Guiana and Guyana, endowed Surinamese Jews with both a corporate status and a circumscribed political sovereignty, ensconced primarily in their own tribunal.

This colonial arrangement, which obligated all local Jews to belong to the Jewish community, had much in common with its counterpart in medieval European Christendom, where Jews had been cast as "servants of the king," assessing and paying a special annual tax directly to the monarch in return for receiving his or her protection and the privilege of governing their lives by their own regulations and court.[26] But in Suriname, Jews paid the same taxes as other colonists (as well as separate levies to their own community). Their relationship with the local authorities, moreover, was predicated not on a royal alliance in which Jews were legally the property of the king or on the medieval theological view that Jews as Christ-killers were to be relegated to the status of servants to Christians. Rather, their relationship to the colonial government was based on a latitude granted because Jews were sorely needed as planters and as white colonists. The situation in Suriname also departed in significant ways from the Jewish experience in early modern Amsterdam and London and in the English or British colonies, where Jews were typically regarded as members of a voluntary religious society and where the municipal or colonial authorities neither mandated nor enforced adherence to Jewish law, much less belonging in the Jewish community. In these locales, Jews experienced a corporate existence very inconsistently, if at all.[27]

Although a tiny minority in the overall Surinamese population, Jews were among whites a sizable and highly visible group. Through the mid-nineteenth century, Jews comprised one- to two-thirds of the white population. From their first permanent settlement in the 1660s to the abolition of their communal autonomy in 1825, Jews in conversation with colonial authorities were leading agents in the construction of the largest outpost of the Dutch Atlantic. The desperate need for such settlers explains the willingness of authorities not only to accommodate the distinctiveness of Jews but in effect to reward them for it. The negotiation of this autonomy, an ongoing conversation between the local colonial rulers and Jewish leaders, on the one hand, and the fatherland and the colony on the other, determined the contours and self-definition of the Jewish community.

Despite their obvious religious nonconformity, it would be a mistake to conceive of Jews primarily in religious terms, not only because of the central role of descent (as opposed to conversion) in determining Jewish group belonging but also because of the community's pronounced ethnolinguistic features.[28] Up until the modern era, nearly all Jewish diasporic groups cultivated Hebrew- and Aramaic-infused spoken and written vernaculars, while the language of the Bible and rabbinical literature was preserved for the sacred realm. The first and numerically largest group of Jews to settle in Suriname were Portuguese, many of whom had been born as New Christians in the Iberian Peninsula, their circumstances a legacy of more than a century of forced apostasy and its diachronic consequences. These Portuguese settlers had recently converted back to their ancestral Jewish faith in Protestant cities like Amsterdam and London, where they identified not as members of a nation-state but rather as extraterritorial nationals, as members of the "Hebrew" or "Portuguese Jewish nation," or simply as members of the *nação*. Portuguese was their primary written and spoken tongue, but it was increasingly over time a "Luso-Hispanic hybrid idiom" noticeably marked by Hebraicisms and the grammatical peculiarities of what linguists call a speech community. It set Jews linguistically apart from other Portuguese speakers in the Iberian Peninsula and Brazil.[29]

Their community in Suriname paved the way for the influx of hundreds of Ashkenazim, Jews of central and eastern European origin, who began to arrive in the late seventeenth century and spoke a variety of Germanic dialects, often with similar Hebrew and Aramaic derivations. The relatively late arrival of Ashkenazim can be explained by their distinctive migratory patterns. Jews originating in the Iberian Peninsula began to restore an open Jewish presence to Europe's Atlantic coast starting in the 1590s, and from there to the New World, while Ashkenazim tended to move eastward beginning in the fifteenth century, a trend that began to reverse for the latter group in a westerly direction only in the mid-seventeenth century. At that point Ashkenazi Jews, fleeing war and persecution, began to migrate to western Europe in significant numbers and some eventually to the Americas. Demographically, then, Suriname was a microcosm of the broader Atlantic Jewish World, where for roughly the first two hundred years of the Atlantic age, most of the Jewish population was of Iberian origin. The Jewish Caribbean was almost entirely of this same provenance during the Atlantic period.[30]

Suriname was the only early modern Dutch colony with a Jewish population that also included a separate, formally organized Ashkenazi community.[31] In 1695, Ashkenazim numbered 75 individuals or nearly 14 percent of a Jewish community of 550; a century later their presence had burgeoned to 430, nearly one-third of a Jewish population 1,330 strong.[32] Both their later arrival in the colony and the exclusionary nature of the already established Portuguese Jewish settlement prevented most Ashkenazim from taking up the spade. The majority of Ashkenazim lived as petty traders or merchants in Paramaribo, where they established a separate congregation called Neve Salom in 1734.[33] The Ashkenazi presence contributed to the fact that at its peak in the late eighteenth century, Suriname's combined Jewish community numbered around 1,400 individuals, representing the largest Jewish community in the Americas in the second half of the eighteenth century.[34]

In the first eighty years of the colony, Ashkenazim were administratively subsumed within the Portuguese Jewish community, and colonial governments did not distinguish between the two groups, referring simply to "Hebrews" or the "Jewish nation." The original privileges granted under the English, and ratified by the Dutch, identified the beneficiaries not as Portuguese Jews but as "Hebrews."[35] Within the community, however, differences were recognized and maintained through, for example, separate burial grounds. Moreover, once organized as an administratively separate community in the 1730s, Ashkenazim in Dutch Suriname did not enjoy the same legal status as their Portuguese coreligionists. While Portuguese Jews in the colony were accorded periodically negotiated "privileges," Ashkenazim were the recipients of mere "tolerance." Despite their steadily growing population, the emerging affluence of some of their leaders, and the group's institutional separation from Portuguese Jews, only by default did Ashkenazim enjoy some of the privileges of the Portuguese.[36] To a certain extent, the generic terms "Hebrew" and "Jewish" allowed Ashkenazim to ride on the legislative coattails of their Portuguese coreligionists. As Jews, Ashkenazim were accorded the liberty of residence, engagement in trade and agriculture, property ownership (including slaves), and inheritance. But they were denied their own tribunal and barred from homeownership in Jodensavanne.[37] The lack of a body of privileges specific to them informed the nature of their communal ordinances, which have survived only in fragmented form, not having been painstakingly reproduced and expanded upon in multiple copies by successive generations of Jewish scribes and colonial government officials. Moreover, they appear to have been much more limited in content and length than those of their Portuguese coreligionists.[38] The experience of Suriname's Ashkenazi Jews, thus, was less as members of a corporate group than as affiliates of a voluntary association, much like their coreligionists of Amsterdam and London and the English or British colonies.

Suriname was the only colony on the South American mainland that fostered the long-term development of a Jewish community. Despite a few short-lived, communal experiments in the 1660s, Jews were officially barred from settlement in Berbice, Essequibo, and Demerara. The occasional presence of individual Portuguese and Ashkenazi Jews in eighteenth-century Berbice, most of them male, is an exception that proves the rule.[39] This uneven immigration policy was the consequence of decentralization in the metropole, which lacked any "consistent Dutch interest or policy" for its Atlantic possessions. This variance meant that no singular "governmental or legal framework" was imposed on the entire Dutch Atlantic. Although each colony was formally directed by a governor, local power was held mainly in the hands of local planters and merchants, and the population was administered under unique legal forms, including placards (*plakaaten*), which were periodically promulgated but never gathered into a single compendium of colonial law.[40] Dutch metropolitan and colonial decentralization, and the consequent administrative and legal diversity, coupled with the pioneering, uninterrupted presence of Jews in the region since the 1650s, secured Suriname as the preeminent homeland of Jews in the Guianas.

*   *   *

The situation of the Jews in Suriname, like that of their coreligionists of Curaçao, was singular among Atlantic Jewries because it endowed Jews with both corporatism and their own legal jurisdiction. Yet in the extent of liberties enjoyed, Surinamese Jewry diverged even from its sister community. For unlike Curaçao's Jewish chiefs, Surinamese Jewish leaders enjoyed a circumscribed say in determining Suriname's colonial governance, specifically, the privilege of voting for members of Suriname's political council or court (Raad van Politie), a body composed of influential planters. Even more astounding was that Suriname was the only place in the Atlantic World (and perhaps on the entire globe) where Jews possessed their own village, a place called Jodensavanne, or Jews' Savanna, whose plots were in

Portuguese Jewish hands and, according to both colonial and Surinamese Jewish law, could not be alienated. Jewish corporatism and autonomy thus found their fullest expression in Suriname. To locate contemporaneous approximations, one must look beyond the Atlantic World to the Council of the Four Lands in the Polish-Lithuanian Commonwealth and perhaps to Leghorn, both of which have been singled out by scholars as pinnacles of Jewish diasporic autonomy but neither of which gave rise to Jewish villages.[41]

Surinamese autonomy was largely possible because unlike other imperial possessions in the Americas, the colony was founded and, until 1816, ruled largely by personal actors and private companies rather than state agents. These private interests included the Chartered Society of Suriname (Geoctroyeerde Sociëteit van Suriname), a Dutch colonial undertaking that sought to profit from the administration of Suriname and ruled the colony from 1683 to 1795. The Society of Suriname was comprised of three voting participants: the Aerssen van Sommelsdijck family, the city of Amsterdam, and the Dutch West India Company (hereafter "West India Company"), a joint stock company that ruled the Dutch colonies and trading stations in the Atlantic World on behalf of the States General (Staten-Generaal), which represented the seven Dutch provinces and was akin to a federal government.

Moreover, a de facto policy of cultural non-incursion reigned in the Dutch overseas possessions. The metropolitan Dutch population of close to two million residents was too small to exert religious or linguistic hegemony over any of its American colonies. This effective non-interference gave rise to African-origin populations in Suriname and Curaçao that shared neither the official creed nor the language of the local colonial government. Thus, people of African descent, like Jews, were linguistic and religious nonconformists, whether "saltwater" slaves, Afro-Creole bondpeople, Maroons (enslaved Africans who self-manumitted by escaping to the surrounding rainforest), or legally free. Possessing what scholars refer to as "cultural autonomy," these individuals spoke a variety of languages native to West Africa, developed several Creole tongues with heavily West African features, and practiced diverse non-Christian spiritual traditions that defy the Western category of "religion."[42]

Despite its distinctive features, Suriname was in other ways both representative of and connected to the broader Atlantic World. This interconnectedness not only facilitated interimperial legal and illegal trade but also transformed Suriname into a major destination for involuntary African migrants.[43] In Suriname, sugar and other export crops were cultivated, harvested, and processed by unfree Africans and then shipped to the markets of the United Provinces of the Netherlands. As such, Suriname constituted part of the Atlantic World, where people, commodities, diseases, ideas, and technology were regularly exchanged among the four continents of North and South America, Europe, and Africa. On land and in water, the region was the intersection of the western hemisphere's great empires, their colonies, and, beginning in the late eighteenth century, emerging nation-states.

That the Atlantic World should have a Jewish inflection has proven of marginal interest to most historians or has escaped their attention altogether. This is true not only for self-identified Atlantic historians, who tend to recognize the role of Jews in largely economic terms, if at all, but most evidently for scholars of the Jewish past, most of whom are still wed to an ethnonational or ethnoregional paradigm that confines the frame of reference to "colonial American Jews," "early American Jews," "Jews in the Caribbean," or "Sephardi Jews."[44] In the last two decades a handful of Jewish studies scholars aware of the Atlantic history paradigm have made some tentative but useful forays, although some tend to conceive of the Atlantic World as a geographical space rather than as a coherent system of interaction and exchange, and therefore do not apply the methodology of Atlantic historiography.[45] The reasons to include Surinamese Jews as a factor in an interconnected world are not just compelling but, arguably, imperative. The Atlantic World was less a geographical space and more a coherent system of exchange and interaction that preceded the rise of globalism in the nineteenth century. To exclude the Jews, particularly those of the Dutch realm, is to unnecessarily narrow our understanding of this richly interconnected world.

Another compelling reason to include Jews is their potential to deepen our understanding of the African diaspora created by the Atlantic slave trade. Atlantic history has traditionally provided a framework that presumes the relevance of Christianity, African and indigenous spiritual traditions, and increasingly Islam but has generally excluded Judaism as irrelevant. The intersection of the African diaspora with Jewish civilization, so clearly manifest in Suriname, erects a signpost for the undertaking of similar studies elsewhere in the Caribbean. To address the promise of this largely unexplored intersection, this book self-consciously sets forth a new methodology for integrating the Jewish past into Atlantic history, one that

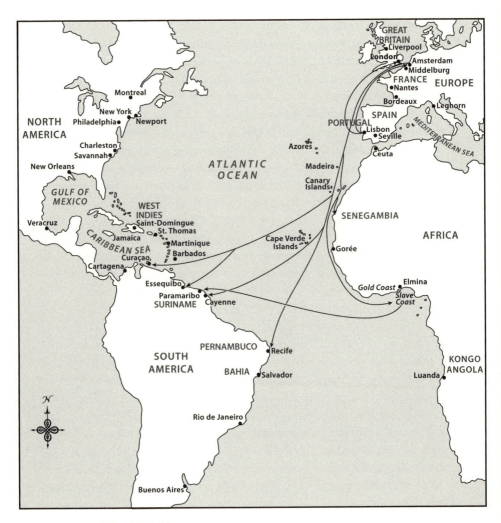

MAP 1. Atlantic World.

combines the obvious religious and economic with less apparent ethnic, racial, linguistic, and especially political approaches. This study thereby proposes four elements that characterize Atlantic Jewish history: the demographic and economic centrality of Caribbean Jewry among hemispheric American Jewries; Portuguese Jewish hegemony among Jews in the Atlantic World; the era of slavery; and the triad of privileges, disabilities, and Jewish Emancipation.[46] The Atlantic Jewish age was a time when the American

Jewish epicenter was not in colonial North America or the United States but in the insular and circum-Caribbean; when for centuries most Atlantic Jews were of Iberian, and not of central or eastern European, origins; when most hemispheric American Jews lived in slave societies; and, beginning in the 1800s, when legal equality gradually began for the first time to be extended to Jews, replacing an earlier system predicated upon an ancien régime of dispensations and restrictions.[47]

David Nassy (1747–1806), the internationally known Surinamese Jewish communal leader, physician, and historian, offered a historiographical model that scholars of the Atlantic Jewish World would still find useful, if not self-evident. In the preface to his *Essai historique sur la colonie de Surinam* (1788), he explained that the history of Surinamese Jews was "so linked and . . . identified with . . . the colony in general," and events involving Jews "so interwoven with those of the other inhabitants of the colony, that it was morally impossible" to separate them.[48] In short, just as one cannot write of Surinamese Jewry without writing of Suriname, one cannot write of the Dutch colony without in some way centering its Jews.

*   *   *

The emergence of a Jewish community in Suriname was intimately tied to its role as an intermediary between the white Christian population and non-white subjugated or pacified groups. In the first place, the colonial government contended with a small but politically significant local Indigenous population, which was at war with the government until the 1680s. Unlike English rule, which practiced divide-and-conquer politics, the Dutch eventually pursued peace with Indigenous people, promoting trade with them and using them as scouts to spot enemy ships. While colonists increasingly enslaved Indigenous people, particularly to replace the rapidly dwindling African population, this tendency was checked by Indigenous uprisings. The tug-of-war ended in 1684, when Governor Sommelsdijck sued for peace, declaring "Indians" free and unenslavable, except in cases of crime.[49] Thereafter, there were no major conflicts between Indigenous peoples and whites.[50] The number of enslaved Indigenous people in the colony fell from 500 in 1671 to 100 in 1684, most of them women.[51] The ban against systematic enslavement and the trade in Indigenous people was pragmatic rather than ideological, a means to keep the peace.[52] Another reason for this limited enslavement is that Indigenous people played a prominent role as intermediaries between colonists and Maroons, sometimes as diplomats, other times as informants for the colonial government.[53]

The colonial government also contended with hundreds of thousands of involuntary African immigrants, as well as Maroons, runaway slaves who established autonomous villages in the rainforest.[54] Dutch authorities strove to thwart the military threat all these non-white groups posed or to exploit their economic potential. For this, European-origin settlers were needed to launch plantations, engage in commerce, and serve as a bulwark against both internal and external forces, particularly along the frontier that divided the tropical forest from land cultivated by slaves and owned by whites.

From a very early stage, the open immigration policy of Suriname included the extension of unsurpassed liberties to Portuguese Jews, who were granted religious freedom and communal autonomy, allowing them to establish their own village, Jodensavanne, which abutted the wilderness, and permitting the operation of Jewish schools and a Jewish court of law responsible for adjudicating all cases involving exclusively Jewish parties and sums up to a fine of ten thousand pounds of sugar. Unlike the situation in other English or British agrarian colonies, notably the islands of Barbados and Jamaica, Jews were hindered neither by restrictions on the number of slaves they could own nor by discriminatory taxes that made their residence nearly impossible. As we have seen, Jewish planters in Suriname also enjoyed the right to vote for members of the Council of Policy, though they could not serve as council members themselves, nor could they ever aspire to become colonial governors. Marriage with Christians was also forbidden them.

Agrarian pursuits also account for the divergence of Suriname's Jewish community from most other Atlantic Jewish settlements. Most Atlantic Jews, including those of the Dutch trading islands of Curaçao and St. Eustatius, were involved in commerce. Like their Huguenot contemporaries, also a primarily urban, exilic group, Portuguese Jews excelled in acquiring the skills needed for large-scale planting and agrarian estate management.[55] The structure of Suriname's Jewish estates and the daily secular life there have been addressed extensively elsewhere, and in most regards, there is nothing to indicate differentiation from Christian-owned plantations.[56] For this reason, this book does not comprehensively explore daily life on Jewish plantations or work relations between Jewish owners and their human property.

On the other hand, observance of the Jewish Sabbath and holidays, the incorporation of select persons of African descent into the community, and the main language of communication among many slaves and their owners did set Jewish estates apart from Christian-owned plantations, distinctions explored primarily in Chapters 3 and 4.

As this book implicitly argues, Jews were neither "kinder" nor exceptionally cruel slave owners. Whether or not they were "better" or "worse" is not even a valid research question for, as Wim Klooster and Gert Oostindie have remarked, all slavery in the Atlantic World "involved a policy of dehumanization and exploitation, and by definition there cannot be anything 'mild' about it."[57] Nor is there any evidence whatsoever that Jewish religious ideology dictated concerns about the suffering of the enslaved. As for other white groups in the Atlantic World whose identity was partly based on spiritual beliefs, including Quakers, participation in slavery was far less an ideological or moral choice than it was a systemic, largely unquestioned reality.[58]

Suriname's capitalistic engine found expression in daily physical torture and a calculus that made it more economically feasible to work Africans to death and replace them with "saltwater slaves" than to ameliorate their conditions in order to lengthen their lives.[59] When the States General assumed partial responsibility for the governance of Suriname in 1682, it stated in a charter that Suriname could not survive without the use of "black slaves or negroes" and guaranteed that the West India Company would import the required number of Africans each year.[60] That same year, 4,000 forced laborers resided in Suriname, a number that swelled to nearly 60,000 by 1774.[61] Due to a combination of high mortality, some of it a function of disease, marronage (the flight of enslaved Africans to the surrounding rainforest), and economic crisis, this figure decreased to 56,000 during the following decade and remained slightly below that range until abolition in 1863. Starting in the late eighteenth century, by one account, 84 to 96 percent of Suriname's population was enslaved. Even on the eve of Emancipation, when the majority of free people in Suriname were of African descent, most residents—69 percent—remained in chains.[62] Long-term statistics forcefully communicate the massive, diachronic loss of life in the colony. At the tail end of the period stretching from 1668 to 1830, during which between 213,000 and 250,000 Africans cumulatively were transported to Suriname, the colony's unfree population hovered in the 50,000s.[63]

Insofar as it gave rise to a deeply ingrained popular awareness of Suriname's destruction of people of African descent, Voltaire's distorted description of brutality was justified. Physical torture was a daily reality in the lives of slaves. Seven distinct street corners in the capital city of Paramaribo, including one intersecting with "Jewish Broadway" (Jodenbreestraat), were reserved for the "Spanish buck" (*Spaansche bok*).[64] This publicly performed infliction entailed positioning the victims cross-handed and cross-legged and, as one visitor described it in the 1770s, tying them to a device, typically a stick looped through the limbs, so that they "could not make the smallest movement." Their backs were then whipped until "their entire skin [was] ripped off" and maggots swarmed on the festering wounds.[65] This form of discipline proved so incendiary that the colonial government restricted its execution to these specific street corners and to the authority of the colonial prosecutor.[66]

Despite restrictive legislation, slaves were tortured by means of the "Spanish buck" on plantations throughout rural Suriname. John Greenwood, a North American artist and chronicler who visited Suriname in the 1750s, once fled an estate because he failed to prevent its master from meting out the torment as punishment for "trivial offences," including the failure of a nursing mother to quiet her baby. After the thrashing, he noted, the flesh was washed with salt and water to prevent putrefaction. But this antiseptic often proved vain, inducing a swarm of larvae and leaving dreadful scars. Greenwood came across horribly disfigured victims of the "Spanish buck" every day.[67] In Jodensavanne, the historic Jewish village of the colony, situated along the banks of the Suriname River, the streets and fence surrounding the synagogue square served as habitual sites for administering the torture.[68] Nor, would it appear, were children spared, although some masters in Suriname deemed a good whipping with a tamarind branch sufficient for the young and tender.[69]

And yet, as common as misery was to the lives of the vast majority of Suriname's residents, plumbing the depths of human suffering does not advance our understanding of the colony's history or of the lives of Africans.[70] Rather, this book takes as its starting point Suriname's Jewish community, and not because it represents the most remarkable or important aggregate of people in the colony or because a study of local Jews necessarily has more explanatory value than any other subject. Suriname's Jews deserve our sustained attention for the following three reasons. First, Jews were the only ethnic group outside of the nominally Dutch Reformed Protestant

FIGURE 1. *The Spanish Buck* (*De spaansche bok*), 1806. Illustration by Christiaan Andriessen. This image depicts Andriessen, a Dutch Christian artist, giving a private tutorial to two pupils while he disciplines their younger brother through mock mimicry of the "Spanish buck" torture. The image communicates awareness in the Dutch metropole of the harsh treatment accorded Africans in Caribbean slave societies.

government who created serial records that stretch across the entire period of slavery and beyond. Second, because Jews formed one-third, and in the first half of the nineteenth century up to one-half to two-thirds, of the white population, their experiences and observations can be considered in many respects representative of life in the colony. Lastly, Surinamese Jews were exceptional among their Atlantic coreligionists in that they admitted a significant number of Eurafricans (and, to a lesser extent, Africans) into their community and regarded them as bona fide Jews. As we will learn, many of these slaves and their descendants articulated their own experiences, particularly if manumitted or freeborn.

Whether any representation of the African experience in the colony of Suriname can ever approach symmetry to its Jewish parallel is highly doubtful, given the paucity of sources written in the voices of the enslaved and their free descendants. Yet their history as refracted through the lenses of Surinamese Jewish sources brings us a bit closer to fulfilling the aspiration of historians to recover subaltern voices. Moreover, Surinamese Jews, like Africans, were a constitutive force in shaping the Atlantic World. They did not simply sustain this world; they helped create it. In sum, the uninterrupted longevity of Jews in the colony, their sustained record-keeping practices, their selective integration of people of African descent, and their statistically significant presence among the white population make Jews a promising entry point for the exploration of the Surinamese colonial past.

*   *   *

This book builds on several generations of excellent scholarship on Jews and Africans of the Atlantic World. Robert Cohen's comparative dissertation on Jewish demography in eighteenth-century London, the West Indies, and early America (1976) broke new ground in his anticipation of the subfield of Atlantic Jewish history, while his *Jews in Another Environment*, a social and cultural study of early modern Suriname (1991), included the first scholarly treatment of a major communal rebellion in the latter half of the eighteenth century led by Jews of African origin.[71] I also owe much to the discernment of Jonathan Schorsch, whose aforementioned opus cast a wide eye on the relationship of Jews to an institution—slavery—that constituted the building blocks of the Atlantic World. The ongoing quest of Natalie Zemon Davis for the "braided histories" of Suriname's African and Jewish populations has served as a beacon to me over the years, while the previously mentioned work by Wieke Vink has proved a touchstone.[72] I have also been deeply influenced by the publications of Gert Oostindie and Alex van Stipriaan on plantation Suriname.[73] Based on a combination of oral history and archival research, the studies of Richard Price provide stunning historical confirmation of the interrelation of Surinamese Maroons and their erstwhile Jewish masters, not to mention a nuanced anthropological analysis of these runaway communities and their present-day descendants.[74] Some of my impressions of Suriname's political history have been shaped or affirmed by the work of Surinamese politician and sociologist Marten Schalkwijk.[75] Many other authors, too numerous to note here, but duly and gratefully cited throughout this book in the endnotes, also helped shape this book in important ways.

Even as I acknowledge these intellectual debts, I am cognizant that *Jewish Autonomy in a Slave Society* departs from previous treatments by approaching Jewishness and Africanness not as essential facts but as by-products of structural signifiers. It is not simply a matter of complementing a nation-based approach to Atlantic history with one that crosses the confines of the nation-state or empire, or acknowledging that religious cultures "also flowed across national boundaries," as Erik Seeman phrases it.[76] The revision that archival investigation demands entails looking beyond essentialist assumptions about what constitutes the characteristics of a specific group. This book's focus on the political lives of Surinamese Jews facilitates their comparison to self-ruling non-white groups, namely Maroons and Indians, and to the autonomous elements of local Afro-Creole cultures and languages. The colonial government's failure to impose the Dutch language and the Protestant Reformed religion on Jews and enslaved Africans allowed these two communities to develop their respective spiritual and linguistic traditions with virtually no outside interference. While it may at first seem incongruous to compare the privileged and protected legal status of Jews with the de facto autonomy of Indians, and of enslaved and free people of African descent, the practical results—civilizations largely free from Dutch cultural influences—are striking.

And there is more, as we can learn from Alex van Stipriaan's exploration of this "unusual parallel." Both Jews and slaves followed a similar trajectory of creolization, a historical process we might define as the creation of "a new culture and new roots."[77] Whereas in the mid-eighteenth century, three-quarters of Suriname's enslaved population had been born in Africa, by the close of the century, these proportions were inverted, marching in step with a parallel phenomenon in the Jewish community. These locally born people of African and Jewish descent regarded Suriname or their individual plantations—and not Africa, Europe, or biblical Israel—as their home and as the land of their ancestors.[78]

One final parallel brings us to the era of enfranchisement. Due to a combination of manumission and high birthrate, the free population of African descent, concentrated in Suriname's only city, burgeoned in the last quarter of the eighteenth century. By the 1790s, nearly one-third of all free persons living in Suriname were freeborn or liberated persons of African ancestry, a proportion that was to nearly double by 1811.[79] The free population of African descent had climbed from 300 in the mid-eighteenth century to 2,889 a half century later, reaching 13,000 by the time of Emancipation in 1863.[80] By the nineteenth century, the majority of manumitters were themselves former slaves or freeborn people with roots in slavery.[81] By law, those who left slavery owed their respect and a certain percentage of their wealth to their previous owners, were enjoined to publicly exhibit submissive behavior before whites, and could be fined or even reenslaved for violating certain social mores, such as appearing in the streets between six in the evening and six in the morning without shoes and stockings.[82] But sumptuary laws and other impediments governing their conduct gradually eroded.[83] In 1799, the evening curfew that restricted their mobility was temporarily lifted and did not recur after 1804.[84] Moreover, all professions except governmental positions were open to free people of African descent, and there were no obstacles to their ownership of land, houses, or slaves.[85] In Paramaribo, males of slave origins entered trades such as carpentry, millwrighting, tailoring, baking, and typesetting, while their female counterparts typically earned their living as seamstresses, ironers, washerwomen, and market sellers. Unlike the experience of their counterparts in the British colonies, free people of African descent in Suriname were permitted to reside anywhere in the city. By 1845, they constituted the largest ethnic group dwelling in the genteel neighborhood of the Gravenstraat, the most affluent quarter of Paramaribo, outnumbering white Christians and Jews by seven to six.[86] Moreover, freeborn people of African origin technically enjoyed the same rights as whites.[87]

The equalizing trend was also manifest within the Jewish community. While any Christian of African descent who could afford it was permitted burial in Paramaribo's Reformed Protestant cemeteries, apparently without ritual distinctions, this was not the case among Jews, who relegated deceased members of African origin to the margins of the cemetery.[88] This began to change at the turn of the nineteenth century. In 1802, for example, Portuguese Jewish leaders banned all distinctions in burial rites between first- and second-class Jews, who were designated by the racially coded terms *jehidim* and *congregantes*, respectively. The practice of reserving separate, and often inferior, cemetery plots for *congregantes*, who were typically African-origin Jews, ceased in 1820. And finally, in 1841, all remaining legal distinctions between the two groups were eliminated in both the Portuguese Jewish and Ashkenazi communities of Suriname.[89] Jews, as a community separate from Christians, were also subject to the new dictates of a society of equals. In 1825, metropolitan authorities abolished communal autonomy in both the Portuguese and Ashkenazi communities, thereby according Jews legal parity with white Christians, at least theoretically.

Upward social and economic mobility increasingly placed free Christians of African descent in direct conflict with indigent whites and particularly with Jews, regardless of class. The relatively recently acquired Christianity of African-origin people gave them social primacy above both white and Eurafrican Jews, even after 1825. While Christians of slave origins were still barred from occupying government positions, as Christians they occupied a first-tier position within the colony to which Jews could not aspire. The rise of free Christians of African descent was for Jews a bitter irony, especially in the numerous cases where Jews themselves had been the manumitters.[90] Thus, the steady enfranchisement of free people of African descent was inversely linked with the emancipation of Jews of whatever background, which was also the case in the British Caribbean.[91]

On the other hand, during the era of enfranchisement the proportion of Jews in the white population increased to two-thirds. This augmentation was mainly due to the tendency of white Christians to return to the fatherland, a reverse migration often triggered by either the making or losing of a fortune. These two groups, free people of African descent and Jews, therefore became the leading localized communities in Paramaribo and, along with the Maroons of the rainforest, the major forces in Suriname the colonial government had to contend with before the abolition of slavery in 1863.

Amelioration laws for the enslaved population were also enacted during the age of enfranchisement. In 1827, the colonial government granted slaves legal status as persons by transferring them from commercial to civil law.[92] Their complete legal release from servile status, however, took an additional thirty-six years, and another decade after that if one includes the period of mandatory apprenticeship. The civic and political improvement of their status, therefore, was never in competition with the legal trajectory of Jews yet still unwittingly followed the same arc toward universal equality that first materialized in the age of Enlightenment.

Alex van Stipriaan is therefore correct that the social and legal evolution of the two groups, whom he refers to in shorthand as "Jews" and "Africans," was "parallel." However, we may go even a step further, for the two populations increasingly intersected as they creolized. This intersection was both an instigator and a by-product of the process of creolization. Whereas previous scholars have imagined the Jewish community as an isolated group until a colony-wide economic crisis in the last quarter of the eighteenth century induced a mass relocation from inland Suriname to the capital city, and have viewed lack of integration into white Christian society as a marker of separateness, *Jewish Autonomy in a Slave Society* envisions the Jewish community as tightly intertwined with Afro-Creole civilization.[93] In short, this book argues that creolization in a slave colony should be assessed by a group's degree of integration into the majority society rather than into the Caribbean's tiny white Christian elite.

*   *   *

This book opens with "A Jewish Village in a Slave Society," which explores the nature and history of Jodensavanne, the colony's Jewish village, misleadingly synonymous with the concentrated presence of Jews in the colony and their supposed communal perfection. Here I also discuss the village's legal and communal antecedents elsewhere in the Caribbean and in Brazil, as well as the use of Amsterdam as a communal launching pad for Jews of the Dutch Atlantic. Chapter 2, "The Paradox of Privilege," explores the legal status of Jews under the successive rule of the English and Dutch and questions how autonomous Jews actually were, whether as a corporate group or as individuals. In Chapter 3, "From Immigrants to Rooted Migrants," I trace the process whereby Jews transformed from newcomers, a large proportion of whom were indigent transients, into a group that left a deep imprint on the colony's cultures and languages and were considered by both natives and visitors as quintessentially local. "The Emergence of Eurafrican Jews" and "The Quest for Eurafrican Jewish Equality," the following two chapters, take an in-depth look into the strongest expression of that localism, namely the ethnogenesis, social consciousness, and political activism of Eurafrican Jews, while Chapter 6, "Purim in the Public Eye," explores how a two-thousand-year-old Jewish holiday became synonymous with Suriname's Afro-Creole Carnival. We taper off with Chapter 7, "The Abolition of Jewish Communal Autonomy," which examines a piece of legislation pertaining specifically to Portuguese and Ashkenazi Jews but is paradigmatic of the gradual legal process that would eventually place all of Suriname's residents on equal footing, at least according to the letter of the law. The Conclusion summarizes the main arguments of the book and advocates for the application of an Atlantic Jewish paradigm.

This book follows three main narrative arcs. The first traces the transformation of Suriname's Jews from former New Christians who envisioned themselves as part of a global Portuguese "nation" to a group whose Portuguese identity was culturally Jewish but not imperial. Second, we will consider the evolution of Jewish legal status, from the patroonship (a type of proprietary microcolony) to the acquisition of communal, political autonomy, and concluding with the shift of Jewish status from privilege and disability to equality before the law. Finally, *Jewish Autonomy in a Slave Society* traces the transformation of Jews from immigrants and transients to a settled and localized group regarded as "native" to the land whose brutality Voltaire immortalized in 1759. As we will see, people of African descent, whether enslaved or free, were tightly intertwined with each of these three trajectories. It is a densely documented story that leaves little room for speculation, and certainly no place for satire.

Notes on Usage

Ethnic Nomenclature

The Jews who constitute the focus of this study traced their origins to the forced conversions to Christianity that occurred in the Iberian Peninsula between the fourteenth and fifteenth centuries. Many left Spain and Portugal as Catholics and formally returned to public Jewish life beginning in the late sixteenth century in Amsterdam and later in London. Before the mid-nineteenth century, they usually referred to themselves as either "Portuguese Jews" or "Spanish Jews" and collectively as members of the "Spanish and Portuguese Jewish nation." The congregations they founded, from Beraha VeSalom, established in Suriname in 1685, to the synagogue eventually called Shearith Israel in Montreal, were called "Spanish and Portuguese congregations."[94] The primacy these Jews gave to Spanish in their congregational names showed deference to the language they often reserved for belles lettres, as well as scripture and liturgy in translation, although most spoke Portuguese as their vernacular, having descended from the forced apostasy of Portugal's Jewish community in 1497.[95]

Members of these exilic, formerly Christian communities did not identify as "Sephardi."[96] As a self-referential term, it never appears in their communal minutes, wills, or letters. They distinguished themselves from Ottoman Jews, whose ancestors had been expelled from Spain in 1492, left the Iberian Peninsula as Jews, and did call themselves "Sefaradím" (סְפָרַדִים), the Hebrew word for "Spaniards," often rendered in English as "Sephardim." Only in the mid- to late nineteenth century, with the influx of thousands of these Ottoman Jews into the metropoles of the Atlantic World and their absorption into Spanish and Portuguese Jewish congregations, did Portuguese Jews gradually begin to apply the term "Sephardi" to themselves. The indiscriminate application by scholars of the term "Sephardi," in its various permutations ("Sephardi," "Sephardic"; plural: "Sephardim," "Western Sephardim"), permeates the historiography, across linguistic boundaries, but obscures the distinctive sense of self cultivated by early modern Portuguese and Spanish Jews and their lack of integration into the Sephardi world.[97] I join the handful of scholars who have chosen nomenclatural historicity over scholarly convention.[98]

Similarly, I have preserved the Latin-scripted Hebrew orthography employed by exilic Spanish and Portuguese Jews and the Ashkenazim who conformed to their coreligionists' culture in the Atlantic World. This distinctive spelling is very different from modern Israeli Hebrew and should not be mistaken as a transcription or pronunciation error. Thus, for example, the names of the synagogues are Beraha VeSalom, Sedek VeSalom, Neveh Salom, and Darhe Jesarim (and not Beracha VeShalom, Tsedek VeShalom, Neveh Shalom, and Darchei Yesharim). The family name of an emissary from the Land of Israel who visited Suriname in 1773 is ACohen and not HaCohen, a pronunciation practice also evident in the Hebrew last name of the Ashkenazi planter known as Gerrit Jacobs or Napthaly Bar Isac aCohen. The Festival of Weeks is Sebuot or Sebuoth and not Shavu'ot. Sabbath is Sabat and not Shabbat. The Hebrew letter "ayin" at the end of a word is rendered in Portuguese transcription as "ang" to indicate the guttural pronunciation held in common with the same letter in Arabic; thus, *milrang* (מלרע). When speaking in abbreviated form, Portuguese Jews tended to eliminate the word "de" in last names like "del Prado" and "da Costa." I have followed this practice when using last names only, referring to Moses Rodrigues del Prado, for example, as "Prado" and Ishac da Costa as "Costa" (rather than "del Prado" and "da Costa").

In the Atlantic World, Jews of central and eastern European origin self-identified as "Ashkenazi" and as members of the "High German Jewish" community, synagogue, or nation, while non-Jews usually preferred the latter term. Portuguese Jews used all of these terms to refer to their Germanic coreligionists as well as "asquenazim," "asquenas," and, more rarely, "tudesco."[99] My preference in this book is for "Ashkenazi." The "High" in "High German" (in Dutch, *hoogduits*) refers not to social class but rather to the language spoken by residents of Germanic highlands, in contrast to the language of the Netherlands, a toponym literally denoting "Low Countries."

The dearth of sources pertaining to the specific origins of Africans has made appropriate reference a much more complex matter. Generally, scholars cannot diachronically verify the provenance of newly arrived Africans, whose traffic across the Atlantic peaked in 1790 and whose population in Suriname reached a high of 60,000 at roughly the same time. According to one estimate, some 41 percent of Africans who lived in Suriname in the mid-eighteenth century originated in the Kormantin ethnic group, while 25 percent were born into either the Mandingo or Loango cultures.[100] The ever-expanding Trans-Atlantic Slave Trade Database has significantly advanced our knowledge on the specific regions whence most Africans embarked during particular years. But whether place of embarkation is synonymous with nativity and whether we can even speak of these groups as ethnicities are onerous questions. Nor, for the most part, were transporters and purchasers of Africans interested in learning of, much less documenting, these origins or cultures.[101]

Of far greater interest in the colonies was the degree of divisible African-ness. Racialized terms describing these individuals proliferated over the course of the eighteenth century. In Dutch sources alone one finds *neger/negerin* (black), *mulat/mulattin* (one-half black, one-half white), *carboeger* or *carboegel* and *mestice* (both terms indicating one-half black, one-half mulatto), *castice* (one-half white, one-half *mestice*), *poestice* (one-half white, one-half *castice*), *de vrij* (the free one); *vrije volkeren* (free people); *slaaf/slavin* (slave); *kleurling/kleurlingen* (colored), and *lieden van gemengde couleur* (individuals of mixed color).[102] Some of these labels were specific to certain periods and then fell into desuetude, while others changed meaning over time or depending on immediate context. In general, the diversity of categories diminished toward the end of the eighteenth century, exhibiting a hardening of the binary between whites and people of sub-Saharan descent.

Scholars of Suriname have handled such linguistic complexity in a variety of ways. Cynthia McLeod, for example, deliberately employs the racial terms exactly as they appear in the original documents in order to convey a sense of social position and degree of degradation.[103] Margot van den Berg, who has studied the juridical records of Suriname, uses "black" as an umbrella term encompassing people native to Africa, as well as individuals of Afro-European and Afro-Indian origin who were slaves, Maroons, or ex-slaves, even as she acknowledges that this usage is "inept."[104] Ellen Neslo, who has studied nineteenth-century elites of slave origin in Paramaribo,

often prefers the all-encompassing term "non-white."[105] All of these scholars have placed considerations of narrative convenience or historical accu-
racy above the power of these terms to offend present-day sensibilities.[106]

Fully appreciative of all of these views, I have chosen, where relevant,
to remain faithful to the original terms, placing them in quotations. But I
have also interspersed "of African origin" and "of African nativity," descrip-
tives that are purposefully vague in terms of social position and precise
ancestry, in order to reflect, where appropriate, the lack of information on
social status or perceived ancestry. To describe individuals publicly known
to be of dual European and African origins, I use "Eurafrican," a term
borrowed from George E. Brooks's work on economic and cultural brokers
in West Africa.[107] Some readers may find this term as applied to a Surinamese context inadequate, since persons denoted as Eurafrican had usually
never set foot in either Europe or Africa. Eurafrican, nonetheless, is the best
choice because it avoids lending facticity to the minutiae of divisible racial
categories and because it acknowledges that this ascribed racial status was
at least one notch in the hierarchy above "negro" or "black." For similar
reasons, I have not refrained from employing the term "slave," denoting
the legal status of a person, but do use it interchangeably with "enslaved,"
the term preferred by scholars (particularly in the Anglophone world) who
wish to stress the humanity of the person above his or her legal position.

The term "Creole" in a Surinamese context (both then and now) refers
to Afro-Surinamese people who trace their origins to manumission or Emancipation, in contradistinction to Maroons, who have historically taken pride
in the fact that their ancestors ran away from slavery rather than continue to
endure it. I use "Creole" interchangeably with "Afro-Creole." In distinguishing between "Bush Negroes" (*bosnegers*), the government's term for Maroon
communities who were immune to enslavement because they had concluded
peace treaties with the colonial authorities, and runaways (*weglopers*),
enslaved people who ran away from their plantations, I use the terms
"Maroons" and "runaways," respectively. When relevant, I use the terms
"Maroons" and "outlaw Maroons" to distinguish between groups who had
concluded peace with the colonial government and those who had not. The
former made frequent visits to Paramaribo to share information and negotiate with the government and, in exchange for "capture ransom" (*vanggeld*),
to turn in runaway slaves who had fled to their village.[108]

The shared language of Suriname, a combination of African, European,
and Hebrew linguistic elements, has been known in the past several decades

as "Suriname Tongue" (Sranan or Sranan Tongo). In eighteenth- and nineteenth-century sources, it is variably referred to as "Negro English," "Negro speech," and "Negro language" (*Neger Engels, Neger Spraak,* and *Neger Taal*). I use all of these terms interchangeably.

One final note on the nomenclature applied to Africans relates to their belief system. As a concept formulated in European antiquity, "religion" is highly problematic when applied to Suriname's African population, if not to most non-Western people (including biblical Israelites and ancient Jews). When discussing Surinamese people of African origin, I therefore prefer "spiritual traditions," a term first suggested to me by Joseph C. Miller in 2009. It is not an ideal term, and thus another expression of the difficulties involved with writing about people who seldom left behind written records in their own voice or hand. On the other hand, I do describe the spiritual tradition of Surinamese Jews as a religion since they themselves accepted this term.

In the early days of colonial rule, being Christian was synonymous with being white, and I sometimes follow this referential practice, particularly for the early colonial period, for the following reason. In Suriname, unlike much of the New World, few Africans were converted to or voluntarily embraced Christianity. The mass conversion of African-origin people to the faith of the Apostles began in Suriname only in the late eighteenth century and then primarily under the prescribed guidance of Moravian missionaries.

The final group that needs terminological explanation comprises the first inhabitants of Suriname. I refer to them alternatively as Indigenous people and Indians or by their specific ethnic markers, including Taíno, Arawak, Carib, and Waraus, which are both self-ascribed and ascribed.[109] Sometimes, I cite the locution used in archival sources, namely *indios* and *indianen*, in Portuguese and Dutch, respectively. Specific details on nomenclature can be found in the endnotes throughout this book. If I have dwelled excessively on ethnic nomenclature it is out of recognition that categorization forms the basis of human thought, perception, and action.[110]

Geographical and Political Terminology, Spelling, and Translations

The spelling of the foremost Dutch colony in the Guianas varies in the sources. In this book I employ "Suriname," which represents the traditional

Dutch orthography as well as the official name of this sovereign state, an independent republic since 1975. Nineteenth-century Hebrew sources and Jewish studies scholarship dating to the late nineteenth through the mid-twentieth century tend to refer to the insular Caribbean and Caribbean mainland with the antiquated terms "West India" and the "West Indies."[111] In this book, "West Indies" is used interchangeably with the "insular Caribbean," while "Caribbean" denotes the "Greater Caribbean," that is, both the islands between North and South America and the South American littoral bordering the Caribbean Sea and Atlantic Ocean.

The name of the metropolitan country that is now the Netherlands changed several times in its history as a result of major political upheavals. Between 1581 (when part of the country threw off Spanish rule) until 1795 (when French revolutionary forces installed the Batavian Republic) the land was called the Dutch Republic, shorthand for the Republic of the United Netherlands or the Republic of the Seven United Provinces. The Batavian Republic endured until 1806, when a monarchy was proclaimed under Louis I (Louis Napoléon Bonaparte), and regained independence only in 1813, when William Frederick was crowned sovereign prince. From at least the late seventeenth century, the Dutch Republic was often termed the "fatherland," a reflection of the family as the dominant metaphor of Dutch colonial life.[112] In this book, for the sake of simplicity and variation, I interchangeably use "Dutch Republic," "metropole," and "homeland" with "fatherland" (*vaderland*) and "motherland" (*moederland*), both of which are commonly found in archival and printed primary sources.[113]

The Atlantic World, as historians understand it, was not a region or geographical space but rather a newly emerging world, a coherent system of regular exchange and interaction of people, commodities, diseases, ideas, and technology among the four continents of North and South America, Europe, and Africa and on their oceans and seas. This world arose around 1500 and relinquished itself to globalism around 1825.[114]

I have shortened the Surinamese title "Gouverneur Generaal," a title first used by G. de Schepper (1738–42), to "governor" and have translated *raad fiscaal* as "colonial prosecutor."[115] I translate Raad van Politie as "Council of Policy," a corrective to much of the historiography, which offers the mistranslation "Court of Police." Suriname, like other colonies and nations in the Caribbean, had no police force until after Emancipation. The Council of Policy combined the features of "an elected colonial parliament, an executive council of ministers, and a judiciary court."[116] The Raad van Civiele Justitie, which administered civil justice, is abbreviated as "Court of Justice."[117]

While many scholars continue to use the term "frontier" synonymously with borderland, others have of late rejected the former word as belittling to peoples unsubjugated by whites, in the case of Suriname, Indians or Maroons inhabiting the rainforest interior.[118] These thinkers also argue that such conflicts paralleled borderland disputes between nation-states and empires and should therefore be elevated to the same level. As sympathetic as I am to this view, I have not hesitated to employ the term "frontier" because that is precisely what the literate people of the time called it in their various languages (*fronteira*; *frontier plaetsen*).[119] Moreover, those words would be rendered either "frontier" or "border" in English, with no appreciable semantic difference. However, I avoid the historic term "bush" (Portuguese, *matos*; Dutch, *bos*), whose early modern connotation as an "untamed wilderness" inhabited by "backward" and "uncivilized" people endures, and in its place use "rainforest" or "the interior."

All translations from foreign languages are mine.

The Nassi/Nassy Family

To distinguish the seventeenth-century colonial entrepreneur David Cohen Nassi from his more famous descendant, philosophe, physician, and communal leader David Cohen Nassy (1747–1806), I have adopted their own idiosyncratic ways of spelling their second family name. Seventeenth-century Surinamese correspondents tended to spell the family name as "Nasi" or "Nassi."[120] By the following century the final "i," already attested to in some earlier government and personal correspondence, had definitively been replaced by a "y." Thus, the birth name of the latter was David de Isaac Cohen Nassy. He legally shortened his name to David Nassy in 1790.[121] To avoid confusion, I refer to him in this book as "David Nassy." Although the title page of the *Essai historique* attributes authorship of this book to a number of Surinamese Portuguese Jewish leaders, including "David de Is. C. Nassy," Nassy identifies himself elsewhere as the true author, while archival and printed primary sources in Portuguese and Dutch indicate that he was either the sole or main writer.[122] In this book, therefore, Nassy is referred to as the sole author of the *Essai historique*.

CHAPTER 1

A Jewish Village in a Slave Society

On Thursday, March 14, 1743, Joan Jacob Mauricius, recently appointed governor of Suriname, set out from the capital city of Paramaribo for his inaugural tour along the Suriname River and its creeks. As he traveled along the shoreline in the shade of his tentboat, gunshots and cannon blasts rang out from riverside plantations, marking his accession to power. Lavish meals and overnight sojourns on the estates of leading government officials and planters punctuated his nine-day journey. Midway, on Monday, March 18, "Jews' Savanna" came into view on the left bank of the river. Known by its Dutch name, Jodensavanne, this village was founded in 1685 some 30 miles (48 kilometers) south of Paramaribo on the upper reaches of the Suriname River. As Mauricius disembarked at the dock known as Nassy's landing place, the *parnassim* (regents or governing officers of the Portuguese Jewish community), along with the local Jewish Civil Guard, came out to greet him, "just as is done among the Christians." They took the Jewish burgher's oath of fealty to their new governor, after which five salvos were fired. They then led Mauricius into the synagogue and honored him with the customary *hommage*. The regents closed the ceremony with a prayer recited for him and his family, and the entire congregation responded with a resonating "Amen."[1]

As Mauricius was to remark a few years later in 1748, Jodensavanne was "the only town in the whole world where only Jews live."[2] While the Amsterdam-born governor was captivated by the novelty of the place, modern-day writers have tended to view Jodensavanne as an idyll.[3] They characterize it as a "promised land before Israel," a verdant utopian settlement that was "a home at last on a paradisiacal patch of earth."[4] In their eyes, the village attests to a "baroque Zionist imagination, *avant la lettre*," and a "Marrano dream of a New World Zion," where the ingathering of

FIGURE 2. *View of a number of houses on the river, possibly Jodensavanne* (*Gezicht op een aantal huizen aan een rivier, mogelijk de Jodensavanne*), Hendrik Huygens, 1850(?). In the foreground is a tentboat. Further in the distance is a *pondo*, a small water vessel covered with banana leaves. Courtesy of Rijksmuseum, Amsterdam.

the exiles was accomplished, albeit on a small scale.[5] One political scientist characterizes Jodensavanne as a Jewish "aristocratic republic" and "'ministate.'"[6] Jewish contemporaries, researchers tell us, though without attribution, called Jodensavanne a "Jerusalem by the riverside"[7] and perceived it as a "provisional Jerusalem of the Savanna."[8] One writer even claims that the Jewish village was the inspiration for the founding of Ararat, a plot of land in upstate New York purchased by U.S. diplomat Mordecai Manuel Noah in 1825 for the purpose of Jewish colonization.[9] Others have mistaken the inland town for a bustling entrepôt, a meeting place for early modern merchants, bankers, and businessmen. They envision Jodensavanne as "recognizably urban," a "Jewish trade center," and a "conduit for the district's plantation exports and imports."[10]

At first glance, this collective portrait of Jodensavanne as a flourishing haven for secret Jews and a proto-Zionist settlement would seem self-evident. After all, the site was the political center of Surinamese Jews, many of whom had been born as New Christians in the Iberian Peninsula, heirs to centuries of religious and racial persecution. An area densely populated with self-governing Jews does poetically evoke a revived Jerusalem. But what if, instead of assuming that Portuguese Jews in Suriname were refugees in search of asylum and political self-determination, we were to instead center the context of the Jewish Atlantic World? Such an approach would force us to think systemically about a migration and settlement undergirded by poverty, slavery, and the hegemony of Portuguese Jewry over other Jewish groups. The Atlantic Jewish paradigm refocuses our attention on a movement of populations that was initially fired by the quest to establish new, economically viable communities intended to relieve the financially dismal situation of western European congregations, a quest inextricably entangled with the unfree labor of many thousands of forced migrants from Africa. Of the numerous attempts by early modern Jews to establish a settlement in Brazil and the Caribbean, Jodensavanne was the only agrarian venture that endured. It is the culmination of a story that began in the first half of the seventeenth century, nearly 1,700 miles southward, in Brazil, the birthplace of America's first Jewish community.

Colonial Entrepreneurs

In 1630, the West India Company invaded Brazil. Its official control over vast areas of the territory would endure until 1645, when the Portuguese began an incursion that ended with the defeat of the Dutch in 1654. Although short-lived, the colony had a decisive impact on the direction of the Dutch overseas empire, which played a dominant role in the slave trade and eventually extended from the homeland in the United Provinces to the Hudson River, and from the Caribbean to the African Gold Coast.

Brazil also had a decisive impact on Jews, whose communities on Europe's Atlantic coast were then undergoing reconstitution following several centuries of expulsions, forced conversions, massacres, and residential bans. In Amsterdam, where Jews had begun to arrive in the 1590s, a Jewish community emerged, comprised primarily of former New Christians, some

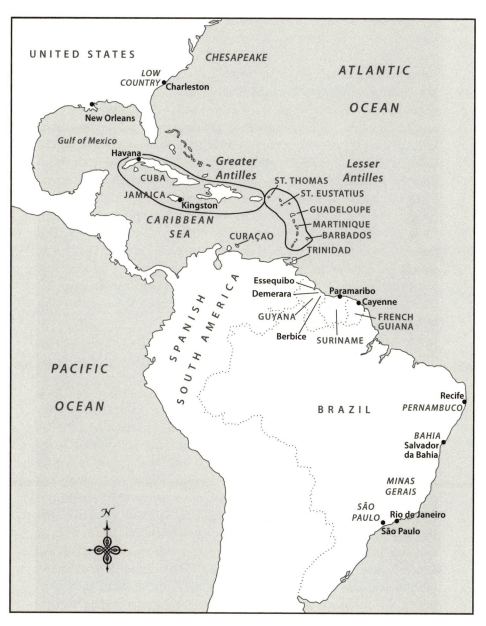

MAP 2. Atlantic America.

of whom soon moved to Dutch Brazil in order to eke out a living as trades-
men. In order to manage the religiously pluralistic population of newly conquered Brazil, the Dutch extended religious liberties to these Portuguese Jews,
leading to the establishment of the first hemispheric American synagogues.[11]
The reversion of Brazil to Portuguese rule in 1654 resulted in a mass exodus
of the Jewish population, most of whom returned to Amsterdam.[12]

The founders of Jodensavanne belonged to a coterie of Jewish colonial
entrepreneurs whose work began in Dutch Brazil and continued in the cir-
cum- and insular Caribbean starting in the 1650s. All of them were of Portuguese New Christian origin, and many had returned to their ancestral faith
in cities such as Amsterdam. Their pragmatic goal was to launch Jewish settlements in the New World in order to relocate the hordes of impoverished New
Christians who were regularly arriving from the Iberian Peninsula, embracing
Judaism, and burdening the community's charitable coffers.[13] The goal of
relocation was deeply imbued with the messianic sentiments of the time. Jews
and Christians widely regarded their age as redemptionist, and many were
convinced that the dispersal of Jews to the four corners of the earth, which
included the newly colonized territories of the Americas, was a divine prerequisite for the coming of the Messiah. For Christians, this Messiah was
expected to be Jesus Christ risen, while for Jews the "Anointed One" would
be a human being and coreligionist of Davidic descent.

While the English also tolerated a Jewish presence in their American
colonies, starting with Barbados in the 1650s, only the Dutch offered a practical means of communal organization in the form of the patroonship. Created in 1628 by the West India Company to encourage colonization in the
New World, the patroonship provided the applicant with land in fief for
cultivation, provided he attracted fifty colonists within three years. The
patroon, a professional colonizer or organizer of a patroonship, was granted
specific freedoms and exemptions and was empowered as the administrative and judicial leader of his fiefdom.[14] His jurisdiction was limited to
sentences involving fines to the value of no more than fifty to one hundred
guilders, depending on the arrangement.[15] These manorial settlements,
established in the Dutch Americas through the 1650s, were one of the various ways Dutch metropolitan authorities sought to populate their overseas
American colonies, develop cash crops, and stake out trade outposts.[16]

In Dutch Brazil, the patroonship played a modest role in creating the
incipient Jewish community. In the Caribbean, by contrast, the patroonship
was essential in paving the way for the large-scale, legal settlement of Jews.

The proliferation of Jewish patroonships was directly related to the fall of Dutch Brazil, shrinking since 1645 due to a Luso-Brazilian uprising. The greater part of the exiles who returned to the Dutch homeland were Christians. Soldiers and sailors deprived of their back pay and livelihood, ministers, comforters of the sick, clerks, lumberjacks, and street sweepers streamed out of the colony, most headed for Amsterdam. Many appealed to the States General and the West India Company for financial assistance, usually in vain.[17] Jewish émigrés suffered financially alongside their Christian peers, but the challenges of the former were more daunting. While Christians could settle wherever they wished, most Dutch towns banned Jewish residence. The cities of Amsterdam and Middelburg, where they were admitted, were already congested and increasingly so.[18] The refugees of Brazil were joined in Amsterdam by other Jewish exiles from the Iberian Peninsula and eastern Europe, where the Chmielnicki uprisings of 1648–52 resulted in the massacre of one-third of the Jewish population. Amsterdam, the only Dutch city at the time that permitted the arrival of indigents, became a preferred destination for many of these displaced persons. Its city council insisted on a continual inflow of low-skilled migrants to stimulate the urban economy and supply the ships of the Dutch East Indies (Verenigde Oostindische Compagnie, or VOC) with sailors and soldiers.[19] But in the Dutch metropole, Jews were collectively excluded from various guilds, as well as from the four trades of industry, agriculture, shipping, and the militia (which included both the army and the navy), significantly narrowing their opportunities to make ends meet.[20]

By the early 1650s, therefore, the urgency to find new areas of settlement for Jews intensified. It was during those years that Jewish leaders first proposed to authorities in Christian Europe the launching of Jewish patroonships in the Caribbean. Of these men, João de Yllán (b. 1609) and David Cohen Nassi (1612–85) are the best documented. Both were deeply entrenched in messianic expectation, and the former was an openly avowed messianist. In 1666, he dispatched a letter to the English king Charles II, requesting safe passage for a Dutch ship that would sail him and "several of [his] Jewish brethren" to Jerusalem during the Second Anglo-Dutch War. De Yllán planned to bring with him fifty "poor families"—reminiscent of the fifty colonists required for a patroonship—in anticipation of God's plan to "gather in his scattered people" under the leadership of a "prophet." That prophet was Sabbatai Zevi, who convinced thousands of Jews he was their messiah before converting to Islam under duress in 1666.[21]

Evidently fueled by redemptionist fervor, Yllán established the first Jewish patroonship in the Caribbean, arriving in Curaçao, a Dutch island off the coast of what is today Venezuela, in 1651.[22] Though Yllán's colony failed, the idea of Jewish settlement in Curaçao was not abandoned. In 1659, Isaac da Costa received permission to establish a patroonship under the assurance of free exercise of religion and protection from the local authorities.[23] The small group of settlers he assembled eventually evolved into a full-fledged Jewish community that by the late eighteenth century came to rival its Surinamese Jewish counterpart in both population size and the reach of its political powers. While neither Yllán nor Cohen Nassi built an enduring community on the island, there is some evidence that they participated in the founding of the Caribbean's oldest Jewish congregation, Mikvé Israel, which apparently emerged during their sojourn there, although as yet without a dedicated building.[24] The congregation's name, "Hope of Israel," is probably a reference to a book of the same name, published in 1650, first in Latin and then in Spanish, by the Amsterdam-based Portuguese *haham* (ordained rabbinical leader) Menasseh ben Israel.[25] The book's Hebrew title, *Mikvé Israel*, carrying the double entendre of "the ingathering of Israel," alluded to ben Israel's messianic hope of extending the Jews' residence to England and the Americas and thereby bringing about their global dispersal, a rabbinical prerequisite for the coming of the Messiah.

Implicitly, messianism also informed the worldview of David Cohen Nassi, who along with his son Samuel was the leading founder of Suriname's Jewish community. Scholars have traditionally argued that the elder Cohen Nassi was born a New Christian in Portugal, where Judaism had been outlawed since 1497, and that he must have publicly returned to his ancestral Judaism in Amsterdam. Bearing the dual aliases of Joseph Nuñez de Fonseca and Christovão de Tavora, he lived in Dutch Brazil in the 1640s before becoming a patroon.[26] Recently unearthed documents raise the possibility that Cohen Nassi may have actually been born in Brazil. The São Carlos sugar plantation in Recife was in the family's possession during the 1620s, at which time Nassi would have still been a child.[27]

Regardless of his birthplace, "David Cohen Nassi" was likely not his birth name. Although some New Christians did secretly assign their children unofficial Hebrew names at birth, Nassi probably selected his Jewish first and last names as an act of self-anointment, announcing himself as both a religious leader and a direct descendant or even incarnation of the messianic king of the Hebrew Bible. Through his first family name,

"Cohen," the colonial entrepreneur asserted his direct descent from the High Priests of the ancient Temple in Jerusalem. This assumed priestly pedigree secured for him special religious status within Jewish ritual and law, particularly through honors accorded descendants of priests during the synagogue service. In identifying himself as a Davidic, messianic leader, Cohen Nassi followed a tradition that had emerged in the Middle Ages among self-appointed Jewish rulers who wished to legitimize their status and authority.[28] Descent for Iberian Jewish notables, who often claimed Davidic origins, constituted a vital source for social status among exilic Portuguese Jews, even though such assertions were often "based on the flimsiest of evidence."[29] The assertion of Davidic descent was also a well-known ruse among Christian monarchs, including those of late medieval France.[30]

His second family name, "Nassi," denotes "patriarch" or "prince," an imperially recognized dynastic office that emerged under the Romans and often served as the title of Jewish leaders in medieval Christian Europe.[31] The appropriation of this princely title was a common practice among provincial leaders in the medieval Jewish world who wished to assert their political authority but could not claim themselves to be kings (מלכים) on the level of a biblical David.[32] The Nasi family of pre-Expulsion Spain (probably unrelated to our David) counted among the land's Jewish aristocracy and possessed "patents, rights and privileges" bestowed by the Crown.[33] In Spain after the forced conversions of 1391, a renewed impulse to invent a noble pedigree trickled down to the New Christian masses and became common among Portuguese Jews, both wealthy and indigent, during the sixteenth and seventeenth centuries.[34] Doña Gracia Mendes Nasi (1510–69), a Portuguese New Christian who became one of the wealthiest and most politically powerful Jewish women of Renaissance Europe, is probably another example of such an assumed identity.[35] Natalie Zemon Davis speculates that David Cohen Nassi "retained the family memory that he was a Cohen," a descendant of ancient Jewish priests.[36] But given the aforementioned historical patterns, it is more likely that the pairing of his two last names was a self-conscious strategy to claim leadership authority from both the Bible and diasporic Jewish tradition.

If this interpretation is correct, it helps explain why Cohen Nassi was not easily dissuaded by his colonizing failures. With the misadventure of Curaçao behind him, he turned to a second region for Jewish colonization, located in the Guianas, north of Brazil and east of what is today Venezuela.

Cohen Nassi trained his eyes on the Dutch settlements of Nova Zeelandia, also called Essequibo (1658), located on the River Pomeroon in what is now Guyana, and Cayenne (1659), in what is today French Guiana. The so-called Essequibo Liberties, a grant of privileges proposed by Portuguese Jews in their maternal language, and ratified by the Dutch government, bestowed upon Cohen Nassi and his Jewish settlers extraordinary benefits, including full religious liberty, exemption from appearing in court on Sabbaths and Jewish holidays, burgher status, political self-rule, representation in colonial governance and trade, the right to bear arms, and freedom to hunt, fish, mine, and engage in the slave trade.[37] In Dutch-ruled Cayenne, Jews cultivated sugar and erected a synagogue. They were offered similar freedoms to those granted in Essequibo, but Dutch Reformed judges withheld from them the privilege of their own tribunal.[38] From admonitions to remain "so far from the [already established] colony on Cajana [Cayenne] that they will not interfere with the inhabitants of that [colony]," we may surmise that the Jews of Cayenne lived in their own village.[39]

The Dutch colony at Cayenne collapsed in 1664 when the French invaded, prompting David Cohen Nassi and his son Samuel to relocate with their coreligionists to Essequibo.[40] Jews on the Essequibo and nearby Pomeroon rivers were expelled in 1666, when English troops "invaded western Guiana and destroyed the colonies."[41] The era of Jewish patroonships came to a close. Jews departed, many of them headed for Suriname, which lay between Essequibo and Cayenne and had been colonized in 1651 under Francis Willoughby, the governor of Barbados.[42] Lord Willoughby and the fellow Barbadian planters who shared his political designs saw in Suriname an opportunity to expand the sphere of power of their sugar-rich island.[43] The movement of Jews from newly conquered French Cayenne and the formerly Dutch Essequibo to English Suriname demonstrated their political flexibility and their willingness to aid in the expansion of the Barbadian sugar frontier. Their welcome reception by the English, particularly after a deadly epidemic took hold of the colony in 1665, bespeaks the desperation of the English to buttress their possession and their rivalry with the Dutch for Jewish settlers.[44] In Suriname, Jews founded what would become the only enduring agrarian Jewish settlement in the Americas.

Collectively, most of the earliest Caribbean Jewish colonies, largely patroonships, were fragile and fleeting and did not create a durable memory outside the Jewish community.[45] Dwelling upon them, as we have done, allows us to appreciate the essential experience they offered in colonization, commerce, planting, governance, and diplomacy, all pivotal in launching the two long-lived Jewish communities of Curaçao and Suriname.[46] The pragmatism of the Jewish colonial entrepreneurs, reflected in their use of slave labor, and in their aggressive negotiation for religious and economic liberties, was tightly intertwined with the messianic fervor of their time.[47]

The Emergence of Suriname's Jewish Community

Jewish settlement along the shores of the Upper Suriname River had already begun in the 1650s, under English rule, almost a quarter of a century before the establishment of the village that came to be known as Jodensavanne. Because English Suriname lacked hydraulic technology to control the swamping of land resulting from the ebb and flow of tides, the first plantations were established far inland, tens of miles south of the Atlantic Ocean on the Suriname River.[48] Jews also established most of their estates in this vicinity but in addition developed a smaller cluster of plantations dotting the Cassewijne Creek, a tributary of the Commewijne River, stretching out to the east of the Suriname River.[49] Because the patroonship was unknown to the English, Jewish immigrants instead relied on land acquisition through purchase and government land grants. The first stirrings of a Jewish community in Suriname date to 1661, when Baruch da Costa and Selomo de Solis conceded to the Portuguese Jewish community one acre of land along the Cassipora Creek, on the Suriname River and in the district of Thorarica, a mile and a half south of the future Jodensavanne.[50] The donation conforms to a pattern by which Jewish agrarian entrepreneurs would launch plantations at their own initiative, prove them viable, and receive as further incentive additional land from the colonial government. In 1665, the English governor augmented the Cassipora Creek settlement with ten acres, situated atop a hillock, near the plantation of Baruch da Costa and the Cassipora Creek.[51] These eleven acres may have coincided with the region identified in 1673 as the Joden-quartier, a Dutch-French conflation denoting "Jews' neighborhood" or "quarter."[52] Judging by its name, Jews' Quarter never achieved the status of a village, though it did bear the telltale attributes of a fledgling population center. Its burial ground, whose earliest surviving epitaph dates to

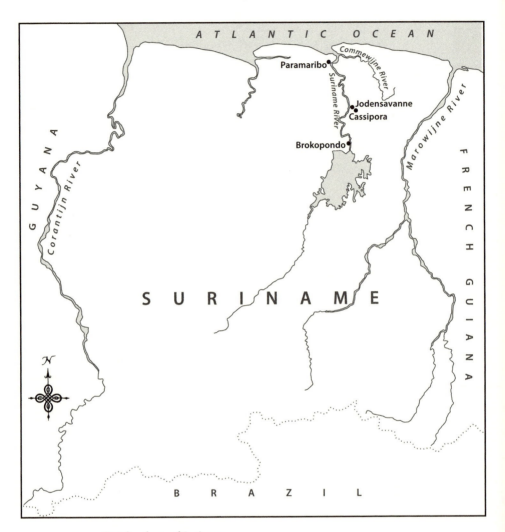

MAP 3. Dutch colony of Suriname.

1666, is known today as the Cassipora Creek Cemetery, while a no-longer-extant synagogue once lay near the Silva estate. Tellingly, the colony's first Jewish birth and circumcision records begin in 1661, suggesting the centrality of land acquisition to the Jewish community's founding.[53]

Simultaneously, Portuguese Jews began to establish plantations further north, in the vicinity of "Torarica Stadt" (Torarica Town), the capital of

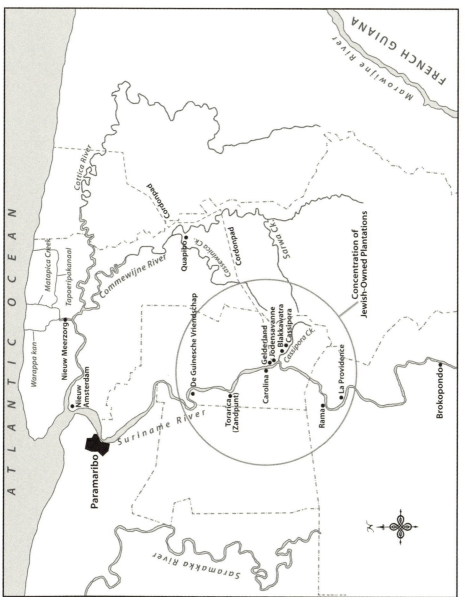

MAP 4. Detail of the Suriname River with relevant plantations and the villages of Jodensavanne and Cassipora.

Suriname under English rule, located six miles south of Paramaribo, along the Suriname River. By 1667, the date of Suriname's earliest land map, a considerable cluster of Jewish settlements had begun to spiral out north and south of the erstwhile capital city. Men bearing the family names of da Silva, de Casseres, Pereira, Mesa, Nunes, de Fonseca, and da Costa launched estates on both banks of the Suriname River.[54] The colony-wide epidemic of 1665, which coincided with the Second Anglo-Dutch War, contributed to the fall of the colony to the Dutch in 1667. One-third of the white colonists immediately departed with the English, but many others stayed behind, probably because they were fettered by debt.[55] The English Crown attempted to evacuate its remaining subjects in 1671 and 1675 but succeeded in removing only the poorest.[56]

Not a single Jewish name appears on the list of 51 English petitioners who in 1671 requested to depart for Barbados, a possible indication of the refusal of Christians to join forces with Jews. With the exception of two "Hebrews" in 1675, no Jews seem to have counted among the émigrés, nor is there direct evidence until that year that Jews wished to depart. That year, ten of the colony's leading Jewish families tried to leave for Jamaica, and "several others," totaling 10 Portuguese Jewish men collectively owning 322 slaves, resolved to "goe when occasion shall present."[57] Acting Governor Pierre Versterre persistently objected to their removal, eager to retain his white colonists.[58] At least some of the ten Jewish families who petitioned to leave Suriname succeeded in doing so in 1677, as David Nassy affirms in his *Essai historique*.[59] But there is no known documentation indicating that any "Hebrews" counted among the 1680 evacuees, who constituted the last mission to ferry English subjects out of Suriname.[60] Thereafter, the sources are silent, suggesting either that the Dutch lost interest in the case or that no additional Jews desired to evacuate.

Yet movement of a different kind was taking place, readily discernible in the geographical shift of Jews away from Torarica Town and the Cassipora Creek. By the 1680s, most of the Jewish plantations just south of Torarica Town, on the western bank of the river, had disappeared and the original ten-acre land grant along the Cassipora Creek was abandoned.[61] Jewish plantations along the Cassipora Creek continued to exist, and Portuguese Jews continued to bury their dead in its Jewish cemetery until 1873.[62] But the center of Jewish gravity had definitively shifted northward, to the area on the Suriname River just north and south of the site that would become known as Jodensavanne.

The Emergence of Jodensavanne

Cartographic evidence and contemporary images show that Jodensavanne was an area of meadowlands and hills adjoining a vast rainforest that dominated the country's terrain and obstructed most overland travel. Nearly all illustrations allow the viewer to gaze up at the village from the water. These nineteenth-century depictions situate the village atop two hills that flanked the riverside. A number of dwelling houses dotted the landscape, foregrounded by the synagogue, the highest building of the landscape and by one account the most magnificent building of the land.[63] Outside observers variably called the site "the Jewish village," "Jews' town," or "Jews' Savanna," while local Jews referred to it simply as "the Savanna."[64]

Some scholars have speculated that the transition to Jodensavanne from the Cassipora region may have been a reaction to malaria or the quest for a generally healthier climate.[65] However, it is more likely that the shift occurred because the ten-acre expanse of the hilltop community at Cassipora Creek was too limited to support communal growth and complex village planning. This would make sense given the ascendance of Jews in the colony after the 1675 departure of the English. The diminishment of the English population enhanced the Jewish role in conducting business, discussing colonial policy with the government, and contributing to the colony's militia.[66] It also resulted in the primacy of religious over ethnic distinctions in Suriname, creating a more pronounced Christian-Jewish divide. At the same time, the shift away from Torarica Stadt and the Cassipora Creek to Jodensavanne resembles the pattern of New England's colonial villages, whose founders established new nuclei as residents dispersed their homesteads away from the original meetinghouse in search of prime pasturelands.[67] The rise of Jodensavanne, then, may have been a function of the quest for new, more extensive grounds along the Suriname River and the subsequent demand for an administrative and religious center in close proximity.[68]

The plots of land that would form the future Jodensavanne were donated to the Jewish community by David Cohen Nassi's son Samuel Cohen Nassi in September 1682. The village was formally established in 1685, the date of its oldest gravestone and the year its synagogue, Holy Congregation Blessing and Peace (Kahal Kados Beraha VeSalom), was consecrated. In August 1691, Cohen Nassi *fils* added twenty-five acres of adjoining land,[69] followed by Governor Johan van Scharpenhuysen's contribution of an additional one hundred acres in the name of the Society of Suriname.[70]

Samuel Cohen Nassi, once an indigent student enrolled in the renowned Portuguese Jewish seminary Ets Haim of Amsterdam, became a ship and slave owner in Suriname and played a central role in transforming the colony "from a contested settlement into a stable plantation colony," pioneering regional trade between Suriname, Barbados, and New York. When slave ships underperformed, he launched several voyages of his own, helping to ensure that deliveries of captive Africans to Suriname became regularized. The profits he reaped on the sale of human beings and sugar made him an extremely wealthy man. Save for the governor himself, no one owned more slaves than Samuel Cohen Nassi.[71] True to the significance of his second family name, Samuel may have aspired to succeed Cornelis van Aerssen van Sommelsdijck as governor, as Julien Wolbers suggests.[72] It would have been a daunting political role. Sommelsdijck, Dutch Suriname's first governor, had arrived in the colony in 1683 and was murdered by mutinous soldiers five years later. The early Dutch colony was beset by internal strife regarding its leadership, and this would not be the last time.[73]

Poverty and Migration

Despite the unusual privilege of autonomy, the village of Jodensavanne emerged within a context of endemic indigence. Poverty in early modern Suriname is notoriously difficult to define, particularly owing to the cultural and temporal distance between the subject and the historian, on the one hand, and the nature of slave societies, on the other, where even owners of human beings could experience food insecurity and deprivation of basic needs.[74] An important study on the Portuguese Jewish community of Amsterdam shows that destitution in the Atlantic World was a prevalent, pressing concern for Jews, one that threatened not only the survival of individuals but also the viability of Jewish institutions. By their own accounts, material scarcity overwhelmed Atlantic Jewish communities until well into the nineteenth century, whether in the Dutch, English, or French realms. The administration of poor relief, earmarked for such basics as food, fuel, and clothing, was a "constant leitmotif" in congregational records.[75] Effective poverty management was the organizing principle that brought the major Portuguese Jewish communities into existence. The

FIGURE 3. A sugar mill, showing slave dwellings and the sugar cooking house. While most Surinamese Jews barely eked out a living, a small percentage owned plantations. Engraving by J. D. Herlein. From J. D. Herlein, *Beschryvinge van de volk-plantinge Zuriname* (Leeuwarden: Meindert Injema, 1718).

communal bylaws of Portuguese Jews, including those of Amsterdam, Bordeaux, London, and Hamburg, all specify the need to cope with indigence as the initial instigator of the founding or corporate merging of their congregations in the seventeenth century.[76]

Another critical gauge of widespread poverty is the incessant movement that characterized the Jewish Atlantic World. Perhaps the majority of the region's Jews periodically relocated to faraway places in quest of their daily bread. This movement was primarily regulated through the *despacho*, a quintessentially Portuguese Jewish institution responsible for the relocation of indigents either voluntarily or against their will to other cities or colonies. Recipients of travel aid had to promise not to return within a prescribed time, typically between one and fifteen years.[77] Because Portuguese Jewish leaders generally lacked the power to expel their members from a particular city, the *despacho* provided a legitimate alternative. In theory, this "sending away" allowed the regents to immediately and perhaps permanently relieve themselves of economically burdensome individuals and families. In practice, however, this genteel form of expulsion operated more like a game of hot potato, producing perpetual transience among the various Atlantic Jewish populations and repetitive strain on communal budgets.[78]

Indigence was no less prevalent in the largest outpost of the Dutch Atlantic, and not only among Jews. While scholarship on the colony's whites tends to exaggerate their purchasing power, most of them in fact had little money and were dependent on charity. These individuals attempted to eke out a living as low-ranking military functionaries, estate servants, boat drivers, peddlers, tailors, bakers, and laundry washers, but their earnings were usually insufficient for survival, in part because they were in direct competition with the larger and ever-growing free population of African descent.[79] In the Jewish community, individuals and families such as these regularly petitioned the *parnassim* for "a piece of clothing to cover their flesh" or were compelled to request or lengthen weekly allowances when illness pushed them further beyond the edge of subsistence level.[80] The Mahamad (the Jewish government, led by the *parnassim*) also responded to the many "poor and miserable" locals who were too penurious to pay their colonial or communal taxes.[81]

Christians and Jews who did manage to own land faced formidable financial obstacles. While arable tracts were more or less freely granted by the governor, operating a plantation was virtually the only potential path to riches and an extremely costly and risky undertaking. The colony was almost completely dependent upon imports and when ships were delayed, prices soared, leading to food and supply shortages.[82] As in the general white population, Jewish estate ownership was not always a secure path to wealth. Jewish plantation owners were often hundreds of guilders in debt to both the colonial administration and the local Jewish community. In any given year, significant numbers of Jews owed substantial taxes to the government for slaves purchased.[83] A list drawn up in 1671 by Portuguese Jewish leaders included a threat of legal prosecution against eight coreligionists who owed a total of 3,495 Surinamese guilders in communal taxes, nearly 7 percent of the community's operating budget.[84] Slaves, of course, bore the brunt of the shortfall. Ishak Arrias, a planter who simultaneously served as the Portuguese community's *haham*, found in the 1670s that he could not feed his Indian and African slaves, much less his own family.[85] Starvation may have been the reason one of his female workers, already ailing from an unspecified illness, consumed mud and subsequently died.[86]

Amid the concern about widespread hunger and a shortage of servile laborers, Portuguese Jews also worried about paying taxes to the colonial government, one a head tax, the other a land tax. During the 1681–82 fiscal years, Jews owed (and not all of them had yet paid) a total of 3,942 Surinamese guilders, just under 10 percent of the total head and land taxes meted out during those years.[87] Of the total of 35 household heads who appear on this list, 21—60 percent—owed no acreage taxes, most likely because they were landless or because their plantations had never launched and were hence abandoned.[88] Nevertheless, it was this planter class that often covered budgetary shortfalls, adorned the synagogue and prayer houses with opulent ritual objects, and created for the broader community a misleading reputation for wealth.[89] As Robert Cohen points out, elite Jews may have shaped the community's image, but it is a "poor index of the community's economic strength."[90]

The presence of indigent Jews in Suriname is hard to quantify because their inability to pay taxes left them unaccounted for in records other than those pertaining to the distribution of charity. Moreover, recently arrived colonists, including transients, were not taxed.[91] Heads of households without land grants were explicitly overlooked in seventeenth-century censuses, though some may have been subsumed among members of more affluent households. We therefore must make do with head counts that earlier scholars have mistaken as representative of the entire Jewish community. A population survey taken in 1684 indicates the presence of 232 Jews in the colony, including 105 men, 58 women, and 69 children, comprising 35 percent of the white population.[92] By the 1690s, the colony's Jewish population, still concentrated along the Suriname River, reportedly numbered 92 Portuguese families, 10 to 12 Ashkenazi families, and 50 bachelors, amounting to a total of 560 to 575 Jews, one-third of the colony's white population. Collectively, they owned 40 sugar plantations, which in 1684 had produced nearly 38 percent of the colony's total sugar exports.[93] If we accept David Nassy's assumption in 1788 that each family averaged 5 members, the total Portuguese Jewish community at the turn of the eighteenth century, not including bachelors, approximated 460 individuals. This estimate does not include illegitimate children born into slavery, or Indians or Africans in the service of Suriname's Jewish families and synagogue. In 1684, these unfree people reportedly numbered 995, of whom 23 were Indian. The implication of this census is that Jews owned just under 30 percent of the colony's unfree people.[94] The earlier observation that Jewish-owned estates produced 38 percent of the land's sugar must reflect the exceptionally large holdings of a handful of individual planters, including Samuel Cohen Nassi.

Despite the early concentration of the colony's Jews along a single stretch of the Suriname River, it is highly doubtful that their village was ever densely populated, even before the mass dislocation of the 1770s and 1780s. Even when Suriname's Jewish population was heading toward its early modern peak of nearly 1,500 individuals during the latter half of the eighteenth century, most Jews in the colony did not live in the Jewish town, at least not full-time. The only known census of Jodensavanne, which dates to 1762, records the presence of 68 individuals (21 men, 14 women, and 33 children under the age of twelve), all of them bearing Portuguese Jewish names, with one, ten years of age, designated as a free "mulatto."[95] As the community approached its demographic height in the second half of the eighteenth century, Jews living along the Suriname River never numbered more than 200 individuals, representing under 17 percent of the colony's total Jewish community. At that point, in 1762, Surinamese Jews resided in at least half of the colony's twelve divisions, including Paramaribo, where the presence of 318 Ashkenazim and Portuguese Jews is documented.[96]

The reason for the sparse population of Jodensavanne has to do with its function as a village. First and foremost, "Jews' Savanna" primarily operated not as a residential quarter but rather as an administrative center, providing a meeting place for the Portuguese Jewish leadership and its institutions. In addition to the synagogue and its nearby cemetery, there were also a court of justice (a largely secular tribunal operated by the Mahamad), a rabbinical court (*bet din*), mutual aid societies, schools and higher institutions for rabbinical study, a residential center for orphans and the poor, and private houses, including one reserved for the *haham*. The gradual dispersion of the colony's Jews away from the Suriname River, to locations at a rowing distance of several hours to a few days from the Jewish village, made Jodensavanne implausible as a full-time residential area.

As early as 1708, the Portuguese Jewish population of Paramaribo was sufficiently large to justify the founding of a prayer house. Portuguese Jewish residents were distressed that they could only experience communal prayer three times a year, and only by making holiday pilgrimages to

FIGURE 4. A view from the Ashkenazi synagogue Neve Salom of Jodenbrees-traat in Paramaribo, 1952(?). Courtesy of the Jacob Rader Marcus Center of the American Jewish Archives, Cincinnati, Ohio, at americanjewisharchives.org.

Jodensavanne. An official prayer house would allow them to engage in daily prayer locally and also educate their children in Judaism.[97] Ashkenazi Jews were permitted to join in prayer, but by 1716, the Mahamad decided they would no longer be part of the Portuguese congregation and designated for them a separate house of prayer on Paramaribo's Keizerstraat. Ashkenazi Jews remained under the communal jurisdiction of the Portuguese Jewish regents until continuing religious disagreements (likely the displeasure of Ashkenazim with their relegation to the second-class status of *congregantes*), led the Portuguese leaders in 1724 to petition the governor for official separation. Finally, in 1734, the division of the two communities was formalized, a sure sign that the general Jewish community had grown large enough to justify the split. Portuguese Jews seceded from Neveh Salom, bequeathed it to the Ashkenazim, and formed another house of prayer in the city called Sedek VeSalom.[98]

By 1762 the spatial distribution of the colony's Jews had further shifted. As we have seen, at least half of the colony's twelve regional divisions now contained Jews. By the mid-eighteenth century, therefore, the only regions where Jews were nowhere to be found were the Commewijne, Upper Commewijne, Lower Cottica, Upper Cottica and Perica, and possibly the Para Divisions.[99] The most remarkable transition was the mushrooming of Paramaribo's Jewish community. While in 1684 the city was home to a single Jew, about half a century later Paramaribo's Jewish division counted 129 heads of household, totaling 318 individuals, including 27 Jews of slave origin.[100] The sizable presence of an urban Portuguese Jewish community may be misleading, though, since several planters had houses and households in the countryside, along the Suriname River, as well as in the city. Some plantation owners who dwelled on their estates maintained a second house in Jodensavanne, as we shall see.

The Development of Jodensavanne

A series of petitions dating from the 1690s through the 1730s speaks to incipient village planning, including the building of new streets, the repair of dilapidated houses, and the erection of private homes carefully choreographed under the watchful eyes of the Mahamad. Unlike Paramaribo, streets in Jodensavanne had no formal names but were rather known according to the leading planters who owned houses there. Jacob Valenssy, for example, requested permission in 1703 to construct a house on "the street of Mr. Selomoh de la Parra or the street of Mr. Abraham Pereira."[101] The regents appointed an overseer, sometimes identified as the *haham*, to ensure that each house was built to code and did not exceed the square footage conceded.[102] Requests to construct new houses provided only the dimension of the facade, a possible indication that the regents were more concerned about regulating the frontage of houses, and hence access to the streets, than they were about the extent of backyards.[103] One senses that Jodensavanne was rapidly becoming densely dotted with claimed plots, as by 1696, parcels that had not been spoken for were hard to come by.[104]

Yet most homeowners clearly intended their domiciles to function not as their primary homes but rather as holiday houses. This was especially true for planters with estates located elsewhere on the Suriname River or its tributaries. Mosseh de Ribas, a cultivator living on the Cassewijne Creek, petitioned the Mahamad in June 1710 for a plot in Jodensavanne measuring forty feet long in order to furnish a house for the upcoming Feast of Tabernacles, four months hence, "to gather [there with] my family."[105] Ribas was writing one day before the Festival of Weeks (Sebuoth) and must have felt particularly isolated on his plantation at that moment. Similar sentiment was expressed by Moseh Henriquez Cotino, who in 1696 petitioned for an empty plot on which to build a house, or that failing, permission to come to Jodensavanne to "congregate on the occasions that offer themselves, as has any *jahid* [dues-paying, first-class member] of this holy congregation." His turn of phrase suggests that *jahid* status was defined or enhanced by landownership. He further disclosed that being deprived of such a plot or of permission to worship in the village made him feel a "great lack of community" (*descomonidad*).[106] In 1719, Ester, widow of Joseph Cohen Nassy, requested a forty-foot plot to build a house since she had no place in the savanna to come and celebrate the holidays (*pascuar*) with her family.[107] In 1704, a Eurafrican Jew named David Judeu requested license to add a twenty-foot extension to his house on the savanna so that he could "celebrate Passover more comfortably."[108]

Just how deserted Jodensavanne became during secular days comes to us from a variety of eyewitness accounts. Abraham Gabay Izidro, Suriname's *haham* in the 1730s, complained that the Mahamad was never at hand for consultation in matters of Jewish law, each *parnas* being on his own plantation.[109] John Greenwood, the aforementioned Bostonian artist and chronicler who visited Suriname in the 1750s, made a similar observation about Jodensavanne in his diary. The village, he wrote, was "as empty as the synagogue is of a Sunday, the Jews being all gone to the plantations."[110] On secular days, he continued, only "a few Vagabones" stayed behind, debtors who had fled from Paramaribo on account of "Debt" or "Misdemeanors." They would hide out in the synagogue, taking advantage of their hilltop location to spy out policing tentboats dispatched from time to time to hound and extradite them. When the outlaws spotted these sheriffs within half an hour from the shore, they would flee into the surrounding rainforest.[111]

Religious functionaries, who were legally contracted to be present in the Jewish village nearly every day, yearned to break free of their workplace. These subordinate officials routinely supplemented their paltry salaries by launching plantations, much to the chagrin of the regents. The student and teacher of Jewish law Jacob de Casseres Brabo is the earliest known example. In 1698, he petitioned the Mahamad for permission to lay aside his duties as rabbinical teacher (*Ruby*) for two days a week in order to devote more time to his plantation, claiming that he otherwise could not subsist. The court granted his request on condition that he secure a substitute and warned him not to use his days off as a pretext for "other trips," perhaps an oblique reference to visits to Paramaribo for the purchase of slaves and access to information on current markets.[112] This would have left Brabo four days to instruct his pupils, shifting the burden of the other two days of the week to assistant teachers. Five years later, a colleague lodged several complaints against Brabo, who allegedly shirked his obligation to lead prayers and study sessions, and often arrived late or not at all to the school. Among his numerous excuses were visits to the "fort in order to purchase negroes."[113]

Similar allegations were made in 1703 against assistant cantor and teacher Jacob Nunes de Almeida, who frequently missed prayers and school for various reasons, including visits to Paramaribo's fort. Like Casseres Brabo, Almeida may have also been drawn to the fort for the purchase of slaves for his plantation. In the city, he evidently met with ritual slaughterers, who may have sought his rabbinical knowledge in return for remuneration. Sometimes he crossed the river separating Jodensavanne from the other shore, undertaking excursions to gather starchy root vegetables (*tayas*), a suggestion of hunger.[114] In the colony's early days, the drive of these functionaries to launch plantations with the aim of supplementing their meager income found its parallel in the colonial government, where everyone from simple bureaucrats to the governor himself speculated in estate ownership, partly because of the unpredictable remittance of paychecks.[115] These concerns deepened as a result of the economic collapse of the mid-1770s. In 1775, long-time assistant cantor David Baruh Louzada began a quarter-century battle with the regents and racked up a series of fines owing to his departure from the village without permission or for exceeding his furlough. During one of his trials in 1787, Louzada claimed that he did not have the means to feed his wife and children and could not bear to witness them clamoring for bread.[116]

The case of Abraham Gabay Izidro follows an even more bathetic trajectory. Izidro, a native of Spain (where he had been born a New Christian), left Amsterdam for Suriname in 1731 to serve as its ordained religious leader (*haham*) in Jodensavanne. Upon arrival in Paramaribo, and later in Jodensavanne, Izidro received the ostentatious reception mandated by Mahamad protocol. In the Jewish village, the *parnassim* and *adjuntos* (former *parnassim*) called an impromptu meeting to formally bestow upon him the title of *haham* and head of the religious tribunal (*ab bet din*) in their names and in the name of the entire congregation. They then summoned an enslaved African fisherman, informing him of his duties to his new master and advising him to behave like a good slave. On a one-year loan, they also presented Izidro with another *negro* to chop wood and carry out other domestic tasks. Later, on the eve of the Jewish Festival of Weeks (Sebuoth), just after delivering his first sermon in synagogue, Izidro was presented with a generous freewill offering, on behalf of the regents, that included 1,542 guilders, 25 hogsheads each of sugar and cacao, several hundred guilders' worth of coffee, five cows, and an enslaved valet (*muleque*). Such extravagant gifts were perfunctory and were designed as much to show off the Mahamad's wealth and power as to encourage the new civil servant to remain in the congregation's service.

Izidro might have already felt himself a rich man. However, from information acquired before leaving the fatherland, he realized that he could not eke out a living on a functionary's salary, even if supplemented by gifts, and that he would need to launch his own plantation. Before signing his contract in Amsterdam, he had also been informed that many of his predecessors had lived not at Jodensavanne, as formally required, but on their own plantations. At his first meeting with the Surinamese Mahamad, Izidro mentioned that Jodensavanne's soil was "inconvenient" and that he therefore intended to be off premises whenever he needed. The leaders did not respond, and Izidro interpreted their silence as assent. Izidro, with almost a dozen slaves, launched a plantation, which flourished, but found that from the beginning the regents sought to impede his freedom of movement outside the savanna. Izidro's interference with the triennial election of regents, and the contact he initiated with the governor (or, according to his own defense, which the governor himself initiated), placed him at odds with his Jewish superiors. His unwelcome interference with Jewish politics, the tropical disease that afflicted both him and his wife within their first year in the colony, and a long trial in which he found himself a defendant against the Mahamad bankrupted Izidro within a year.[117]

Subsequent clerics continued to show awareness that salaried officials could not make a living at Jodensavanne. Izidro's successor, Aaron Ledesma, recruited from Amsterdam in 1736, was wise enough to secure approval for his secondary employment beforehand. The contract appointing him *haham* of the Beraha VeSalom synagogue also permitted him to carry on his duties as a doctor (*medico*) anywhere in the colony.[118] In

August 1764 a new *haham* was imported from Amsterdam.[119] Just two years later, this ordained leader resolved to move to Paramaribo because he could not sustain himself on the savanna.[120]

Needless to say, Jodensavanne had no export economy. Wealthy residents survived on the surplus of their private plantations, while the poor subsisted on a combination of charitable donations, local timber production (destined for internal consumption only), and petty trade. Some residents served as bakers and purveyors of provisions, while others, including enslaved women, roamed the streets selling bread and cheese. David Pereira Brandon is typical of the Jewish jack-of-all-trades who struggled to make ends meet in Jodensavanne. In 1760, he applied to the Mahamad for a license to bake bread and to sell provisions, textiles, tools, and foodstuffs to local residents.[121] Civil servants, including ritual slaughterers, and synagogue functionaries, who did not pay taxes to the Portuguese Jewish community on their annual salaries, were part of this small service economy. A contraband economy also existed. In 1781, Jewish residents were taken to task for sending their female slaves (*negras*) to sell merchandise, some of it smuggled, on Sabbaths.[122] Soldiers of the free corps (*negros soldados*), comprised of former slaves who had engaged in military service in exchange for manumission, as well as Indigenous people, often purchased strong drinks from Jews, even though such transactions were strictly banned by both colonial and Jewish ordinances beginning in at least the 1750s.[123]

Nor did Jodensavanne's location on the banks of the colony's main waterway mean that the village was easily connected to either the rest of the colony or the capital city, as some scholars have imagined.[124] Lack of transportation was a constant predicament, even among the elite. In 1727, Portuguese Jews founded a pious brotherhood called Neveh Sedek and unanimously elected Moses Nunes Henriquez its president (*roos*). Gathering in October to contemplate their upcoming meeting just before the Festival of Weeks, members decided that if Henriquez was not able to attend due to lack of river transport, they would bring his lower-ranking colleague, Joseph Cohen Nassy, to the savanna for that holiday.[125] Communal ordinances dating to the mid-eighteenth century allowed families whose infants were born outside of the savanna six weeks (instead of the usual few days) to celebrate their occasion in the synagogue, in consideration of the "inconveniences of the colony," a likely reference to transportation challenges.[126]

In later years, the impossibility of securing embarkation to Jodensavanne resulted in the cancellation of scheduled meetings of the Mahamad,

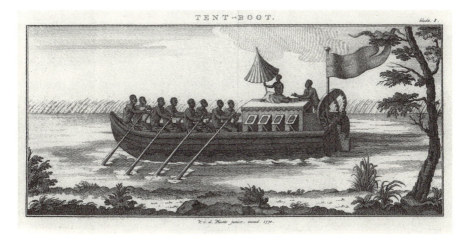

FIGURE 5. *Tent-Boot.* Detail of a tentboat, a partially covered water vehicle navigated by six to eight enslaved men, 1770. Surinamese planters used tentboats for transport to and from the city of Paramaribo. A journey from Paramaribo to Jodensavanne in such a vessel would have taken ten hours. Illustration by Phillippe Fermin. *Nieuwe algemeene beschryving van de colonie van Surinam* (Harlingen: V. van der Plaats Junior, 1770), 8. Courtesy of the John Carter Brown Library, Providence, R.I.

a problem exacerbated by the colony-wide economic crisis and the consequent transition of most of the rural Portuguese Jewish population to Paramaribo beginning in the 1780s.[127] Even with a tentboat, the trip from the capital city to Jodensavanne took ten hours and required the expensive rental of slaves as rowers.[128] In 1795, two community members with business affairs in Paramaribo requested that their legal cases be tried in Paramaribo rather than in Jodensavanne, given the "inconvenience of securing passage and slaves [*negros*] to go to Jodensavanne."[129] By the 1810s, regents regularly canceled their sessions in Jodensavanne, opting instead to meet in Paramaribo in order to save the expense of leasing a river transport vehicle and enslaved rowers. These cancellations cost the regents much angst, given the "indispensable obligation" to maintain scheduled sessions at Jodensavanne.[130]

The source of Jodensavanne's wealth, therefore, was not in the village itself. What affluence Jodensavanne enjoyed, manifested in its few magnificent houses, crossroads, and the costly accoutrements that adorned the synagogue, was dependent on the taxation of earnings from Jewish plantations

clustered mostly north and south of Jodensavanne. The *parnassim* of Jodensavanne enjoyed the power of levying taxes on all agricultural export products produced by community members and determining the amounts owed
by each household head. Another vital source of income for the village was
the freewill offerings (*promesas*) or honorary functions bestowed during
ritual prayer that were usually pledged by the well-to-do. Privately occupied
plots of land in Jodensavanne never appear as estates taxed for profits. The
village's land was owned by the community, not by individuals.[131]

Making ends meet in Jodensavanne, as was the case elsewhere in the
colony, was an ongoing challenge for the majority of residents. Taxes periodically levied by the synagogue are an eloquent barometer of the skewed
economic status of the village's residents. A tax reformation imposed in
1733 in response to the urgency of supporting the congregation's coffers
instituted a levy of 2 percent on *jehidim* (typically white, taxpaying members of the community) who produced sugar, coffee, cacao, honey, rum,
and wooden planks. These tax returns show huge economic discrepancies
between *jehidim*, the most modest generating 1,200 pounds of sugar annually and the wealthiest 56,750 pounds.[132] Landless Jews were as usual not
mentioned in this list. The congregation's charity chest was always on the
brink of depletion, well before the economic crisis of the 1770s. As in other
hemispheric American colonies, the cost of living in Suriname was high
and the burden of operating the synagogue heavy. When, in 1761, the
regents resolved to bring a new *haham* to Jodensavanne from Amsterdam,
they solicited several wealthy members to commit to five consecutive years
of contributions. Even that would not cover the expenses of transport to
Suriname, salary, and amenities. The regents therefore instituted, in addition, a general collection among all *jehidim*.[133]

The generation of charity funds from plantations was therefore vital to
Jodensavanne's existence. From early on, a handful of enterprising Jews in
Suriname established plantations whose revenues were earmarked for the
support of local Jewish paupers. The communal minutes make several references to the administration of such estates.[134] Among the longest lived
was the timberland Quapibo, located on the Cassewinica Creek. In operation since 1696, it earmarked a portion of its profits for impoverished Portuguese Jews.[135] In 1770 the Portuguese Jewish community derived a total
of 1,069.31 Surinamese guilders from six separate charity estates, almost 19
percent of its annual capitation tax.[136]

Jodensavanne sorely needed the benefits of local estates. According to Adriaan van Berkel, a Dutchman who visited the colony in the 1680s, the colony's best plantations were located in the environs of the Jewish village.[137] By the 1720s, dozens of manors owned by Portuguese Jews had sprung up north and south of the Jewish village. A map of 1737 is the earliest showing detailed plots. The Jewish population had significantly expanded, with 31 Jewish-owned estates north of Jodensavanne and 41 to the south, representing 18 percent of all colonial estates. In comparison, 25 percent of planters had a French (Huguenot) family name, while another 7 percent had English or German names, an indication that at least half of all plantations were in the hands of people originating outside the Dutch political-economic elite.[138] The 1737 map is also the earliest to show the distinction between Jodensavanne's village square and its immediate surroundings, on the one hand, and its adjoining "great prairie," abutting the wilderness, on the other. Compared to the mid-eighteenth-century estates in its environs, Jodensavanne's nucleus was tiny, amounting to 135 acres.[139] Upper Ajo and Lower Ajo, owned respectively by Isaac Henriquez de Barrios and Isaac Uziel de Avilar, each measured 800 acres, while La Diligencia to the north, in the hands of Samuel d'Avilar, stretched out to 1,775 acres.[140] This distinction is significant for, as we have seen, Jodensavanne did not produce agricultural products for export.[141] This had not only to do with its small size (300 acres was the minimum required to establish a coffee plantation) but more importantly with the quality of its soil, which in geological terms was savanna, defined as an area covered by white sand or clay and vulnerable to desiccation during the dry season.[142]

Despite the relative infertility of its soil, some residents did experiment in small-scale agriculture at Jodensavanne. Abraham de Quiros Costa started cultivating coffee plants next to his house in 1731, in the same decade that planters in Suriname began extensive cultivation of that crop.[143] Three years later, he petitioned for an additional 200 feet of land adjoining his house for the same purpose.[144] We know that Costa did not aspire to substantial production because commercial coffee production, like cacao, required a much larger expanse of land: 300–500 acres.[145] Other agricultural endeavors at Jodensavanne seem to have been ornamental and possibly medicinal. Abraham Raphael Arrias, who was living in the Jewish village in 1723, requested land for a garden.[146] Residents of Jodensavanne, particularly those inhabiting houses lining the Suriname River and the two valleys of

FIGURE 6. "View of Jodensavanne," undated, engraving by J. H. Hottinger, after drawing by Johan Anthoni Kaldenbach, undated. Note the ornamental gardens flanking the river. From Richard Gottheil, "Contributions to the History of the Jews in Surinam," *PAJHS* 9 (1901): 129–42, frontmatter.

the mountain on which it was built, took great pride in their ornamental and medicinal gardens, as David Nassy noted in 1788.[147]

Even the name of the Jewish village, as contrasted with the names of nearby plantations, underscores awareness of the difference between the relative infertility or uncultivated state of Jodensavanne and the fecundity of agricultural estates. "Savanna," a word that entered European languages from the Taíno Indigenous culture, denotes a grassy plain sparsely dotted with trees and shrubs.[148] In the French Caribbean, a *libre de savanne* (free person of the savanna) was an enslaved person informally freed by his owner and permitted to establish residence in the savanna or outlying area of the plantation.[149] By contrast, a number of plantations established by Jews near Jodensavanne bore biblical names, such as Mahanaim, Sucot, Gosen, Carmel, Petah Enaim, Kayam, and Rama. These toponyms suggest that Suriname's early Portuguese planters viewed their agricultural undertaking as a link to biblical ancestors, who communicated directly with God and received His blessings of plenty. Mahanaim, for example, was the land the sons of Jacob found to be the best in Egypt, suitable for both crops and livestock, after famine forced them out of the Land of Israel (Genesis 46:28–34, 47:1–6). Mount Carmel, located in the northern Kingdom of Israel, is described as a place of beauty and fertility (Isaiah 35:2). Sucot, meaning "tabernacles," is the harvest feast commemorating the exodus from Egypt and God's bounty as well as a city bordering Egypt and the Promised Land (Leviticus 23:42–43; Exodus 12:37).[150]

If Jodensavanne could not provide abundant crops, it did offer comfortable living space. Petitions to build house extensions explicitly mention the desire for "comfort" to accommodate expanding families. Implicitly, they indicate a changing sense of living standards conditioned by increased material wealth. In 1710, Ishac Pinto complained that his house in the savanna was only 38 feet long. Given that he had a family living very narrowly in that house, he wished to lengthen it by 25 feet.[151] Again in 1721 he petitioned the regents for permission to enlarge his house, facing the Suriname River, by 20 to 30 feet. Pinto considered this not a luxury but something he "needed."[152] Both requests appear to have been granted, and if they pertain to the same house at Jodensavanne, the finished product would have stretched 93 feet, a bit longer than the local synagogue. By then, Pinto's plantation La Estrella, which he shared with his brother Dr. Abraham Pinto, was valued at 74,000 guilders. His domestic slaves, who might have accompanied him during holidays to Jodensavanne, numbered sixteen.[153] The increasing tendency of Jodensavanne's elites to display their wealth through lavish residences was part of a material transformation that took place over the course of the eighteenth century, witnessed among families of means in Europe, North America, and the urban centers of colonial Africa and Asia. Large rooms previously undifferentiated in purpose made way for smaller spaces demarcated for specialized use, such as entrance halls, reception rooms, dining rooms, and the parlor, which became the focal point of family life.[154] In the absence of interior descriptions of Jodensavanne's houses, we may rely on this global trend to imagine rooms never described in the petitions.

Plots along the synagogue square were the choicest, parceled out to leading members of the community. Imanuel de Solis, among the first *jehidim* of the congregation and, by 1715, an *adjunto* (former *parnas*), received permission from the Mahamad to build a house on the synagogue square in 1708.[155] Elites also used their clout and wealth to leave their mark on the Jodensavanne Cemetery. Samuel and Baruh Cohen Nassi, among the founders of the colony's Jewish community, received permission in 1706 to build and furnish a house in the burial ground in order to hold there an annual memorial service (*escava*) for their late mother. The house was to

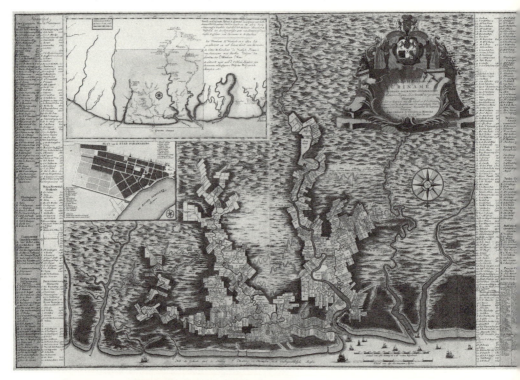

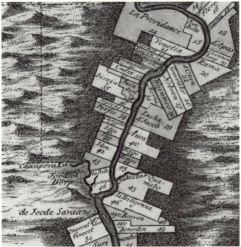

FIGURE 7. *General Map of the Colony or Province of Suriname (Algemeene Kaart van de Colonie of Provintie van Suriname)*, 1758. Until the last decades of the eighteenth century, Jewish-owned plantations, with their Hebrew, Portuguese, and Spanish names, dominated a long stretch of the Suriname River. Directly northeast of Jodensavanne ("Joodsch Dorp") are "la Dilegensa" (46), "Lucha d'Jacob" (39), and "Rama" (20). Courtesy of the John Carter Brown Library, Providence, R.I.

be substantial, 25 by 20 feet, seven feet high, covered with shingles or tiles, surrounded by columns, and furnished with benches, but lacking embroidery decor to avoid the risk of theft,[156] a precaution that hints at the village's desertion on secular days.

Yet the vast majority of building projects were modest in dimension and probably also in structure, as Nassy's comments in 1788 about "mediocre architecture" and the "thrift of our ancestors" hint.[157] Houses typically measured forty feet across their front, mirroring the dimension of the synagogue's facade and perhaps revealing an attempt at symmetry. Although the Mahamad liberally distributed plots, actual construction was extremely precarious. Several petitioners for lots in Jodensavanne declared they needed many years to complete their houses because the land was "inconvenient."[158] Both elders and newcomers to the community regarded Jodensavanne, with its persistent lack of "comfort and food," as "a desert."[159] The cost of building houses was enormous, particularly when it involved the manufacture of shingles, which for reasons of fire prevention were preferable to thatch.[160] The reconstruction of Jodensavanne's dilapidated charity house, occupied by its caretaker, Abraham Ysrael, in 1692, tallied over 3,000 pounds of sugar, not counting the cement foundation, which was still intact.[161] This sum represents the total annual revenue of a low-income member of Jodensavanne's community, according to a 1732 tax roll.[162] Slightly more than half the total amount of construction on the charity house represented labor carried out by four enslaved Africans, including a skilled "negro" carpenter, an indication of how valuable ownership in human beings was in the colony.[163]

From its early days, then, Jodensavanne functioned not as a center of commerce or passage to the extralocal economy but rather as a holiday resort. Its soil was relatively unfertile and its land mass too inadequate to support the large-scale cultivation upon which planters depended. In this sense, Jodensavanne parallels the Sabbath and nooning houses of Puritan New England, which the faithful constructed near the village meeting-house so that they would not be compelled to travel a long distance on Sunday for worship. Colonial New England's Sabbath houses were often constructed collectively by several farmers, whereas in Jodensavanne holiday homes tended to be private and were a sign of an individual's lofty status as a *jahid*.[164] Jodensavanne would not even have existed had it not been for the surrounding estates, which provided both a tax base for the communal poverty chest and charitable contributions for residents.

Wealth, however, was not the only differentiating marker among Jews in this village.

Social Hierarchies in Jodensavanne

Aside from economic status, ethnic distinctions were also key to the status of Jodensavanne's Jewish residents and sojourners. Recipients of plots owned only the physical structures they built thereupon. The plots themselves were the legal property of Suriname's Portuguese Jewish community and could not be alienated. Moreover, according to communal bylaws, houses could be sold only to fellow Portuguese and Spanish Jews.[165] With occasional exceptions and special permission from the *parnassim*, no one outside the Portuguese Jewish nation was permitted to even lease a home in Jodensavanne, not even Ashkenazim.[166] In 1754, an Ashkenazi Jew who signed his name only as "Mordecai" petitioned for a plot on which to build a house, even though he was not a *jahid*. He described himself as a resident and stated that he could not find lodging during the holidays. Mordecai probably occupied a room or house made vacant only during secular days. He was careful to secure the permission of his prospective neighbors before submitting his petition. The regents assented to his plan but under strict orders that he rent out his house only to members "of our nation" (that is, Iberian-origin Jews) and never sell the plot to anyone, as it belonged to the Portuguese Jewish charity chest.[167]

The occasional presence of an Ashkenazi Jew served to reinforce the time-honored law that such persons did not really belong. As late as 1824, during the Feast of Tabernacles (*sukkot*), an altercation broke out between David Jacob de Vries, an Ashkenazi Jew, and Moses Henriquez Cotino Junior. When Cotino reported his aggravation about De Vries's behavior, he reminded the Mahamad in Portuguese that his aggressor, as "an individual of the Ashkenazi nation," was "only tolerated in the savanna and in no way . . . considered an owner of the savanna, as each individual of the Portuguese nation is."[168] Such exclusivist policies helped to ensure that Jodensavanne and its environs remained a Portuguese Jewish enclave.

The ethnically exclusive nature of Jodensavanne seems to have been initiated by Portuguese Jews themselves. Governor van Scharpenhuysen's 1691 land grant identified the recipients as members of the "Jewish nation," not as Portuguese Jews.[169] This generality may be a reflection of the general indifference with which white Christians regarded Jewish ethnic distinctions through roughly the first half of the seventeenth century or of the relatively insignificant numbers of Ashkenazim then present in the colony. It may also hint at a lingering desire among Portuguese Jews to distance themselves from Portugal and the atrocities committed against New Christians and Jews during and after the fall of Dutch Brazil. Governors who succeeded Van Scharpenhuysen reinforced ethnically exclusivist policies, a sign of the power Portuguese Jews wielded to determine the contours of the colony's Jewish community. Once Ashkenazi Jews formed their own congregation in Paramaribo in the 1730s, they duplicated those exclusivist policies in mirror image, barring Portuguese Jews from participating in Ashkenazi public worship, a regulation the Portuguese Jewish regents both initiated and enforced. This separatist practice gradually, but only provisionally and exceptionally, began to relax during the last quarter of the eighteenth century, but only in the city (and not at the Jodensavanne synagogue).[170]

Fierce competition for residential plots in Jodensavanne helped create other social distinctions. In theory, all taxpaying, Portuguese Jews, including, through the first half of the eighteenth century, many Eurafricans (*mulatos*), were classified as *jehidim*, that is, taxpaying, first-class members of the community. However, native-born Jews felt themselves to be superior in rank to recent arrivals. In 1707, Dr. Abraham Pinto and Ishac Pinto expressed concern that the choice plots they had laid their eyes on could be claimed by "new *jehidim* who might come to this holy congregation." The petitioners argued that given their status as long-standing members of the community (*jehidim antigos*), they deserved to enjoy more commodious housing than newcomers.[171] Imanuel de Solis insisted on the basis of being among the first *jehidim* of the congregation that he be allowed to build his house on a plot along the synagogue square. The time lapse between concession (1703) and planned construction (1708) did not diminish his sense of entitlement.[172] The distinction these men were drawing on the basis of recency of arrival underscores the finding of sociologists Norbert Elias and John L. Scotson, namely that the formation of hierarchies can manifest even within economically, religiously, and ethnically homogeneous populations.[173] The anxiety-ridden petition of the Pintos, meanwhile, attests to the regular influx of Jews from Amsterdam, the major transit city for early modern Portuguese Jews migrating to the New World.[174] However circular migration was in the Jewish Atlantic, the strongest flow was toward and not away from the Americas.[175] The Portuguese Mahamad in Suriname dispatched fewer destitute Jews back to Amsterdam than it received.[176]

Interestingly, communal leaders in the first half of the eighteenth century did not seem to discriminate against Jews of Eurafrican origin. Such
Jews both requested and received plots on which to build their homes. At
the time of her petition in 1728, Simha Peregrino was living with her family
in her father's home and had no house of her own. She requested and was
granted a forty-foot plot on which to build her own house. She does not
mention a husband, and it is likely that hers was a matrilocal family, as
most Eurafrican families at the time seem to have been. Peregrino requested
a plot in between those of Mosseh Prado and Jacob Abenacar, fellow
Eurafricans, suggesting residential solidarity and perhaps a subtle form of
exclusion by the white Portuguese Jewish caste.[177] But the very fact that
Eurafricans requested and received plots for building their houses suggests
that they shared a sense of native belonging in the Jewish community and,
more specifically, to its village. In 1704, David Judeu, who was circumcised
in the colony in 1663, petitioned the regents for a twenty-foot extension to
his already existing house in order to celebrate the Passover holiday "more
comfortably," a possible indication of his growing family (and fortunes).[178]
Jahacob Pelengrino also felt sufficiently at ease to petition for a forty-foot
extension to the house of his sister Simha Peregrina (perhaps the aforementioned petitioner Simha Peregrino). The twenty-foot house he already
owned was no longer large enough to accommodate his increasing clan.[179]

In concluding this section, it would be remiss not to mention the hierarchies implicitly embedded within the architecture of the synagogue, situated in the center of the village square. On one level, the design of the
building suggests the harmonious peace and solidarity that according to
Jewish tradition will precede the end of days. Architect Rachel Frankel was
the first to hypothesize that the layout of Jodensavanne's central plaza and
architecture of its synagogue were messianic, a persuasive theory given what
we know about the eschatological inclinations of David Cohen Nassi and
fellow colonial entrepreneur João de Yllán.[180] Four roads, positioned in parallel and perpendicular pairs beside the riverfront, came together to form
the synagogue plaza, a quadrilateral site plan remarkably similar to that of
colonial New Haven (1638) and the fanciful utopian state described in
Johann Valentin Andreae's *Christianopolis* (1619), though it was rectangular
rather than square.[181] Like its predecessor to the north, Jodensavanne seems
to draw inspiration directly from biblical directives for building a "new
Jerusalem."[182] The quadri-directional layout brings to mind one of the three
passages in the Hebrew Bible where "ideal (i.e., not extant) town planning

is described." In the first, Numbers 2:1–31, the Lord directed each tribe "to encamp by its own standard, three tribes each on the north, south, east and west sides of a square in the center of which was the tent of meeting." The congregation's name, Beraha VeSalom, seems to allude to a commentary on the *Zohar* (Book of Splendor), which many scholars attribute to a Jewish mystic of thirteenth-century Castile and which in early modernity was accepted as a sacred text by many learned Portuguese Jews. The medieval commentary indicates that Eden is to be located in the place of "the secrets of life, *blessing, and peace [beraha ve-salom]*" (italics added).[183]

Unlike any other synagogue in the Portuguese diaspora, one entered Beraha VeSalom through an open plaza—unencumbered and exposed. This imposing layout compensated for the modest size of the synagogue, as if the town planners were focusing less on projected population size and more on emphasizing the autonomy and environment of Jodensavanne, unprecedented in Jewish diasporic history. An outer perimeter wall invited approach to the synagogue plaza from all cardinal directions through four separate entrances. One of these entrances led to a separate door reserved for enslaved Africans (*porta dos Negros*), perhaps a reference to the so-called *negros da sedaca*, property of the communal charity chest, branded with the initials of the congregation ("B.V.S."), and tasked with the upkeep of the synagogue and its immediate surroundings.[184] Despite the threat of slave revolts and attacks from Maroons, Indians, or invading European powers, the synagogue was laid out as if in a perfect world.[185] As the foregoing details suggest, and as the next two sections confirm, a great distance separated the messianic ideals of the village's founders from the lived reality of its dwellers.

The Demographic Owners of Jodensavanne

Because Jodensavanne was a Jewish village it is easy to lose sight of the fact that the majority of its residents were enslaved Africans.[186] One would not come upon this fact except through inference, as people of African ancestry are rarely mentioned in records pertaining to the Jewish village. Suriname, as we have seen, was among the largest slave societies in the Americas, relative to its free population. In the last few decades of the seventeenth century, the import of enslaved Africans burgeoned to keep pace with the proliferation of the colony's sugar plantations. By 1684, the number of enslaved Africans reached around 4,000, dwarfing the white Christian and Jewish population of around 800 by 5 to 1. The spread of coffee cultivation after 1725 further prompted the importation of Africans to the colony. In the 1730s, their population had risen to 40,000, while by 1774, nearly 60,000 of their number were living in Suriname.[187] Between 1668 and 1830, between 213,000 and 250,000 Africans were introduced into the colony, and for much of that period over 90 percent of the colony's residents were both enslaved and of African origin.[188]

The stretch of the Suriname River dominated by Jews was thus also dominated by people of African descent. In 1684, one year prior to the construction of Beraha VeSalom, the village and its surrounding Portuguese Jewish plantations were home to 1,158 people, with Africans outnumbering Jews by at least 6 to 1.[189] The domestics who counted among these unfree people accompanied their owners to Jodensavanne and were perhaps left behind during secular days, as were the slaves tasked with the upkeep of the synagogue. David Nassy observed in 1788 that each Jewish family residing in Jodensavanne lived with four to six slaves.[190] As we have noted, it was not only the fabulously wealthy who were slave owners. That decade, several slave-owning heads of house turned to the Mahamad for support, unable to maintain their families or pay their colonial taxes. Mosseh Jessurun, for example, earned a meager living from his pen (he was perhaps a scribe) and struggled to support a wife and three children, while coping with his illness. He owned "only one *negra*." Selomoh Romanel, also afflicted with a disease, had to support a wife and two children. He owned two *negros* and earned a pittance selling chickens and flour provided by his brother-in-law. Isaac Bueno de Mesquita, a cobbler, husband, and father of six children, had "nothing but the benefit of a dwelling house" and two *negras*.[191]

Although there was little cultivation in Jodensavanne, people of African ancestry were given plenty to do. Scattered references document their unceasing role in the upkeep of Jodensavanne, even if their labor on nearby plantations, the backbreaking work that maintained Jodensavanne as a functioning village, is usually only implicit. David Nassy observed in 1788 that adjacent plantations regularly provided the residents of Jodensavanne with foodstuffs. These provisions could only have been produced by slaves.[192] In the village itself, slaves were responsible for manufacturing wood planks and beams for local consumption and for executing building and road projects.[193] Planters were largely dependent on the success of their estates, worked by African slaves. Some plots in Jodensavanne claimed by Portuguese Jews stood empty for years if the occupier had not yet launched a plantation or if his estate had not yet turned a profit.[194] Imanuel de Soliz received permission to build a house 51 feet long in 1703 but could not gather the necessary funds before the three-year window closed because he—and, by implication, his slaves—were occupied with building a polder, an endeavor that demanded almost more work "than my strength can withstand."[195] By 1708, Soliz had still not constructed the house.[196]

Enslaved females also had a supervised role in the synagogue. The *ascamot* of 1748 include a repeatedly violated prohibition against the attendance of "Negras, Molattas [ou] Indias," with or without children, and indicate the responsibility of their masters to remove them.[197] These women were no doubt tending to the needs of their owners during worship. But for many of them, the synagogue was also a locus for socializing. In 1772, these three groups became so consistently disruptive to worshippers that the regents designated a so-called charity slave to keep fellow servile workers quiet during services.[198] Later that decade, slaves who accompanied their masters and mistresses to the house of worship during Yom Kippur day were so threatening to the order and tranquility of the region that the Mahamad hired guards at the gates of the synagogue and patrols around the savanna to quiet them.[199]

According to communal legislation, both slaves and servants of Jews were not to work on Sabbath. These ordinances also prohibited *jehidim* from working or having their slaves or domestics, whether owned or rented, labor on holidays, including the Festival of Weeks (Sebuoth), Passover, and the intermediary days of these holidays.[200] This was enforced as a religious principle and ratified by the *haham*.[201] A Jew who contravened this law was considered a Sabbath violator (*haver quebrantado Sabath*).[202] These examples underscore the observation of Jonathan Schorsch that slaves owned by Jews experienced Jewish life communally and created their own communalism, whose rhythms paralleled and at times intersected with Jewish ritual life.[203]

Through the generations, unfree people of African descent were trained to defend, construct, landscape, clean, and paint Jodensavanne and were mandated to tidy and supervise the synagogue as "charity slaves." Many of them were fixed residents of Jodensavanne and demographically dominated as continual dwellers of the Jewish village. Some, like the ten-year-old free "mulatto" who appeared in a 1762 census of Jodensavanne, were themselves of Jewish parentage. The "trusted slaves" or manumitted people who stayed behind to watch over the property of their masters or former owners after mass relocation to Paramaribo were probably those responsible for preventing the theft of the costly accoutrements listed in synagogue inventories of the 1820s through 1840s.[204] Like other unfree people living in Suriname's countryside, for whom the plantation was home and the domicile of their ancestors' spirits, it is plausible that Jodensavanne's slaves regarded the Jewish village as their own.[205]

Jodensavanne as a Paramilitary Outpost

Because it existed on the frontier, on the borderland between colonial settlements and autonomous or outlaw non-white populations, Jodensavanne increasingly assumed the function of a paramilitary outpost, an informal garrison that, although not part of the colony's professional armed forces, functioned similarly. To be sure, any plantation or village situated alongside the frontier, an extensive area that abutted virtually all riverine settlements, was similarly situated. But Jews, or at least so they claimed in a petition to Governor Van Sommelsdijck in 1684, tended to remain in place and defend their settlements against attacks, while other whites fled.[206] In 1689, the Jewish militia (civil guard) helped defend the colony against a French attack, despite the fact that it was Sabbath.[207] Defense carried out by private citizens was crucial to the colony's survival. Suriname's standing army was traditionally oriented toward fighting off external enemies. But in general, internal threats were dealt with by several regional militias manned by volunteer forces. These included four companies of whites, one company of free "mulattoes," and another of free "negroes," all stationed in Paramaribo, plus six to ten rural militias, one assigned to each region. The rural companies included a Jewish Division, in operation since at least 1671. Starting in the 1730s, as the threat of Maroons to plantation life intensified, the standing army was also mustered to combat runaways, alongside the volunteer companies.[208] It was this standing army that was made famous to Anglophone readers through the memoir of one of its soldiers, John Gabriel Stedman. As Stedman's account affirms, the paramilitary character of Jodensavanne became more pronounced as the threat posed by Maroons mounted, with patrols constantly cruising between the Jewish village and nearby plantations.[209]

In the early decades of the colony, slave rebellions were relatively minor and did not seriously threaten the colony's agricultural estates. But in 1690, a mutiny broke out that triggered a long era of large-scale uprisings.[210] The rebellion occurred on a plantation owned by the Portuguese Jew Emmanuel Machado and located on the Cassewijne Creek, "behind," or directly northeast of, Jodensavanne. Like most owners, plantation directors, and overseers, Machado was known for inflicting excruciating torture on slaves who committed the most minor offenses. In 1690, he was murdered by his slaves, who fled to the wilderness, taking with them necessities and leaving the plantation in flames.[211] Instead of financing a retaliatory expedition out of the colonial coffers, Governor Johan van Scharpenhuysen insisted the Portuguese Jewish community take full responsibility for avenging Machado's death. Jewish leaders dispatched an expedition to the nearest Maroon settlement, where they killed many of its residents, including several women and children, whom they tortured before execution.[212]

Machado's grave, if the fire spared any cadaver to inter, is unknown. But the Jodensavanne Cemetery preserves the memory of two other Portuguese Jewish men who lost their lives in similar slave uprisings in 1738 and 1739, respectively: Emmanuel Pereyra and David Rodrigues Monsanto.[213] Of the latter nothing other than his epitaph is yet known, but Pereyra was murdered in 1738 when enslaved Africans on his plantation near the Sarwa Creek (due east of Jodensavanne) staged a violent rebellion, killing their master and pillaging his property. The runaways set on a rampage through the savanna, destroying all neighboring estates. Independent of the colonial Dutch authorities, the Jewish Civil Guard sought its own vengeance by attempting to track down, punish, and kill the escaped slaves. Their pursuit was successful; they returned after six weeks with forty-seven captives and six hands severed from the bodies of the vanquished fugitives.[214]

The cemetery at Jodensavanne served as a perpetual reminder of these mutinies. Both Pereyra and Monsanto received epitaphs indicating the cause of death and intoning prayers for divine retribution against the rebels, disparaged on Monsanto's gravestone as "cruel, uprising negroes" (*crueys negros alevantados*). The opening verse carved on the respective monuments of Pereyra and Monsanto is identical: "O Lord God, to whom vengeance belongs; O God, to whom vengeance belongs, shine forth!" (Psalms 94:1).[215]

Similarly, when Jacob, son of Abraham Meijer, of the "Ashkenazi nation," perished in a Maroon attack in 1789, David Hizkiahu Baruh Louzada (1750–1825), the cantor of Congregation Beraha VeSalom and keeper of Jodensavanne's cemetery and its register, described the killers as "our cruel and rebellious enemies" (*Nossos Crueis & rebeldes Enemigos*), concluding the entry with the curse, "may his blood be avenged."[216]

In 1743, yet another David Cohen Nassy, this one an elderly officer in the Jewish militia, led an expedition against runaway slaves. According to his epitaph in the nearby Cassipora Creek Cemetery, he departed this world "after he returned from beating the black rebelling slaves."[217] The David Nassy of *Essai historique* fame noted, again with bitterness, that this officer died of a fever around the age of sixty-seven, after returning from a Maroon expedition to face a trial that convicted him of excesses during the attack.[218]

The nature of Jodensavanne as a holiday resort, largely forsaken during secular days, increased the village's vulnerability to such Maroon incursions, particularly after 1712, when slave desertions increased in frequency.[219] Jewish plantations, so prominently represented in the region, were often targeted.[220] The Jewish village and its neighboring plantations lay adjacent to a thick rainforest where bands of runaway slaves could launch attacks. In 1753, the Jewish regents of the Mahamad instituted a 10 percent tax hike on all Jews residing along the Suriname River, at Jodensavanne, and along the Cassewinica Creek to fund the rental of slaves who would clear the overgrowth that could serve to camouflage the outlaws.[221]

The pacification of certain runaway communities in the second half of the eighteenth century, including the Djuka in 1760, the Saramakka two years later, and the Matawai in 1767, did not eliminate the threat posed by individual absconders or other Maroon groups, which intermittently arose, particularly in reaction to worsening treatment.[222] The threat became more pressing after the formation of the Boni, a group of uncertain origins who by 1765 had grown large enough to launch attacks on plantations. Named after a locally born man whose mother had been a runaway slave, these Maroons concentrated their assaults on the Cassipora Creek region and by 1772 had successfully attacked five plantations.[223] In 1780, two enslaved women known as Diana van Isak Mesias and Lucretia van Pinto were at Jodensavanne with their master, who sent them into the surrounding forest to chop wood. Suddenly, six runaways accosted the pair with a lance, covering their mouths to stifle their screams. The women were then spirited away to a Boni Maroon village, at a five-day distance. There is no indication how

Diana and Lucretia returned to offer their testimony to government officials, but hostage swapping may have been involved.[224]

The Portuguese Jewish regents were highly conscious of the vulnerability of their village to such attacks. In 1782, they pointed out to the governor
that the particular topography of Jodensavanne made it an inviting target
for a military takeover. Perched between two ravines, the village offered a
secure hideout if conquered by Maroons, while the synagogue could be
transformed into a small citadel.[225] At the time of the major Maroon uprisings of the 1770s and 1780s, the dread of attacks was especially heightened
during holidays, when Jodensavanne's population was at its densest,
because worshipping Jews could be caught unawares. The regents made
sure to station military guards at the synagogue gates during the High Holy
night and day.[226] In 1789, following a Maroon attack on the Clarenbeek
plantation in the Commewijne area and the kidnapping of its rector, Jean
Merla, the Boni announced their plans to attack plantations near Jodensavanne.[227] The regents responded by creating a large opening in the forest
nearest to the dwelling houses of Jodensavanne. All residents of the
savanna, as well as planters, were compelled to lease out ten to twelve of
their "good negroes" to accomplish the work, which would be reflected in
a discount to their taxes. Thereafter, two slaves would be permanently
leased to clear the surroundings.[228]

During the culmination of the Maroon wars in the 1770s, Jodensavanne's strategic location and topography attracted the notice of military
officials. In that same decade, various military leaders from Suriname and
abroad announced their intention to visit Jodensavanne with their entou-
rages, as part of reconnaissance tours to restore the colony against the rebellious slaves, "our affirmed enemies."[229] By the late 1770s, colonial officials
had completed a new defense line (*linie de defensie*) or military path, dotted
with fortified outposts, to combat Maroon incursions and to protect
adjoining plantations from attack. Also known as the *cordonpad* (cordon
path), it purposefully traversed a corner of Jodensavanne. Soldiers stationed
there could purchase provisions from the inhabitants of Jodensavanne, and
visiting military officials could impose on the Jewish community for free
lodging as needed.[230] By early 1780, the post featured a supply store and
horse stall, and was manned by a sergeant, corporal, and thirteen general
officers, as well as a store clerk, baker, barn boy, lawnmower, and six
enslaved men from nearby plantations.[231] Stretching from Jodensavanne to
just short of the Atlantic Ocean, the *cordonpad* passed through swamps and

rainforests and extended ninety-four kilometers. Portions of the defense line were still in operation in as late as 1842.[232]

Portuguese Jewish records affirm that the rebel threat did not end in the eighteenth century. During the Hebrew year coinciding with 1805–6, David Baruh Louzada, then cantor of Congregation Beraha VeSalom, followed the directives of the regents and composed a prayer to be read on Sabbath days, imploring God for the "triumph of the militia of this colony dispatched against our enemies, the rebelling, uprising Negroes."[233] As it turns out, this supplication was not a response to typical outlaw Maroons but rather to three Eurafrican detachments that revolted in 1804 during the British Interregnum (1799–1802, 1804–16). These militias were composed of Red Barets (or the Black Chasseurs, as the British called them) who had been serving along the cordon defense line. They executed some white officers and the surgeon, raided a plantation, absconded with thirty slaves, and headed toward the Marowijne River, where they joined the Boni and received some assistance from the Djuka. All told, sixty to seventy men rebelled, perhaps emboldened by the massacre of whites and the declaration of an independent Haiti under Jean-Jacques Dessalines in 1804.[234] The late date of this Surinamese revolt, which concluded with a new peace treaty between the colonial government and the Djuka, is evidence that military incursions continued to menace the Jewish village into the nineteenth century.[235]

By the turn of the nineteenth century, the era of the British Interregnum, the village's paramilitary and patriotic functions had fully merged. In November 1804, the Portuguese Mahamad learned of Governor Charles Green's upcoming visit to the savanna in order to view the defense line. They resolved to receive him as was customary and proceeded to compose long shopping and guest lists. The governor, accompanied by three commissioners of the Council of Policy, was received with full fanfare. He and his entourage proceeded to the synagogue, where they received the "honors and ceremonies proper for this occasion."[236] By the time German soldier August Kappler was stationed at Jodensavanne in the 1830s and 1840s, the village had become synonymous with a military outpost.[237]

The foregoing evidence does much to dispute the scholarly image of Jodensavanne as a village idyll, developed and persistently repeated over the past century. However, one cannot fault these scholars alone. When David Nassy, Samuel Cohen Nassi's great-grandnephew, sat down to describe his native Jodensavanne in 1788, no chronicler of the Dutch colony had deigned to say much more about the place, except that it was "a village of Jews."[238] David Nassy was, in fact, the first writer to extensively describe Jodensa-vanne in any published venue. He devoted eight full pages to the village in his *Essai historique*, a survey of the Dutch colony that doubled as an apolo-gia of its Jewish community.[239] His idealized depiction focused on the built landscape and the natural setting and emphasized the village's remoteness and tranquility. Nassy began his description with the dwelling places of the village's elites. Their homes, some "large and commodious," were erected around a rectangular central square measuring 450 by 300 feet wide and intersected by four cross streets. More modest houses, of a "mediocre archi-tecture," lay adjacent, reflecting the "thrift of our ancestors." Houses abut-ting the riverbank were flanked on each side by little gardens "shaped in the form of a slope, planted with shrubbery and with pot-herbs for the house." In the center of the village square was the "Blessing and Peace" synagogue, consecrated in 1685. Standing 90 feet long, 40 feet wide, and 33 feet high, it was built of brick and supported by large wooden columns topped by a vaulted ceiling. Although modest in size, everything about the synagogue was "so properly built," Nassy mused, and communicated "such an indescribably majesty," that although quite ordinary in size, "it elicits the admiration of those who see it for the first time."[240]

Nature seemed to confirm Jodensavanne's sublime aura. Its air was "the healthiest in the entire colony." In a nearby spring, cascading from the top of the mountain, bubbled pleasant-tasting water used to combat tertian fevers and constipation. Even in the hottest season, this water source never appeared to dry up.[241] Its remote setting on the upper reaches of the Suri-name River, Nassy elsewhere explained, secured Jodensavanne as a haven from "the inquisitorial spirit that had made them [Iberian New Christians] flee Spain and Portugal."[242] The village was, according to him, "the sole place of retreat where one can sojourn and conduct one's household with all imaginable liberty."[243]

As Nassy wrote these words, a major change in Suriname was already underway, a colony-wide debt crisis, triggered in part by the stock market crash of 1773 and inflated plantation appraisals that did not coincide with production capacity. A long period of economic decline ensued, and by the late 1780s most of the inland Jewish population had relocated to Paramar-ibo.[244] Because their estates were the oldest, and thus more vulnerable to soil depletion, Jews were affected disproportionately compared to their Christian counterparts. Two-thirds of the Jewish community now relied on the communal poverty chest. Around 1730, 115 of Suriname's 401 plantations (almost 30 percent) were owned by Jews. By 1788 that number had declined to 46 of 591 (nearly 8 percent). Only sixteen of them were cotton or coffee estates. The remainder were provision estates or generally less lucrative lumber plantations.[245] The investment craze had largely done away with sugar cultivation for the time. The mass removal to Paramaribo first became noticeable in the early 1780s, by which time 620 Portuguese Jews lived in Paramaribo, leaving just 250 residing on plantations.[246] As the Jewish presence in the capital city augmented, so did anti-Jewish sentiment and acts among various sectors of Suriname's population, whether free or enslaved.[247]

By dint of Nassy's pen, Jodensavanne was recast from a rather obscure settlement into a blissful one. The Jewish hamlet became a perfect world in miniature, where ideal town planning combined with the bounty of nature to produce a peaceful, orderly existence amid Edenic abundance. In the late 1770s and 1780s, other Portuguese Jewish regents joined in by lauding Jodensavanne as the community's "Jewish patrimony" and "perpetual and incontestable inheritance."[248] This new regard for Jodensavanne was based on the type of collective amnesia scholars understand as integral to alienation from the present and a concomitant quest for a future embedded within a fictional past.[249] The displacement of most of the riverine Jewish population to Paramaribo, the precipitous economic downfall of their elites, and a rising incidence of anti-Jewish thought and deed encouraged David Nassy to portray Jodensavanne as symbolic of the fulfillment of Suriname's economic promise, a vibrant religious and flourishing settlement that highlighted the progress and potential of Suriname, while at the same time demonstrating that its Jews were benevolent, enlightened, and unappreciated by their Christian cohorts.[250]

David Nassy based most of his assertions on archival sources, which were easily accessible to him as a communal leader, and diligently transcribed and inserted several of them in his book as *pièces justificatives*. An Enlightenment figure, Nassy was a documentary historian who pioneered a scholarly methodology for Suriname before the rise of History as a professional field. The same trove of archival sources from which he drew confirms most of his factual assertions but significantly alters his assessment of the Jewish village as a place of freedom, peace, and prosperity. For, just as in the colony at large, so too in Jodensavanne was liberty closely intertwined with coercion, tranquility with violence, and widespread poverty with fabulous wealth.

Conclusion

This chapter has examined the village of Jodensavanne in terms of its political, economic, and religious functions and in light of its characterization in secondary sources as an Edenic, economically bustling, proto-Zionist settlement. There is some indirect evidence that the village's founding generation were imbued with messianic impulses. The spurt of redemptionist fervor that accompanied early Jewish colonization in the Caribbean during the 1650s and 1660s finds echoes in the mystical name of Jodensavanne's congregation, "Blessing and Peace," an oblique allusion to the Garden of Eden, and is perhaps hinted at in the synagogue's architecture and in the quadrilateral layout of its plaza.

However, unlike early Puritan leaders who formed their own settlements, Portuguese Jewish leaders did not leave behind any verbal articulation of their early eschatological vision for Jodensavanne. The phrases "Jerusalem by the Riverside" and "New Jerusalem," which many researchers have attributed to early modern residents of Jodensavanne, are nowhere attested to in the communal archives.[251] Rather, these epithets are later interpolations, coinciding with the rise of the modern, political Zionist movement in the nineteenth century. As Tuvia Preschel reminds us, the ascription of the "Jerusalem" moniker to locales where it was never used contemporaneously is a common tendency of latter generations, born "of a desire to emphasize . . . [the] importance and influence" of such Jewish communities.[252] Even the biblical names of plantations launched by Portuguese Jews in Jodensavanne's environs are more an expression of Suriname's Protestant environment than Jewish eschatology. Because Protestant Christians, after the rise of their denomination in the sixteenth century, largely abandoned the practice of pilgrimage to Jerusalem, they lost their physical connection to the earthly site. The holy city for them increasingly became a "theological ideal" rather than a real place, a shift in perspective evidenced by such common toponyms as "Salem," "New Canaan," and "Zion," inscribed on English, Dutch, and German colonial maps, whether in North America, Africa, or the Pacific.[253]

Moreover, contemporaneous residents tended to stress the uncertainty of the colony's survival and the community's precarious endurance. Insecurity, violence, and deprivation were the central themes of daily existence. Purposefully built on the frontier, Jodensavanne existed as an embattled, militarized settlement near plantations owned by Portuguese Jews, where enslaved Africans generated wealth for the colony and where white settlers fended off attacks by Indigenous people, rebellious slaves, and outlaw Maroons. Mirroring violence elsewhere in the colony, African slaves were routinely tortured on the village's roadsides or along the fence enclosing the synagogue square. Whether nearly abandoned, as on profane days, or on holidays, when the population swelled, Jodensavanne was extremely vulnerable to Maroon incursions. In the last quarter of the eighteenth century, the primary function of Jodensavanne became ever more militaristic. The *cordonpad*, constructed in the mid-1770s to deter Maroon incursions, purposefully intersected a corner of Jodensavanne. Over time, the Jewish village increasingly functioned as a paramilitary outpost. Residents were compelled to offer lodging and provisions to visiting soldiers, and communal leaders were pressured into providing perfunctory ceremonies to greet colonial governors and military officials who came to survey the cordon path. The liberty Jews enjoyed in Jodensavanne to live and die as members of their ancestral faith was inextricably intertwined with violent coercion.

Nor can Jodensavanne be characterized as a prosperous village. Along with its surrounding plantations, Jodensavanne functioned in part as a receiving center for Amsterdam's indigents, men, women, and children who were seeking better fortunes elsewhere in the Atlantic World, Jews who were economically superfluous at home and had few alternative destinations. The general neglect of Jodensavanne in surveys of the colony owes much to the fact that it was neither a bustling commercial town nor, for most Portuguese Jews, a full-time residential center. The village emptied out on profane days because there was no certain way to make a living there. The majority of Jewish residents at Jodensavanne were impoverished, surviving on a subsistence economy supplemented by the manufacture of wooden planks, donations from relatives or the wealthy, contraband trade, and taxes on the Jewish plantations that framed the Jewish village to the north and south. Even well-to-do residents of Jodensavanne admitted that the village was a "desert," an allusion to its sandy, infertile soil. Out of economic necessity the congregation's clerics routinely shirked their duties in order to tend to their plantations or business matters in Paramaribo. Private dwellings at Jodensavanne paralleled the Sabbath and nooning houses of Puritan New England, which the faithful constructed near the village meetinghouse to avoid a long walk to Sunday worship. On secular days, the village was so desolate that fugitives used the synagogue as a hideaway from which to spot law enforcers or creditors approaching on the Suriname River.

Yet Jodensavanne does exemplify a stronghold of Portuguese Jewish culture and self-determination. The village was entirely under the jurisdiction of Portuguese Jews and housed the headquarters of Jewish communal governance and its autonomous court. This Jewish tribunal gathered periodically through the early 1800s to administer the village, regulate diplomatic relations with colonial authorities, and execute judgments pertaining to Portuguese Jews everywhere in the colony. There, during the three major pilgrimage holidays of the Jewish calendar, worshippers and even some Christian observers flocked to experience the "comonidad" and vibrancy of Portuguese Jewish ritual life and culture.[254] Near the synagogue, at the Jodensavanne burial ground, and a few miles downriver along the Cassipora Creek, lay the colony's two oldest Jewish cemeteries, where Portuguese Jews continued to bury their relations through the 1870s, in hallowed ground that linked them back to some of the first immigrants in Suriname. It was the place where rich and poor Jews alike, including manumitted slaves, willed their bodies be laid to rest, many preferring burial in these inland plots over internment on local plantations or in the Paramaribo cemeteries that had been in use since at least the early eighteenth century.[255] Tied as it was to the industrious plantations operating directly north and south, Jodensavanne functioned as a barometer of sorts, testifying to the viability of Suriname's agrarian Jewish community and the strength of its political autonomy. As such, Jodensavanne offers a microcosmic view of how Suriname's Jewish community emerged, functioned, and shaped the lives of both residents and visitors.

What economic advantages Jodensavanne did enjoy were almost entirely dependent on the wealth generated on nearby plantations and funneled to the village in the form of taxes and charitable donations. Jodensavanne, and Jewish settlement on the upper reaches of the Suriname River in general, constituted a colonial project aimed at populating the region with whites who would serve as a human bulwark against Indian and Maroon attacks and produce prodigious wealth derived from tropical agriculture. As this chapter has hinted and as the next will further detail, the privilege of Jewish autonomy in Suriname always functioned in the service of empire.

CHAPTER 2

The Paradox of Privilege

Nearly every diasporic Jewish community in early modern times, during extended periods of peace and prosperity, has extolled its civic and political status as unparalleled in the Jewish world.[1] Portuguese Jewish leaders of Suriname were no different in arguing that their community was exceptional, "more distinguished than [in any of] the other colonies inhabited by Jews."[2] Perhaps nowhere else in the world, David Nassy proclaimed in 1788, did one find religious tolerance more extensively and more strictly observed "without there having ever been any discussion or controversy whatsoever."[3] Thanks to this religious tolerance, Portuguese Jewry was "established in Suriname upon a foundation happier and more favorable than any other place in the universe."[4]

Several non-Jews in Suriname also remarked on the Jewish community's unusual legal status. Within the colony, Governor Joan Jacob Mauricius marveled in 1748 at the existence of two synagogues in Paramaribo and one in Jodensavanne, where Jews freely and openly practiced their religion. Equally astonishing to him was their immunity from being served sentences on Jewish holidays and Sabbaths, permission to take oaths according to their customs, and their own civil military guard and orphan chamber. But most remarkable in his eyes was the possession of their own court of justice and their privileges, conferred and periodically ratified since 1665 without any contradiction from governors or the local councils.[5] Somewhat less sympathetically, George Bruce, an Englishman serving in the Dutch colonial military in 1751, commented: "It is a rhapsody of inhabitants here; the greatest canaille [riffraff] that one can find among all Jewry, who have more freedom than elsewhere on the surface of the earth. The Lutherans complain because they are not treated similarly."[6] John Gabriel Stedman, a soldier of mixed Scottish and Dutch parentage who served in the colony during the 1770s, remarked without animus: "such are these privileges I never knew Jews to possess in any other part of the world whatever."[7] Similarly, military intendant V. P. Malouet, who visited the colony in 1777, noted that nowhere else did Jews "enjoy such great privileges."[8] Finally, Floris Visscher Heshuysen, comptroller of colonial finances during the British takeover in 1799, called the village of Jodensavanne "perhaps the only one of its kind on the entire face of the earth."[9]

The political situation of Surinamese Jews even attracted attention outside of the colony. The French writer Guillaume-Thomas Raynal remarked in the 1770s: "There is perhaps no empire on earth where this unfortunate nation is so well treated. Not only has it been granted the freedom of professing its religion, of land ownership, of itself settling the differences that arise among its members. It enjoys also the right common to all citizens, of taking part in general governance, of participating in the elections of the public magistrates. Such is the progress of the spirit of commerce that it silences all national or religious prejudices in the face of the general interest which should bind men together."[10]

Scholars have tended to accept this characterization of Suriname's Jewish legal position wholesale. Wieke Vink describes the "high degree of autonomy and full freedom of worship" that Surinamese Jews enjoyed as "unique in its time."[11] Jacob Rader Marcus argued that the privileges Jews enjoyed under Dutch rule in Suriname were possibly the most liberal that Jews had ever received under Christendom and paralleled the favorable political status they had enjoyed in polytheistic Rome, which bestowed citizenship on all of its free subjects in the third century C.E.[12] In my own writings, I have reinforced these views, though with a steadily intensifying question mark.[13]

Now that we have dismantled the myth that Jodensavanne was a proto-Zionist village where most of the colony's Jews resided and enjoyed a harmonious existence in materially comfortable conditions, we can shift our investigation to another legacy, this one pertaining to the legal status of Surinamese Jews. Painted in broad strokes, our inquiry is three-pronged. First, what precisely were the nature and full scope of the Jewish privileges? Second, is it true that the status of Jews was unparalleled in the Jewish world, and perhaps even surpassed concessions granted other religiously nonconforming whites in the colony? And lastly, were David Nassy and Joan Jacob Mauricius accurate when they observed that Jewish privileges were readily conferred and enjoyed without any discussion or controversy

whatsoever? We begin our inquiry in the early 1660s, the moment Surinamese Jews emerged as a corporate group, and continue through 1825, the
year the Jewish privileges were legally abolished.

The Beginning of Communal Autonomy in Suriname

As we have seen, Jews established their first official community in Suriname
in 1661 under Governor William Byam (1654–67), where some of them lived
alongside Christians in the town of Thorarica.[14] On the eve of the Dutch
conquest, the town was the site of 100 homes, dozens of sugar plantations,
a sugar mill, and 4,000 inhabitants, among them 1,000 whites and 3,000
African slaves.[15] At the time, Jews were limited to a de facto legal status in
the colony. No document regarding their position vis-à-vis the English
colonial government before 1665 has survived, and no subsequent generations of local Jews possessed or recalled any laws bearing on their earliest
legal position. It is clear, however, that even before 1665 Jews regarded their
situation as secure enough to merit secular leaders and communal bylaws.
Portuguese sources refer to a *Livro Politico*, written in the years of the
Hebrew calendar coinciding with 1661/1662, as well as a legal ordinance
(*escama*) from 1662/1663, authored by the nascent rulers of the congregation
(*kaal*). The former permitted the existence of only one Jewish congregation
in the colony, while the latter forbade *jehidim* (first-class community members) from circumcising the children of fellow *jehidim* who had been
demoted from their *jahid* status, probably for marrying Jewish women of
African ancestry.[16]

In August 1665, five months after the outbreak of the Second Anglo-
Dutch War, English authorities formally accorded Jews privileges, in desperation to retain these religious nonconformists during crisis time. These
liberties, which for the first time officially confirmed the favors Jews were
already de facto enjoying, were no doubt directly informed by the
"Essequibo liberties," issued in Portuguese and Dutch in 1657. A translation
of these liberties, undated but written in archaic English, suggests that Suriname's first colonial rulers were keenly interested in retaining and attracting Jewish settlement by mimicking the privileges earlier extended in the
Dutch colony of Essequibo, in what is today Guyana.[17]

The 1665 privileges granted Suriname's Jews legal status as "English-
born," freedom of conscience, landownership, exemption from holding

public office and serving in the military (except in case of war), freedom to trade and plant, and their own court of justice for cases not exceeding fines to the value of ten thousand pounds of sugar.[18] The same document granted them ten acres in the district of Thorarica (*divisie Thorarica*), not to be confused with the trading town of that name, which was renamed "Zand-punt" under the Dutch.[19] The land grant, which spurred the establishment of the Cassipora Creek Jewish community, was intended for the construction of "houses of religion and schools as well as a burial place of its deceased."[20] These favors were consistent with the English government's general practice with respect to its Caribbean holdings: to extend religious liberties to Protestant nonconformists, Catholics, and Jews. The policy had a number of pragmatic motivations, including relocating potentially irksome religious minorities, counting on their residence as a bulwark against foreign invasion, and encouraging others in the mother country to become immigrants themselves.[21]

The colony transitioned to Dutch rule in 1667, following the conquest by a Zeeland squadron during the Second Anglo-Dutch War and the confirmation of Dutch rule at the Treaty of Breda. For its first century and a half under Dutch rule, Suriname was under the control of the Society of Suriname, jointly owned and administered by the West India Company, the city of Amsterdam, and the Van Aerssen van Sommelsdijck family. Although the society officially governed Suriname, the local governor was tasked with the daily administration of the colony. Assisting him was the Council of Policy, a political council representing the planter elite and comprised of ten white Christian males who served for life or until their departure from the colony. This council exercised a great deal of authority. The governor was obligated to consult with it on all matters of import and promulgate its resolutions. The ultimate power lay in the Society of Suriname, which could annul any Council of Policy resolution or governmental decree.[22] Legislative power over Suriname was thus divided between a number of stakeholders both within the colony and in the fatherland. Surinamese Jews quickly learned to play these authorities off each other.

While most English planters attempted to liquidate their immovable assets, pay their debts, and abandon the newly Dutch colony with their slaves, the majority of Jews seem to have remained.[23] Acting Governor Pieter Versterre (1671–77) was reluctant to release them, due to their "considerable" numbers and their "fortune." Capitalizing on the nebulous legal position of Jews in the English metropole, where over the course of the

seventeenth century their status shifted from connivance to a loose tolerance not inscribed in law, and on their consequently dubious standing in
the colony as "English-born," Versterre claimed that the Jews, unless they
had received English denization, were not English subjects. Rather, he
argued, they belonged to the Hebrew nation and were thus subjects of the
States General, the current rulers of Suriname.[24] In 1675, the States General
followed Versterre's ruling and refused to recognize the Jews as English
citizens.[25] The Amsterdam roots of many Surinamese Jews reinforced the
Dutch polity's position.

The exodus of Christians had a devastating demographic effect on the
colony, especially because a sufficient number of new Dutch settlers did
not arrive to replace the exiles. This exodus augmented the economic and
political value of the Jews who remained, strengthening their bargaining
position when it came to negotiating their freedoms. But because of the
"manifold troubles" associated with political transition, Portuguese Jews
had no opportunity to appeal to Acting Governor Abraham Crijnssen
(1668–69) for the reinstitution of their former status. Just before Crijnssen, three leaders had governed Suriname in rapid succession from 1667
to February of the following year. The post-conquest shift to Dutch rule
in 1667 disrupted all the privileges Jews had negotiated under English
rule.[26]

In 1669 the Jewish community, headed by sixteen representatives,
including David Cohen Nassi and his son Samuel, initiated negotiations
with the new governor, Philip Julius Lichtenberg.[27] Following the precedent
of the English, who had conferred upon Jews the status of "burghers and
residents of this colony . . . as if they were born Englishmen," Lichtenberg
declared Jews and their descendants as "true vassals of the Republic of Holland" and as "burghers."[28] This status was simultaneously a carryover of
an edict promulgated in 1657 by the States General and States of Holland
proclaiming the republic's Portuguese Jews as subjects (onderdaanen) of the
Dutch Republic. It also paralleled one of the privileges embedded within
the aforementioned "Essequibo Liberties."[29]

The Jewish leaders continued with more specific requests. As a pream-
ble, they mentioned the protections the English government had given
them and their property in Suriname.[30] Gesturing to the urgent need for
white colonists, they also made reference to inquiries they had lately
received from overseas coreligionists who were "inclined to come and settle
here," provided that the treatment and legal status of Jews were favorable.[31]

Interestingly, the majority of their requests concerned problems with enforcing *internal* governance, a foreshadowing of the essential challenge to Jewish communal autonomy in Suriname in future years. First, David Cohen Nassi and his cohorts grumbled that Jewish settlers were not adhering to the laws that had been set down by the Jewish leaders. The petitioners appealed to Governor Lichtenberg to reinforce Jewish self-rule by punishing those who disobeyed.[32] Second, they requested he expel coreligionists who brought "scandal to the Jewish community."[33] And finally, they asked him to retain the Jewish privilege of working on Sundays, to allow their slaves to toil, and to permit them all to pass by the river marshals on those days without harassment. The governor provisionally approved these requests in 1669.[34] These three elements, the enforceability of Jewish law, the exclusion of troublemakers, and public non-observance of Christian holidays, comprised the cornerstone of Jewish privileges until the abolition of communal autonomy in 1825.

The Nature of Privileges and Communal Bylaws

Before we investigate the long-term experience of these concessions, the distinction between privileges and bylaws merits explanation. Secondary literature often treats "privileges" (*privilegios*; *privilegiën*; *privilèges*) as synonymous with bylaws (*ascamot* or *escamot*), the latter two terms denoting "agreements" in Portuguese-inflected Hebrew and referring to communal regulations.[35] This confusion is augmented by some of the primary sources themselves, which tend to conflate the two.[36] Moreover, one of the cornerstone privileges, the colonial government's pledge to reinforce Jewish rule, implicitly meant that governors would uphold the *ascamot*. In this respect, privileges and bylaws bled into each other.

In practice, however, privileges more often referred to the relationship between the colonial government and the Jews, whereas bylaws, translated to Dutch as "ecclesiastical institutions" (*kerkelijke instellingen*), tended to be restricted to internal governance, that is, behavioral expectations for Portuguese Jews within their ethnoreligious community. Thus, two major streams of governance dictated the lives of Jews in Suriname: legislation flowing from the colonial and metropolitan governments to the Jewish community, ensconced in the privileges, and regulations formulated by local Jewish leaders and imposed upon their local constituents, embedded within communal bylaws. In addition, Jews were expected to follow all pertinent placards issued by the colonial government and by which all residents of the colony were bound. Privileges, earned through negotiations between Surinamese Jewish leaders and the state, could be issued by the governor, the Council of Policy, or the States General. They encompassed both time-bound rulings, including the 1741 expulsion of Abraham Shiprout Gabay from the colony for disobedience to the Mahamad, to more permanent and far-reaching ordinances, such as the establishment of a Jewish court, the validity of Jewish marriage contracts, and the status of Jodensavanne as a Jewish village collectively owned by Suriname's Portuguese Jews.[37] In contrast, bylaws were typically promulgated by the Mahamad, ratified by its Amsterdam counterpart, and confirmed by the Dutch Crown. Even in documents where privileges and bylaws appear within the same bookbinding, the former precede and remain spatially separate from the bylaws. The colonial government could not have cared less about most of these bylaws, as it was uninterested in the intricacies of internal Jewish governance, such as the order of ceremonial processions during synagogue services.[38]

One final distinction between the two bodies of law is linguistic. Until the nineteenth century, the bylaws or *ascamot* were first written in Portuguese and then translated for the colonial authorities into Dutch. The privileges, by contrast, were written in Dutch and were rarely translated to Portuguese, perhaps a reflection of the second-language linguistic competency of the Portuguese Jewish leaders who negotiated with Dutch colonial authorities, a fluency that spread through the community over the course of the eighteenth century.[39]

The steadily expanding privileges of Suriname's Jewish community survive in various copies from 1665 through the abolition of communal autonomy in 1825. While these privileges were faithfully reproduced and cited in each generation, almost nothing is known about the *ascamot* that governed the community in its first century, from 1661 through the mid-1700s. Communal bylaws exist only in fragmentary form during that period, after which several complete copies survive. Despite their initially fragmentary nature, there are several indications that these bylaws steadily expanded after the 1660s.[40]

To understand the somewhat inconsistent status of Surinamese Jews as members of a nonconforming minority group, two structural realities are important to keep in mind. First is the corporate status of Jews, that is, their existence as an aggregate outside of their immediate communal context. This means that the state legally treated Jews as such even outside the confines of their own community. Second is the juridical autonomy of Jews, that is, the group was subject to its own mandatory arbitration that replaced the jurisdiction of state authorities over their Jewish residents.[41] In our framework, this meant that it was the Jewish court that most immediately and consistently mediated the secular and religious behavior of its Portuguese Jewish constituents. Because of competing legal systems and situational imperatives, however, neither corporatism nor juridical autonomy in Suriname was a constant. For example, Portuguese Jews in Suriname fought in a separate militia since the 1660s. However, they were also permitted to serve in a mixed Jewish-Christian militia in Paramaribo until 1758, when a conflict between soldiers erupted.[42]

The Fragility of Privilege

The cornerstones of Surinamese Jewish privileges (the enforceability of Jewish law, the exclusion of troublemakers, and public non-observance of Christian holidays), conferred in 1669 by Governor Lichtenberg, immediately came under fire, an anticipation of the periodic undermining of Jewish autonomy through the ages. That same year, the regents warned the governor that a certain Salomon de Rocha, a person "of great disadvantage and prejudice to the welfare of our conservation," was en route to Suriname aboard the ship *Jongen Abraham*. The regents asked the governor to expel Rocha from the colony, which he pledged to do, but not until over a year later.[43] In 1675, Acting Governor Pieter Versterre issued a law that barred all work on Sundays. Jewish leaders challenged the ruling the following year, though without immediate success.[44] Then, in 1680, under the rule of Acting Governor Laurens Verboom, Portuguese Jewish regents complained that several dozen *jehidim* had failed to pay the annual head tax they owed to the congregation. The governor promptly signed an order commanding the debtors to pay under pain of seizure.[45] Thus, already in the first two decades of the Dutch colony, we can see that government enforcement of Jewish privileges was conditioned by the length of time authorities took to act.

The privileges of Surinamese Jews were summarized in nine categories or "titles" assembled in the mid-eighteenth century and dating from 1669.[46]

Ironically, this compendium includes the suspension of certain privileges, even those that threatened the basic guarantors of Jewish communal life. The liberty of Jews to labor and to put their slaves to work on the Christian Sunday, confirmed in 1669, is paradigmatic. The successive violation of this freedom beginning in 1675 is illustrative of both the precarious nature of Jewish privileges in Suriname and the persistence of Jews to ensure their enforcement. One influencing factor was the clerics, who strove to uphold the Christian nature of the colony and at times held great sway over colonial governors.

After Governor Versterre banned all work on Sundays in 1675, thirty-six Jewish planters drafted a twelve-point petition, advancing theological, social, and political arguments. They first argued that God had mandated their observance of the Jewish Sabbath, and forcing them and their slaves to observe the Christian day of rest was tantamount to spiritual and "anti-synagogal" coercion. Their next points placed the colony's economic interests at heart. If they followed the Sunday law, their slaves would be inactive and unprofitable the entire weekend and would therefore pose a threat to the colony at large. Moreover, if slaves owned by Jews had up to three days free each week, their counterparts laboring under Christian masters would become envious and behave rebelliously. This was especially the case since slaves owned by Jews ceased laboring early on Friday, while those laboring for Christian owners insisted on beginning work late on Monday. Besides, Jews already had to observe seventy-eight Sabbaths and holidays, which God commanded them to follow without dispensation. Should they be obligated to also observe Sundays and Christian holidays, there would be no working days remaining, if one took into account the rainy season, which brought all agricultural activity to a standstill. Finally, the petitioners threatened to take their case to the States General or leave the colony altogether. The colony could not survive without Jewish planters, some thirty to forty in number, they pointed out. Even though Suriname was a "desert" where dearth was widespread and dangers abounded, they would still choose to remain if compensated by good treatment and complete freedom based on the privileges.[47]

Even this forcefully argued polemic did not definitively resolve the issue for the Jewish community. A decade later, Governor Van Sommelsdijck (1683–88) again formally revoked their privilege, forbidding Jews to work, conduct business, or keep their shops open on Sundays. The regulation was reissued under Sommelsdijck's successors. Only in 1696, after the intervention of Emanuel Baron de Belmonte, agent of the Spanish king in the Dutch Republic, and Samuel Cohen Nassi before the directors of the Society of Suriname in Amsterdam, were Jews once again permitted to travel on the rivers and work on their plantations on the Christian day of rest.[48]

With the steady rise of a significant Jewish community in Paramaribo during the eighteenth century's first half, the Sunday issue posed more acute challenges, if only because Jewish behavior was more visible in the city than on rural plantations relatively isolated one from the other. In 1718, the consistories (ecclesiastical bodies) of the Dutch and French communities in Paramaribo complained that Jews in the city were keeping their shops open on Sundays, carrying their merchandise through the streets, and allowing their women to knit and sew at the doors of their houses "as if with a premeditated plan . . . to vilify our placards and denigrate our religion."[49] The placard banning Sunday work in the city, reissued in 1721, suggests that Jews were as defiant as they were ineffectual in arguing against the decree.[50] Similar decrees were issued by the Council of Policy in 1771 and 1784, and Jewish leaders protested them in their customary way, digging up copies of privileges and resolutions nearly a century old and presenting them to the Society of Suriname, which had veto power over colonial bodies.[51] These periodic repeals of a basic Jewish privilege may have masked intentions to ruin Jews economically, for if they and their slaves could not work on Sundays, in addition to Jewish Sabbaths and holidays, nearly half of the year would pass without income-generating labor, as the Portuguese regents pointed out in 1784. Implicitly, the ruin of the Jews was also the ruin of the colony.[52] The annulments hint at the vicious economic competitiveness between white communities and underscore the reality that privileges were not simply conceded as a measure of entitlement. Jews could never take them for granted. Retaining them demanded ongoing vigilance and negotiation, like exercising a muscle in order to retain its bulk. The fragility of Jewish privileges honed the political skills of Jews and contributed to their acute historical consciousness and awareness. Archival documents, stored in a special room in the Beraha VeSalom synagogue, were not merely pieces of paper to be deposited and passed down as heirlooms. Rather, they were essential documents to be periodically consulted, documents with a vital afterlife, with the power to defend the status of Jews in the colony and to justify their very presence in the colony.

The banishment of troublemakers, the second cornerstone privilege, also placed the Jewish community at odds with colonial authorities.[53] As

Robert Cohen notes, the Jewish privileges were the only body of law in the colony containing an ordinance that "expressly permitted political banishment due to 'an evil life.'"[54] Christian leaders could also recommend banishment, but for them the grounds on which to do so were much more specific, applying only to crimes that endangered the moral and political stability of the colony. These crimes included sedition, selling liquor to soldiers, and falsely claiming to be free.[55] During the seventeenth century, adultery committed by whites, sexual relations between white women and enslaved men, and "whoredom" sometimes occasioned deportation whether in the Dutch metropole or in its colonies.[56] By contrast, the occasion for the expulsion of Jews was much closer to the failure on the part of liberated slaves to exhibit subservience and respect toward whites. Increasingly over the course of the eighteenth century, Jewish leaders interpreted "an evil life" as any persistent challenge to their authority.

In general, forced exile typically involved the removal of an individual from the colony. However, disobedient Jews could also be expelled from Paramaribo to Jodensavanne, to the *cordonpad* (a military defense line constructed in the mid-1770s), or even to the colony's frontier land, where in one case a white Jewish man was sent to live and trade in exile among Indians and Maroons, perhaps doubling as a spy to ensure that one pacified Maroon group did not join forces with another.[57] Individuals subject to Jewish banishment also included non-Jewish free or enslaved persons of African descent who lived in the Jewish community.[58] Almost all forced Jewish exiles were poor, and nearly all deportees, whether free or enslaved, were also male. Social and political discipline in the colony was almost entirely a male affair, suggesting that women had their own methods of social discipline, albeit extralegal and informal.[59]

The vague concept of an "evil life" enabled the Mahamad to threaten with expulsion anyone who refused to repent and accept correction. But enforced exile was a last resort, even for the governor, and was usually used as a threat to prevent the persistence of bad behavior and to encourage obedience because actual expulsion was both difficult and costly to carry out. In 1770, for example, the Portuguese Jewish regents placed Moses Henriquez Coutinho in the Zeeland fort for nine days on a diet of bread and water, warning him to amend his behavior so that the leaders would not have to involve the colonial prosecutor and create "nuisances for our superiors."[60] The same year, David Martines Ledesma verbally attacked the First Parnas of the Portuguese synagogue in Paramaribo and resolved to do the same to other members of the *collegio*. The governor then intervened and placed him in the fort, perhaps overriding the regents' banishment order. In 1772, Ledesma repeated his earlier behavior, and the regents resolved to allow him to confess his guilt. If he did not, they threatened to place him in the fort on bread and water and have him forever banished from the colony. Ledesma repented.[61] In 1780, Treves, a silver worker identified only by his last name, was also threatened with banishment for selling counterfeit precious metals. He apparently heeded the warning.[62]

These examples, based on an exhaustive reading of surviving communal minutes, which date from the mid-eighteenth century, make plausible David Nassy's assertion that banishment of Jews from the colony was extremely rare. In 1788, he affirmed that from the founding year of the Jewish community in 1661 there had been only sixteen cases of forced exile, half of them due to crimes of a religious nature and "disobedience to the established authorities, and not for offenses and crimes."[63] His distinction is telling. Robert Cohen argues that after the mid-eighteenth century, incidents of attempted banishment became increasingly frequent, a clear indication for him that the authority of the Portuguese Jewish regents "was seriously challenged."[64] The absence of communal minutes predating the 1750s does not permit us to verify this statement. But even if Cohen is correct, focusing on the extreme disciplinary measure of banishment as a gauge of Jewish obeisance to leaders may be misguided, for lesser acts of rebellion, which we will explore later in the chapter, were fairly constant.

The Jewish power to recommend forced exile was substantially altered in 1751 as a result of the intervention of the metropolitan authorities, as Cohen himself notes. In 1747, during the term of Governor Mauricius, a faction developed between those who represented the Society of Suriname and the governor and an opposing party that wished to make its own mark on the colony's administration. Ishak Carrilho, an *adjunto* and captain of the Jewish Civil Guard, closely allied himself with the opposition and put his signature on a petition to the Society of Suriname that criticized Mauricius's administration. The *parnassim* were aghast at such intervention and reported Carrilho to Mauricius, who summarily dismissed Carrilho from his captaincy. The regents then began litigation against Carrilho on the grounds that he falsely represented the Jewish community and placed its privileges at risk. Upon their recommendation, the governor expelled Carrilho from the colony.[65] Once in Holland, Carrilho leveraged his wealth and litigiousness in the Dutch courts, arguing rather speciously that the power of banishment no longer existed because the 1682 charter (mentioned in the Introduction to this book) had established the entire colony on a new legal basis.[66] If Carrilho's argumentation was faulty, his timing was not. The States General, already displeased with the governor's administration of the colony, removed Mauricius from office and allowed Carrilho to return to Suriname and to his position as captain of the Civil Guard.[67]

The *parnassim* countersued, dispatching their own representative to Holland. After protracted negotiation, the States General arrived at a resolution. Carrilho was forced to relinquish his captaincy and Princess Anne, who assumed the position of regent of the United Provinces in 1751 on behalf of her three-year-old son, appointed new *parnassim*. More radically, she slightly reformulated the Mahamad's power to recommend deportation, adding a class component. From thereon, only "poor, shabby people and those who are fugitives from elsewhere" were subject to a recommendation for banishment. Colonists such as Carrilho, "who have established themselves in Surinam and have property," were immune, except if an extraordinary Jewish tribunal, composed of all *parnassim* and *adjuntos*, voted by a two-thirds margin in favor of expulsion.[68] In theory, the newly revised privilege created a loophole protecting the civil disobedience of propertied members of the Jewish community. In practice, the efficacy of the altered privilege depended upon three unpredictable forces: the regents, the governor, and, if a defendant was sufficiently wealthy and resourceful, the metropolitan authorities. Moreover, the decree of banishment, like all privileges, was potentially retractable.

The case of Moses Rodrigues del Prado clearly illustrates this last principle. In 1775, Prado, a Eurafrican Jew, was banished from Jodensavanne for verbally insulting the sexual honor of certain *jehidim*, an act forbidden by communal regulations. The hypocrisy of the decree, issued by powerful men intimately familiar with the practice of concubinage, must have deeply embittered Prado, a plantation overseer and himself the product of at least one generation of so-called "Suriname marriage," the informal sexual relationships between white men and African-origin women that lasted until the departure or death of the former.[69] But economic necessity may have been a more decisive factor in his decision a week before the Jewish holiday of Hanukkah in 1778 to illegally return to Jodensavanne. There, he ran through the streets, shouting imprecations against the Mahamad, which had banished him from the village three years before. He finally prevailed against the Mahamad the following year, when the Council of Policy ruled that the regency had no authority to expel anyone from the savanna. His appeal before the court benefited from the intercession of the plantation owner on whose estate Prado had once served. The regents considered the ruling a contradiction of a mandate signed by Governor Wigbold Crommelin in 1757 but were powerless to counter.[70]

Appealing directly to authorities in the fatherland was another option. Shortly after his arrival in the colony in 1756, Selomoh Montel was prosecuted by both the Jewish tribunal and the Council of Policy for loaning money on interest to a fellow Portuguese Jew, a violation of biblical and colonial law. Montel refused to carry out his prescribed Jewish penance, which included an interdiction against shaving his beard, the payment of a fine, and the recitation of a formulaic apology before the congregation.[71] The regents showed great leniency, repeatedly urging him to repent. But Montel was recalcitrant, insisting that he would not open his wallet even if he were to be excommunicated three times a day. With a "heavy heart," the regents resolved to banish Montel from the colony.[72] Montel retaliated by initiating a campaign in Holland and appealing to the States General. They found for him, completely reversing the decision of Surinamese *parnassim* and undermining their right (and that of the governor) to banish troublemakers from the colony. Montel returned to Suriname and died there in old age.[73]

Even if a banishment decree remained uncontested, it was difficult to keep it in force over time, for many exiles returned to Suriname as if guided by a magnet. Jacob Rodriguez Campos, first prosecuted by the Mahamad in 1753 for insulting the sexual honor of the deceased Rahel, wife of Jacob Henriquez Fereira, was ejected from the colony for unspecified reasons in 1765.[74] He returned five years later, claiming he was suffering from poverty and at his advanced age could not support himself and his wife elsewhere.[75] Abraham Mendes Cunha, who had been exiled from Suriname in 1793 for selling counterfeit gold for letters of exchange, returned to the colony in 1798.[76]

Robert Cohen and other scholars have assumed that the challenges the Mahamad faced in asserting its authority over its constituents intensified after the mid-eighteenth century. Cohen partly attributes the weakening of the Surinamese Mahamad to the gradual transfer of the Jewish population from the rural plantations surrounding Jodensavanne to the capital city of Paramaribo. But this view assumes first of all that the majority of Suriname's Portuguese Jewish community lived on the Suriname River until the

1770s, which they did not, and second that the Mahamad had experienced a golden period of authoritative rule, which it in fact never enjoyed.[77] Government rule was too unsteady, Jews too mobile, and the accused too resourceful to allow for a resolutely hegemonic Mahamad.

Thus the cornerstone privileges of Jews were periodically challenged from both within and without. Sometimes, these forces converged. Several times in the 1770s and 1780s, government officials visited Jodensavanne shortly before or on Jewish holidays to deliver citations. In Paramaribo, lawyers began to execute judgments against Jews on days when adherents of the Mosaic faith were forbidden to take action. Jewish communal authorities filled the pages of their minute books agonizing over such breaches of their privileges and how to appropriately respond.[78] In 1772, the judicial deputy arrived in the savanna during the High Holy Days to hand out several citations to Jews celebrating there. What complicated matters is that Samuel Uziel de Avilar, captain of the Jewish Civil Guard, had allegedly directed the government official to serve the sentences during that holiday, perhaps because he knew the recipients would be at home. The regents excommunicated Avilar and resolved to submit a list of Jewish holidays annually to the governor so that he would know when not to send his representatives to deliver citations to Portuguese Jews.[79] Surinamese almanacs, first published in the colony in 1788,[80] included a list of Jewish holidays, a reflection of the prominence of Jews in the colony but probably also an attempt to keep holiday infringers at bay.[81]

Clearly, these preventive measures were ineffective. In 1780, Moses Pereira de Leon complained that one day before the Jewish New Year, colonial commissioners entered his home by force and removed a female slave (*negra*) he owned in execution of a judgment against him.[82] A similar case arose in 1815.[83] To the very last, Portuguese Jews were obligated to defend their privilege not to be disturbed with legal matters on Jewish holidays. In 1825, on the eve of the abolition of Jewish communal autonomy, the First Parnas was forced to remind the governor about not serving Jews sentences during the festival of Passover.[84] Jews themselves were responsible for increasing the likelihood of such infringements, for the privileges they negotiated extended the duration of Jewish holidays by a total of six days. This meant that Jews could not be presented with citations for a period of time commencing three days before a holiday and ending three days after.[85]

The *parnassim* always attributed the governor's violation of religious privileges to ignorance, a reasonable conclusion given the frequency of regime change and the fact that Jewish holidays fall each year on a different date in the Christian calendar. On the other hand, not all governors could have been as ignorant as they claimed about the holidays of Jews, who constituted one-third (and by the first decades of the 1800s, two-thirds) of the white population. Rather, it seems that a governor's violations of privileges were intended as a ritual to remind Jews at whose mercy they lived, if not to tentatively challenge Jewish autonomy itself. Because the regents typically prevailed, these periodic challenges to Jewish sovereignty, sometimes resulting in political intercession from the fatherland, functioned as a theater, testing Jewish status in the colony, or even keeping it in check, but ultimately reinforcing it.

At the same time, privileges could also be expanded. In 1757, the Mahamad reflected that in their century, the Jews had always been permitted to "amplify" their privileges.[86] In 1799, for example, when the sale of a house on public auction in Paramaribo coincided with the Festival of Weeks (Sebuoth), Jews were prevented from bidding and signing. The regent Moses Robles de Medina requested that Governor Juriaan François Friderici prohibit all sales at public auction on Jewish sacred days. The governor responded that it was his desire to benefit the nation in the "augmentation of its privileges" and invited the Mahamad to request in writing the banning of all sorts of public auctions on Sabbaths and holidays, promising to find the means to make this possible.[87] Thus the nature of Jewish privileges of the colony was elastic, pulled in either direction by competing authorities and stakeholders. The Jewish community was by no means always united as to which direction to tug.

Bylaws Under Fire

Internal communal governance was also a volatile matter. Bylaws underwent modification several times after the 1660s, usually at the initiation of the Surinamese Portuguese Mahamad. The subjection of these ordinances to periodic alteration was first mandated with the Hebrew year coinciding with 1680/1681, when the gentlemen of the Mahamad issued an *ascama* calling for the "revision of the bylaws that they made since the institution of his holy congregation until the present day."[88] The timing had the potential to set the precedence for such reformation to occur every twenty years. In practice, however, communal bylaws were irregularly subject to amendment, and apparently coincided with changes made to the privileges by the colonial governor and subsequently approved by the States General, Society of Suriname, or the Dutch Crown. In addition, a bylaw in force by at least the mid-eighteenth century permitted amendments any time there was a unanimously voting *junta* (a special meeting of *parnassim* and former *adjuntos*).[89] Typically, leaders initiated revisions in response to internal conflicts or what they termed "confusion."[90] Surviving compendia of modified bylaws cluster around the 1660s, 1680s, 1750s, and 1780s.[91] At their numerical pinnacle in the mid-eighteenth century, the bylaws of Portuguese Jews reached 59; by the late 1780s, they had dwindled to 26.[92]

If privileges tended to be challenged from without, bylaws were always threatened from within. From the earliest surviving communal minutes of the mid-eighteenth century, rebellious impulse is evident on nearly every page of the communal minutes, and not only from the underclass. Class and other social conflicts were certainly a phenomenon in other contemporaneous Jewish communities.[93] But one wonders if the degree of intracommunal contentiousness reached new levels in Suriname, as well as in its sister community of Curaçao, equally notorious for communal strife that interfered with colonial governance and the conduct of trade.[94] In Suriname, Jewish communal governance was unremunerated, was highly time-consuming, and often demanded coercive "freewill offerings."[95] It was perhaps because of these factors that in 1760, all of the elders (*adjuntos* or former *parnassim*) of the Portuguese Jewish community resigned and there was no pool left from which to draw new *parnassim*. A similar crisis had already once occurred, when no eligible *jahid* was willing to serve as a regent, and the *ascamot* were duly revised to allow elders to be reelected. But the new ordinance did not anticipate the resignation of all elders. The outgoing regents resolved to amend the *ascamot*, annulling those resignations and requiring elders to serve, with the exception of David Uziel de Avilar, who, as captain of the Jewish militia, could not be present for most meetings and was permitted to attend only when he could. No one else was permitted to resign.[96]

Most other internal protests in Suriname's Portuguese Jewish community involved a layman insulting the regents of the Mahamad or flaunting their authority, a violation of the second bylaw.[97] These affronts were of such a trivial and repetitive nature that the recording secretary rarely included details. The following three examples illustrate both the frivolity and the atmosphere of satire that pervaded many of the cases. One day in April 1789, the *parnas* Yosef Arrias was standing in Paramaribo outside the tavern door chatting about business matters when he overheard Moses Rodriguez complaining about recent political events in Holland. "Did you see how they cut the head off of a soldier who killed his official? It was cut off just like the head of a *parnas*, and that is precisely how . . . Parnas Arrias should have his head cut off." When Rodriguez was summoned to appear before the Jewish tribunal he denied everything, claiming, "I did not say the head of the *parnas*, but rather the head of the *ananas* [pineapple]." The communal minutes obscured all of Rodriguez's exact words, for fear of re-creating the shocking affront. But one can imagine the great fun Rodriguez had with his ridiculing pineapple rhyme: "Parnas, Arrias, Ananas!"[98]

Just after the Jewish New Year in 1794, Abraham de Samuel Robles de Medina appeared before the regents on a charge that he had slapped David de Haim Sarruco during synagogue services. When asked to account for himself, Robles composed a complicated statement filled with "specious reasons and sophisms" in which he attributed the slap he had discharged to a different movement he had tried to make with his body. After some discussion, the regents concluded that it was impossible for a person to touch the face of another without the faculties of the aggressor agreeing to bring his limb into movement. Robles was commanded to beg forgiveness at the lectern of the Paramaribo synagogue and was fined five hundred guilders. Robles refused to complete his penance and the regents duly stripped him of his *jahid* status and, with the governor's authority, dispatched him to the fort for further punishment. In 1795, Robles took the case to the States General, and the regents were ordered to admit him once again to the synagogue until they further deliberated the case.[99] The incident underscores both the power and the limits of the Mahamad's authority, as well as the canniness of Jewish laymen intent on exposing the vulnerability of Jewish jurisdiction.

Most challenges against Portuguese Jewish authority remained within the community. Typical was an incident that occurred in 1798 during synagogue service, when a worshipper named David de Abraham Bueno de Mesquita tossed a piece of coconut at the reader's lectern, where the assistant cantor was leading prayers. Under oath, Mesquita denied throwing anything, claiming that while he was attempting to exit the synagogue, he had accidentally fallen onto the *theba*. The *hazan*, meanwhile, presented the court with the chunk of tropical fruit thrown at him and also mentioned that someone among the worshippers had called him "Jojo," the deprecatory name of a slave. Mesquita was fined one hundred guilders and the case was closed.[100] The minutes are silent about Mesquita's reasons for challenging and ridiculing this synagogue functionary, who as a salaried official could not have formed part of the Mahamad.

As the foregoing examples suggest, challenges to Portuguese Jewish self-rule cannot be reduced to expressions of class conflict or protest against the oligarchical leadership of the *parnassim* and *adjuntos* or simply attributed to the spirit of revolution that gripped the Atlantic World in the last decades of the eighteenth century, though these elements could play a role in certain contexts. More decidedly, the environment of legal pluralism in Suriname, intensified by the physical distance from the metropole, rendered communal governance inherently disputable, a reflection of the broader colonial situation. As G. W. van der Meiden has argued, much of the conflict between colonists and the Surinamese government stemmed from the nebulous demarcation of responsibilities and powers between the various institutions and parties exercising authority over the colony.[101]

While some conflict was triggered by substantive issues, arguably the most pervasive expression of disputed authority, among Jews or otherwise, was simply a contest of wills. One unusually explicit articulation supporting this argument occurred in 1750, when Johanna Carolina Bedloo, widow of Everhardus Brouwer, decided to throw a ball in her Paramaribo home for her five-year-old daughter's birthday.[102] When it became clear that the celebration would take place on Sunday, the local Dutch Reformed authorities warned her to desist. Widow Brouwer assured the church that the party was only for children and would be brief, beginning at six o'clock in the evening. However, once the event began, a huge crowd of white adults and children appeared, along with numerous slaves tending to their owners, and trumpets blared. When authorities protested, carousers threw oranges at them. The revelry and music continued until after midnight, in violation of the 8:00 slave curfew. When government officials ordered the widow to make the musicians stop playing, she replied tartly, "The Governor is master in his house, and I am master in mine." In the wake of the scandalous ball, colonial officials could only retort meekly: "If a governor is master only in his own house, it would not be necessary to send a governor to the colony."[103]

If the communal bylaws are any indication, the real subversion of Jewish communal governance came not from without but rather from within. It was the virtually incessant, petty challenges to Jewish authority and violations of decorum inside and outside the synagogue walls that drained the leadership's time and energy and deflected its attention from content-related issues. Self-governance may have been in theory a highly valued concession, but it was frequently experienced as both oppressive and worthy of derision.

Jewish Privileges as Unparalleled

As we have seen, the privileges Jews enjoyed were regarded as remarkable among both the colony's residents and its visitors, and by Jews as well as by Christians. In time, these liberties came to function as a litmus test for Christian status. In one case in 1748, the Reformed Protestant Minister Lambertus de Ronde protested to the governor that on the Saturday before he was to preach, a sworn clerk interrupted his "study day" and read him a very long legal indictment submitted by the widow Audra. De Ronde argued before the governor that on the day he customarily reserved to prepare his Sunday sermon, he was "entitled to at least the same privileges as the Jews enjoy, that on their Sabbath and holidays they should be free from judicial interpolations."[104] The minister's a fortiori argument, which the governor upheld, acknowledged that in terms of their religious privileges, Jews occupied a rung slightly higher than that of Christians. By demanding legal immunity on both Saturday and Sunday, Minister De Ronde not only mimicked Jews' legal lengthening of their holidays but also appropriated the Jewish Sabbath for himself in order to correct what he experienced as a skewed hierarchy. Viewed in another way, this religious rivalry led not to the curtailment of Jewish privileges, as it might have in Christian Europe or in the British Caribbean, but to the "judaizing" of Reformed Protestantism.

The assessment that Surinamese Jews enjoyed a favored status among other whites is also borne out when one considers the range of ecclesiastical congregations and their religious officials. In the 1730s or 1740s, there were only three churches in the colony, presumably all Dutch Reformed: one in Paramaribo in the Oranjetuin, and two others in the remote countryside, in Cottica on the corner of the Perica Creek, and on the Commewijne River.[105] By the same decades, there were two places of Jewish worship in Paramaribo alone, one of which was reserved for Ashkenazi Jews. Toward the second half of the eighteenth century, these were joined by a third, reserved for Eurafrican Jews. The fourth was the Beraha VeSalom synagogue, located in Jodensavanne.

FIGURE 8. Portuguese Jewish prayer house Sedek VeSalom, Paramaribo, 2009.
Courtesy of Stichting Gebouwd Erfgoed Suriname.

Other nonconforming religious groups lagged far behind. In 1741, Lutherans secured permission to build a church on the condition that they proffer a yearly tax of six hundred guilders to the colonial hospital. Construction began that year and the building was completed in 1744. The first preacher had arrived in 1742, by which time Surinamese Jews had lived under the guidance of their ordained clerics for seventy years.[106] Roman Catholics did not receive permission to assemble in Suriname until 1785, the year Suriname's Jews celebrated the centennial of their congregation in Jodensavanne. Even then, Catholics' right to worship was restricted to Paramaribo, where they were forbidden to erect a church building and had to worship in an ordinary house. Moreover, they were allowed no ordained priests or public processions and were banned from converting their slaves to their religion.[107] Moravians, keenly invested in the conversion of the enslaved population, were even more suspiciously regarded. In 1740, the Council of Policy forbade Moravians from publicly professing their religion. Only in the 1760s, in response to the colonial government's conclusion of peace with the Saramakka Maroons, were the brothers permitted to convert slaves to their faith.[108] As for the residual English ethnic minority,

FIGURE 9. Ashkenazi prayer house, Paramaribo, 1952(?). Courtesy of the Jacob Rader Marcus Center of the American Jewish Archives, Cincinnati, Ohio, at americanjewisharchives.org.

no known Anglican church ever existed under Dutch rule.[109] In comparison to Jews, organized nonconformist Christianity lacked both longevity in the colony and a body of legal concessions that might be used as a bargaining chip for further liberties. Even Reformed Protestantism, the official faith of the colony, could not boast the visibility and institutional vibrancy of Jews in the capital city.

Another attribute that set Jews apart from other whites was their territorial autonomy—no other white group collectively owned a village. Although sparsely inhabited and not the home of most of the colony's Jews, the village of Jodensavanne was the clearest expression of Jewish corporate status and a state-within-a-state. To be sure, other white groups in Suriname were at times offered ethnic or religious enclaves of their own under partial self-rule starting in the seventeenth century, but none of them lasted. To maintain its political supremacy, the colonial government instituted such villages on the frontier, in a buffer zone situated between outlaw

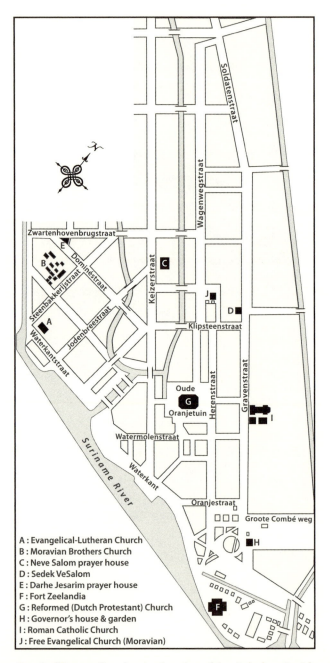

MAP 5. Detail of Paramaribo, showing location of the city's three Jewish prayer houses. Until 1744, there was only one church in Paramaribo but already two Jewish prayer houses.

Maroons and settlements colonized by whites.[110] Stakeholders in the Dutch Republic preferred Protestant and Catholic recruits, but these settlements were short-lived. They included the Labadists, a pietistic Protestant sect founded by Jean de Labadie (1610–74), who established their community on the Suriname River at the La Providence plantation in 1683.[111] The Piedmontese physician Louis de Bussy established a village of Swiss immigrants along the Para Creek in 1747, which succumbed to internal dissension, famine, and Maroon attacks by 1753.[112] Perhaps inspired by Jodensavanne's centennial, Governor Wichers proposed a scheme to create "a sort of village or city" near Paramaribo or the Nieuw Amsterdam Fort shortly after 1785, to be settled by twenty to twenty-five immigrant families.[113] Of these experiments in autonomous enclaves, only Jodensavanne prevailed.

We must therefore look outside the white population for parallels to Jewish territorial autonomy in Suriname. Somewhat counterintuitively, they are found among the Maroons and Indigenous people, who lived in the colony's rainforest. Certainly, the comparison is imperfect, for the government's relationship to these groups differed from its conduct toward Jews. Neither Maroons nor Indians were counted in colonial censuses. To the government, only the names of the leaders were of consequence. By contrast, Surinamese Jews (unless they were vagabonds or transients) were both burghers and residents who were regularly counted in censuses. Moreover, neither Maroons nor Indians were governed by a list of bylaws detailing internal mores that were subject to periodic government approval. Rather, treaties composed with ink, blood, and paper dictated the mutual obligations between certain Maroon groups (beginning in the 1760s) and Indians (from the seventeenth century), on the one hand, and the colonial government on the other. As we have seen, colonial law since 1684 specified that Indians were unenslavable by the state, except in cases of crime.[114] Maroons pledged not to attack plantations, and both they and Indians were contracted to assist the colonial government in the capture of runaway slaves, for which they received one-time rewards and annual tributes from the colonial government in the form of necessities and luxury items. These tributes were typically presented by government officials in the rainforest homelands of the recipients, though the government preferred to meet in Paramaribo, where non-whites could be impressed by the "capability and superiority" of the whites.[115]

Non-monetary tribute also informed diplomatic relations between Jews and the government, further underscoring the parallel between the three groups. However, it was Jews, rather than the state, who proffered this tribute. Treatise 39 of the *ascamot* obligated Jews to present an annual offering, which manifested as a lavish present, typically worth three hundred guilders, to each governor upon his accession to power.[116] The first preserved description of such a gift dates to 1750, when the Mahamad gathered to discuss an appropriate offering for the new interim governor, General Major Hendrik Ernst Baron van Spörcke, and the colonial cabinet (1751–52), who were mobilized in those years to suppress outlaw Maroons.[117] The Jewish leaders settled on an array of six Caribbean pine saplings and four fine sheep, accompanied by an assortment of chocolate and dried preserves arranged on an adorned silver tray. The *parnassim* and *adjuntos* traveled to Paramaribo to present these gifts in person and to congratulate the new governor and his entourage on their arrival.[118] Perhaps because all colonists were mandated to receive Spörcke just as they would a governor, the regency convened once again in April 1751 and unanimously resolved to purchase six cows and personally transport them to Paramaribo as a separate gift.[119]

The foregoing examples demonstrate that the collective social status of the Jews as a separate corporate and juridically autonomous entity fell somewhere in between that of a non-white and a white, religiously nonconformist group. Like Christian dissenters, Surinamese Jews occupied a deferential position vis-à-vis the governor and his cabinet, symbolized in the tribute they owed them. Yet this tribute was not monetary (as it was for Lutherans), bringing Jews symbolically closer to Maroons and Indians. Like Indigenous people and pacified Maroons, Jews possessed territorial autonomy, that is, ownership and jurisdiction over their own village. Yet the governor did not reward Jews with gifts for their role in guarding the frontier. One possible explanation for the discrepancy is that there were no preexisting scripts for dealing with Maroons or Indians in this unprecedented colonial environment. For all the parties involved, the dance of diplomacy had to be improvised from scratch, while in the case of the Jews, the colonial government could fall back on deeply imprinted European models, where tributes from religiously nonconforming groups to the government were standard.[120] Moreover, Jews, unlike their Indian and Maroon contemporaries, were not in a position to exact retribution or violate their legal relationship with the government, for they were integrated into the economy and thus had nowhere to run within the colony. Collectively abandoning the colony was not much more than a rhetorical threat. In this sense, Jews, unlike Maroons and Indians, were completely at the mercy of colonial and metropolitan authorities.

Outside of the Atlantic World, the Jewish community of Leghorn constitutes a possible rival to Surinamese Jewry in terms of its political status. Non-Jews frequently equated the Italian port city with a "paradise" or quasi Jerusalem for its Jews.[121] The Livornia charter, in effect almost uninterruptedly from the late sixteenth century until 1861, sheltered former *conversos* from the Inquisition and legally protected Jewish children from kidnapping and forced baptism. Jews were exempt from donning distinguishing markers, could purchase real estate, enjoyed freedom of movement, not being confined to any ghetto, and were permitted to enter any trade, save for peddling in secondhand clothes. They existed as a corporate group and were empowered with their own jurisdiction over civil disputes and lower-level criminal cases involving only Jewish parties. These port Jews functioned as a state-within-a-state, electing their own leaders, assessing taxes for their community, and negotiating with the governor, the Grand Duke, and his ministers on behalf of their community. In the eighteenth century, they were also extended the privilege of significant political participation in the running of the city's local government.[122] This great latitude, nonetheless, did not translate into generalized wealth; the great majority of Jews were "earning low wages or living in poverty," a characteristic of all sizable early modern Jewish communities.[123] The Jewish community of Leghorn therefore constitutes a striking parallel to the Surinamese situation, albeit in an urban environment saturated with other privileged, nonconforming minorities, all of whom lacked territorial autonomy.

Because Surinamese Jews existed and circulated primarily within an Atlantic orbit, a comparison with other Jewish communities in the Atlantic World may be more informative. The short-lived Jewish community of Dutch Brazil (1624–54) was accorded religious freedom, including permission to build two synagogues, representing one unified congregation, the first in both the New World and the Dutch realm. Their most important leader, Abraham d'Azevedo, served as a deputy alongside other whites in the colony's government. Brazil's Jews could also own land and trade in slaves and own them. Although they could engage in commerce, certain handicrafts and manual labor were off-limits to them, as becomes clear in a petition a group of Portuguese Jews dispatched to the West India Company two months before the fall of Brazil. In their communication, they requested the freedom of "enjoying the same privileges and benefits of shop-keeping, commerce, artisanal trades, handiwork, business, and all the other means in order to obtain their support there." The board received the appeal but postponed their decision until it was too late.[124]

In Amsterdam, in both England/Britain and its Caribbean colonies, and in southwestern France, Jews formed something akin to a society but were not a corporate group (that is, a community apart outside of the synagogue) and thus did not enjoy juridical autonomy. Although congregational leaders were empowered to enforce religious conformity and to assess internal taxes owed to the congregation, their authority was not reinforced by the state. Both the British and Dutch metropolitan governments considered the Jewish community a voluntary religious association.[125] This lack of formal corporate status, however, could be inconsistent. In the English and British Caribbean, for example, Jewish soldiers in Jamaica fought alongside non-Jews by at least the 1690s but in the early 1800s had their own separate militias, parallel to those reserved for free people of African descent. Whether or not integration into white society was an advantage to Jewish existence is debatable. When Jamaican Jews in the 1760s protested the colonial government's order to appear in arms on Sabbath, both their petition and their request for intervention from London's Portuguese Jewish leaders failed. The latter advised Jamaica's Jews to desist from asking for a military exemption on Sabbath and holy days.[126]

In fact, the governance of Jews under the same body of law that regulated white Christians often attracted accusations of unfair advantage and stimulated negative corporate treatment. In 1772, for example, Thomas Dicey, commissioner of Jamaica's Board of Customs, petitioned the metropolitan treasury to introduce a special annual tax to be levied on all non-naturalized Jews present in the British Caribbean colonies, once upon registration and annually thereafter. Dicey complained of the "unmolested privileges which they now enjoy, equal to any Christians whatever."[127] His suggestion was not innovative; Jamaica had instituted a discriminatory "Jew tax" in 1692 for similar reasons. In Barbados, meanwhile, Jews between 1688 and 1706 were restricted in the number of male slaves they could own, a strong disincentive against estate ownership.[128] In both Jamaica and Barbados, from the 1660s through 1786, non-endenized Jews living in urban areas were periodically banned from purchasing more than one slave.[129] Between 1680 and 1780, Bridgetown's Jews, never more than 10 percent of the white population, paid 20–57 percent of the town's taxes, in addition to what they owed on land, house, and commercial surtax, not to mention the monetary gifts, known as "Jew pies," which they presented the colonial government to ensure its favor. Pedro Welch calculates that Bridgetown's Jews thus paid "what amounted to a quintuple taxation."[130] To conclude that disproportionate taxation of Jews on the islands of Barbados and Jamaica is a sign of the community's general prosperity is to overlook the general destitution of Anglo-Caribbean Jewries, their legal vulnerability, and their small size relative to the total white population.[131]

Erik Seeman attributes the relatively small population of Jews among other whites in the English colonies to a "climate of intolerance." In contrast to the Dutch Caribbean, where as we have noted Jews formed one-third to two-thirds of the white population, Jews in Jamaica constituted 10 percent of the white population, while only reaching the 3 percent mark among Barbados whites.[132] However appealing this interpretation may be in light of Suriname's generous Jewish privileges, it is probably not the main factor. The large proportion of Jews among whites in the Dutch Caribbean had more to do with economic opportunities available in the Dutch Republic, which were ample for Christians but extremely limited for Jews, and the general reluctance of Dutch Christians to immigrate to the colonies. To be sure, broad liberties accorded to Jews in Suriname made possible the formation of a strong Jewish community headed by a handful of elites who provisioned the synagogue's charitable coffer. But Jews were not drawn to Suriname because of their unparalleled legal status there, which in any case did not translate into generalized economic well-being for Jews.

Moreover, the corollary of privileges, that is, the liberty of Suriname's Portuguese Jews to promulgate state-enforced Jewish bylaws that mandated in minutia the secular and religious behavior of their constituents, and demanded uncompromised obedience to the Mahamad, did not constitute ipso facto a freedom for the laity. The verbally and socially mutinous behavior of the colony's Portuguese Jews, heretofore discussed, indicates quite the contrary. In fact, many Jews may have viewed the *lack* of Jewish juridical autonomy as freedom, as a letter dispatched from Amsterdam's Ashkenazi leaders to their Surinamese counterparts in 1786 suggests. It concerns the widespread practice of married Jewish women who, with the permission of their husbands, appeared in public with their hair uncovered. The correspondent admitted that there was nothing Jewish leaders could do against this rabbinically forbidden behavior, since they lived in a "free republic."[133] For these Jews, whether laypeople or leaders, freedom was understood as the absence of internal religious coercion.

Even the possession of both corporate status and a specific body of law recognized and enforced by the state did not entirely immunize Surinamese Jews from some of the legal challenges their coreligionists faced elsewhere in the Caribbean, as we have seen. Nor could the lofty legal position of Surinamese Jews protect them from the progressive social demotion that set in by the late eighteenth century. By the time of the British Interregnum (1799–1802, 1804–16), the social standing of Jews in the colony had significantly declined. Their bathetic status was apparently well known in the colony. Shortly after capitulation, a senior British official reported that although Jews were "the first settlers of Surinam" and settled there "with their own laws and privileges granted them by the Sovereign," they were now "considered as the very lowest class of the white people."[134] One Englishman who visited Suriname at the turn of the nineteenth century noticed that the "wives of the richest Jews were not invited to the official festivals and balls of the Dutch governors," a most powerful denigration of men through their women that at the same time disputed the very rootedness of Jews in the colony.[135]

The collapse of Suriname's inland plantation economy in the 1770s, which triggered the mass relocation of riverine Jews to Paramaribo, including the Portuguese Jewish oligarchy, provided new justifications for disobedience. By the 1780s, it was no longer practical for the Mahamad to adjudicate its cases at Jodensavanne, putting into question the reach of the regents' sovereignty. Community members were quick to pick up on this vulnerability. In 1778, when Samuel Cohen Nassy was called before the Mahamad to testify against Moses Fernandes in an adultery case, he refused, claiming he was not obligated to do so unless the alleged crime had taken place in Jodensavanne, where the court adjourned. Nassy was fined ten guilders, but no further action against him was taken.[136] The regents eventually acknowledged the infeasibility of calling Paramaribo residents to testify or stand trial in faraway Jodensavanne by reducing the number of court adjournments to four times a year.[137]

During British Interregnum rule, inaugural governors continued to visit Jodensavanne to formally confirm Jewish privileges and autonomy. But these official visits began to wane over time. After the official appearance of Governor Charles Green at the Jewish village in 1804, the next recorded occasion was not until 1822, under restored Dutch suzerainty.[138] Rather than a largely symbolic affair, in which Portuguese Jewish leaders ceremoniously presented the governor a copy of their ecclesiastic and political privileges, newly inaugurated governor Abraham de Veer inquired whether the Jews wished to maintain their privileges and, if so, how to revise them.[139] On the horizon lurked the possibility of a Jewish existence in Suriname without privileges. In this charged atmosphere, the *parnassim* and *adjuntos* proceeded to deliberate over amending the *ascamot*. After a lengthy process of discussion and revision, the new bylaws were finally approved in February 1823, the last time a sovereign would ever ratify the communal ordinances of Surinamese Jews.[140]

Conclusion

Generations of contemporary observers and modern historians have noted that the privileges accorded Portuguese Jews in Suriname were unparalleled in their nature and extent, both in comparison to Jews living at the time elsewhere in the world and from a diachronic, diasporic perspective. Some observers even perceived a Jewish legal advantage over other white colonists. The ownership Jews enjoyed of their own village in Jodensavanne, their power to subject their constituents to a Jewish tribunal, and the say they were given in the appointment of colonial magistrates were chief among these liberties. It is difficult to dispute the claim of unsurpassed latitude, particularly if the comparative purview remains Europe and the Americas. However, the exaltation of Jewish status in Suriname fails to take into account three fundamental caveats.

First, the privileges of Portuguese Jews were periodically contested from without. They were challenged not only by successive governments, which sometimes concluded that the concessions were too great, but also by clergymen, who wished to preserve the Christian nature of Sundays. Second, the chief privilege, a broadly conceived self-jurisdiction ensconced in the communal bylaws, was inexorably disputed from within. Precisely why many Jews continually rejected the authority of their ethnoreligious leaders is difficult to surmise from a description of the conflicts themselves, which articulate the offense but usually not the motivation. Perhaps Jews felt harnessed by the wide array of bylaws to which they were bound or bore personal grudges against their leaders. Some of the discontent may have been class based. Or perhaps, like so many Jews and other religious minorities elsewhere who possessed a strong degree of juridical autonomy, Jewish rebelliousness in Suriname masked an unspoken belief that the court arbitrating the lives of the general population was more just or advantageous.[141] Contesting the Portuguese Jewish court was also an expression of "forum shopping" or "jurisdictional jockeying."[142] Finally, Surinamese Jews lived in an environment of competing authorities, where Jewish communal autonomy was mediated not only by the colonial government but also by the Society of Suriname, the States General, and the Dutch Crown, and where the wheels of justice turned very slowly as a consequence of the lengthy travel time from the Caribbean to Europe. Politically savvy and financially able Jews who had time on their hands were able to mobilize these negotiated authorities to their advantage.

In the end it may be uninformed to ask which Jewish community in the world enjoyed the most extensive liberties or the highest status, for the experience of these concessions was always highly contextual, not to mention constantly negotiated. There are, as well, certain conditions we should consider that seem to be particular to the Dutch Atlantic. Government enforcement of decrees related to nonconforming groups was much more usual there than elsewhere in the Atlantic World. Dutch municipal authorities routinely intervened in the religious matters of all denominations. This tendency was commonplace in the United Provinces and carried over to the Dutch colonies.[143] By contrast, in most other European Jewish communities, Jewish secular leaders largely conferred with their own tribunals, and their "internal disputes remained concealed from the surrounding society."[144] This invasiveness, generally absent from the English and British realms, also helped diminish the self-determination of Suriname's Portuguese communal leadership.

The Surinamese Jewish situation thus closely parallels its counterpart in the Polish-Lithuanian Commonwealth, where early modern Jews also enjoyed a high degree of communal autonomy through the so-called Council of the Four Lands (Va'ad Arba Ha-Aratsot). On the one hand, their special status provided a platform for the participation of Jewish notables in the broader politics of the land, as Judith Kalik has noted. On the other hand, Jewish autonomy gave license to the secular authorities to intrude into Jewish affairs "at a national level."[145] In the highest-profile cases, the government intrusion that sabotaged the self-rule of Jews in Suriname allowed dissenters who opposed the Mahamad's rulings to triumph and shape Jewish life in their own ways. As the regents discovered in the case of the Portuguese Jewish communal leader Ishac Carrilho and the moneylending Selomoh Montel, banishment from the colony brought about the unintended consequence of reopening in the metropolitan court disputes that had already been resolved in the colony. Both Carrilho and Montel prevailed, a reminder to the Jewish community that some of its more affluent or resourceful members had the potential power of diminishing the Mahamad's authority, setting unwanted legal precedents, and (in the case of Carrilho) revising the very bylaw that empowered the regents to recommend banishment in the first place.

The extreme litigiousness of Carrilho and Montel, however, was unusual for Surinamese Jews. Typical proceedings of the Portuguese Jewish tribunal involved minor offenses impinging on the respect due to the Mahamad. The repetitive nature and vagueness of such wrongdoings, and the inevitable fines and acts of contrition that usually followed, suggest that the Portuguese Jewish court functioned largely as a theater, whereby Jewish laymen (and sometimes leaders) tested the authority of the Mahamad and the validity of some Jewish privileges. In almost all cases, the Mahamad prevailed. In this sense, the daily workings of Suriname's Jewish tribunal approximate what Ken Stow, in the context of the Roman ghetto, characterized as a theater, a performance. While the Jews of Rome's ghetto used Jewish jurisprudence to convince themselves that they were in control, when in fact they were at "the whims of the pope's Roman Vicar,"[146] the Surinamese Mahamad usually possessed real power over its constituents, however delimited it may have been in certain contexts. In the challenges they presented against the *parnassim*, litigious Portuguese Jews strove to lay bare the identity of the true director running the show, to expose the underlying vulnerability of the Jewish court to its colonial and metropolitan patrons. Their actions brought to the fore the difference between autonomy, which presumes the presence of an external, higher authority, and sovereignty, which indicates political independence.

This political situation in Suriname differed in the extreme from the tiny North American Jewish communities, where lack of external enforcement fundamentally shaped Jewish congregations. In 1786, for example, one Martin Prager of Philadelphia, "a Hebrew who left England" a few years before, disclaimed "all title to his religion," apparently without conversion to Christianity.[147] Prager took advantage of a society that allowed nonconformists to express their religious views within the compartmentalized space of private organizations but not in the public sphere.[148] In the North American colonies and in the early American Republic, Jews (including several communal leaders in Montreal) routinely married Christian spouses without formally abandoning their religion for another.[149] Certainly, the colonial and U.S. government could and did intervene in Jewish religious matters, as recent research has shown.[150] But their interference was only occasional and not, as in Suriname, systematic and written into the apparatus of colonial law.

In Suriname, by contrast, Jews were not only *permitted* to live according to their biblical and rabbinical mandates but *obliged* to do so. This held true in the early modern metropole only to a certain extent. The Portuguese Jewish ordinance mandating communal membership and conformity for all Portuguese Jews who lived locally was technically in force in London and Amsterdam, at least in the earliest bylaws, but was much more difficult to implement than in Suriname. Only in Leghorn, where Jewish leaders reserved the right to vote foreign Jews into the community and thereby entitle them to the privileges of the Livornina, did the situation approximate that of Suriname.[151]

In Suriname, thus, Jews were governed not by the principle of "the right to be different," defined as the entitlement of ethnoreligious collectivities to deviate from the norms of the ruling class, but rather by the "mandate to be different."[152] This mandate meant behaving Jewishly not just on Jewish holidays but on every day of the year, which entailed working on plantations and carrying out business on Christian holy days, except when the influence of the church convinced a governor to repeal this Jewish privilege. In multiple spheres of life, the jurisdictional status of individual Jews was forcibly subsumed under Jewish corporate status. Thus, not only was Jewishness theoretically protected, but its practice was enforced by both the local Jewish government and the colonial state. The nearly all-encompassing nature of the Jewish mandate to be different in Suriname helps explain the prodigious output of minutes recorded by the Portuguese Mahamad, which met weekly and sometimes daily to conduct its business, far more extensively than its counterparts elsewhere in the diaspora, or local Ashkenazim, who left behind comparatively meager communal records.[153]

In the final analysis, Jews in Suriname were collectively integrated into the economy and their elites even had a limited say in the administration of the colony's government. In their access to governance and the colony's system of production, distribution, and consumption, and the freedom to publicly practice their religion, Jews approached the legal status of white Protestants. In their territorial and judicial autonomy, Jews paralleled the legal status of Indians and Maroon groups who were officially recognized by the colonial government. The latitude the Jewish community enjoyed, however, did not prevent many of its constituents from resenting their legal protections, nor did it prevent the majority from languishing in poverty. For most, legal privilege or parity did not translate into freedom from coercion, nor did it lead to economic upward mobility. Privileges may therefore have been of more consequence to the community's rulers than to its masses. Yet the ongoing negotiation of these leaders with the Dutch colonial government for the confirmation of Jewish privileges first bestowed in the seventeenth century, and for the ongoing quest for new privileges, was the legal expression of a rootedness the wealthy shared with the poor. As we shall now see, this rootedness manifested not only in age-old legislation but also in more subtle ways, at times more perceptible to historians than to the actors themselves.

CHAPTER 3

From Immigrants to Rooted Migrants

In the early 1740s, Governor Mauricius remarked that most of Suriname's white population were "foreigners . . . and thus have no patriotic feelings, because the United Provinces are not their native country . . . they will always preserve the *animus revertendi* [impetus to return]."[1] The same could not be said of Jews. As they themselves noted, and as scholars have since affirmed, Jews did not relocate to the Caribbean "to make their fortunes and then to return to Europe."[2] Despite their strong ties with Jewish metropolitan communities, and ongoing migration, Suriname's Jews did not regard their new home as a "temporary abode."[3] Their tendency to remain was in part a response to constraint. Unlike Christians, they had fewer options for settlement elsewhere in the Americas.[4] Catholic territories, including Portuguese Brazil, the Spanish Americas, and by 1685 the French Caribbean, were off-limits to Jews. Moreover, in the Dutch Republic, whose economy was booming, mostly due to European commerce, opportunities for Jews were narrow. In the Dutch metropole, Jews were collectively excluded from various guilds, as well as from industry, agriculture, shipping, the army, and the navy.[5] Certain cities, such as Deventer, Gouda, Groningen, and Utrecht, forbade them the right of residence through much of the eighteenth century. Amsterdam was the only city that had tolerated a Jewish presence since the 1590s.[6]

At the same time the poverty that was endemic to Jewish communities everywhere in the Atlantic World created a widespread transience.[7] Successive relocation of Jews was by at least the first half of the seventeenth century institutionalized in the *despacho*, a congregational method of sending indigent Jews away from an urban center or colony with the necessary travel funds and a mandate not to return for a specific period of time.[8] If we focus our attention on Suriname, an obvious paradox emerges. How could Jews constitute quintessential locals of the colony while a significant proportion of their community was always in flux? Was "true settler" status a creation of the elite, who financed permanent structures like synagogues and carved out the landscape with plantations and urban businesses, or did the transient poor also play a role? In this chapter, we shall address the seeming contradiction embedded within Jewish settler status and explore its concrete and intangible manifestations. Finally, we shall consider the consequences of Jewish localism for broader society.

True Settlers Among Transients

David Nassy noted in his *Essai historique* that "it is only the Jews who are indeed the true citizens and inhabitants of Suriname."[9] On one level, such assertions were rhetorical. Self-portrayal as faithful colonists was an important means through which Jewish leaders argued for the continuation and expansion of their privileges in the colony. In 1684, Portuguese Jewish leaders reminded the governor that during the recent wars against local Indigenous people, Jews had remained at the frontier out of loyalty, placing their "persons and goods at risk" and suffering "very great damage" for the defense of the colony, while most of their (white Christian) neighbors had "abandoned their posts and plantations."[10] This tendency, Portuguese Jews claimed, had been the pattern since they first founded their community in 1661. As the Portuguese Jewish regents recalled over a century later: "from 1661 onward there have been Jews here and they have not, as is commonly said about all new colonies, established themselves here as adventurers, but on the contrary, have come with huge riches from Portugal and especially Brazil. The Jews have melted the treasures that they took along with them in order to continue agriculture. No one has ever tried to make a fortune and return to Europe."[11] Their awareness of a precise year reflects an oral tradition bolstered by habitual referencing of communal archives. Leaders of each generation of Portuguese Jews carefully preserved their archives, largely motivated by the "afterlife" of legal documents that ratified and served as precedents for Jewish privileges in the colony.[12] True settler status was closely intertwined with this profusion of paper and moved the tendency of Jews to remain in the colony beyond mere rhetoric. Documents demonstrated to authorities that Jews had been among the pioneering colonists, solid proof against various arguments that arose, particularly during the Jewish Emancipation era, that Jews were a wandering people who did not really belong in any civic society. True settler status also finds confirmation in recent scholarship. A study on marriage patterns among Portuguese Jews in Suriname between 1788 and 1818 shows that of 196 locally married couples, only 39 men and 19 women were born elsewhere, particularly in Amsterdam. Viewed another way, 334 (just over 85 percent) of the newlyweds were Surinamese natives, as compared to 58 foreign born. If these records are representative, Surinamese Portuguese Jews were largely a native-born group by the late eighteenth and early nineteenth centuries.[13]

On the other hand, Suriname's Jewish community was not too far removed in time from its immigrant roots in Amsterdam and other places in the Atlantic World, and to a lesser extent in the Mediterranean. Marriage intentions filed with the colonial Dutch authorities during the 1740s, mostly by foreign-born Portuguese Jews in their twenties, indicate birthplaces as varied as Amsterdam, The Hague, London, Bayonne, Bordeaux, Spain, Portugal, Saleh (in what is today Morocco), Curaçao, Jamaica, St. Thomas, and New York.[14] A comprehensive survey of surviving tombstones in the four oldest Jewish cemeteries of Suriname, dating mostly to the eighteenth century, speak to birthplaces as diverse as Altona, Amsterdam, Leghorn, Barbados, England, Fez, London, and St. Eustatius, as well as Saint-Esprit (near Bayonne), Bayonne, and Bordeaux, the latter three in southwestern France.[15] The natal lands memorialized in the contemporaneous Old Ashkenazi Cemetery of Paramaribo are not as geographically wide-ranging but also speak strongly to immigrant origins. Most of these coreligionists arrived from the hundreds of distinct political territories that are today part of Germany, France, and Switzerland.[16] Epitaphs reference Altona, Amsterdam, Belgrade, Calabria, Courland, Hamburg, Hamelberg, Königsberg, Lyon, Naarden, Prague, and Prussia.[17]

The so-called High German Jews were introduced into the Atlantic World in significant numbers about a century after their Iberian coreligionists. To my knowledge, no Ashkenazi *despacho* institution systematically regulated or encouraged their dispersion.[18] In the geographically constricted nature of their origins, Ashkenazi Jews were similar to the colony's white Christians, who hailed largely from western and northwestern Europe. J. D. Herlein noted in 1718 that Paramaribo's white inhabitants were "divided among Netherlanders, French, Germans, and Jews."[19] Although Jews are the only non-national group mentioned in this listing, they, too, were largely natives of Europe at this time. Only in the mid-eighteenth century do the epitaphs of Suriname's oldest Jewish cemeteries begin to specify Suriname as the birthplace.[20]

The institution of the *despacho* played a central role in sustaining the immigrant dimension of Suriname's Jewish community. The highly irregular manner in which *despachos* were documented in Atlantic Jewish communities, with references to the individuals affected typically dispersed haphazardly through minute books and other records, has thus far prevented compilation of systematic surveys. Still, the work that has been carried out thus far for Amsterdam, London, New York, and Suriname is suggestive. One database, based on two registers specifically devoted to *despachos* from Amsterdam and collectively covering the period from 1759 to 1814, lists a total of 404 heads of family or individuals, of which nearly 35 percent (141) were sent to Suriname, by far the most popular destination.[21] This percentage roughly accorded with the counsel Portuguese Jewish economist Isaac de Pinto provided in 1748 to solve the indigence problem of the Amsterdam community.[22] The second and third most popular destinations for these evacuees were the Dutch Caribbean islands and London. Amsterdam's Portuguese Jewish community dispatched 90 heads of house or individuals to the first region and 56 to the British capital. Other destinations included Bordeaux, Bayonne, The Hague, Hamburg, Rotterdam, Gibraltar, Mogador, Tunis, Leghorn, Venice, Trieste, Istanbul, Izmir, and Jerusalem. New York's Jewish community sent its poor to London and helped circulate others to and from Suriname, Curaçao, Barbados, Jamaica, and St. Eustatius. Communities with greater financial resources tended to dispatch more individuals than they received.[23]

Beginning in the late seventeenth century, Suriname became a major receiving station for the penurious of the Atlantic Jewish World. Aside from the ongoing *despacho*, a significant factor in the 1730s and 1740s was a mass migration scheme first inspired by the founding of the British colony of Georgia in 1732 as a haven for Protestant refugees. The plan, collaboratively executed by Portuguese Jewish leaders in London and Amsterdam, was in part triggered by worsening conditions within their communities.[24] In those decades, the income of Amsterdam's Portuguese Jewish congregation fell and its deficit skyrocketed.[25] European port cities, including those in the British and Dutch metropoles, contended during the 1720s and 1730s with an influx of Portuguese refugees fleeing the Inquisition. Under King João V (r. 1706–50), the country became intolerable for many New Christians. The Church secured enormous power, enriched by huge quantities of jewels and silver. The king's religious zeal led to the construction of numerous convents and monasteries. At the time, over 10 percent of the population of two million served in Holy Orders or other religious institutions.[26] Consequently, the Inquisition was able to renew its scrutiny of New Christians for alleged adherence to Judaism. In cities and towns across the Dutch Republic, the *parnassim* asked local authorities "not to admit poor Jews or even practitioners of crafts," such as butchers, which were already sufficiently represented.[27] One member of Amsterdam's Portuguese Jewish community commented in 1732 that there was "so much poverty coming to us from all parts" to his city that there was no possibility of helping supplicants as they would wish.[28]

Mass colonization of Jews in Suriname seemed to promise a quick solution. It was the brainchild of the *parnassim* of London and Amsterdam, who consulted with each other on the method and the timing.[29] In the latter city, Portuguese Jewish leaders secured the cooperation of the Society of Suriname and the financial support of extremely wealthy Jews.[30] The plan as devised in 1733 was to dispatch over the course of three years one-third of Amsterdam's indigent Portuguese Jews, numbering 500 to 700 individuals, to found a new agricultural community in Suriname.[31] The new arrivals would be permitted to become either petty merchants or cocoa and coffee planters. They would be free to trade or engage in any manual labor they wished, including baking and selling bread.[32] The plots would be carved out near Jodensavanne, adjacent to each other in order to provide protection against attacks by runaway slaves.[33] Using the same calculus applied to the *despacho*, the Portuguese Jewish regents reasoned that it would be more economically expedient to arrange for the mass sending away of indigents than to continue to support them indefinitely out of the charitable coffers.

Negotiations between the Amsterdam leaders and their Surinamese counterparts reveal that the *parnassim* in the fatherland were well aware of the "uncertainty of success." They instructed communal leaders in Suriname to throw themselves on the mercy of God's benevolence to the poor and the divine merit of demonstrating charity to the feeble.[34] Messianism may have undergirded their faith, as it had in the case of the Lutheran refugees in Savannah, Georgia. The projected sum of 25,000 acres to be distributed to prospective colonists in Suriname mirrors the biblical Ezekiel's vision of the Jerusalem Temple. The layout of this hallowed ground, on which both the sanctuary and the city lay, was circumscribed as 25,000 cubits square (Ezekiel 42, 45, 48), one of the three occasions in the Hebrew Bible where "ideal (i.e., not extant) town planning is described."[35]

The colonization strategy, intended to go into effect in 1734, was foiled, in part by unnamed disputes between the Portuguese regents and elders in Suriname.[36] According to Isaac de Pinto, the poor refused to go.[37] But it is more likely that the failure stemmed from the extended financial crisis and ongoing conflict between Surinamese colonials and the local government over who should pay for the construction of a much-needed fort at the confluence of the Suriname and Commewine rivers (the structure was finally completed in 1747).[38] It is also plausible that the plan failed due to the lack of strong local government to enforce it.[39] Between January 1734 and March 1735, Suriname's governorship turned over three times, before passing under the authority of the Council of Policy from March 1735 until the end of that year. Not until 1742 did any governor serve more than five years. That leader was Joan Jacob Mauricius, under whom the scheme was renewed.[40]

In 1748, the Portuguese regents of Amsterdam convened to formally resurrect the contract of 1733. As in 1733, Portuguese Jewish leaders stated as their goal the removal from Amsterdam of one-third of their paupers.[41] In a pamphlet written in Portuguese in 1748, Isaac de Pinto anticipated that sending away the poor to the colonies, particularly to Suriname, would lessen the burden on the community's poor chest, reduce the annual financial obligation of *jehidim*, and alleviate competition among remaining indigents. Pinto also gestured to the promise of finding a fortune in the colonies, a benefit that would prove largely chimerical.[42] The 1740s was a decade marked by economic decline, warfare, harsh winters, and the introduction of new restrictions in welfare remittances. From 1747 to 1748, a series of unsuccessful insurrections to democratize local government broke out across the country.[43] These factors increased the urgency of removing indigents from Amsterdam's Portuguese Jewish community, whose leaders "became less open-minded and hospitable," and their immigration policy stricter.[44]

Prospective colonists reacted to the immigration scheme with a mixture of economic desperation and naivete. Several applications survive. All but one (written in Spanish) were penned by Portuguese Jews, a testament to the renewed ferocity of Portugal's Inquisition.[45] The petitions, all submitted by men, are filled with allusions to illness, hunger, and lack of clothing. Moses, son of Abraham de Aguilar, disclosed that he had nothing to pass from his hand to his mouth, while Josseph de Minhana found himself without means to earn a piece of bread for his five children.[46] Izchac de Abraham Palache, who described himself as an itinerant worker, gestured to a debilitating condition that left him, his wife, and two small children in "great poverty."[47] Jacho Martenes testified that his wife and three children were suffering from "much hunger and much nakedness."[48] The gullibility of the applicants is manifest in several of the petitions, which referred to the colony as a newly discovered land or "new island of Suriname."[49] Some of the immigrant hopefuls who enlisted in the initial mass colonization scheme in 1733 had previously resided in Brazil, Spain, and Portugal and believed that their experience there in viticulture and, in one case, mining would serve them well in Suriname.[50]

Due to the absence of documentation, neither the biographies of the applicants nor the total number of émigrés who were actually dispatched to Suriname is clear. According to Tirtsah Levie Bernfeld, a mass migration was never carried out.[51] Yet record fragments do refer to a significant number of immigrants. Jacob Rodrigues Morran, for example, was dispatched with his wife, their seven children, and 300 guilders.[52] "Abrao Lopes Grasía" was sent off with a spouse, five children, and 250 guilders.[53] Other documents suggest that seventeen applicants, including fourteen heads of house, were directed to Suriname, totaling about seventy individuals.[54]

The experience of a handful of colonists in 1747 gives some indication of the scheme's discouraging results. In February of that year, a group of fourteen Jewish settlers composed a letter to the regents of Amsterdam's Portuguese Jewish community. They disclosed that due to the "inconveniences of the colony," they were not able to fulfill their contract. The most fertile and secure plots along the Suriname River were already carved out by wealthy plantation owners who monopolized local agrarian production, a pattern generally characteristic of Caribbean sugar colonies.[55] It was impossible to subsist further upriver owing to the "continual attacks" of Maroons. The latter had not only murdered the settlers' principal slaves, rendering the plantations inoperable, but also "barbarically and cruelly" executed whites on several occasions. Losses such as these forced Jews to abandon their estates and leave their enslaved laborers behind, fully at liberty to escape.[56]

The group asked Amsterdam's regents to intercede with the authorities in the nearby Dutch colony of Berbice and negotiate privileges that would allow them to freely farm and trade there as both Jews and burghers, anticipating a suggestion Portuguese Jewish leader Isaac de Pinto would offer a few months later.[57] What became of these individuals is unknown, but no Jewish community protected by legal privileges was ever established in the Dutch colony of Berbice. Jewish settlement there had been strictly prohibited since the onset of Dutch colonization. A momentary relaxation of this policy in the 1750s was immediately reversed when Berbice's colonial officials discovered that the prospective Jewish immigrants were financially needy.[58] Metropolitan Jewish leaders offered little sympathy for the failed planters. From his home in Amsterdam, Pinto dismissed the petition as "spoiled children's tantrums, caused by a slight lowering of their standard of living," which he viewed as a clear indication of their success in the colony, since only the wealthy complained of deteriorating conditions. He recommended that émigrés from Amsterdam be barred from returning for a period of twelve years.[59]

By July 1748, Amsterdam's *parnassim* realized that the amount of start-up funds they had allotted the immigrants was insufficient. They resolved to raise a separate collection, but just two months later, for unspecified reasons, they reversed their position, firmly convinced that no more monies should be dispensed for the dispatched families, nor assistance given for any reason whatsoever, leaving the new immigrants at the mercy of Suriname's Jewish authorities. If any family requested dispatch to another place, only Amsterdam would be considered. Far from providing a solution to poverty among Jews in northern Europe's port cities, the 1747 colonization attempt encouraged a return exodus and confirmed Suriname's reputation as an "inconvenient" land.

Nevertheless, Jewish arrivals in Suriname after 1750 exceeded departures, a testament to what Seymour Drescher calls "a semicoerced migration from Amsterdam."[60] Soon after the publication of Pinto's 1747–48 pamphlet, the Amsterdam regents implemented all of his suggestions, and even increased his recommended twelve-year period to fifteen years.[61] As we have noted, over four hundred Portuguese Jewish heads of house, many with wives and children in tow, left Amsterdam between 1759 and 1814 as *despachados*, more than half of them destined for the Americas. Of these, most settled in Suriname.[62] There are no records that systematically capture the demographic growth or shrinkage of the Jewish community of Suriname or elsewhere in the Caribbean. But scattered information suggests that for a community to remain viable, around 40 percent of its members had to remain in place until their dying day.[63] This was certainly the case for Suriname as well as for Curaçao, and seems to have held true for the smaller communities of Jamaica and Barbados. Suriname was a consistent receiving center for Jews, given the function of Amsterdam and Curaçao as points of transit. The overall effect of the *despacho* and the mass migration scheme of the 1740s was a community of extremely diverse origins and native lands, stretching from the Ottoman Empire and Italy to southwestern Europe. At the same time, relocation policies expanded the sector of the Surinamese community that had no possibility or desire to leave.

The synagogue was an important channel through which Surinamese Jews claimed a local identity. Patterns of charity giving suggest that they were more strongly identified with their local houses of worship than were their Christian contemporaries. While the colony's Christians tended to bequeath to both local causes and benevolent institutions on the other side of the Atlantic, Suriname's Jews overwhelmingly devised solely to their local synagogue, a finding Holly Snyder has also found true of Jamaica.[64] These synagogues, in turn, tended to favor native-born Jews as alms recipients. "Sons" and "daughters of the land" (*filhos da terra*) received priority for funds distributed in response to individual petitions. In 1776, for example, the Portuguese Jewish regents in Suriname passed a resolution giving priority to the native-born in the apportioning of charity. This worked against the widow of Haim Saruco, who in 1785 requested an annuity but did not qualify for it since she was not a "daughter of the land" (*filha da terra*).[65] Isaac Lopes Nunes and Ester Gabay Izidro, who applied for an annual pension later that decade, were granted fifty and one hundred guilders, respectively, as a "son" and "daughter of the land."[66]

One reason Suriname's Portuguese Jews of all classes strongly identified with their synagogue was that it functioned as a material receptacle attesting to the longevity of Jews in the colony. Special prayers, variously known in Portuguese-inflected Hebrew as *escavot*, *escabot*, or *ascabot*, were recited annually for large donors or synagogue functionaries. The mandate of the congregation to periodically invoke the names of these distinguished individuals did not expire, even after the bequests had been expended, and therefore promised those honored symbolic immortality.[67] Implicitly, synagogues elsewhere in hemispheric America, including Philadelphia, Curaçao, and Montreal, served a similar function.[68] At the end of the eighteenth century, a number of Surinamese religious functionaries were still memorialized by the congregation, although by then they were remembered only by their last names: Netto, [Abraham] Gabay Izidro, [Ishac] Meatob, Oliveira, Ledesma, Aellyon, Casseres, Abendana de Britto, Aboab, [Ishak] Meatob,

Sasportas, and Mendes Quiros.[69] One list of *escavot* represents the leading founders of Suriname's Jewish community, including Semuel Cohen Nassi and Ishak Arrias, a planter who also served as *haham*.[70] An *escava* was also reserved for "David Nassy ACohen," who is remembered in the memorial prayer not as the author of the *Essai historique* or as a communal leader but rather for his occupation as a physician (*arofeh*).[71] Such lists reinforced awareness of the Jews' uninterrupted longevity in a colony.

Prayers specially devised in response to the Surinamese environment are another indication that Jewish culture was transforming through the development of new roots. One of these prayers, as we have seen, was composed by the congregation's cantor David Hizkiahu Baruh Louzada (1750–1825) on the occasion of an uprising of a Eurafrican military detachment that in 1804 attacked white officers and a plantation and found common cause with the Boni Maroons and Djuka.[72] Largely consisting of biblical verses forming an acrostic of the author's name, the invocation also incorporated secular references, most strikingly its description of the runaway rebels as "our enemies, the cruel and rebellious Blacks [השחורים]."[73] The phrase is a slight variation of the Jodensavanne epitaph of an elderly officer in the Jewish militia who led an expedition against runaway slaves and died in 1743 after returning from "beating the black rebelling Negroes [הכושים]."[74] As Zvi Loker and Robert Cohen have noted, Louzada's prayer attests to the "degree of Jewish culture" in Suriname's Jewish community and the "quality of its Hebrew usage."[75] It is also a reminder that religion is not always about the wolf learning to dwell with the lamb.

The striking verses bring to mind two other epitaphs found in the Jodensavanne Cemetery, this time in the Portuguese language. Both Emmanuel Pereyra and David Rodrigues Monsanto lost their lives in slave uprisings in 1738 and 1739, respectively.[76] Their inscriptions call on God to exact retribution against the rebels, disparaged on Monsanto's gravestone as "cruel uprising negroes" (*crueys negros alevantados*). Similarly, when Jacob, son of Abraham Meijer, of the "Ashkenazi nation," perished in a Maroon attack in 1789, Cantor Louzada, who also served as keeper of the Jodensavanne Cemetery and its register, described the killers as "our cruel and rebellious enemies" (*Nossos Crueis & rebeldes Enemigos*), concluding the entry with the Portuguese curse "may his blood be avenged" (*sua Sangre seije Vengada, Amen*).[77]

Another innovation to Surinamese Jewish ritual reflected the condition of new masterhood. Surinamese Jews had recourse to prayer books, published in Amsterdam, that mandated the recitation of certain prayers upon the purchase of slaves. *Order of Prayers* (*Orden de Bendiciones*) is the earliest known Jewish prayer book that mentions slave regulations. Published in Amsterdam in the Hebrew year coinciding with 1686/1687, it contains a special formula used in the purchase of slaves (*bendición de quando compran siervos*) but probably refers to an intermediary conversion, without conferring full Jewish status, that made it ritually permissible for slaves to prepare kosher food and drink.[78] Michael Studemund-Halévy argues that the Hebrew locution of the prayer—*avadim*, the same word that in the Hebrew Bible denotes the unfree Israelites who labored under the pharaohs of ancient Egypt—confirms that slaves, rather than domestic servants, were the prospective converts.[79]

A successor, *Covenant of Isaac* (*Sefer Berith Yitshak*), published in the same city in 1720, includes instructions for the full conversion of slaves to Judaism, which required ceremonial wine, Hebrew prayers, circumcision for males, and ritual immersion for both sexes. Instructions for welcoming slaves into the bosom of Judaism are preceded by the explanation that this ceremony was practiced "when the Temple [still] stood."[80] Although clearly a consequence of the Atlantic slave trade, the roots of these prayers trace back to at least medieval Europe, speaking to the ubiquity of servile labor in premodern Europe. One Hebrew prayer dating to twelfth-century central Europe instructs Jews who purchased non-Jewish slaves from Christians to circumcise the former upon purchase. The ceremony included imbibing a glass of wine,[81] perhaps to underscore that circumcised slaves were now intermediary Jews and the drink could be consumed in their presence without becoming ritually defiled.

While the use of *Sefer Berith Yitshak* in Suriname has not yet been definitively attested, the appendix at the back of the book, listing the names of ritual circumcisers, includes seven living in Suriname.[82] The circumcisers are listed according to their city of residence, all within the Atlantic orbit. In Europe, these include Amsterdam, The Hague, Naarden, London, Hamburg, and Bayonne. Curaçao and Suriname are the only Caribbean locations. Another Amsterdam edition from 1764/1765, reprinted in 1803/1804, does not include a list of ritual circumcisers but does incorporate the slave conversion ceremony. This volume, discovered in the attic of Curaçao's Congregation Mikvé Israel, is strongly suggestive of the continuing relevance of slave conversions for Caribbean Jewish communities into the nineteenth century.[83]

Arguably, the synagogue building was the strongest and most public indication of Jewish rootedness in a particular locale. Such an edifice was a symbol that Jews were not merely tolerated, as were Christian dissenters in the Dutch metropole and the colonies, but rather followers of a legally recognized and publicly protected faith. In the English and later British and Dutch realms, the erection of synagogue buildings placed Jews a notch above their Catholic contemporaries, who were forced to worship in private homes and contend with complaints over the crowds that gathered outside after services or how many worshippers were invited to attend.[84] In Suriname by the 1730s, Jews enjoyed the use of two synagogues in the capital city of Paramaribo, at a time when Lutherans had no church building of their own and members of the dominant Reformed Protestant faith prayed in a single house of worship.[85] One can therefore readily appreciate the significance Jews attached to their sacred objects emblazoned with the name of the donor, or the silver trays, bearing the congregation's monogram and presented as gifts to colonial governors. More than an expression of personal piety, wealth, or realpolitik, these precious objects were a statement about the permanence and highly exceptional privileges enjoyed by an entire community. These artifacts became vectors of memory for the longevity and purported former glory of Suriname's Jews, outliving the community itself. When Marten Douwes Teenstra, a Dutch agricultural advisor in Suriname, visited the nearly abandoned village of Jodensavanne in 1828, the names of benefactors were still clearly visible on the copper crowns, candelabra, silver wash basin, and ewer he admired in the synagogue.[86] Surinamese Jews had thus proven that objects, even more than people, were the anchors of historical memory.

The establishment of charity plantations endowed Surinamese Jews with a marker of belonging that extended to the poor. The revenues of these estates were earmarked for local Jewish paupers, a practice mirrored in the Christian community.[87] These estates helped counter the equation of outsider status with poverty. The timberland Quapibo, located on the Cassewinica Creek, was founded on March 7, 1696. On the eve of Emancipation in 1863, it was cultivated by 66 slaves and jointly owned by Rachel Bueno de Mesquita, widow of Abraham Gabay Fonseca, and the estate of Sara da Silva. A portion of its profits was reserved for indigent Portuguese Jews.[88] Other charity plantations owned by Portuguese Jews were Waicoribo, Mamre, Gelderland, Amsterdam, and Dotan. In 1770, the Portuguese Jewish community raked in a total of 1,069.31

Surinamese guilders from these six charity estates, almost 19 percent of its annual capitation tax.[89]

The Ashkenazi Jew Gerrit Jacobs (1674–1754), a native of the village of Zager in what is today Lithuania, established a parallel charity plantation for members of his own ethnoreligious group. Nieuw Meerzorg, located on the Matapica Creek due east of the Suriname River, produced mostly coffee but also the root vegetables tayer and cassava. In the mid-eighteenth century, this 1,000-acre plantation, whose name euphemistically denotes "more care" (in the sense of exertion or worry), enslaved 171 persons of African descent, one of the largest slave conglomerates in Suriname. As he felt death approaching in 1754, Jacobs penned a will mandating that his plantation should never be sold and that its revenues benefit both friends and relatives, the latter, if indigent, being entitled to a double allotment. Later, at least a portion of the proceeds was parceled out as poor relief to the Ashkenazi synagogues of Suriname and Amsterdam. His design to transform his plantation into a charity factory after his death is clear from his mandate that the number of slaves be increased to "200 or more." Jacobs's descendants remained faithful to his instructions; by 1863, 279 slaves were held captive on that estate.[90] Such charity plantations sent the implicit message that the indigent of the community deserved to be supported locally rather than shipped out of the colony. Jewish-owned charity estates endowed the Jewish poor with an aura of permanence and belonging. Ownership of a charity estate also helped Gerrit Jacobs acquire a local status in Suriname. Since Ashkenazi Jews were barred from owning land in Jodensavanne and, de facto, in its environs, Jacobs launched his plantations far from the Suriname River. Eventually, he adopted the name of the colony as his family name, becoming Gerrit Suriname. His local family members became known to relatives in Europe as the "Surinamese millionaires."[91] The exploitation of slave labor, therefore, played a pivotal role in the creation of a local Jewish identity.

In Suriname, membership in a Portuguese Jewish community was established either through birth or by formal allegiance to a congregation. Every Portuguese Jew who settled in the colony automatically became affiliated with the local Portuguese Jewish community, a practice at least nominally in force in Dutch Brazil, Curaçao, London, Amsterdam, and Leghorn, the five other centralized Portuguese Jewish communities of the Atlantic World and Mediterranean.[92] By at least the 1670s, Suriname's Portuguese Jewish regents decreed that there could be only one synagogue in the colony, and by the middle of the following century the bylaws explicitly stated that all residents of Suriname who belonged to "our nation," whether Portuguese or Spanish, were automatically considered *jehidim* and subject to all the *escamoth*, echoing the policy of forced membership in those other colonies and metropoles, and in Leghorn. So long as Iberian-origin Jews lived in the colony, they could not recuse themselves from membership.[93] With the exception of the poor, each head of household was expected to pay a capitation tax to the Portuguese Jewish congregation, in addition to a separate tax to the governor, assessed at the same rate as for Christians. Newcomers to the colony were expected to register themselves with the local Jewish community within six weeks of arrival to ensure they would be entitled to privileges and protections.[94]

The social ramifications of a slave society nuanced this bylaw. Already by the Hebrew year coinciding with 1662–63, the founders of Suriname's Jewish community had instituted the categories *jehidim* and *congregantes*, which clearly communicated status differentiation. The overt racial dimension of this distinction is first attested to in surviving sources from the mid-eighteenth century. Eurafrican Jews as well as whites who married *mulatas* were stripped of their *jahid* status but were still subject to all the ordinances, including fines for transgressing communal law.[95] These Eurafricans were apparently exempt from the community's capitation tax until 1784, when the *parnassim* resolved to mandate their annual assessment if they wanted the protection of communal privileges.[96] This new policy, part of what Wieke Vink refers to as "aggressive inclusionary politics towards poor and coloured Jews," was likely more a response to economic crisis than egalitarian ideals.[97]

Suriname's Jewry theoretically always remained a centralized community, with only one official congregation, that of Beraha VeSalom. However, this exclusivist mandate began to weaken in the early 1700s with the growth of Paramaribo's Jewish community and eventually gave way to the legal fiction that additional devotional centers were permitted, so long as they were considered houses of worship rather than congregations. Thus, in 1708, Portuguese Jews in the city secured permission from the Mahamad to launch a house of prayer (*caza de oraçao*), which Ashkenazim, then numbering about fifty individuals, were permitted to join.[98] This open-door policy repeated an ecumenical pattern characteristic of other early Jewish communities of the Atlantic World, including those of seventeenth-century London and North America.

From the 1730s, when Ashkenazim formally seceded to form their own Jewish congregation, named Neveh Salom ("Oasis of Peace"), strict ritual separation was established between the two communities. The bylaws of the Portuguese Jewish community forbade its constituents from praying in the Ashkenazi house of worship, an ordinance the latter congregation reciprocated. As a rule, Portuguese and Ashkenazi Jews were banned from worshipping or serving in each other's prayer houses.[99] But there was a clear double standard. Portuguese Jews could in special circumstances serve as religious functionaries in Neveh Salom.[100] In 1781, the Portuguese Mahamad grudgingly granted Ashkenazim permission to hire a Portuguese Jewish cantor for the High Holy Days. Their biting rationale for the concession was based on the Jewish principle of beautifying a religious commandment (*adorno & graça para ofesejo da ley*), a supercilious implication that the religious mores of Ashkenazim were not as aesthetically pleasing.[101] Intramarriage with a Jew from the other community resulted in relegation to *congregante* status.[102] Patrilineal descent determined congregational belonging. The last names listed on Portuguese synagogue membership rolls, all of Iberian Jewish origin, suggest strict adherence to this rule. With the exception of the Sanches family, of enigmatic origin, the rule also obtained in the Ashkenazi community, whose members bore Hebrew or Germanic family names through the eighteenth century.

The terms *jahid* (or *yahid*) and *congregante* deserve special attention. To understand their application in Suriname, it is useful to provide a contrast with other Portuguese Jewries in the Atlantic World. *Yahid*, as it was spelled in the Anglophone world, a word whose etymology probably derives from the Hebrew root "yahad," denoting "together," occurs in the Talmud in reference to a person worthy enough to be appointed manager of a community.[103] In Britain and her colonies, the terms *yahid* and *congregante* seem to have been exclusively economic in nature. In London, as in Barbados, a *yahid* was an assessed member of the congregation who attended meetings and possessed the right to vote.[104] In London, a *congregante*, translated into English as *congregator*, applied to "a person who frequents the Synagogue, but is not of the status, or possessed of the privilege of a Yahid,"[105] and typically was too poor to pay the minimal *finta*. The term *congregante* seems not to have existed in the British North American colonies. In New York, nonpaying affiliates were referred to in the negative, as "any other person not a Yaheed, tho Congregating with us."[106] The non-"Yaheed" in New York was still eligible for "Right, benefit or Priviledge."[107] Such individuals lacked

an assigned seat and were required to stand during worship.[108] The apparent absence of a discrete term for a non-*yahid* speaks to the tenuous size of
the North American Jewish settlements.

In the Dutch Atlantic, by contrast, the terms *jehidim* and *congregantes*
combined economic with ethnic and racial elements. In Amsterdam's Portuguese Jewish community, Ashkenazim were entirely excluded from membership, despite some early exceptions in the 1600s. Other Jews with no
documented Iberian origin, such as Italians, were admitted as *congregantes*,
though social standing and some evidence of "Portuguese" roots could
qualify them for *jahid* status. *Congregantes* were intermediary members of
the community. They were assessed a *finta* but were not given an assigned
seat in the synagogue, were banned from participating in most honorary
functions in the synagogue, and in the cemetery were relegated to the
"common row." Portuguese Jews of African origin (*negros* and *mulatos*)
were treated similarly and suffered harsher ritual exclusions in the synagogue, but there is no published evidence that they were formally classified
as *congregantes*. In Amsterdam, therefore, the *congregante/jahid* dichotomy
was primarily ethnic (not racial) in nature.[109]

By contrast, in Suriname and probably also in Curaçao, the terms *jahid*
and *congregante* were explicitly racial in nature but retained some of the
ethnic and economic elements that first emerged in Amsterdam. *Jehidim* in
Suriname paid their annual *finta* and were presumed to be white. As in the
metropole, Ashkenazim were excluded from membership. Intermarriage
with an Ashkenazi woman would result in the relegation of a Portuguese
jahid to *congregante* status. Ironically, "mulatto Jews," the strongest symbol
of Jewish settler status, were routinely assigned *congregante* status by the
mid-eighteenth century, overturning previous practice, by which they could
under certain circumstances become *jehidim*. A "whitening" clause was
simultaneously introduced. Though a *branco* who married a "mulatto" Jewess was demoted to *congregante* status, his family could recapture its former
jahid status by marrying the sons off to white women for two consecutive
generations.[110]

Although the communal minutes of Curaçao predating the mid-
eighteenth century have not survived, bylaws from 1755 refer to both *jehidim* and *congregantes*. Since both groups were subject to taxation, and could
qualify as either locals (*moradores*) or strangers (*forasteiros*), the distinction
between the two was probably racial.[111] When the Surinamese regents
stripped "mulattoes" of their *jahid* status in 1748, in conformance with the

practice in "other Jewish congregations" (*como em outras Kehilot*), they may have had Curaçao in mind.[112] In 1772, the Ashkenazi regents issued an identical ordinance, repeating the phrase "as in other Jewish congregations."[113] As these examples demonstrate, both whiteness and economic means were guarantors of full citizenship in Suriname's Jewish community but not clear indicators of rootedness.

Language

Language is a compelling example of Jewish rootedness in the colony because it demonstrates how Jewish localism became generalized in Surinamese society. As this final section will show, Portuguese was by far the most important form of communication among Jews and many of their slaves until the late eighteenth century. The Lusitanian tongue was the lingua franca of most Jews and overwhelmingly the main written language used in their record keeping through the early 1800s. This Portuguese linguistic tenacity can be explained by the significant size of the Jewish community within the white population and, concurrently, the small number of Dutch speakers within the multinational white settler society. Moreover, Jews tended to eschew conversion to Christianity and intermarriage with white Christians, possessed the liberty to maintain their records in Portuguese, and had the right to extend the reach of their culture by converting select members of the majority population (people of African origins) to a Judaism that was thoroughly Iberian in its cultural orientation.

The impact of Portuguese on the colony's majority, African-descendant population played a significant role in the language's entrenchment and dispersion within the colony. An anonymous description of Suriname, penned in Dutch in the 1730s or 1740s, indicates that many slaves living on Jewish-owned plantations had Spanish and Portuguese "ways of talking" and that often slaves understood nothing but Spanish or Portuguese. The unnamed author, himself a planter, implies that slaves learned these languages from their owners, just as servile workers who lived on estates originally founded by French masters were familiar with many French words.[114] But the impact of Portuguese on the enslaved, unlike French, was widely attested through the generations. Scholars, following the observations of contemporaries, identify the Portuguese-inflected tongue of enslaved Africans in Suriname as a "mixed language with Portuguese words" that had developed by 1740.[115] Some denote the language more specifically as Dju-tongo ("Jewish tongue") or Saramakkan, which emerged in 1680 and incorporated a lexicon of Portuguese, West African languages, and English with an African grammatical structure.[116]

The Dju-tongo Creole first developed on Jewish-owned plantations and was distinct from "the more fully English-based Ningre Tongo or Neger Engels (now known as Sranan or Sranan Tongo) on the other plantations"[117] and in the capital city of Paramaribo. If slaves on Jewish plantations were involved in lawsuits, an ensign (*vaandrig*) from among the Jews, someone fluent in either Portuguese or the local Afro-Portuguese Creole, was obligated to interpret on the slaves' behalf.[118] The communal archives of Suriname's Portuguese Jewish community also confirm the knowledge of Portuguese among domestic slaves owned by Jews. In 1779, Jacob Henriquez de Barrios Junior, the provisional jurator of the Jewish nation in Suriname, visited the house of Jacob Bueno de Mesquita, a defendant in a legal case. When he knocked on the door, Barrios was greeted by an African slave (*negra*), who responded in fluent Portuguese: "se havia ido ariba," indicating that he had gone upriver. Her words are underlined, in order to represent a direct quote.[119] Similarly, Chape, a woman owned by Isaac Vaz Farro, showed at least a passive knowledge of Portuguese when she was summoned before the Mahamad in 1769 to give testimony in a case of the illegal sale of killdevil, a kind of rum (*drama*). Since the records do not indicate that the regents used any other language but Portuguese in her presence, or employed an interpreter, we may surmise that Chape knew enough Portuguese to inform the Mahamad that she was in the service of Mordechay Cohen del Monte, who had instructed her to sell the drink to whoever desired it.[120]

Portuguese also had a strong presence among Eurafrican Jews. The *mulato* Isaac de Semha (Simha) de Meza, accused in 1797 of contravening the orders of the Second Hazan Samuel Jessurun Lobo to return to his proper synagogue seat, defended himself in fluent Portuguese, claiming that since Lobo was a mere salaried employee, and not a regent of the Mahamad, he did not have to obey him (*Eu nao conheço Sampy Lobo senao pr Hazan que ganha sallario*).[121] The free "mulattresses" Maria de Prado, also known as Mariana del Prado, and Simcha Judia both passed their wills in the Portuguese language in the 1780s and 1790s, respectively.[122] Hana Pelengrino, the daughter of a Jewish slave, and herself born a *congregante*, dictated her last will in 1786 in the Portuguese language, given her ignorance of Dutch (*vermits de testatrice de Neederduytse taal niet magtig is, is alle het selve aan haar in de Portugeesche taal geinterpreteerd gewoorden*).[123] Her brother Daniel Pelengrino (1736–87) served as the ritual inspector (*somer*) of the Paramaribo Jewish slaughterhouse, a position that would have required fluency in Portuguese,[124] and in 1787 also dictated a will in Portuguese.[125] Daniel owned an African slave (*negro*) named Avantuur, who at the time was being leased out to the Eurafrican Jew Abraham Ismael Judeo.[126] Judeo, a former slave fluent in Dutch who could sign his name, was very close to Daniel. In his own will, passed in Dutch in 1780, he had named Daniel as a legal guardian (*voogd*) of his minor heirs.[127] Judeo's aunt Roza Judia was a wealthy plantation owner who carried out her business correspondence with Eurafrican Moses de Oliveira in Portuguese and owned a Spanish prayer book.[128] If these intertwined Eurafrican families are representative, we may conclude that most Eurafrican Jews preferred to communicate in Portuguese or, secondarily, in Dutch, a language widely spoken or at least understood by Suriname's Jews by the late eighteenth century.[129] Together, these languages connected Eurafrican Jews to the Portuguese Jewish and Christian white populations, and simultaneously distanced them from the colony's enslaved people and their descendants, most of whom spoke a variety of African languages or, particularly if native born, Sranan.

A systematic survey of wills written during the eighteenth century confirms that, by a narrow margin, most testating Eurafrican Jews tended to speak not Sranan, the language of most wills passed by former slaves, but rather Portuguese or Dutch as their strongest languages. This evidence encourages us to reconsider the findings of Wieke Vink, who has argued that by the last quarter of the eighteenth century, most of the colony's Jews spoke Sranan Tongo exclusively and were thus "Creole Jews."[130] The implication of this statement is that Eurafrican Jews would have been in the vanguard of a linguistic shift from Portuguese to Sranan Tongo. In fact, Dutch and Portuguese appear to have been the strongest languages among precisely those Jews whom one might expect to be most creolized: Eurafricans.

The strong imprint of Portuguese on Jewish-owned people of African descent in Suriname may have much to do with Portuguese Jewish identity, which encompassed both religion and ethnicity, and therefore enjoyed a wider domain than other languages that transcended ethnicity or religious traditions. Other factors were the Surinamese custom of keeping enslaved families intact, recognizing spousal relations among slaves, the colonial law that barred Portuguese Jews from selling their houses in Jodensavanne to anyone but fellow Portuguese Jews, and the fact that thousands of enslaved Africans labored on plantations along the Suriname River densely populated by Jewish owners.[131] Portuguese may have functioned as a parallel to Suriname's lingua franca, Sranan Tongo, serving as a common language spoken by Jews, their African-born slaves, and their Eurafrican progeny.

The strength of Portuguese in Suriname owes much to the fact that in the vast majority of Dutch colonies, whether in the West or East Indies, neither the imperial language nor the official religion was imposed upon the masses.[132] While in general the governor and highly placed officials were expected to be fluent in Dutch, and Dutch migrants (and possibly their offspring) spoke the language, "the share of Dutch speakers was always small," even among whites.[133] The main reason was the small population size of the originating community: a million and a half people lived in the United Provinces and very few of them settled in the colonies. Whether as transients or settlers, most immigrants in the Dutch colonies did not hail from the republic, although many had passed through the fatherland, where some had gained knowledge of the language.[134]

The outcome of this demographic reality is the weak imprint of Dutch on the Creole languages of Suriname. This unusual colonial situation also influenced the majority population's spiritual traditions, which was not Dutch Reformed Protestantism. Although governors and high officials in the Dutch colonial world were generally obligated to espouse that faith, there was no official effort to nominally bring all residents under a common religious umbrella. To one nineteenth-century observer, Dutch culture in the colonies (whether in the West or East Indies) resembled a "Cork on which the Netherlands Floats."[135] By contrast, in the Spanish, British, and French colonies, as well as in the United States, the majority populations shared the religion and linguistic marker of the colonial administration. The anomalous situation in Suriname helped create a space for the reception among some of Suriname's enslaved population of both the Portuguese language and its locally corresponding religious faith, Judaism.

It is also possible, as most linguists now agree, that many slaves arrived in the colony with prior Portuguese knowledge. In the last quarter of the seventeenth century and roughly the next forty years, 38.5 and 25.8 percent, respectively, of the slaves shipped by the West India Company originated in Loango-Angola, a region colonized by the Portuguese since the late sixteenth century. During the free trade (1730–1803), the period when other companies became involved in the commerce in slaves, 34.5 percent of the forced immigrants came from Loango.[136] The "vast majority" of the so-called Charter Generation, the earliest newcomers, who also arrived in New England, Barbados, New Amsterdam, Brazil, and elsewhere in the Guianas, spoke closely related Bantu languages, while others who settled in Suriname spoke Gbe tongues. But many, in addition, had knowledge of a creolized version of Portuguese.[137]

Smaller numbers of Africans who ended up in Suriname originated in Portuguese-influenced Upper Guinea, and thus bore Portuguese names, were baptized Catholics, or were trained as Portuguese interpreters.[138] Occasionally, by happenstance, colonial records acknowledge the Lusitanian heritage of specific slaves. In 1824, the Surinamese press reported a runaway African-born slave (*Neger*) named Emanuel, who spoke little "Negro English" but was fluent in "truer Portuguese" (*echter Portugeesch*). The owner who posted the announcement, Jacobus Lemmers, was a wealthy, white Christian planter.[139] Although the largest contingency of Africans who arrived in Suriname probably spoke Ewe and did not come from regions colonized by Portugal, the Portuguese and its West African variants that existed among the broader slave community may have predisposed some of them toward the acquisition of Surinamese Portuguese Jewish culture.[140]

This strength of Portuguese as spoken in Suriname is also witnessed through the colony's Creole languages. Sranan, historically called "Black English" or "Negro Speech" (*Neger Engels* or *Neger Spraak*), first emerged on plantations when the colony was under English rule (1651–67) and therefore contains a noticeable Anglophone foundation.[141] Yet some 4 percent of the basic vocabulary of Suriname's national language is Portuguese. Among Maroon languages, Saramakkan, developed by slaves who fled their owners between 1690 and 1710, shows the broadest "watermark" of Portuguese, with some 35 percent of its basic vocabulary derived from that language.[142]

The problem for linguists, given the geographical origins of Africans transported to Suriname, is etiology. What, precisely, are the *origins* of the Portuguese component of these Creole languages? Did the Portuguese imprint originate from West Africa or from Suriname's Jews? In answering this question, linguists have necessarily relied on informed speculation rather than diachronic documentary evidence, which is largely missing for the enslaved population and its manumitted descendants.[143] The indirect evidence scholars posit for a Jewish origin is demographic: Jews formed at least one-third of the white population and the majority, through most of the eighteenth century, were involved in plantation agriculture.[144] The evidence for a West African imprint of Portuguese is more speculative. The natal regions of an unknown percentage of Suriname's West Africans had been colonized by the Portuguese since the late sixteenth century. While this did not necessarily mean that a significant percentage already spoke Portuguese or were familiar with Lusitanian culture, some may have been, which could have predisposed them toward Portuguese Jewish culture. At the very least, communication with Portuguese owners would have been simpler for many of these slaves in comparison to unfree laborers sold to Dutch- or French-speaking masters.[145]

Given the incorporation of select West Africans into the Jewish community since the seventeenth century and the fact that an indeterminable percentage of African-born slaves carried with them a preexisting Afro-Portuguese culture, it is quite problematic to trace the Portuguese strand of Creole languages to a single cultural group. Moreover, the etiological approach obscures the complicated, intersecting historical processes that produced the colony's Creole languages, as well as the social, cultural, and economic context that only documentary evidence can provide. Finally, Creole tongues, much more so than European languages, were highly unstable because they were overwhelmingly oral languages seldom committed to paper. Arguably, writing systems tend to have a conservative effect on languages, retarding linguistic change over the generations.[146] The intense evolutionary quality of Sranan and other Creoles means that it is particularly problematic to trace origins or align the provenance of these languages with a specific community. Particularly in hemispheric American slave societies, language is rarely transmitted through a single path, as the occurrence of Portuguese and Spanish in Suriname's Arawak language attests.[147] Unwritten languages in Suriname were dynamic, changing from generation to generation, now absorbing or casting off, then reforming. Whether the Portuguese came from West African Creole or via Surinamese Jews, from the other side of Suriname's southern border via migrant Indians, or from all of these directions, the incidence of Portuguese in multilingual Suriname testifies to an overlapping heritage that tied these communities together and to varying degrees facilitated cross-cultural communication.

The presence of Portuguese vocabulary in Suriname's national Creole language, Sranan Tongo, and more substantially in Saramakkan, the Maroon Creole, at first glance seems to be an additional expression of the impact of Jews on the majority population. Most linguists, however, argue that the incidence of Portuguese in these new languages originates in regions of West Africa colonized by the Portuguese. Both scenarios are built largely on speculation, as I have argued. It may be expedient, therefore, to conceptualize the Portuguese present in Sranan and Saramakkan as transmitted through the linguistic process of anastomosis, defined in this case as the coming together again of language branches separated in the distant past.[148] That is, since both West African and Surinamese Jewish Portuguese were imported from the Iberian Peninsula, it is just as likely that they reunited in Suriname, resulting in an interconnection between two largely similar branches of a language family. Viewed in this way, it may be misguided to even ask whether the Portuguese of Suriname's Creoles came from West Africans or from Portuguese Jews. The Portuguese spoken in Suriname was always a combined result of Jewish exile, Iberian colonization, and the Atlantic slave trade.

One component of Afro-Creole civilizations in Suriname clearly derived from Jewish culture concerns the biblical and rabbinical concept of *taref* (commonly rendered in English as "traif"), an animal or object ritually unfit for consumption or use by Jews. In traditional Judaism, such animal products included fish without scales, shellfish, pork, and any dish combining milk with meat. Already in the 1770s, John Gabriel Stedman noted among the enslaved population "a direct prohibition in every family, handed down from father to son, against the eating of some one kind of animal food, which they call *treff*."[149] Although enslaved Africans sometimes described their prohibition as *treff*, and it could coincide with Jewish religious practice (such as the avoidance of unscaled fish), the taboo among slaves could be inherited from a parent or acquired, was individualized, and was supernatural (rather than ritual) in origin. The use of the word and concept among slaves and their descendants showed a remarkable continuity into the next two centuries.[150] Whether or not the word and practice of "treff" were imposed by Jews on their slaves, or enslaved people adopted the word to describe a preexisting system of taboos that had originated in West Africa, as some scholars have argued, the phenomenon is further evidence of the blurry boundaries of cultural exchange, a phenomenon we will further explore in Chapter 5.[151]

Conclusion

Since the seventeenth century, Suriname's Portuguese Jewish leaders had taken pride in their rootedness, pointing to their refusal to abandon their frontier settlements under threat and their status as faithful colonists who regarded Suriname as their true home. These leaders exerted the strongest hand in creating a sense of entrenchment through the building of their rural synagogue and urban houses of worship and the plantations they carved out along the Suriname and Commewijne rivers. Eventually, their longevity in the colony was also expressed through successively legislated privileges, memorial prayers dedicated to cumulative generations of leaders and donors and regularly recited in synagogue, and ritual objects, engraved with the initials or names of pioneering philanthropists. The small proportion of Dutch colonists within the multinational white population, and the general tendency of white Christians to return to the fatherland once their fortunes were won or lost, accentuated the visibility of Suriname's Jews as true settlers.

On the other hand, widespread poverty, which for Portuguese Jews of the Atlantic World went hand in hand with transience, vitiated this sense of permanence. Indigence in Amsterdam was more extreme among Jews than their Christian counterparts, since many guilds and economic sectors were closed to them. This factor encouraged Jewish immigration to Suriname, which threatened true settler status. The *despacho*, a Portuguese Jewish institution created as a response to poverty, reinforced the transience of a large portion of Atlantic Jewry. Mass-migration schemes of the 1730s and 1740s, even though they did not succeed on the scale initially intended, deepened the immigrant dimension of Suriname's Jewish community.

Within Suriname, Portuguese Jewish leaders possessed the power to reinforce the transient, outsider status of the second class by creating the social categories of *congregantes*, foreigners, and vagabonds who did not enjoy full citizenship in the Jewish community and therefore did not completely belong. Simultaneously and conversely, these same elite men helped to make indigent people locals through the launching of charity plantations, whose proceeds were funneled to supporting the poor, and by giving priority in alms distribution to Jews native to the land (*filhos da terra*).

As transient as a significant portion of Atlantic Jewry was, the settling of Jews in Suriname beginning in the seventeenth century was a dramatic departure from the previous century, when most European Jewish families

Table 1. Jewish Population of Suriname

Year	Population
1684	232
1690	560–75
1695	550
1788	1,411
1791	1,350/1,430
1845	1,363

Sources: Nassy, *Essai historique*, part 1, 48, 83–84, part 2, 39; NAN, Sociëteit van Suriname, inv. nr. 213, Suriname Lijste tot den 31en decembr 1684, pp. 223–24, 224; Goslinga, *The Dutch in the Caribbean and the Guianas*, 309; Schnurmann, *Atlantische Welten*, 382; Klooster and Oostindie, *Realm Between Empires*, 277n21); Kruijtzer, "European Migration," 119; Van Lier, *Frontier Society*, 85–86, 90–82; Vink, *Creole Jews*, 27.

had resided in the same city for just one generation.[152] The Jewish community of Suriname provides the quintessential example of Jewish rootedness in the Dutch Atlantic, since both Amsterdam and Curaçao continued to function as transit points. Ultimately, more Jews left Amsterdam for Suriname than the reverse, helping the community to grow and strike roots. Through their uninterrupted longevity in the colony, significant size (one- to two-thirds of the white population), resistance to intermarriage with white Christians, and engagement with the local African-origin population, the Portuguese Jews of Suriname rendered Jewishness nearly synonymous with settler society. Jewish entrenchment in the colony was thus the combined result of regularized transience, unusual privileges, and extreme coercion.

The clearest example of non-elite localism is the use of Portuguese as a lingua franca between Jewish owners and their slaves and among Eurafrican Jews. From the late seventeenth century, Portuguese was an important language of communication between Jews and Africans, some of whom may have brought a Lusitanian linguistic tradition with them from West Africa. Wills passed over the course of the eighteenth century and other records suggest that most Eurafrican Jews spoke Portuguese (and secondarily, Dutch) as their strongest language, rather than Sranan Tongo, as previously thought. So significant was the Lusitanian tongue that it came to form the basic vocabulary of some 4 percent of Sranan, and 35 percent of Saramakkan, spoken by a group of Maroons, some of whom traced their immediate origins to Jewish-owned plantations. These findings suggest that the creolization process among Jews and people of African origin remained strongly

Portuguese in its character. The imprint of Portuguese on the colony is an implicit sign of Jewish localism. If the tendency of their Christian counterparts to return to the fatherland accentuated the entrenchment of the Jewish community in the colony, Creole languages confirm it. At the same time, the possible introduction into Suriname of the Portuguese language and its dialects from West Africa (and possibly Brazil's indigenous migrants) reminds us that anastomosis, rather than etiology, may be the best model for understanding the emerging cultures of Atlantic slave societies. Given the chaotic forced and voluntary migration streams circulating within the Atlantic World, and the equally unpredictable merging and transformation of local cultures, the tracing of single strands of culture back through time becomes an increasingly ambiguous undertaking.

As Jews became rooted in Suriname, they adapted to their new environment in ways that can be captured by the concept of creolization, defined as the distinctive manifestation of human civilization as produced by the encounter or mixture of two or more cultural groups. Jews changed as a community, especially in reaction to new economic and social contexts deeply informed by African slavery. They launched dozens of plantations on which enslaved Africans produced tropical crops intended for export to Europe, devised Jewish prayers to implore divine aid against Maroon incursions, and introduced communal regulations pertaining to the growing number of enslaved and manumitted progeny living in their community. Sub-Saharans and their locally born descendants, the most disadvantaged of Suriname's human populations, exerted the strongest impact on the colony's Jewish community, a saga considered in the next two chapters.

CHAPTER 4

The Emergence of Eurafrican Jews

In the 1720s, four Portuguese Jewish couples in Suriname wed according to rabbinical law. Jahacob bar Abraham, Jahacob Mesias Pelengrino, Josseph Rodrigues del Prado, and Ismael Judeu were joined in matrimonial union, respectively, to Miriam Mashiah Pelegrino, Ribca de Mattos, Yael Israel da Costa, and Hana, daughter of Gabriel de Mattos.[1] Their Jewish marriage contracts are all drafted in accordance with the traditional Hebrew/Aramaic text and are bound in a volume of two hundred similar *ketubot* drawn up over the course of the century's first half.[2] The dowries of the four brides collectively included thousands of Surinamese guilders, dwelling houses, jewelry, cattle, a wagon, and several slaves. None of these possessions were unusual among affluent Jews living along the Suriname River in the eighteenth century. What does stand out is the fact that seven of the eight partners had themselves been born in bondage.

These Eurafrican Jews, referred to in archival sources as "mulatto Jews," "Jewish mulattoes," or simply as "mulattoes," were typically descendants of an enslaved African mother and a white Portuguese Jewish father who decided to formally convert his children to Judaism, either during or after their enslavement. Both historiography and communal self-representations have tended to dismiss such conversion as a phenomenon limited to "a few Jewish slaveholders."[3] R. A. J. van Lier concludes that most Jewish males "were so orthodox in their religious views that they were not easily induced to enter into an extra-marital relationship."[4] Historian Wieke Vink estimates that no more than 10 percent of Suriname's Jewish community by the late eighteenth century constituted "coloureds," and half that by the middle of the following century.[5] Even Robert Cohen, who studied a major social uprising among Eurafrican Jews dating to the 1790s, understood the

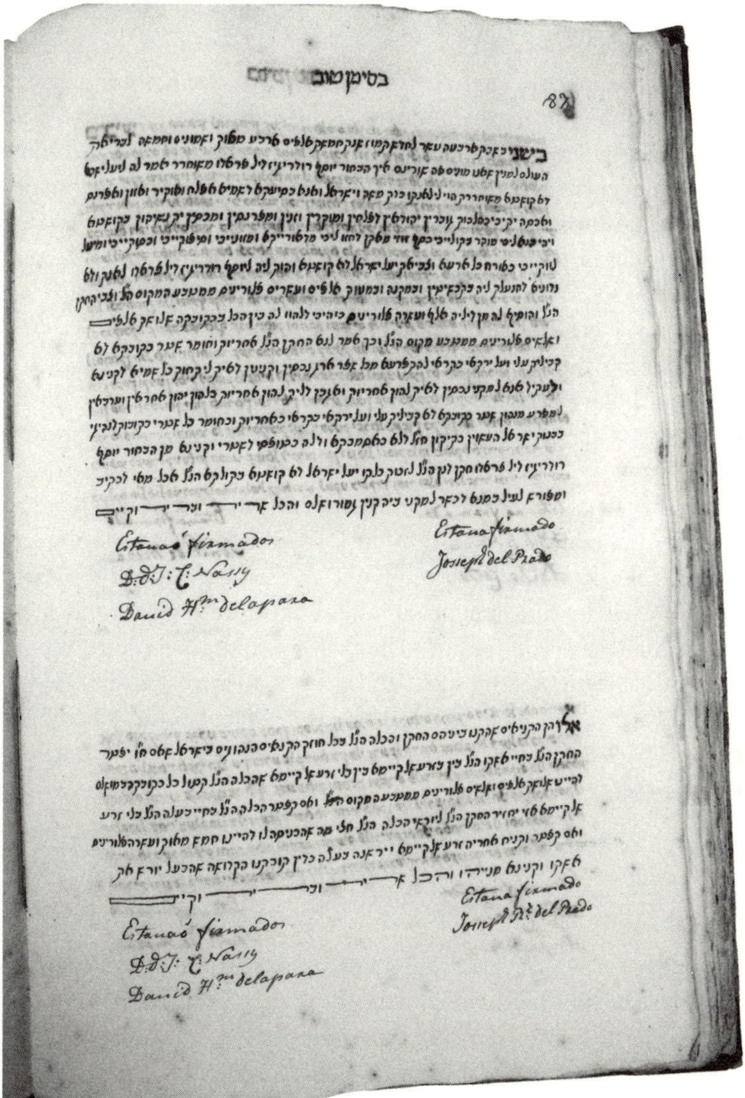

FIGURE 10. Jewish marriage contract (*ketubah*) of Josseph Rodrigues del Prado and Yael Israel da Costa, 1725, written in Hebrew/Aramaic. Both the bride and the groom are identified as former slaves. This is one of four surviving Hebrew/Aramaic marriage contracts from Suriname that explicitly mention former slave status. NAN, inv. nr. 1552, 1929 xiv, p. 87. Courtesy of Nationaal Archief Nederland.

impact of "mulatto Jews" as confined to that decade.[6] He further argues that "concubinage and marriage Surinam-style were rare among the Jews."[7]

In fact, Jews of African descent were far more significant in Suriname's Jewish community, from the moment of their first emergence in the 1660s. Their growing presence is evident in the bylaws of both Jewish communities, which regulated their presence in the synagogue and the cemetery, their social position among other Jews, and the status of white Jews affiliated with them through matrimony. Systematic examination of the records demonstrates their vital role in the survival and creolization of Surinamese Jews as a collective group. The leadership initiatives Eurafrican Jews undertook beginning in the second half of the eighteenth century, much of it devoted to the achievement of social and political equality, intensified the institutional diversity of Suriname's Jewish community and stimulated social reforms.

This chapter considers the ethnogenesis of Eurafrican Jews, their population size, and their legal status. In the following chapter, we shall consider their cultural orientation, their economic and social roles, and the strategies they employed to gain membership, collective autonomy, and first-tier status in the Jewish community. The uneven, transgenerational process of their eventual attainment of social equality is a microcosmic example of the struggle of slaves and their manumitted descendants in the Atlantic World to better their social and economic position and to achieve a status equal to that of whites.

Ethnogenesis

The ethnogenesis of Suriname's Eurafrican Jews was a factor of two constants: the legal status of slaves and the liberties embedded within the Jewish privileges. First, as theorists have observed, enslavement renders the owner the proprietor of both the labor and the body of the slave.[8] Second, colonial law, ensconced in the Jewish privileges, allowed Jews to freely practice their religion, a liberty that included the conversion to Judaism of non-Christians. These two constants, together with what one scholar calls the "imperious drive of sex," made the initiation of carnal relations with enslaved women almost inevitable.[9] Sexual access to enslaved females was the unquestioned prerogative of the master, a truism enforced by traditional religious values, as well as by rabbinical law and behavior in the

Atlantic World.[10] De facto behavior and Jewish religious tradition, which did not explicitly forbid sex between a master and his female slave, were mirrored in colonial law. The 1686 Surinamese statute banning white male *servants and artisans* from engaging in sexual relations with enslaved females, periodically reissued through 1784, has been misunderstood by scholars as a ban imposed on all white men.[11] However, the law never restricted the sexual behavior of male *planters*, who enjoyed full liberty to handle their human property as they wished.[12] While the ordinance first had white servants and artisans in mind, free male artisans of slave origins (*vrije ambagtslieden*) were also included by as early as 1725. The law, on the books until 1814, may represent an attempt by the colonial government to prevent solidarity between the enslaved and the white lower class, who were deprived of many of the privileges of whiteness.[13] Its successive reissue for over a century is probably an indication of its continual breach, and it may have been largely a symbolic law, a perfunctory regulation that gestured toward an ideal, white (though non-planter) sexual morality, without the intention to enforce it.

Suriname's population rapidly Africanized over the centuries. By 1684, 4,200 African slaves resided in Suriname. In 1705, the number of African-origin slaves in the colony climbed to nearly 10,000 and in the 1770s and 1780s peaked at 60,000 people, captive on some 400 plantations.[14] In 1690, there lived in Suriname five individuals of African descent to every white. By 1775, that gap had increased to almost 25 to 1.[15] Viewed another way, the percentage of whites in the total population declined from 16.4 in 1684 to 5.8 in 1791, an indication in part of the exponential proliferation of sugar plantations. While the real number of whites increased by four and a half, the real number of black slaves increased 13 or 14 times, meaning that over 90 percent of the Surinamese population was both enslaved and of African origin.[16] The numerical dominance of slaves in Suriname remained stable through the abolition of slavery in 1863, though the population of free people of African origin steadily increased as a result of manumissions, mostly involving women and children.[17]

The sharp growth of the African population vis-à-vis whites dramatically increased sexual contact between white men (including Jews) and enslaved women. In the early period of colonial rule, Jews collectively owned proportionately more slaves than their Christian counterparts. By 1684, 232 Jewish householders, comprising 28.6 percent of Suriname's European-origin population, owned 30.3 percent (or 1,298) of the colony's enslaved Africans. Sexual relationships between European-origin Jews and enslaved women of African origin must have been especially common on Jewish plantations, as the same census suggests. On larger agricultural plots, particularly those owned by Jews, the ratio between male and female slaves was more or less equal, supplying more African-origin females vulnerable to sexual exploitation.[18] One historian, writing in the final years of Suriname's slave regime, estimated that whites and free men of African descent maintained non-consensual sexual relations with seven or eight enslaved women at a time.[19]

Gender imbalance within the Jewish community made the conversion of Eurafrican children to Judaism expedient for survival. Like many early settlements in the hemispheric Americas, the Jewish community suffered a dearth of women. About 64 percent of Suriname's Jewish population in 1684 was adult male, almost double the size of the adult female population. This approximates patterns in the white Christian population, where 74 percent of the community was male.[20] This gender imbalance likely continued until the late eighteenth century.[21] The preponderance of men as beneficiaries of the *despacho* system contributed to the skewed ratio. Official marriage between enslaved women and free men was impossible, again leaving concubinage as an obvious resort.[22] African-origin women were thus a key component in the growth, survival, and redefinition of the colony's Portuguese Jewish population.

By contrast, white Christians in Suriname were generally less inclined to convert their human property to the household religion. An ordinance of 1733 required that masters instruct their slaves in Christianity *after* manumission, an indication that some conversion to Christianity was occurring during bondage.[23] However, white Christians typically did not baptize their slaves until the late eighteenth or early nineteenth century.[24] The scattered references to the Christian conversion of African slaves beginning in the late seventeenth century specifically characterize the conversion phenomenon as rare.[25] Rosemary Brana-Shute found that only 8 percent of the 1,346 slaves she examined who were manumitted between 1760 and 1828 "indicated any experience of, education in, or commitment to Christianity."[26] Planters in particular objected to slave baptisms, threatened by a gospel that preached equality, and regarded slaves as inferior creatures by virtue of their "heathenism."[27] Among Europeans, concludes Johannes Postma, the Dutch "may well have been the least interested in efforts to educate and Christianize the African population."[28]

The impulse to formally introduce the progeny of master-slave relations into the Jewish community developed early. In the Hebrew year coinciding with 1662–63, Suriname's Portuguese Jewish leaders already distinguished between *jehidim*, a Hebrew word denoting "individuals," and *congregantes*, Portuguese for "congregants." The former were banned from circumcising the children of fellow *jehidim* who had been demoted from their *jahid* status.[29] The passing allusion to this bylaw, which does not survive, does not define the two italicized terms, nor does it explain why a *jahid* would have been demoted, but later evidence and precedents elsewhere in the Atlantic World, as we shall see, suggest that the relegation was connected to the African ancestry of the children.

The conversion of slaves to Judaism appears to have always been regulated by Suriname's rabbinical leaders. The earliest known descriptions of actual conversions, both of which date to the 1720s, indicate that the procedure was carried out by the community's "teacher" (*leraar*), according to the regulations of the Jewish "nation," and that it involved circumcision for males and ritual immersion for both sexes.[30] The officiator may have had recourse to a prayer book similar to the aforementioned *Covenant of Isaac*, which included instructions for circumcising and ritually immersing male and female slaves for conversion to Judaism. The ceremony closely followed the biblical commandment, "He that is born in thy house, and he that is bought with thy money, must needs be circumcised: and my covenant shall be in your flesh for an everlasting covenant."[31] The ceremony attests to the non-racial rabbinical approach to slave conversion in the Caribbean.

By at least the mid-eighteenth century, rabbinical leaders in Suriname also enjoyed jurisdiction over formalizing the liberation of slaves converted to Judaism. The Portuguese Jewish bylaws of 1752 specifically directed *jehidim* who wished to free their Jewish slaves to first secure a ruling from the *haham* and have it submitted to and stored in the communal archives. The bylaw was understood to be in compliance with the directives of "our divine sages" (*nossos Divinos Sabios*), likely a reference to the rabbis of the Talmud (a text canonized around 550 C.E.) and the rabbinical sages of twelfth-century Spain. The use of these texts, which predate the rise of the Atlantic slave trade, once again underscores the non-racialized approach to slavery embraced by Jewish legal decisors of the Atlantic World.[32]

David Nassy, author of the *Essai historique*, brought up at least seven of his "mulatte" slaves in the Jewish religion: Moses, Ismael, Marianne and her daughters Jema and Simha (all of whom he bequeathed to his daughter

Sarah in 1777), and Simha's children Isaac and Sarah.[33] Portuguese Jewish
leaders writing to Governor J. F. Friderici in 1794 explained the provenience
of Eurafrican Jews euphemistically, notably obscuring the perspectives of
the mothers and children. Several men of the "Portuguese Jewish Nation,"
they explained, "out of private affection, begot children with some of their
female slaves or mulattoes," and "out of special love for the Jewish religion,
had the boys properly circumcised and the girls ritually immersed by the
rabbinical teacher," and so on through the generations. Some of these
enslaved or liberated mothers, they continued, brought their children up
with Judaism.[34] As we shall see, there are hints that African mothers and
their Eurafrican children had both utilitarian and spiritual reasons for evincing an interest in embracing Judaism.

The two earliest known descriptions of slave conversion to Judaism further help us understand the social context of Eurafrican Jewish ethnogenesis in Suriname. In his 1725 will, Ishac da Costa identified himself as the
"legitimate" son of Moses and Ribca da Costa and husband to his first
cousin, also named Ribca. His own marriage was unfruitful, a problem
often noted in Portuguese Jewish records and possibly exacerbated by the
coupling of successive generations of first cousins. Avunculate and first-
cousin unions, outlawed by the States of Holland in 1580, were one of the
privileges early on accorded Surinamese Jews.[35] Costa himself was not infertile. Implicitly, he procreated six young Eurafricans with two or more of
his slaves beginning in 1703, if not earlier: Rosa (21), Ismael (19), Simha
(10), David (7), Hana (5), and a *muleca* (enslaved valet) named Aquariba,
daughter of his late "negress, Assiba." Costa affirmed that they all merited
manumission by virtue of being "born in my house and from my female
slaves, [by virtue of] the good service and loyalty that I had from their
mothers, and [by virtue of] the inclination of said mulattoes to be obser-
vant of our Holy Law and having received it willingly and with love."[36]
Costa had these children formally converted to Judaism during their
enslavement, the boys being circumcised, the girls ritually bathed (*baña-
das*).[37] Conversion, then, was a stepping stone to liberation.

For affluent Jewish men like Costa, conversion followed by manumission was the obligatory prerequisite to the creation of direct legal heirs.
After fulfilling these two steps, Costa then declared his children slave owners in their own right. Ismael was bequeathed the *negra* Beatriz and her
children, while David inherited the *negra* Serafina and her progeny, along
with the *negro* Piche. His daughters, Rosa, Simha, and Hana, also became

slave owners, but Costa's non-human property went to the boys. Ismael and David received one-half of Costa's house furniture, clothing, and half of his cattle, plus the cultivated land and buildings he owned in Paramaribo (the master's nephews received the other half). Costa's will embodies the key elements of the phenomenon of "bywives" in slaveholding societies of the Atlantic World: the "legitimate" wife is mentioned and made a benefi-ciary, while the birth mother is left enslaved and is rewarded only through the rising fortunes of her children. Out of a sense of public decency, prog-eny are never explicitly referred to as their master's offspring. But their status as "mulattoes" and their inheritance of the bulk of the testator's wealth loudly announces their filial connection.[38]

The case of Joseph Pelegrino of Suriname follows a similar pattern. In 1720, he appealed to the local municipal authorities to recognize the manumission of his three children, Simha, Jacob, and Mariana, all procre-ated during enslavement and converted to Judaism by the community's teacher (leraar). Since the colonial government's jurisdiction over manu-mission did not commence until 1733, Pelegrino had liberated his children according to the regulations of the Jewish "nation," and therefore worried that the local municipal authorities would not recognize their freedom. The court declared the three children "free of all slavery" and legitimized them as Pelegrino's true descendants.[39] Pelegrino, like many other Portuguese Jewish masters/fathers, seems to have been himself of African descent, per-haps a reason he was forthcoming about his paternity. Although Joseph Pelegrino's petition does not include information on his racial status, the legal position of his descendants suggests that he himself was either "mulatto" or "black." Joseph's son Jacob was classified as a carboeger (denoting a child of a mulatto and a black) and was buried in the Eurafrican section of the Jodensavanne Cemetery, while his grandson Daniel Pelegrino was described as a negro.[40]

Similarly, Benjamin Musaphia, the mulato son of Samuel Musaphia and the manumitted Semja Pelegrina, expressed his desire in his 1764 will that his two "adopted" children Dina and Mariana Musaphia, procreated by the free "negress" Beatrice, be raised in the Jewish religion.[41] Since ownership of property was a status marker that at this time distinguished free people from slaves, the quest for legal heirs was of central concern to Jews who had been born enslaved or who were but one generation removed from bondage. This preoccupation is mirrored among similarly situated persons living in agrarian slave societies elsewhere in the Americas. In Sabará, Brazil, for example, manumission for the sake of legation was a leading motivation of slaveholders who made their fortunes in the eighteenth century, although these men were typically unmarried. Such Brazilian slave owners tended to acknowledge their paternity, more often of sons than daughters.[42]

At the same time, the conversion of slaves to Judaism cannot be reduced to an economic calculus. Ishak Mesias, owner of the Goede Delijansa plantation on the Suriname River, reasoned in his 1759 will that since he and his wife, Lea, had not merited progeny, they should recall that good works were also children in that they "not only perpetuated the name and notoriety" of the decedent but were also "lights that accompany the soul and allow it to reach the place God reserves for those who fear Him." In this same testament, Mesias manumitted Simha, his *mulata* slave (and likely also his daughter), whom Hazan Mordehai Mendes Quiros had already ritually immersed and converted to Judaism. At his death, Mesias left her an annual bequest of fifty guilders.[43] Mesias's will reminds us that the conversion of slaves to Judaism reflected the personal relationship between the master and his human property and that Eurafrican children were much more likely to be manumitted than African men and women.[44]

The family name "Peregrino" helps us to appreciate the ethos of Eurafrican Jews, who were typically fluent in Portuguese or Spanish. Peregrino denotes "pilgrim" in both languages and was used in Atlantic Jewish communities to denote a foreigner or convert to Judaism. In bilingual Spanish/Hebrew prayer books of the 1680s, reissued through the generations, "peregrinos" were men who were already circumcised (as were many West Africans) and who therefore had to be formally converted to Judaism through the symbolic extraction of a drop of blood from their penises.[45] In the Atlantic World, *peregrino* acquired a transcendental meaning, perhaps derived from medieval Christianity, where the *peregrinus* had been a spiritual wanderer who underwent a series of challenges on a quest for salvation.[46] New Christians who returned to Judaism sometimes chose the family name Peregrino or Pelegrino, an implicit reference to Abraham, the Bible's first pilgrim and convert to the Israelite religion, which eventually evolved into Judaism.[47] In Suriname, the last name seems to have functioned as a parallel to *congregante*. "Peregrino" (variably spelled within the same Surinamese family as Pelengrino, Pellengrino, Pelegrino, or Pellegrino) effectively stood in for three epithets, one marking reversion to Judaism, another indicating a second-class racial status, and the third the transition from enslaved to free status.

The Peregrinos of Suriname were themselves aware of the multi-layered resonance of their name. This is plain to see in the 1758 petition of Miriam Pelengrino (who identified as Mirian Pelengrina), daughter of the late Joseph Pelengrino. Describing herself as the most unfortunate person in the land, she explained to the regents that she had just recovered from a three-month illness that had left her unable to continue to earn her living as a seamstress. She evoked the memory of her late father, known for his charity, and asked her leaders to recall the biblical admonition not to turn away the pilgrim (*nao largues ao Pelengrino*).[48] Pelengrino was evidently paraphrasing Exodus 23:9 ("Do not oppress the stranger"). Given the familial connections of Eurafrican Jews to Christians of slave origins, Miriam may even have been inspired by the New Testament's Book of Matthew (5:42), which urged its students to "Give to the one who asks you, and do not turn away from the one who wants to borrow from you."[49] The timing of the petition, written just as Eurafrican Jews who had secured *jahid* status were experiencing a new communal policy that demoted them to the position of *congregantes*, also suggests that Pelengrino was trying to negotiate a racial status as well.

Miriam's brother Jahacob, who petitioned the *parnassim* for charity sometime before his death in 1750, likewise evoked the memory of his charitable late father. Quoting from the Book of Leviticus, he urged the regents to recall that God's "holy law says that you are to have the same law for the foreigner and the native-born" (*hua [ley] tanto para o pelengrino como o natural entre vos*).[50] Almost half a century later, members of the Eurafrican Jewish brotherhood Darhe Jesarim leveraged a similar biblical passage in their petition to the governor, pointing out that their second-class status in the Portuguese Jewish community contradicted the Mosaic law affirming "one ordinance shall be both for you of the congregation and also for the stranger that sojourneth with you."[51] The resonance of "pilgrim" differed markedly from its meaning for white Portuguese Jews. In their letters to Europe dating to the 1670s, Portuguese Jewish colonists spoke of their sojourn in Suriname as a collective peregrination (*peregrinasão*).[52] For white Portuguese Jews, pilgrimage was a shared condition that implicitly constituted part of God's plan for the Jewish people, while for their Eurafrican counterparts, pilgrim status was stigmatized and thus contravened God's law.

Parallel to the Peregrinos was the Judeu family (sometimes rendered in Spanish as "Judio" and feminized as "Judea" or "Judia"). The Judeus were also Eurafrican Jews with a family name referring to their outsider/insider status. "Judeu" means Jew in Portuguese, and also indicates conversion to Judaism because it is not a traditionally Jewish patronymic. On the Jewish marriage contract of Ismael Judeu it is rendered in Hebrew as *yehudi* (יהודי).[53] Like many other Eurafricans through the mid-eighteenth century, the Judeus enjoyed full Jewish status. The first known member of the clan, born in 1663 and circumcised by David Messias, is not distinguished by a racial category in that record book.[54] A man of the same name was living on the Suriname River by 1701 and three years later requested a twenty-foot extension to his house at Jodensavanne.[55]

Although Jewishness as a diasporic birthright has been typically passed on through the mother, it is important to recall that the patriarchal strain of Jewish identity transmission, which first emerged in antiquity, never fully disappeared. It is attested to elsewhere in the Atlantic Jewish World, including Jewish centers in North America that were not slave societies and where Jews engaged mostly in commerce. In British North America, Samson Levy and Michael Judah both outmarried with white Christians and ritually circumcised their children.[56] Several Portuguese Jews in early nineteenth-century London circumcised their own children, born to local Christian women, or requested that their infants so conceived be buried in the Jewish cemetery. Both acts were contrary to the policy of London's Mahamad. The tendency to evade rabbinical authorities is also witnessed in the eighteenth-century Dutch Republic, where a number of Ashkenazi male criminals, organized into bands, became involved with Gypsy women and informally converted them to Judaism. Criminal proceedings reveal that the Gypsy Fisone "had become a Jewess" during her relationship with the Jew, Levi Abrahams, and one of her children by a previous involvement with a Christian man was given a new, Jewish name. Florike Egmond classifies this phenomenon as the adoption by a Christian/Jewish group of Jewish customs.[57] The men in these very different settings seem to have adhered to the understanding in broader Christian society that the husband/father determined the religious identity of their children, particularly sons. The patrilineal principle in Suriname's Jewish community, though practiced with formal conversion as a mandatory stipulation, thus did not constitute a radical break with the past, nor was it unusual in the Atlantic World. Nonetheless, the patrilineal principle did not remain dominant in Suriname, largely because of the diachronic effects of concubinage across the generations.

The Shift to Matriarchal Judaism

Increasingly after the destruction of the Second Temple in 70 C.E., patriarchal Judaism was overshadowed by a rabbinical Judaism that made Jewish mothers the sole determinants of their children's religious identity. This shift occurred largely in response to the laws of Christian Europe, which banned Jewish proselytism. The pattern we have heretofore considered allots most of the transmission of Judaism to the father, who was the initiator of the formal conversion process. As the number of child slave conversions to Judaism proliferated through the generations, there arose a sizable group of enslaved and free women who had been born Jewish and could therefore, according to diasporic rabbinical law, automatically transmit their Jewishness to their children, regardless of the father's identity. This shift to matriarchal Judaism in the ethnogenesis of Eurafrican Jews became perceptible by around the mid-eighteenth century and is attested to in birth and burial records that identify most Eurafrican Jewish families as matrilocal.[58]

Theoretically, the matriarchal transmission precept should have also applied to white Jewish women who procreated children with unfree Africans, but sexual double standards in the colony prevented this from happening. In slave societies generally, white women were assigned the sole responsibility for maintaining racial purity.[59] Sexual intercourse between white women and *negros* or *indios* was regarded as a heinous crime by the larger ruling society. Colonial authorities in the Dutch Caribbean reserved harsh punishment for such behavior, considering it, in a placard issued in 1711, "unnatural whoredom and adultery." Unmarried violators were to be flogged and banished for life, and married women also branded, a punishment generally reserved for slaves.[60] The promulgation of this law hints that such illicit unions did occur, and it is thus not surprising that two white Christian women were so accused in 1721. Ten years later, the daughter of a Jewish planter admitted to a sexual relationship with an Indigenous male and was duly expelled from the colony.[61] Thus the punishment of a white woman consorting with an African or Indian entailed not merely a loss of social status but also her local eradication: complete elimination from community membership as well as physical removal from the colony. By the 1760s, such unions were still unusual, but not censured, as suggested by Philippe Fermin, a Dutch-born physician who spent many years in Suriname. A white woman having "commerce" with a *Negre* was "rare," he

FIGURE 11. Five female slaves on their way to their respective houses of worship on Palm Sunday, which coincided in 1829 (the year of the artist's arrival in Suriname) with the second day of the Jewish holiday of Passover. From right to left are a Lutheran, a Jewess (dressed in white), a Calvinist, a Moravian, and, in the background, an (Afro-)Creole Christian. (The caption reads: *Cinq femmes esclaves se rendant à leur église un jour de fête. A droite une luthérienne, à côté une juive, une calviniste, une morave. Dans le fond une jeune esclave créole chrétienne, se rendant à l'église le jour des Rameaux.*) Illustration by Pierre Jacques Benoit, 1829(?). From Pierre Jacques Benoit, *Voyage à Surinam: Description des possessions Néerlandaises dans la Guyane* (Brussels: Société des Beaux-Arts, 1839), 75.

observed, but "not without example."[62] Yet none of the Jewish bylaws accounts for the possibility of children produced by white women and African slaves.

Like Dutch colonial law, communal regulations governing Suriname's Jews included no restrictions against *extramarital* sexual intercourse between white males and female slaves (with the technical exception, as we have seen, of male servants and artisans, likely honored in the breach). Only when Portuguese Jewish men attempted to *formalize* unions with manumitted slaves did penalties accrue. By the mid-eighteenth century, Jewish ordinances stipulated that white men who married *mulatas*, "whether through our Holy Law or solely before the Magistrate, will then be discharged from their status as *jehidim*, and immediately recorded as *congregantes*, and in every single way considered mulatto."[63] Marriage to a free Jewish woman of African descent thus conferred a racial stigma on her white husband.

As in broader colonial society, marital hypergamy provided a possibility for a "fallen" family to restore its white status. The Mahamad stipulated that a demoted *jahid* could be readmitted with his family to his former social status provided that his sons and grandsons all married white Jewish women, an interesting reversal that placed the responsibility for sexual purity on males.[64] Thus, formal marriage between white men and free Eurafrican Jews was not at this point forbidden, only discouraged through status disincentive. It is important to emphasize that surviving bylaws never prohibited formal marriage between white Jews and free Jewesses of African origin, nor did they exclude the offending couple from legitimate communal membership. It merely discouraged such relations through a social demotion that barred the husband from prestigious functions (and thus political influence) in the community, a relegation that may have also affected his business endeavors. Enslaved women are passed over in silence, communicating the legal impossibility of formalizing such a union.

The union of a white Jewish woman with a free Eurafrican Jew is not addressed in any of the ordinances until the 1780s. To some extent, the previous silence is a reflection of the typically androcentric locution of the communal records. The lives of Jewish women were largely regulated by an unwritten moral code enforced through fathers, husbands, or other male family members with coercive authority, and perhaps also by the pressure of fellow women. The sudden reference to white women's demotion through marriage by the 1780s may be an indication that the previous gender gap had significantly narrowed. The reference to Jewish marriages between white women and Eurafrican Jewish men by the 1780s is an indication of a burgeoning population of Eurafricans, male and female, who were Jewish from birth by virtue of having been born of Eurafrican Jewish mothers. The emergence of a critical mass of slaves and free people of African descent who were born Jewish could not have been possible without the intensifying observance of the matrilineal principle of Judaism. The rise of this class of Jews stimulated a change in the way members of the Jewish community were classified and documented, a change that makes it possible to estimate both their numbers and their proportion within the white Jewish population.

Counting Eurafrican Jews

If the collection of *ketubot* alluded to at the opening of this chapter is statistically representative, just 2 percent of Suriname's Jewish community in the first half of the eighteenth century consisted of slave-origin Jews. However, this sample is misleading because most Eurafrican Jews did not legally marry and because Eurafrican Jews were often considered white and admitted as *jehidim* through the mid-eighteenth century. A colony-wide census taken in 1762 indicates the existence of numerous Eurafrican Jews scattered throughout the land who, because of their landownership, are classified as whites (*blanken*). One of these was David Judeu Silva, whose slaves, consisting of eight adults and three children, produced 525 pounds of sugar in 1702.[65] In the 1790s, Eurafrican Jews would recall that in "earlier years," Jews of slave origins, including not only *mulatten* (half white and half black) but also *carboegers* (one-half black, one-half mulatto), enjoyed rights and privileges equal to those of other members of the Jewish congregations.[66] Two of these named individuals, Joseph Rodrigues del Prado and Jacob Pelegrino, both died in the mid-eighteenth century.[67]

Over the course of the eighteenth century, as we have seen, increasing numbers of Eurafrican Jews were conceived outside the bounds of formal marriage, born to single Eurafrican women who were themselves Jewish by birth. Communal birth and death records help us pinpoint the general time period in which the shift to matrilineal descent commenced among Eurafrican Jews. Before 1777, the starting date of the most comprehensive of these registers, individuals in the Portuguese Jewish community were almost never identified racially.[68] In birth and death listings, matrilineal descent was also irrelevant: in terms of identifying parentage, only the father was mentioned. But in 1777, cantor Mordehai Mendes Quiros died and passed on his administrative staff to his successor, David Baruh Hezkiahu Louzada. Cantor Louzada began to carefully note racial and social status, as well as the identity of both fathers and mothers. In the case of most Eurafrican Jews, only the mother was mentioned, an indication that these women tended to procreate outside the bounds of legal matrimony and raise matrilocal families.

The death registers maintained by cantor Louzada help us approach an estimate of the Eurafrican Jewish population in the fifty years that bridge the eighteenth and nineteenth centuries. The 1,371 entries span from 1778 to 1835. Between 1779 and 1824, the deaths of 98 Jews of non-*jahid* status were recorded. Of these, the overwhelming majority were identified as *congreg-antes*, while three were named as "mulattoes" and one as a Jewish slave.[69] Alas, Louzada did not differentiate in his records between born *congregantes* and, conversely, *jehidim* demoted to *congregante* status due to their marriage with a Eurafrican Jewess or (by contrast) because of their violation of communal law and refusal to complete the prescribed penance. However, discussions in the communal minutes indicate that social relegation of whites due to legal infraction was rare and that those demoted due to noncompliance with the Mahamad's directives fairly quickly repented and were restored to *jahid* status.[70] The statistics of this community profile show that, at least officially, between 1778 and 1835, 7.1 percent of the members were lower-status members, most likely of African origin. Phrased another way, roughly one out of every fourteen Portuguese Jews in Suriname over the course of half a century was likely of African origin.

Yet, it is clear from other sources that the presence of Eurafrican Jews was more widespread. To begin with, the register necessarily does not take into account the "whitening" clause operative in Suriname's Jewish community, which effectively concealed countless Jews of more attenuated slave origins. The statistic also omits a sizable group of fringe people who were active in the Eurafrican Jewish community in the 1790s but hovered between Jewish and outsider status. In fact, the majority of Eurafricans who signed a petition to the governor in 1793 demanding equality in the Portuguese Jewish community appear nowhere in the birth or death records because they apparently never officially registered. These include Jacob [*sic*] Jessurun, Jacob [*sic*] Nahar, Abraham Levy, Aron Nunes Henriquez, Abraham Goosen, E. P. Jacobs, Moses de Pina, David Jossiao Pardo, Abraham Gabay Fonseca, David H. Goedman, Moses de Robles, Samuel Gabay Fonseca, and Moses de Torres.[71] Another example of a person who hovered between official Jewish and non-Jewish status is the "molata" Mirjam Judia de Meza, who is listed in the birth records but only because in 1821, at the age of fifty, she was ritually immersed and formally became a convert (*gerá banhada*).[72] Many individuals who do not appear in the death registers may have chosen interment on private property rather than be relegated to the humiliating, muddy margins of Portuguese Jewish cemeteries. The free Simcha Pinto, who left five guilders to the Eurafrican Jewish Darhe Jesarim ("Path of the Righteous") society in 1790, may have been among them. Her last wish was that her executors bury her body on her estate, located next to her grandmother's residential property.[73] Starting

in the late 1700s, dozens of additional persons are mentioned in the communal archives in the context of their *congregante* status or conversion to
Judaism but are absent from the birth and death records. Their erasure was
in part self-imposed, as one regent noted in 1797. "Born *congregantes*" of
illegitimate unions often failed in their obligation to make known to the
cantors of the two synagogues the birth of their children, thus contravening
orders the Mahamad issued in 1790.[74]

Obfuscation of the Jewish community's African origins was also imposed by communal leaders concerned with public image. One official estimate of Suriname's population, dating to 1817, claiming to be precise only
for the Jewish community, and particularly for the Portuguese, stretches
the boundaries of common sense. The "coloured" population among Jews
and Christians, respectively, was supposedly 1 percent, including 30 *kleurlingen* living among an urban white Portuguese Jewish population of 592.
(The estimated percentage among Christians was 2.5 percent.)[75] The first
calculation is rendered all the more dubious in the remark on the very
next pages, where an anonymous author contradictorily explains that the
ongoing dearth of white women has resulted in the reality that white men
"generally . . . live with women of color so that the closest relationships
come about between white men and women of color."[76] The census also
claims to have found no *enslaved* Jews in the Portuguese Jewish community,
a statement patently challenged by the communal minutes, which capture
discussions on the burial of circumcised slaves.[77] Clearly, these collective
details encourage historians to revise previous estimates of the Eurafrican
Jewish population, as well as their strict, halakhic definition of what constituted a Jew in early modern Suriname.

An estimate by a mid-nineteenth-century historian helps us come closer
to reality. According to Julien Wolbers, nearly one-third of all free persons
living in Suriname by the 1790s were of slave origins (either freeborn or
liberated blacks and mulattoes), a proportion that was to nearly double by
1811. In real numbers, that translated to 1,760 free people of African descent
and 2,900 whites, dwarfed by an enslaved population of 53,000.[78] Assuming
that the presence of Jews among free people of slave origins mirrored the
overall proportion of Jews within the white population, at least one-third
of all free persons of African origin in Suriname by the 1810s—that is to
say, roughly 586 individuals—were in some way members of a Jewish community previously estimated at 1,411 strong in 1788. This tabulation, which

FIGURE 12. Family portrait with Isaac Fernandes and his wife, the *mulattin* Clasina Vroom, dressed in "kotomisi," the traditional Afro-Surinamese women's dress. Clasina was born on the Guinese Vriendschap plantation, which in 1889 was managed by S. D. Fernandes and by an overseer listed as "I. Fernandes," possibly the same man who appears in this photo. Collectie Familie Fernandes-Vroom. Courtesy of Beppie Versol-Fernandes.

significantly increases the estimated Jewish population at its peak to approximately 2,000, only accounts for families recently emerging from slavery. Were we to include Jews with more distant African ancestry, namely families whose members had taken advantage of the "whitening clause" by marrying hypergamously for two or more generations and thus recapturing their formal *jahid* status, the percentage of Jews with sub-Saharan ancestry would be significantly higher than the 7.1 percent calculated based on surviving birth and death records of the late eighteenth through early nineteenth century. If this supposition is correct, perhaps the majority of Suriname's Jewish community by the turn of the eighteenth century would have been descended from an African mother.[79]

The Legal Status of Eurafrican Jews

The legal status of Eurafrican Jews in Suriname was informed by two separate domains: rabbinical law and colonial legislation. Even as rabbinical law was deployed in the midst of a color-based society, it remained remarkably conservative in its non-racial nature. The secular aspect of Jewish legislation, meanwhile, ensconced in communal bylaws, did respond to the stigma associated with African origin and was receptive to both colonial law and secular practices elsewhere in the Jewish Atlantic World.

The impermeability of rabbinical law to race-based slavery is evident in the aforementioned Jewish marriage contracts of four Eurafrican couples. These newlyweds of the 1720s all bore Jewish names. With the exception of Jahacob bar Abraham, who married Miriam Mashiah Pelegrino, each is described in Hebrew as a manumitted male or female: *meshuhrar* or *meshuhreret* (משוחררת or משוחרר). An unknown indexer of the *ketubah* compendium, perhaps an Anglophone researcher of the early twentieth century, handwrote the English words "negro" and "negress" next to each of their names, an inaccurate editorial comment, for the terms *meshuhrar* and *meshuhreret* have nothing to do with race or color and thus faithfully adhere to the rabbinical non-recognition of early modern racial distinctions.[80] Rather, the two terms communicate the relevance rabbinical law assigns to the juridical status of manumitted people, who (in theory) could only marry fellow liberated slaves.

The Portuguese family names of seven of these individuals (Rodrigues del Prado, Judeu, Costa, Mattos, and Pelegrino/Pelengrino) suggest not African nativity but rather descent from a Portuguese Jewish father. The sole freeborn Jew, Jahacob bar Abraham, judging from his patronymic, could have been African, Ashkenazi (a Jew of Germanic ancestry), or a white convert from Christianity who had been incorporated into Suriname's Portuguese Jewish community.[81] His family name—a reference to the biblical Abraham, the first Israelite and therefore a convert—suggests a second-class status that played a factor in restricting Jahacob's matrimonial options to a Eurafrican Jewess. Despite his apparently underdog status, Abraham was educated enough to sign his name in Rashi script, an ability that supports the possibility of an Ashkenazi background (Ashkenazim in Suriname were far more likely than Portuguese Jews to be literate in Hebrew).

In everyday life, secular Jewish law in the colony had far more influence than rabbinical ordinances. The concern with circumcision, conveyed in the 1662 bylaw that barred *jehidim* from circumcising boys born to fallen *jehidim*, may hint at the fear that children would be converted to Judaism as slaves and then sold to non-Jews. Bylaw 32 of Brazil's Portuguese Jewish congregation, promulgated a few years before the community's dissolution in 1654, stipulated as much. In order to prevent the sale of a circumcised slave, no one was permitted to carry out the ritual without the master first manumitting him.[82]

Although there is nearly a century's gap between the fragments of Surinamese communal ordinances that have survived from the 1660s and the complete bylaws of the mid-eighteenth century, the latter suggest that the status of Eurafrican Jews in Suriname steadily declined over time. Ordinances from 1748 constitute the earliest surviving definitions of *jahid* and *congregante* status. A *jahid* was a full member of the Jewish community by virtue of his or her European descent, while the second-class *congregante* denoted either a Eurafrican Jew, typically a convert to Judaism, or a first-class member who had been relegated to a lower social status as a penalty for marrying a Jewish female of African descent.[83] Until the mid-eighteenth century, as we have seen, certain Eurafrican Jews were admitted to *jahid* status. Bylaws recorded in 1752 clarify that the privilege was accorded only to Eurafricans born within a legitimate marriage, whether the product of a *branco* and a *negra* or a *mulata*, or of two *mulatos*. Nevertheless, the ritual honors they could receive in the synagogue were restricted in number or to certain times of the day.[84] The loophole extended to legitimately born Eurafricans does not appear in other surviving versions of the bylaws, and within a few years the permissive clause was replaced with a cautionary tale: "Experience having demonstrated how dangerous and inappropriate it is to admit mulattoes as Jehidim, and place them within this community, in which a few have interfered in cases of communal governance, it is established that from now on they will no longer be considered nor admitted as Jehidim, but rather solely Congregantes."[85]

Ordinances from the Ashkenazi community, which tended to closely imitate the legislation of Portuguese Jews, provide evidence that Eurafrican Jews occupied a second-class status within the community by 1734. In that year, Neveh Salom, the newly autonomous Ashkenazi congregation in Paramaribo, included in its bylaws a stipulation that *mulatten* were barred from receiving honors in the synagogue on Sabbaths and holidays and were obliged to sit behind the reader's lectern.[86] In 1772, the Ashkenazi community banned *mulatten* from *jahid* status, relegating them to the position of *congregantes*, following a similar motion that had been effected in the Portuguese Jewish community in the mid-eighteenth century.[87]

The cohort of non-whites in the community was clearly growing, and how to treat them in communal matters was never entirely clear. In 1803 the treasurer of the Liviat Hen burial society asked the regents how he should conduct himself in the case of the death of "circumcised slaves" (*escravos circunciadados*).[88] Women also counted among these marginal individuals. In 1832, Abraham de Leon requested that his "mulatta" slave, Louise (a.k.a. Louisa), be permitted to convert to Judaism. Since colonial regulations now obligated slaves to espouse a religion in order to be eligible for manumission, Leon promised to manumit her as soon as she became a Jew. Given her "inclination" to adopt Judaism, the regents instructed cantor Moses Jona to carry out the ceremony in the presence of the required witnesses.[89]

By the 1810s, Suriname had earned a reputation in the Atlantic Jewish World as a place that facilitated the conversion of Eurafricans to Judaism. A case in point is Isaac Lopez Brandon, familiar to students of U.S. Jewish history through the oil on ivory miniature depicting his likeness.[90] Brandon, an "early American Jew," was the Barbadian son of a woman of slave origins and an affluent Portuguese Jewish sugar planter, Abraham Rodrigues Brandon, who had manumitted him in 1801.[91] Brandon *fils* was likely aware that Suriname's Jewish community included a significant sector of Eurafricans accorded bona fide Jewish status, and may have also heard of the Eurafrican Jewish house of worship in Paramaribo, whose congregation was first founded in 1759 and, by the late eighteenth century, convened in its own dedicated building. In 1812, Brandon arrived in Suriname from Barbados to undergo circumcision and be admitted as "a Jew of the Portuguese Jewish nation." Like many Jewish communities in North America at the time, the Barbados congregation apparently lacked a qualified ritual circumciser, and influential leaders were unwilling to retain Brandon as a congregational member despite his and his father's largesse to the communal coffer.[92] Since Brandon *fils* was technically a non-Jew according to the matrilineal principle, and as a foreigner could possibly be taken for a Christian, the Surinamese regents made certain to contact the colonial prosecutor (*fiscaal*) for permission. The latter official instructed Brandon to submit a statement in which he declared himself willing to be circumcised and be "considered as a Portuguese Jew professing the Judaic religion."[93]

By all accounts, Brandon was deeply inspired by his sojourn in Suriname's Jewish community. By 1819, he was back in Barbados, raising money to establish a synagogue in Philadelphia, which, according to some of his coreligionists on the island, was intended for his "colord [sic] connexions."[94] Rather than a "conspiracy theory," as some scholars have supposed, this report (however surly) could have been accurate.[95] Brandon and his white Jewish father had very good reasons for wishing to participate in the organization of a separate place of worship for Eurafrican Jews in Philadelphia, which already had a Portuguese Jewish congregation, established during the Revolutionary War. Between 1791 and 1809, 25,000 Dominguan refugees, including 15,000 whites, 4,000 free people of African descent, and 6,000 slaves, arrived in the United States.[96] In North American synagogues, the steady exodus of Jews from this and other slave colonies, spurred by the age of Atlantic revolutions, stimulated a tightening of racial boundaries.[97] The constitution of the Charleston, South Carolina, Jewish congregation, first published in 1820 and amended in 1836, resolved to accept proselytes provided they were "not people of color."[98] It is conceivable that similar barriers were also introduced into the existing Philadelphian congregation.

Jewish authorities in Suriname, by contrast, remained accepting of Jews of slave origins. By the 1840s, communal leaders were overwhelmed with requests from free persons and slaves, not born of "Israelite parents," who wished to convert to Judaism and resolved to draft bylaws regulating such cases. Suspecting that financial gain or coercion could be a factor in the desire to become Jewish, the regents obligated the sponsor of the conversion to contribute an amount of money to the poverty chest for the benefit of such individuals and, within six months, to file for manumission papers. Children born of female slaves already members of the Portuguese Jewish community would also be considered members and would be "circumcised or admitted according to our doctrine." Masters who owned such children were obliged to request their freedom within six months of birth.[99] In March 1841, after careful consideration, the regents concluded that the slave Wilhelmina wished to convert out of "pure affection" and resolved to admit her as a member (lidmaat) of the Jewish community.[100] A similar surge manifested in the Ashkenazi community. After 1802, the year the Portuguese Mahamad introduced equal treatment of decedents in burial rites, the number of requests by Eurafricans to be admitted as congregantes tripled. Some large families submitted collective applications for admission. In 1839, Lea Jacob Levy successfully petitioned for the admission of her eight children and grandchildren as congregantes of the Ashkenazi community. Requests presented on behalf of slaves also proliferated.[101]

What is crucial about the deliberations of the Portuguese regents is that their main qualm was not the admittance of people of color or persons of unfree status but rather that such individuals would become an economic burden to the community. As derided as slaves and free people of slave ancestry were in the colony, such a stigma did not impede the most power-ful leaders from opening the doors of their community to them. One rea-son, by the early nineteenth century, seems clear: many or most Portuguese Jewish leaders were of African origin themselves. They probably also recalled the economic exigency of creating legitimate heirs in a colony with a dearth of white women. The rise of an affluent planter class born of African women, and their transition to commerce in the city, demonstrated the wisdom of such inclusion. On a more basic economic level, Eurafrican Jews were sorely needed to increase the tax base of the Jewish community. In 1784, the Surinamese regents had resolved that all free mulatto Jews who wished to be recognized as *congregantes* of the Portuguese Jewish commu-nity and enjoy its privileges had to formally enlist and thereby be obligated to pay an annual *finta* for the expenditures of the synagogue.[102]

While illegitimate birth did not bar Jews of African descent from mem-bership in the Jewish community, as we have seen, their African ancestry did confine them to a second-class social status, a phenomenon I have termed "peripheral inclusion."[103] *Congregantes* existed both metaphorically and literally at the limits of Portuguese Jewish society. Membership in the Jewish community subjected them to Jewish communal law and entitled them to the same privileges and protections as other Jews in the colony. On the other hand, their daily lives were filled with reminders of their marginal status as descendants of African slaves. This manifested itself most prominently in the ritual sphere. In the men's section of the synagogue, the most coveted seats were between the pillars, and even *jehidim*, who had a theoretical right to be seated there, were obliged to petition the Mahamad for an official seat. In 1752, the Mahamad added an ordinance stipulating that seating for Eurafrican Jews was limited to the mourner's bench, just as in times past, and not anywhere else in the synagogue. Above, in the wom-en's gallery, female Eurafricans were relegated to the back rows, where the view of the main sanctuary was obstructed.[104]

Second-class status followed the manumitted and their descendants to the grave, though this had not always been the case. In the Jodensavanne Cemetery, where some 460 grave markers are preserved, Eurafrican Jews were originally buried alongside their white coreligionists. This changed in the mid-eighteenth century. The cemetery is spread out over terrain that gently slopes downward from "top to bottom" (northwest to southeast) and from right to left (northeast to southwest). In the southeast extreme, the limits of the burial ground, near a no longer extant fence, three tombstones, submerged several feet beneath the soil's surface, were unearthed by a cemetery expedition in 1999.[105] The individuals buried below, Jacob Peregrino (d. 1750), Joseph Pelengrino, and Joseph de Mattos (both d. 1751), bear family names of Jewish slaves manumitted by the first two decades of the 1720s and are likely direct descendants. Pelengrino is perhaps the aforementioned petitioner who manumitted his three children. Communal archives describing the relative position of deceased Eurafrican Jews in this cemetery reveal a concatenation of *congregantes*, stretching from Luna (died 1816), daughter of David Haim del Monte, to Joseph Pelengrino, all buried along the fence on the southerly slope of the hill.[106]

This liminal spot continued to be reserved for manumitted slaves through at least the late eighteenth century. In May 1791 the free "mulatta" Simha, who had been enslaved to Joseph Gabay Farro, was also buried in the southern part of the cemetery, near the fence. She was laid to rest with feet pointing to the east, in accordance with Jewish law, near the grave of the aforementioned Joseph, son of Gabriel de Mattos. The next month her sister, Jahel, also a free Eurafrican who had once served the same master, was buried at Simha's feet. Both graves were marked with a (presumably wooden) stake, rather than a carved stone slab, and have since disintegrated. Only the burial register and a passing reference to their manumission preserve their memory.[107] In the Cassipora Cemetery, the oldest known Jewish cemetery of the colony, *congregantes* were also relegated to the margins of the burial ground.[108]

A similar pattern of peripheral inclusion operated in Paramaribo's oldest Portuguese Jewish burial ground. A plot book of that cemetery lists "rows of congregantes," where the socially inferior were interred. The decedents bear distinctly Eurafrican Jewish family names, such as Judio/Judia and Pelegrino, as well as names of founding Portuguese Jewish families, such as d'Avilar, Cohen Nassy, and Mendes Meza, attesting to an increasingly intertwined African and European lineage.[109] A few Ashkenazi names, such as Samson and Goedschalk, also appear, indicating the ability of Portuguese Eurafrican Jews to breach Jewish intraethnic boundaries. By the 1780s, the colony's Ashkenazi Mahamad resolved to designate a special row for the burial of Jewish mulattoes "belonging to . . . our yachidim [*sic*] and not being a congregant," and yet another one for "mulatto congregants."[110] The former group appears to have possessed an intermediary Jewish status, while the latter were considered full Jews. Although the Old Ashkenazi Cemetery of Paramaribo has not yet been analyzed in terms of a *congregante* presence, a membership roster of the colony's Ashkenazi synagogue, dating to the late 1850s, shows the presence of two such Eurafricans, both with Portuguese Jewish names (Jacob Isak de Meza and Simha Isak Jacob de Meza), a further indication that the breakdown of communal borders between the two Jewish groups was instigated by Eurafricans who produced children out of wedlock.[111]

The phenomenon of peripheral inclusion in Suriname finds its parallel in the colony's Christian community, where from at least 1737 persons of African origin were similarly marginalized in both the church and the cemetery.[112] Elsewhere in the Caribbean and in colonial North America, by the eighteenth century, people of non-European origin, including slaves owned by Jews, were buried in cemeteries separate from those of whites or in sections reserved for criminals or "strangers."[113]

Scholars have tended to characterize the phenomenon of Eurafrican Jews in the early Americas as unique to Suriname. They assert that even in the parallel Portuguese Jewish community of Curaçao, no evidence of formal conversion of slaves to Judaism has surfaced.[114] However, the island's communal minutes from 1755 specifically refer to *jehidim* and *congregantes*, and require both classes, whether residents of the islands (*moradores da isla*) or transients (*forasteiros que venhao de pasagem*), to pay one-fourth of 1 percent on all of their profits as a tax to the local Portuguese Jewish "nation." *Congregantes* were also obligated to pay an annual capitation tax (*finta*) to the synagogue and were permitted to make freewill offerings.[115] It is hard to imagine that the distinction between *jehidim* and *congregantes* could have been anything but racial. The often intentional destruction of Curaçao's communal minutes predating 1810 leaves this question largely conjectural for now, preserving for Suriname the status as *the* beacon for Eurafrican Jews of the Atlantic World.[116]

Conclusion

The ethnogenesis of Eurafrican Jews in Suriname began immediately, as a corollary of a slave society that endowed Jews with the freedom to own human beings as property. Ubiquitous sexual contact between masters and enslaved African females, probably most often initiated by owners, was an expression of the imperious drive of sex, combined with sharply skewed power relations, the demographic majority of servile people of sub-Saharan nativity, and the social pressure among males in hemispheric American slave societies to exhibit both masculinity and masterhood.[117] This behavior was by no means unique to either Suriname or the Caribbean but was rather a function of the essential state of a servile human being whose master, by both law and practice, owned both her labor and her body.

The widespread, formal conversion of Eurafrican progeny to Judaism, however, was not inevitable. It was in fact extremely rare among Atlantic Jewries, although limited occurrences are either explicitly or implicitly documented for Amsterdam, Barbados, Curaçao, Charleston (South Carolina), and Senegambia. None of these other occurrences ever resulted in a subcommunity with an autonomous cultural or institutional identity. Until the late eighteenth and early nineteenth centuries, conversion of slaves to the household religion was also unusual among white Christians, who feared that doing so would pose a threat to the authority of the master. Thus Suriname is the only land in the Atlantic World where full and intermediary conversion of slaves to Judaism was so common that Jews of Eurafrican descent likely came to constitute the majority of community members by the early 1800s.

Accounting for the Surinamese divergence is no simple matter. The concentration of Jews in the agrarian economy, as masters and employees of plantations (where Africans vastly outnumbered whites), provided many opportunities for Jewish men to associate with enslaved females, particularly within the framework of sexual exploitation. The corporate status of Jews, together with a juridical autonomy enforced by colonial law, legalized and therefore facilitated the conversion of slaves to Judaism. The tendency of many Surinamese Jewish masters to convert their slaves to Judaism and recognize them as heirs partly resulted from the paucity of white women in the community, infertility among some biologically related white Jewish couples, and the predominance of males in the *despacho* system. Another factor was the non-racial rabbinical approach to conversion, a carryover from Europe and the Senegambian coast. Why Suriname developed a fully defined, autonomous Eurafrican Jewish community, while its sister congregation in Curaçao seems to have not, also speaks to Suriname's European-origin segment, which was less stable than that of the Dutch island.[118] As

Daniel Livesay has remarked for Jamaica, the inclusion of "mixed race" people into white families was a response to the demographic failure of white settler society.[119] The instability of white families, often diminished by disease and transience, may have encouraged Jews to lower the bar to communal inclusion. In Suriname, such inclusion manifested not only within families but within the two ethnic Jewish communities at large, Portuguese Jews and Ashkenazim. Why Surinamese Jews were outliers among local Christians in terms of slave conversion may be partly explained by the fact that Jews were more rooted as a community than Christians, who tended to return to the fatherland once fortunes were made or lost. The presence of a highly visible and active Eurafrican class of Jews in Suriname is thus likely a combination of the longevity of the colony's Jewish community, juridical autonomy, agrarian slavery, and an unstable white population. As a manifestation distinct to Suriname, Eurafrican Jews are therefore a strong example of the colony's localism.

Initially, white Jewish men had almost complete control over the transmission of Judaism to their slaves, via the formal conversion of their progeny to Judaism. Colonial laws in Suriname called for the banishment of white women who had sexual relations with slaves. If Portuguese Jewish men had not sought to bring their enslaved children into the Jewish fold, the community would have had few, if any, "Jewish mulattoes." The Surinamese phenomenon of African-origin Jews during the century that began in 1650 was thus wholly an expression of a patriarchy that suppressed one of the main matriarchal aspects of rabbinical Judaism. By the second half of the eighteenth century, the Eurafrican group so created, as we shall further explore in the next chapter, had achieved a critical mass that allowed a return to the matrilineal principle of Judaism, whereby Jewishness was transmitted through Eurafrican women who had been born Jewish and, like people of slave origins generally, typically formed matrilocal families.

In Suriname, African converts to Judaism and the more numerous Eurafrican Jews, who were increasingly born Jewish by the last quarter of the eighteenth century, are detectable in the records both through their legal status (as *judeus negros*, *judeus mulatos*, and *congregantes*) and sometimes through their unusual family names (such as Pelegrino and Judeu), which communicate a second-class status. Both the Portuguese and Ashkenazi Jewish communities possessed a legal apparatus that included African and Eurafrican Jews as bona fide (albeit second-class) members of the Jewish community. This regulation also countenanced marriages between white men and Eurafrican females and ensured that the memory of slave origins would be eventually entirely erased provided that the progeny of the "mixed marriage" would marry whites through the following two generations. It is this clause that makes African descent particularly difficult to ascertain in genealogies.

The servile status of Suriname's slaves severely limited the agency of females within the context of sexual advances by their masters. Nonetheless, restricted agency does not eliminate the possibility that some enslaved females may have used these relationships to negotiate for privileges for themselves or for their progeny. Nor should we assume that sexual coercion would have necessarily prevented enslaved women and their Eurafrican children from evincing a spiritual interest in Judaism. The wills and epistolary testimonies discussed in this chapter suggest that African and Eurafrican Jews sometimes initiated their own conversion to Judaism and that their devotion to and identification with Judaism and the Jewish people was genuine, rather than purely utilitarian. As the next chapter will demonstrate, these sentiments frequently undergirded the political activism of Suriname's Eurafrican Jewish population.

CHAPTER 5

The Quest for Eurafrican Jewish Equality

In early 1954, a U.S.-born rabbi and Zionist named Israel Goldstein embarked on a visit to Suriname. Goldstein had recently been appointed as associate chairman of the Tercentenary Committee, a New York–based initiative to commemorate the arrival of the first Jews in North America three hundred years earlier via Brazil, and had been dispatched to South America and to the insular Caribbean to spread word of the celebration to other diasporic Jewish communities. In his memoirs, published two years before his death, Goldstein observed that the greatest threats to Jewish life and continuity in the Caribbean were intermarriage and what he called "assimilation." His critique of Caribbean Jewries reached a pinnacle in Suriname, where he remarked drily: "A glance at some of these descendants of the early Jewish settlers is enough to make one realize that there has been a good deal of intermarriage with the native population."[1]

But what Goldstein failed to appreciate is that the Eurafrican heritage of Surinamese Jewry did not undermine the continuity of the community. Rather, the incorporation of people of sub-Saharan ancestry was the community's own creolized response to the realities of living in a slave society where whites were vastly outnumbered and where Jews were accorded unusual privileges that both invigorated and preserved their communal identity. Nor was the visible imprint of African heritage on Jews simply a demographic phenomenon. Over the generations, people of African descent had taken an active role in asserting their belonging in the Jewish community and in petitioning for a less marginal status for themselves and their progeny. In their first century and a half of existence in the colony, engagement with the social boundaries and hierarchical structures in place took place mostly on an individual basis. But by the last quarter of the eighteenth

century, attempts at self-betterment among people of slave origins transformed into group activism.

In this chapter, we explore the changing demographics and political
revolutions of the Caribbean that served as the context for challenging and
eventually effacing the second-class legal status of free people of slave origins. The trajectory toward equality did not progress in linear fashion, as
Eurafrican Jews themselves recognized. Their awareness of their uneven
historic position within the Jewish community encouraged them to question the norms of their own time.

Challenges to Peripheral Inclusion

Historians commonly agree that the status of free Eurafricans in the colonial state and in the metropole was relatively porous through the early
eighteenth century, only giving way to a more fixed and binary position in
the mid- to late eighteenth century. Even so, the boundaries between white
and so-called "mixed race" colonists never entirely lost their early fluidity
and ambiguity.[2] In Saint-Domingue, during the more flexible period, many
free people of African descent had become indistinguishable from those of
exclusively European ancestry, particularly if prosperous.[3] On other islands,
such as Jamaica and Curaçao, colonial authorities experimented with the
elevation to white status of select persons of Eurafrican descent.[4] In 1752,
Curaçao's council argued that a number of free, prosperous, and powerful
families of African origin who had intermarried with whites should be
granted equal treatment. In 1769, the West India Company's military com-
manders and the civil militia officers began a dispute about which organization should accept a group of some twenty to thirty soldiers of mixed
African-European descent. The white militia officers maintained that these
soldiers were not truly mulattoes and should thus not be incorporated into
the free black and free mulatto militias but rather into the white militia. By
1789, 214 mulattoes (known on the island as *mustiesen*) were accordingly
admitted into the white militia unit, comprised of 1,063 soldiers.[5] Similarly,
in the Danish West Indies legislators over the course of the second half of
the eighteenth century grappled with the concept of "nearly white" and
sometimes proposed that the status of Eurafricans be legally changed to
white. Tellingly, the government never took a definitive position on this

matter, an indication of its controversial nature, but also leaving open a potential loophole.[6]

A similar combination of integration tempered by distinctive treatment also manifested in Suriname's Portuguese Jewish community. As we have seen, manumitted Jewish slaves in the 1720s could contract Jewish marriages, attend synagogue, receive charity, build and enlarge houses in Jodensavanne, and be buried in the Jewish cemeteries. Certain *mulatos* and *carboegers* in the first half of the eighteenth century enjoyed the same rights and privileges as white Jews and some had briefly attained leadership positions in the Mahamad.[7] It also appears that some Eurafrican worshippers in the synagogue managed to secure seats in the coveted space between the pillars.[8]

The exponential rise of the Eurafrican Jewish population beginning in the mid-eighteenth century, part of the demographic and economic empowerment of free people of color in cities throughout the Atlantic world, led to a tightening of racial restrictions. The regents' decision by at least 1748 to classify Eurafrican Jews exclusively as *congregantes* emanated from "the impropriety of admitting Mulattos as jehidim, and elevating them in this community, in which some have advanced themselves and intervened in cases of government of the congregation."[9] Six years later this locution was intensified to "the *harm* and impropriety of admitting mulattoes as jehidim" (italics added). Thereafter, according to the new bylaws, no *mulatos* would ever be "considered or admitted" as *jehidim* and would be solely *congregantes*, "as in other congregations," a likely reference to the practice in the Portuguese Jewish community of Curaçao.[10] As per the 1754 ordinances, all *congregantes* would henceforth be confined to the area behind the lectern, on the mourner's bench.[11] In 1772, the Ashkenazi regents issued a similar ordinance, that henceforth no mulattoes would be admitted as *jehidim* but rather considered *congreganten*, "as in other Jewish congregations [kehilot]."[12]

Eurafrican Jewish protest against distinctive treatment began on an individual basis in the 1770s, by which time the group had grown large and confident enough to challenge the racial status quo on an ad hoc basis. In the communal minutes, *congregantes* emerge as particularly vulnerable to the accusation of verbal crimes, the charge that in casual conversation they imputed sexual immorality to *jehidim*. The Mahamad severely prosecuted such transgressors. Abraham Garsia, a Eurafrican Jew living on the savanna, attempted to preempt prosecution in 1775 when he overheard murmurs that he had insulted the sexual virtue of various Jewish women. One of these was Ribca de la Parra, widow of Solomon de la Parra, described variably as a "white woman" and "a noted lady . . . from a family so esteemed." The Mahamad's investigation uncovered a tortuous chain of rumors transmitted mostly from man to man.[13]

Garsia, backed up by a number of other Jewish witnesses, displaced the blame onto Moses Rodrigues del Prado (d. 1797).[14] Prado, the third son of the "mulatta" Maria or Mariana del Prado, was classified in the Portuguese Jewish community as a *congregante*.[15] After calling witnesses and finding Prado to be the guilty party, the Mahamad swiftly resolved to forever banish him from the savanna, a measure never before or after meted out to a white Jew similarly convicted.[16] During his trial Prado was ordered to "behave humbly and recognize the prodigious difference between him and whites." The regents then decided that the penalty of banishment from Jodensavanne was not harsh enough and asked the governor to apply corporal punishment, a deep insult, for its recipients in the Jewish community were almost always slaves or white children who were ordered to be disciplined by their parents. By contrast, verbal crimes among whites were treated relatively leniently by the Mahamad, never resulting in expulsion.[17]

Prado apparently could not make his peace with the discrepancy. In 1778, three years after his forced exile, he unlawfully returned to the savanna brandishing a sword and accompanied by two enslaved valets (*muleques*) who were armed with pistols. When the beadle (*samas*) ordered him to leave the savanna, Prado answered that he had come to carry out some business affairs and would leave when finished. He then proclaimed that he was well known by the governor as a *homem de bem*, a Portuguese term that implies good behavior, wealth, philanthropy, and political power all at once.

Then, reportedly without incitement, Prado began to walk through the streets of Jodensavanne, shouting that the judges who had presided over his case in 1775 had been biased (*apaixoados*) and that if any one of them had the courage, Prado would fight him. Just as the community's treasurer (*gabay*) Samuel de la Parra was passing by, Prado approached him with one of his enslaved valets, who extended an unsheathed sword toward Parra. Parra preempted attack by grabbing the sword from the slave's hand and called for a patrol to arrest Prado and detain him in the Zeeland fort in Paramaribo.[18]

Prado's visit to the savanna was arguably not to carry out business but rather to rectify perceived injustice. During his three-year absence from Jodensavanne, Prado had clearly rallied a powerful network of supporters.

The day after the altercation at Jodensavanne, a *jahid* named Benjamin Robles de Medina learned of the arrest. He stated that Prado was the director of his plantation and that his prolonged detention would cause the estate much damage, an indication of the crucial economic role Eurafricans like Prado played in Suriname's plantation economy.[19] Furthermore, Medina explained that Prado's inebriated state was to blame for the "liberty" he took in the Jewish village. The regents agreed to release Prado, on condition that his behavior in the future prove him deserving.[20] Meanwhile, the Council of Policy deliberated the case, soliciting an account by Prado and a parallel report from the Mahamad, with comments on Prado's testimony.[21] To the regency's shock, the Council of Policy ruled in favor of Prado, declaring that the Mahamad did not have authority to banish any person from Jodensavanne. The Council made this assertion despite the fact that the Mahamad had presented a document from the erstwhile governor, dating to 1757, that conferred upon the regency the power of expulsion. Moreover, the council decided not to punish Prado for insulting the Mahamad.[22] Moses Rodrigues del Prado displayed a canny ability to harness the clout of allies of wealth and power, demonstrating that even Eurafricans could maneuver legal pluralism to their advantage.[23]

In the next decade, ad hoc challenges to the racial status quo moved into the cemetery. On November 20, 1787, anticipating his looming death, the *congregante* Daniel Pelengrino (1736–87), grandson of the aforementioned Joseph Peregrino who in 1720 manumitted his three children, petitioned the regents for permission to be carried in a funeral procession by his disciples. Evasively, the regents decided not to answer, instead placing the question in the hands of the governing leaders of the Liviat Hen burial society, who refused the request. Implicitly, such a funeral procession would have elevated Pelengrino to the status of a white leader, which is probably why the society denied his dying wish. He was buried in the *congregante* row of the oldest Portuguese Jewish Cemetery of Paramaribo, alongside his sisters and heirs, Marjana and Simcha. The desire of Pelengrino to allow his "disciples" to carry his body in a special procession suggests an internal political structure that consciously mimicked that of the white Jewish community.[24]

Another prominent Eurafrican Jewish leader similarly treated was Joseph, son of David Nassy. When Joseph died in April 1790, Eurafrican mourners resolved to inter him with the ceremonies reserved for a Portuguese First Parnas (*parnas presidente*).[25] As carefully dictated in communal ordinances, such a burial entailed a procession with wax candles in which the mourners—rather than the cantor—would sing the memorial prayers.[26] The problem was that Joseph was a *congregante* and therefore ineligible for such an honor. As an archival annotation suggests, at least one communal leader further undermined Nassy's position by denying his *congregante* status and designating him as a mere "Molato" who implicitly had only an intermediary standing in the Portuguese Jewish community.[27] A regent present at the funeral observed this breach of social propriety and intervened to forbid the procession "as being contrary to the bylaws of the community." Tensions resurfaced during the actual burial. The Eurafrican mourners were horrified to discover that Nassy's intended grave was located "in a swamp and only one foot deep." Their objections were silenced with the Mahamad's curt response: "You cannot give orders here, and if you are not silent, we will silence you."[28] The grave's condition confirms there was a designated location for deceased *congregantes* at the outer limits of the Paramaribo cemetery—similar to the burial ground in Jodensavanne. To the Eurafricans, it also demonstrated the Mahamad's discriminatory neglect of Eurafrican burial sites. The regents rejected the latter allegation, pointing to weather conditions in the months of April and May, which assured that "there will always be water on the outer grounds which are lying low and in which a hole has to be dug to serve as a grave."[29]

A few months later, in December 1790, yet another Eurafrican Jew was stripped of dignity in death. The *congregante* Simon de Meza passed away just before the Jewish Sabbath. The First Parnas of Jodensavanne's Congregation Beraha VeSalom dispatched beadle Solomon Fereyra to order a shroud and coffin for Meza. But when Fereyra presented the request before the Liviat Hen burial society, the brotherhood official refused to comply, pointing to article 10 of the organization's bylaws—approved by the Mahamad itself—whereby only members of the Portuguese Jewish nation, who were *jehidim*, or *congregantes* from a "legitimate marriage," could receive such funereal amenities. Meza, either conceived out of wedlock to free Eurafrican Jewish parents or born to an enslaved concubine, fell into neither of these categories.[30]

So as not to be "considered disobedient," the Liviat Hen brotherhood official paid a personal visit to the president of the Mahamad and reminded him of the articles that prevented the request from being fulfilled. In what was likely a heated argument, the president asked and then commanded that the order be carried out that one time, without consequences for the future, promising to provide an explanation later. With no time to convene an ad hoc meeting (*junta*), the brotherhood leadership recognized the Mahamad as its superior and begrudgingly carried out the order.[31] The anecdote shows how regents could use their discretionary power arbitrarily to contravene official ordinances. Perhaps they feared further provoking the Eurafrican Jewish community, which had eight months earlier protested the indignities suffered during Joseph Cohen Nassy's funeral. Clearly some Eurafrican Jews enjoyed the support of the highest authorities of the Portuguese Jewish community. The reaction also illustrates that white leaders were internally divided about the ritual treatment of Eurafrican Jews. The Tuesday following Meza's death, the Liviat Hen convened a *junta* at which it was resolved to respectfully ask the Mahamad to allow the burial society to follow its own articles. One member of the *junta*, Abraham Bueno Bibaz, requested to be exempt from the meeting, suggesting a fear of repercussions or his sympathy with his Eurafrican Jewish coreligionists.[32]

Thus far, we have considered spontaneous disruptions occasioned by the demands of a few isolated individuals. Early in 1790, Eurafrican Jews began to protest collectively, for the first time in their history, by forming a society or brotherhood (*siva*, *jesiba*, or *irmandade*) whose activities included Jewish prayer services with a quorum of ten men. Although, according to their testimony, the fraternity had been formed in 1759,[33] for its first few decades of existence it was evidently a very loosely organized group that did not hold formal prayer services. A Eurafrican Jewish brotherhood is nowhere mentioned in the surviving Portuguese Jewish communal minutes that predate 1790. Moreover, the Mahamad strictly adhered to the first communal bylaw, which since at least 1678 had prohibited private prayer quorums and had recognized Jodensavanne's Beraha VeSalom synagogue as the colony's sole congregation, with the city's Sedek VeSalom synagogue accorded the status of a mere prayer house under the congregation's jurisdiction.[34]

Developments outside the Jewish community also support the latter date as the year of the fraternity's formal founding. In 1787, an elder of the Portuguese Jewish community reported that free and enslaved *negros* in Jodensavanne (whose religious identity was not specified) had founded a "special fraternity" for the interment of their dead. Their gatherings consisted of marching with banners and pikes, clandestine gatherings every Friday night, and inebriation. Further, the former regent noted, members had "impertinently" arrogated for themselves the title of "chiefs of the colony" (*Proceres da colonia*).[35] The report demonstrates the importance of burial societies among enslaved and manumitted people of African origin, particularly during the Atlantic age of revolutions, which commenced in the late 1780s. The timing of the Eurafrican Jewish protest occurred precisely at the moment that the Declaration of the Rights of Man and of the Citizen, promulgated in France in 1789, provoked free people of color throughout the Caribbean to fight for full legal equality.[36]

In their own words, in 1790, the impetus to action among Eurafrican Jews had been the devaluation of some of their eminent members in public ceremonies, an obvious reference to the denigrating funerals to which their late leaders had been subjected, starting with Daniel Pelengrino in 1787. Through their *jesiba*, Eurafrican Jews hoped to "recuperate the spiritual satisfaction that they lose among the whites."[37] Their non-material quest suggests that economic deprivation was no longer their central concern. Joseph de David Nassy, whose controversial burial in April 1790 triggered the Eurafrican Jewish protest, owned three houses in Paramaribo as well as slaves and clothes made of linen, wool, and silk.[38] His father, who is probably none other than the David Nassy of *Essai historique* fame, was at the time bankrupt, his estate abandoned.[39]

Indeed, many Eurafrican Jewish leaders were by the 1790s among the wealthier members of the community, according to the communal tax lists. In January 1790, six of them came forward to present themselves for taxation as *congregantes* of the Portuguese nation. In the Hebrew year coinciding with 1793/1794, most Eurafrican Jews owed well above the minimum single guilder in annual taxation (*finta*) required for congregational membership.[40] These findings confirm those of Wieke Vink, who observes that the Eurafrican Jewish petitioners of the early 1790s were "well-educated and worldly," with extensive knowledge of Jewish law and ritual and fluent in the "rules of engagement of political elite life in the colony," in short, "clearly the exponents of an emerging coloured elite."[41] As Norbert Elias and John Scotson note, the attainment of economic self-sufficiency allows outsider groups to shift their focus from the fulfillment of basic, material needs to the human requirement for respect and dignity.[42] Their rise above subsistence level is precisely what enabled Eurafrican Jewish leaders to keenly feel and resent their social inferiority.

The power of these recent burials to trigger activism among Eurafrican Jews relates not just to their desire to be honored in the public sphere but also to the inevitable reshuffling of internal governance that occurred with the demise of each *mulato* leader. Figuratively speaking, a new generation of Eurafrican Jews was born in the late 1780s and early 1790s. It was a period of much introspection, when these second-tier members of the Jewish community recalled earlier generations who lived with fewer racial restrictions on their communal lives. In the late 1780s, the *parnassim* had revised the communal bylaws, a number of which perpetuated the restricted status of Jews of African origin. The new Eurafrican Jewish leadership that emerged during the age of revolutions demanded ritual equality, and when that proved out of reach, autonomy, thus paralleling the contradictory struggle of the organized Jewish community for both privileges as Jews and parity with colonial Christians.

Demographically, the Jewish population had considerably changed by the 1780s, owing to the growth of a *kleurlingen* population that was born Jewish, a reflection of a shift to matrilineal descent. Since these born Jews presumably helped to balance a skewed gender ratio, Jewish women, whether white or of African descent, now had a broader selection of "colored" Jews to choose from as marital partners. The new communal ordinances of 1787 reflect this shift, indicating that Jewish women who married "negroes, mulattoes or castices" were to be considered *congregantes*. Another ordinance forcibly included in the Jewish community all "Jewish mulattos, blacks, mestices and castices who carry the name of, or are known to be descended of the Portuguese or Spanish nation," regardless of their circumstance of birth. These were to be categorized as *congregantes*. All other "Negroes and Mulatto Jews" who wished to join the "Portuguese Jewish persuasion as *Congregant*" were obliged to state their intention with their signature "at the time of their acceptance once and for all and on equal terms." *Kleurlingen* who were legitimately married or the progeny of a legitimate union had a higher Jewish status than *kleurlingen* born outside of wedlock or who themselves carried on common-law unions.[43]

The birth of most Eurafrican Jews outside the bonds of marriage, together with the intensification of the matrilineal principle of Jewish descent, helped to erode the boundaries between the Portuguese and Ashkenazi Jewish communities, since Eurafricans had no disincentive to cross the boundary lines of the two ethnic Jewish communities. The transmission of Jewish status now largely paralleled the transmission of enslaved status: a Jewish bondwoman automatically passed on both her Jewishness and her enslaved condition to her children. Free Eurafrican Jewish women also automatically transmitted their ethnic Jewish identity to their progeny. In 1814, the *parnassim* confirmed that *mulatos* born of Portuguese Eurafrican women should share their mother's identity even if they carried the Ash-kenazi last name of their presumed fathers. Thus Abigail Abenacar, who had been active in the Eurafrican Jewish community in the 1790s, had chil-dren who were officially members of the Portuguese Jewish community, even though they bore the Ashkenazi family name Goedschalk.[44] The ordi-nance responded to the reality of Suriname marriage, where the father typi-cally did not recognize or remain with his biological children. This also meant that Eurafrican Jewish women had more power to determine the communal affiliation of their progeny than did men. What one colonial administrator noted for the Dutch Cape colony in South Africa also rings true for Suriname's Jewish community: the acquisition of a male slave was "a life interest," that of a female "a perpetual heritage."[45]

The threat posed by the Eurafrican Jews starting in the 1780s lay not merely in their ritual challenge to time-honored traditions, or even their public flaunting of "ecclesiastical" distinctions in the synagogue and ceme-tery. The very existence of Jewish Eurafricans and their liminal racial posi-tion destabilized the borders between the two Jewish communities and between white and non-white status. The communal bylaws, which since the late seventeenth century had bifurcated members into the categories of *jahid* and *congregante*, were ill-suited to deal with the more complex social reality of the 1780s. Even if Eurafrican Jews referred to themselves simply as "koleurlingen," communal leaders insisted upon more gradient distinc-tions, however confounding. Ribca Marcus Samson, for example, the third or possibly fourth generation of a Portuguese Jewish family to carry a *con-gregante* status, was listed as a "castissa" (one-half white, one-half *mestice*) at birth but died in 1823 a "postissa" (one-half white, one-half *castice*).[46] The issue of "legitimate marriage" further clouded the social status of second-class Jews. Finally, a white Jewish leader's personal sentiment or conviction, as we have seen, could overturn the Mahamad's very regula-tions. In this panoply of ancestry, circumstances of birth, and personal bias, what precisely defined a Jew, a *jahid*, or a *congregante*?

In April 1790, the regents learned that the "free mulatto Jewish *congreg-antes*" of the community had illegally held a "public *jesiba*" without the knowledge of the Mahamad, in direct violation of the first communal bylaw, which prohibited Portuguese Jewish prayer quorums outside of the colony's Jewish congregation (Beraha VeSalom in Jodensavanne) and its offshoot prayer house (Sedek VeSalom in Paramaribo). The regents had no objections to the formation of a Eurafrican Jewish brotherhood, provided that its bylaws were revised and approved by the Mahamad and patently manifested the group's second-class position. The Eurafrican Jewish leaders attempted to bypass the authority of the Mahamad, claiming that they were just *mulatos*, with a right to act completely independently, and not *congregantes*, subject to the regulations of the Portuguese Jewish community. But the regents countered that all *mulatos*, *musties*, and *casties* who carried the family names of Spanish and Portuguese Jews were to be considered *congregantes* of Congregation Beraha VeSalom, subject to all the penalties imposed on *jehidim* and entitled to all the privileges of legitimate *congregantes* of the nation.[47] Thus, in February 1791, the Eurafrican Jew Reuben Mendes Meza, along with several unnamed colleagues, formally requested permission to establish a *"jesiba* under the title of Darhe Jesarim." This brotherhood or society would allow Eurafrican Jews to "meditate and recite the mourner's prayer [*kadiz*]" in their own space. Meza promised to submit proposed bylaws to the regents for their approval within three months. The regents granted the request without recorded controversy.[48]

The real dispute surrounding Darhe Jesarim began in June 1791, when the regents discovered that many of the bylaws the society submitted for approval contradicted the customs of the Portuguese Jewish community, empowering *congregantes* to ritually behave as equals to white Jews. The brothers agreed to convene an extraordinary session (*junta*) to revise the ordinances within six weeks but by August had reneged on their promise, irritating the regents.[49] In December 1791, the Eurafrican Jewish leaders presented not the revised bylaws as requested but rather a petition demanding certain "prerogatives and other immunities," which were not only offensive to *jehidim* (as they implicitly compromised the ritual superiority of white Jews) but also contradicted the privileges given to the Jewish community, which included bylaws upholding the second-tier status of non-white Jews. The regents resolved to send the *congregantes* excerpts of the *escamoth*, as approved by the metropolitan sovereigns, and a list the regents had compiled explaining how the Eurafrican demands were transgressive. The *parnassim* further demanded that the Eurafrican leaders submit their revised bylaws within four to six weeks, else face penalty.[50]

At this point, in September 1792, certain individual regents initiated litigation against the Darhe Jesarim society, but the governor refused to intervene.[51] Later that month, the Mahamad received a petition signed by Reuben Mendes Meza and Ismael de Britto, attached to new bylaws. The regents were greatly offended, interpreting the submission (now lost) as defamatory of the Mahamad. They sent for the two, demanding to know who had authored the unsigned documents. Protectively, Meza and Britto insisted that all members of the brotherhood had authored the bylaws, thus making it impossible for the regents to identify and punish the culprits. The regents then ordered all members to sign the bylaws, or else sign a declaration indicating their refusal.[52] By December 1792, the Mahamad had received no response.[53]

When Reuben Mendes Meza was again summoned before the regents, he dared to proclaim that he and the others refused to sign the bylaws because the Mahamad had promised them prerogatives but had not followed through. One of their complaints was that the regents had agreed to extend privileges only to *mulatos* conceived in legitimate marriages and not to the majority of Eurafrican Jews, who were born out of wedlock. The regents balked, reading such criticism as a request for complete equality with *jehidim*.[54] Passive-aggressively, the brothers then informed the regents that they wished to revert to their previous intermediary status as *mulatos* born out of wedlock to Portuguese Jewish fathers, as the *jesiba* was no longer of importance to them, and to turn over the administration of Darhe Jesarim to Ashkenazi "mulattoes" (*mulatos tudescos*), clearly an attempt to divide and conquer by pitting the two ethnic Jewish Surinamese congregations against each other. When the regents reiterated their demand that the brothers identify themselves in writing, Meza proclaimed that he was not a *congregante*, that is, just a *mulato*, and thus not an official second-class member of the congregation. He further threatened that if the regents did not give the *jesiba* prerogatives, the brothers would refuse to pay their annual taxes, they would become Ashkenazim (*se fariao tudescos*), and he himself would convert to Christianity.[55]

As radical as it may seem, the threat to circumvent the Mahamad's authority by seceding or turning coat was not new. Portuguese Jews in both metropolitan and colonial communities had made similar threats during the eighteenth century when they found their leaders unsatisfactory.[56] For Meza in particular, conversion to the state religion would not have been unfamiliar turf, given that his half brother Gerrit Evert de Courval, captain of Suriname's colored militia, was a Christian.[57] That the Eurafrican Jews could make such threats at all shows that by the 1790s, their social and biological ties intersected with a wide swath of the colonial population.[58]

The composition of the society's membership shows how complex a group Eurafrican Jews in Suriname had become. The Mahamad correctly suspected that among the brothers were "Ashkenazi slaves and mulattoes," whose presence could complicate the regency's administration of the *jesiba*, since these individuals did not fall under the jurisdiction of the Portuguese Mahamad.[59] Moreover, many of the Portuguese Jewish members were still legally enslaved, a key point overlooked in previous scholarship.[60] One of the society's principal leaders, Isaac Gabay Fonseca, was the master of his own brother, Jacob Nahar, whom he had purchased in order to eventually free him. From time to time, Jacob submitted allowances to his brother as reimbursement for manumission costs. By August 1792, payment was complete and Isaac was ready to liberate his brother and serve as his guarantor-sponsor (*straat voogd*), a position the colonial government had created to prevent former slaves from becoming public charges.[61] The Eurafrican Jewish community thus straddled the boundaries between white and black, Portuguese and Ashkenazi, enslaved and free.

During the first few years of Darhe Jesarim's formal existence, the leadership of the brotherhood was confrontational and demanding. Only three members, Isaac Gabay Fonseca, Reuben Mendes Meza, and Ismael de Britto, had dared to sign the brotherhood's proposed bylaws, a passive-aggressive act that allowed the regents to outlaw the *jesiba* on the grounds that a brotherhood had to have more than three members in order to be viable.[62] By early 1793, the regents initiated legal prosecution against the Eurafricans for claiming themselves to be *congregantes*, when they were merely *mulatos*, for defaulting on their communal taxes (*finta*), and for holding a clandestine prayer quorum.[63] Although this prosecution was a direct attack against Eurafrican Jews, it was just as much an aggressive attempt to enforce their inclusion within the Portuguese Jewish community. Previous scholars, who claim that the Mahamad's main goal was to dismantle Darhe Jesarim, are far from the mark.[64]

Later that year, the Eurafricans again attempted to bypass the regents by presenting a long petition to the governor to pray in their own societies. Moses Rodrigues del Prado, the exiled Eurafrican Jew who staged a violent attack in Jodensavanne in 1778, was among the thirty-one signatories.[65] The use of the plural to describe these societies (*jesibot*), which recurs several times in the minutes, shows how institutionally prolific the Jewish *mulatos* had become.[66] Their population in both the savanna and in Paramaribo continued to surge. The urgency to accommodate them became manifest in 1794, just as some of the *ascamot* of the Portuguese Jewish community were being revised anew. That year, the regents noted that the bench reserved for Eurafrican worshippers in Paramaribo's Sedek VeSalom syna-gogue was very full and there was no alternative space, save for the bench designated for the beadle (*samas*). However, seating *congregantes* alongside *jehidim* on the beadle's bench had created numerous disturbances, which the regents promised to address by broadening the space reserved for the displaced *jehidim*.[67] In September 1797, the Mahamad approved a seating arrangement, which reserved for all "born congregantes" (*congregantes de nacimento*) the bench behind the lectern (*theba*), in addition to the bench where the beadle sat.[68]

Simultaneously, certain first-class members of the congregation under-took to bridge the social distance between *jehidim* and *congregantes*. In 1796, the regents of Beraha VeSalom complained of disorderly conduct among the *congregantes* who frequently claimed seats in the section reserved for *jehidim*. The resolution, imposing a fine of one hundred guilders on any transgressor, also warned that the same punishment would be the lot of *jehidim*—male or female—who attempted to occupy the seats of *congreg-antes* or insisted on having second-class Jews sit beside them. The Mahamad believed that those in question were interested in "offending the orders of this College."[69] But this was no mere rebellion. Like the aforementioned white Portuguese Jews who manumitted and devised to their Eurafrican children more than half a century earlier, many European-origin Jews evi-dently wished to publicly claim *congregantes* as their own flesh and blood.

In 1797, the regents similarly complained that certain "persons" lacking discretion had made forbidden prayer offerings (*misvot*) for *mulatos* in the Beraha VeSalom synagogue in Jodensavanne, intending to ridicule their *jahid* neighbors by implying the latter were "bastard mulattoes or of slave extraction." An offering for a Eurafrican Jew that directly followed a dona-tion in honor of a white Jew implied that the two persons were associated by status. Here again, the expression of family solidarity, rather than mock-ery, may have been the actual intention of such donations. Veteran cantor David Baruh Louzada not only consented to and executed these *misvot* but also permitted *congregantes* to recite the hymns (*hazaroth*) within the synagogue outside of their accustomed seats, an action forbidden even to *jehidim*. The regents decided to exempt Louzada from punishment, out of consideration for his position, and were willing to assume that the cantor acted inadvertently or with excessive indulgence. But Louzada was on the cusp of celebrating twenty-five years of service in the congregation and it is quite unlikely that he acted out of negligence.[70] Rather, the elderly cantor was probably operating within the concentric social circles that made the distinctions between the two classes increasingly meaningless, particularly at a time when the majority of the riverine community (and hence, the de facto seat of its jurisprudence) had relocated to Paramaribo, possibly turning the congregation they left behind in Jodensavanne into a Eurafrican-majority synagogue.

By 1794, the leaders of Darhe Jesarim lost their legal struggle against the regents, and it is easy to imagine why. It was inconceivable at that moment in time for the governor to sanction equality for persons of African ancestry. Moreover, the brotherhood itself showed signs of internal division. In 1793, Roza Pereyra, mother of Jahacob Jessurun, proclaimed to the regents that Reuben Mendes Meza had taken her son "into his hands" and deceptively convinced him to sign the petition the Eurafricans had addressed to the governor. Since the petition had already been submitted, the regents could only advise her to approach the governor directly for clemency.[71] The qualms she evidently harbored about the petition suggest a profound fear of the Mahamad and possibly repercussions from the governor as well.

The litigation that reached the governor's desk created exorbitant costs for both the Mahamad and the Eurafrican Jewish brotherhood. The Mahamad complained to the governor that the case was burdening their poverty chest, since all documents had to be translated to and from Portuguese and Dutch and then legally certified. The case was even costlier for Eurafrican Jews, who, as losers of a civil suit, had to cover all legal expenditures of the Portuguese Jewish community. In 1794, David Judeo and Abigail Abenacar, both of whom had served as guarantors for the Eurafrican party, requested of the Mahamad a three-month payment plan. They renewed their request when the term was up. The regents, "moved by many considerations," granted both requests.[72] The court case must have also presented a financial setback for the fiery Reuben Mendes Meza. In 1794, he requested of the regents a diminution of his taxes from 10 to 7.10 guilders.[73]

Now defeated, three Eurafrican Jewish leaders (Isaac Gabay Fonseca, Reuben Mendes Meza, and Samuel de Robles) submitted revised bylaws of their *jesiba*, signed by eleven members. The bylaws curbed Eurafrican Jewish privileges in three areas: burial rites, financial aid, and *jahid* involvement in the running of Darhe Jesarim. No *congregante* would ever be buried in a procession where mourners carried wax candles, and the funeral liturgy (*ascaba*) was to be received by the cantor, not the mourners. Furthermore, these prayers were to be uttered in the seclusion of the fraternity house, not in public view within the cemetery. Lastly, the Mahamad withdrew virtually all financial assistance to and involvement in the brotherhood. Together, such strictures helped ensure that Darhe Jesarim would remain a brotherhood and not morph into a separate religious congregation. It was now September 1794, four and a half years after the first formal emergence of the brotherhood. The Mahamad inserted in the margins alterations, corrections, and amplifications but otherwise approved the regulations. The governor then ratified these ordinances, rendering Darhe Jesarim an official society of the Portuguese Jewish community.[74]

Going forward, Darhe Jesarim operated like any other Portuguese Jewish society. When internal dissension over leadership plagued the brotherhood in 1795, an official from within brought the case to the attention of the Mahamad, and the regents intervened to resolve the conflict.[75] The response of the regents characterizes their consistent approach to Eurafrican Jewish political activism: support tempered by demand for deference and strict adherence to the Portuguese Jewish communal laws.

For the rest of its existence, Darhe Jesarim continued to operate as a law-abiding organization within the Portuguese Jewish community. In 1798, for example, the founding members of the brotherhood requested permission to make a collection in favor of their institution on the eve of each Festival of Weeks (Sebuoth).[76] In 1807, when its leaders saw the need to amplify certain articles of their bylaws, they duly submitted to the Mahamad proposed changes for approval.[77] And when brotherhood members violated any of the bylaws, leaders brought the case to the attention of the Mahamad.[78] From the start, the regents took pains to publicly recognize Darhe Jesarim as an integral part of the Portuguese Jewish community. In August 1791, for example, the regents invited the society's members to attend the funeral of a recently deceased *parnas* in Paramaribo.[79] Their official recognition of the society and the privilege for its members to participate in their own prayer quorum should not be taken lightly. Only in very special cases, such as a gathering in the house of a deceased person or the establishment of a meritorious mutual aid society, did the regents make exceptions to the first bylaw banning private prayer quorums. The establishment of Darhe Jesarim and the conferral of official status underscore the full support of the Portuguese Jewish leadership and the prominent standing of Eurafrican Jews within the Portuguese Jewish community. At all times, the regents invested their efforts in the continued survival of the *jesiba*, even after they withdrew financial aid.

Despite its ethnic nature, Darhe Jesarim did not strive to be an exclusi-vist society, and at one point even sought an exception to the regulations forbidding *jehidim* from attending Eurafrican High Holy celebrations. In October 1794, they successfully petitioned for permission to appoint a *jahid*, Isaac Ledesma Meatob, as the society's head (*ros*) and asked that he in turn be granted power to appoint a *jahid* as the organization's beadle (*samas*).[80] These requests may have been attempts to increase the prestige and finan-cial support of the organization but may also be further expressions of the concentric circles that characterized the Jewish community by the eigh-teenth century's end.

Nevertheless, the sponsorship of white Jews could not entirely protect the members of Darhe Jesarim from humiliating treatment in the realm of the cemetery. In 1805, the brothers complained that the funeral of *congreg-ante* Imanuel de Britto was at the last minute postponed by the Liviat Hen society because officials from that burial society had decided to bury a *jahid* first. Three hours after Britto's funeral should have begun, the *congregantes* found that there were too few gravediggers at work and offered to assist them in order to speed up the process. But the Liviat Hen officials refused, saying they did not wish to work with *mulatos*. Nor did they furnish the *congregantes* with the customary black cloth to cover the coffin, forcing the Eurafrican Jews to fetch someone to look for the missing object. The regents responded in a way that implicitly gave license for at least some discriminatory behavior to continue. The Liviat Hen officials were urged to follow their organization's constitution "without distinction of persons," and each individual who refused to dig alongside the *congregantes* was fined fifty guilders. Meanwhile, the Darhe Jesarim brothers were chastised for acting against the established orders and were advised in the future to report any irregularities to the regents "without losing decorum" for those in authority.[81] In subsequent years, similar problems continued to disrupt the funerals of Eurafrican Jews.[82]

By the close of the century, internal weakness threatened the survival of the brotherhood. In 1798, founding members complained of the distur-bances that occurred during holiday prayer time, "caused by the little atten-tion and respect" showed by some *jehidim* and *congregantes*, who preferred to crack jokes, violating the sacredness of the prayer and eliciting criticism from passersby. The regents took the complaint seriously, ordering the wor-shippers to maintain the utmost decorum and respect for those elected as the brotherhood's leaders, under pain of a one-hundred-guilder fine.[83] The deathblow to Darhe Jesarim was this very depreciation of Judaism, followed by complete apathy.

In 1815, brotherhood member Jacob Nahar reported to the regents that Reuben Mendes Meza, E. P. Jacobs, and Jacob Abenacar, recently elected to the leadership, had neglected to fulfill the obligations of their posts. When called before the Mahamad to testify, Jacobs referred to scandals and disorders that took place on the nights the brotherhood held its prayer vigils. Jacobs referred to the "little respect and attention" many individuals in both congregations (Portuguese and Ashkenazi) showed for the divine cult and for orders given by the regency.[84] Reuben Mendes Meza also referred to recurring disorders during prayer vigils and to spiritual disaffection among most brothers.[85]

But the Mahamad refused to accept the resignations of Meza and Jacobs and ordered the officials of Darhe Jesarim to hand over their accounts and a list of members who lived in Paramaribo and elsewhere in the colony. By July 1816, it was clear to the regents that the brotherhood was no longer holding prayer gatherings or meetings.[86] One by one, the regents summoned each member to testify whether they wished their organization to continue. Five replied that they did not, while the other four declared their wish to soldier on, with the support of additional members who had not attended the hearing.[87] But the absent members refused to present themselves before the Mahamad, despite repeated orders and pecuniary threats. Still, the regents refused to dissolve the brotherhood, and out of "extra supra abundance" authorized one of the members to bring the signatures of those who refused to appear but wished to continue the organization.[88] In the last days of 1816, Jacob Abenacar wrote a letter to the Mahamad, indicating he no longer wished to continue as a member of the Darhe Jesarim brotherhood, and resigned.[89] Every other member responded with an apathetic silence. Finally, in 1817, the Mahamad determined to disband the Darhe Jesarim brotherhood.[90] After a quarter of a century, the Eurafrican Jewish moment was over.

The End of Peripheral Inclusion

A decade after Eurafrican Jews formally established an autonomous fraternity, the Portuguese Mahamad began to gradually abolish all legal distinctions between white and non-white Jews. In April 1802, the regents banned all distinctions in burial rites between *jehidim* and *congregantes*.[91] Jewish leaders reasoned that "pious deeds must be carried out without prejudice," and that in the administration of last rites to the dead, "every distinction is improper and disagreeable." All charitable institutions, those already existing (Gemilut Hasadim, Liviat Hen, and Hozer Holim) and those to be established in the future, were to identically serve *jehidim* and *congregantes* with respect to coffin, shroud, and the procession and burial in the cemetery, without exception.[92] By January 1820 the practice of relegating deceased *congregantes* to specific cemetery rows ceased. The Mahamad decreed that all baptized *congregantes* (referring to Eurafricans who had undergone Jewish ritual immersion) be interred throughout the cemeteries, "without stipulation of the place of their graves."[93] In May 1841, all remaining legal distinctions between *congregantes* and *jehidim* were eliminated in both the Portuguese and Ashkenazi communities "in accordance with the spirit of times of the present age."[94]

It would be a mistake to locate the impetus for these changes solely in the Mahamad. The new legislation responded to the ever-increasing presence in the two communities of Jewish slaves and their manumitted descendants, and especially their intensifying activism and quest for spiritual satisfaction. While it would seem that the relaxation of discriminatory laws in the Jewish community, beginning in 1802, produced more Eurafrican Jews, in actuality the law was simply reflecting a growing gap between the official caste system in the colony and the practice on the ground. The new legislation did not encourage the acceptance of non-white Jews as equals. Rather, it was catching up with existing reality.

The boundaries between Christians and Jews were also growing increasingly indistinct. David del Prado, who had been a signatory of the Darhe Jesarim petition in 1793, and is identified in records as a *castice* and a *congregante*, became the first Jew in the colony to wed a Christian. In 1820, he married the mulatta Simcha Pardo, a Portuguese Jew who had been recently baptized in the Lutheran faith. Prado was not only a taxpaying member of the Portuguese Jewish community through at least 1825 but also served as ritual slaughterer and inspector (*sohet* and *bodek*) for his congregation in 1822. The regents of the Ashkenazi congregation complained that many of their *jehidim* refused to eat the meat Prado slaughtered because they considered him a "scandalizer of and profaner of Jewish law, not only by having married someone of another religion . . . but also because he promised that the children of this marriage would be Lutheran." Pardo's personal politics seemed to have posed less of a problem for Portuguese Jews. He continued to be an active member of the community and in 1822 donated wooden planks to repair the Jodensavanne Cemetery.[95] He was buried in the oldest Portuguese Jewish Cemetery of Paramaribo. His high economic status may have played a role in the tolerance he enjoyed. In 1817, the regents assessed him almost 352 guilders as his annual *finta*.[96] In 1823, his tax assessment rose to 477.[97]

By the early 1800s, Surinamese society was well on its way to becoming a land celebrated for the harmonious mingling of its ethnically and religiously diverse population. David Nassy famously observed that several religions and ethnic groups were often represented within one nuclear family or household.[98] Censuses confirm this assessment.[99] It was not unusual for a single testator to leave legacies to the five or six major religious groups of the colony: Reformed, Lutheran, Roman Catholic, Moravian, Portuguese Jewish, and Ashkenazi.[100] Were one to include "Winti," the spiritual tradition of most enslaved and free people of slave origins, which was not recognized as a religion in the records, the multiplicity of heritage in a single household would be greater still. The social profile of the Surinamese population by the early nineteenth century affirms the observation discussed in the Introduction to this book, namely that slave societies tend to produce a complex intermixture of peoples and their civilizations.

Conclusion

From the moment of their emergence in the 1660s, Eurafrican Jews in Suriname played a critical role in determining the relationship of the Jewish community to both slavery and whiteness. Their presence as a distinct class endured well into the nineteenth century. Beginning in the 1770s, Eurafrican Jews protested their second-class status only intermittently, on an individual basis. But by the early 1790s, the era of Atlantic revolutions, the group had grown so large, and its leaders sufficiently well-to-do and influential, that they began to protest discriminatory treatment in the Portuguese Jewish community, particularly as experienced in the synagogues and cemeteries. These protests also responded to the expanding gap between the official caste system in the colony and the practice on the ground, speaking to the concentric circles that increasingly compromised the boundaries between racial groups. In 1794, implicitly buoyed by the revolutions of the Atlantic World, Eurafrican activists successfully petitioned the Mahamad and the governor to officialize their own society, known as the Darhe Jesarim ("Path of the Righteous") brotherhood, first constituted in 1759, albeit only informally. By the 1790s, this society reasserted itself by instituting autonomous communal prayer and, at the Mahamad's order, composing institutional bylaws. Darhe Jesarim constituted the only Afro-Jewish fraternal organization in the Atlantic World.

A careful examination of archival documents dismisses earlier scholarly assertions that the brotherhood was subject to continual attack or was viewed as a "potential cult" that the Mahamad effectively rooted out.[101] On the contrary, the leaders of the Mahamad showed consistent support for the institution, albeit patronizing. They reacted harshly only against attempts to circumvent their authority or remove all signs of ritual inequality. In the end, Darhe Jesarim was dissolved in 1817, despite the persistent endeavors of the regents, a victim of the general disrespect or apathy of Surinamese Jews for their own ritual traditions and organizations and the gradual removal of ritual and legal inequality in the broader Jewish community.[102] Far from a society in which whites were uniformly pitted against kleurlingen, Portuguese Jewish regents and the laity over which they ruled were conflicted about ritual distinctions and judicial discrimination. By the 1780s, concentric circles, rather than separate spheres, increasingly characterized the social fiber of Suriname's Portuguese Jewish community, a geometry that paralleled the intertwined branches of family trees.

While the Darhe Jesarim movement was in part a rebellion against the authority of the Mahamad, and an attempt to achieve the dignity and spiritual satisfaction of which Eurafrican Jews were deprived, their activism was in keeping with the historic political behavior of Surinamese Jewry as a corporate body. In appealing to Governor Friderici, Eurafrican Jews displayed the same political practices as did white Jews, who periodically challenged the authority of their regents by appealing to alternative or higher powers. The Eurafrican demand for autonomy, made simultaneously with an insistence on equal treatment, paralleled the contradictory struggle of the organized Jewish community for both privileges as Jews and legal parity with local Christians. Both this activism, born of the Atlantic age of revolutions, and the visit to the island of the Eurafrican Isaac Lopez Brandon for the purpose of Jewish conversion (explored in Chapter 4) reflect the geopolitical literacy that Eurafrican Jews shared with other enslaved and free people of the Atlantic World.[103]

Because they generally bore children out of wedlock, and increasingly did so across communal boundaries, Eurafrican Jewish women were at the forefront of breaking down the divisions between the Portuguese and Ashkenazi communities. While white Jews also married across intracommunal lines, legislation in both congregations that consequently demoted them to *congregante* status served as a strong disincentive.[104] Eurafrican Jews, by contrast, were already *congregantes* or unaccounted-for *mulatos*, occupying an even more liminal space with the Jewish community. While the Portuguese Mahamad resolved to consider the children of such intramarriages as members of the Portuguese nation, the progeny typically bore the family names of their Ashkenazi fathers. Ashkenazi influences thereby increasingly seeped into the community, most audibly in the Hebrew pronunciation of Portuguese Jews, which progressively conformed to Ashkenazi traditions. In communal records, for example, "Beraha VeSalom" and "Sedek VeSalom" became "Beracha VeShalom" and "Tsedek VeShalom," respectively, a phenomenon further considered in Chapter 7.

Scholars who have dismissed African and Eurafrican Jews in Suriname as nonexistent or their impact as minimal have overlooked the prodigious archival record documenting conversions of slaves and their manumitted descendants to Judaism. They have also largely ignored the growth of the Jewish-born Eurafrican population and have been entirely unaware of the existence of circumcised or ritually unimmersed slaves, born out of wedlock, who existed on the fringes of the Jewish community, considered themselves Jewish, and became disruptive political activists beginning in the late eighteenth century. These individuals were finally invited to become official members of the Portuguese Jewish community beginning in the 1780s, in part to broaden the tax base of the economically foundering Portuguese Jewish congregation. By overly focusing on a halakhic approach to conversion, which normatively demands circumcision for males and ritual immersion for both sexes, previous scholarship has overlooked the localism of Suriname's Jewish community, where leaders in consort with the laity developed alternative forms of communal membership.

In this sense, the rise of a distinct, Eurafrican Jewish class can be largely ascribed to the juridical autonomy of Suriname's Jews and their unprecedented New World environment, an agrarian slave society with no Jewish precedents. The development of conversion practices and communal inclusion in Suriname, however, did not defy traditional rabbinical law (*halakha*) but rather exposed diasporic halakhic practices that have heretofore largely escaped scholarly appreciation.[105] The primacy of localist inclusion practices over supposedly mainstream rabbinical conversion laws may be an expression of the geographical distance of Surinamese Jews from European metropolitan centers. But it is just as much a product of the ascendancy of the secular Jewish elite over religious leaders, a phenomenon David Ruderman attributes to the rise of early modern capitalism.[106]

Eurafrican Jews deserve our close attention for several reasons. These individuals are quite literally the human products of a slave society. In both legal theory and in practice, as we have seen, ownership in humans entailed possession of the person's labor as well as her body.[107] In Suriname, where virtually from the onset of colonization the majority of the population was enslaved, and polygynous sexual behavior was both countenanced and widespread among white males, intercourse between master and slave was inevitable. Although the vast majority of servile people did not leave behind records in their own voice, many of their literate or politically active Eurafrican children did. Suriname's Eurafrican Jews, both as individuals and as members of a self-consciously organized subcommunity, provide detailed accounts of the struggle of an African-origin people to achieve social and political equality and, when that failed, organizational autonomy in a slave society.

The Jewish *kleurlingen* of Suriname also expand our understanding of religion in the early modern African diaspora, one that further develops a counternarrative to the Christian Atlantic World.[108] The prodigious archival record pertaining to these Jews demonstrates that scholars ought not to heavily rely on ancient rabbinical sources or conflate rabbinical prescription with lived reality.[109] These neglected primary sources help us contextualize Olaudah Equiano, a former slave and abolitionist who in 1759 contemplated converting to Judaism during a sojourn in London, which would become arguably "the largest 'African port'" by the late eighteenth century. In an Atlantic history framework, his testimony that "he had recourse to the Jews," but ultimately rejected their religion due to his "fear of eternity," can no longer be dismissed as mere rhetoric.[110] Judaism was one of the Atlantic religions variously forced upon, embraced by, consciously rejected by, or inherited by peoples of African descent. The Portuguese ethnicity it also sometimes imparted, in the form of first and last names and language knowledge, helps to explain the persistent nature of Jewish identity among slaves and their manumitted descendants into the 1800s. The memory of Eurafrican Jews, whether or not they officially subscribed their names to the Jewish community's roster, outlived the foremost autonomous institution

FIGURE 13. Storefront in Paramaribo identifying the plaza as the "SivaPlein," a reference to the Eurafrican Jewish prayer house known as the *siva* ("society" or "brotherhood") Darhe Jesarim ("Path of the Righteous"). This Eurafrican Jewish brotherhood was officially disbanded in 1817. The site upon which it stood is still known as the *sivaplein* ("society square" or "plaza"). The original building, located at the intersection of Zwartenhovenbrugstraat and Dominéstraat, does not survive. In the foreground is the *Dankbaarheidsmonument*, by Dutch sculptor Mari(e) Silvester Andriessen, showing three girls representative of, from a colonial perspective, the most prominent groups of mid-twentieth-century Suriname: Javanese (Indonesian), Hindustani (Asian Indian), and Creole (Eurafrican). The sculpture was presented in 1955 to thank Suriname for its support of the Netherlands during and after World War II. Courtesy of Stephen Fokké, 2019.

they established in the colony. Members of the Darhe Jesarim society, known as a *siva* (from the Hebrew word *yesiva*, or institution of higher learning), worshipped in a building in Paramaribo situated at the end of Dominéstraat, at the intersection of Zwartenhovenbrugstraat (see map 5).[111] Formally known as the "prayer house of the Mulatto Jews," the building was thrice advertised for sale in 1794. It was still standing in 1804 and at some point thereafter demolished.[112] The plaza on which it was constructed is still known as the Siva Square (*sivaplein*).[113]

While their periodic self-assertion and attempts to improve their position challenged the legal distinctions between whites and people of Eurafrican descent, at no point did Eurafrican Jews question the institution of slavery or colonial rule. As such, these Jews were fully aligned with the Dutch Empire but confident enough to negotiate their status within it. Although clearly a burgeoning class beginning in the mid-eighteenth century, they were by no means representative of the colony's majority population, enslaved Africans. Many among this latter population also intersected intensely with Jewish culture. It is to this population that we now turn.

CHAPTER 6

Purim in the Public Eye

The Jewish holiday of Purim as celebrated in Suriname in the eighteenth and early nineteenth centuries was neither a private occasion nor limited to Jews.[1] Instead, Jews and Christians, along with the enslaved and manumitted peoples who vastly outnumbered them, participated in the holiday revelry with public abandon. In Suriname, Purim lasted nearly a week and sometimes longer. Crowds of masked Jews, young and old, poured into the streets of Paramaribo, yelling out obscene declarations against Christianity. Surrounding them were bands of slaves pulling wagons laden with costumed Jews and their domestic bondmen. Sometimes, groups of these unfree people circled the masqueraded Jews, shouting and singing through the streets. Intoxicated Jewish men dressed up as armed soldiers, sailors, Maroons, and Indians, while women donned men's clothing and their female slaves followed suit. Christians purchased masks from Jewish vendors and disguised themselves with the suspected intention of attacking their enemies incognito.[2]

Similarly, in Curaçao, Jews stretched out the observance of Purim so that it lasted eight to eleven days.[3] Each year, masked youths paraded through the streets of Willemstad, dancing and singing to the tune of an accompanying band and visiting Jewish homes. The carousing was accompanied by magnificent pyrotechnics, with firecrackers bursting into the air or zigzagging erratically across the ground.[4] Purim in Curaçao, one observer remarked in 1853, "constituted carnival."[5] In 1890, Purim festivities on the island consisted of several impromptu parties and a "Grand Ball" with "dances, fireworks, supper, licors [sic] and other refreshments," attended by 250 guests, who rollicked until the break of day.[6] In both Dutch colonies, the Mahamad as well as successive colonial governors stepped in to curb these public displays of boisterous commotion and intemperance.[7]

Purim is the annual celebration of the deliverance of the Jews of ancient Persia from annihilation in the fifth or fourth century B.C.E., as narrated in the Book or Scroll of Esther. The story's heroes, Mordechai and Esther, together triumphed over a high-ranking political advisor named Haman, who had convinced the Persian king Ahasuerus to blot out the Jews. Purim, which can fall in late February, March, or April, begins on the eve of the fourteenth day of the Hebrew month Adar and in most diasporic Jewish communities is observed for just one day.[8] The festival is preceded by the "Fast of Esther," lasting twenty-five hours and commemorating in short-ened form the three-day period of food abstinence the story's protagonist took upon herself before presenting herself to the king with a plea to halt his decree against her people. Since late antiquity, the holiday of Purim has been marked by a spirited merriment that encouraged inebriation, inver-sion, and, by the early modern period, masquerade. For this reason, Chris-tian theologians called the holiday "Jewish carnival," or *bacchanalia Judaeorum*.[9]

The participation of non-Jews in an unambiguously Jewish holiday may surprise some readers, but the ecumenical celebration of Purim is not an unusual phenomenon in the Jewish diaspora.[10] Even in early mod-ern Italian cities, where the world's first ghettos were instituted, Chris-tians took part in Jewish festivities, especially Purim, which Roni Weinstein likens to a "Jewish version of a carnival." In those neighbor-hoods, hermetically sealed between dusk and dawn, Jewish and Christian men and women danced together on Purim, their masks blurring the borders between the two groups.[11] While on the surface Purim would appear to be an essentially religious holiday, in the context of the Dutch colony the festival is better understood as one of the multiple ways free and enslaved peoples amused themselves when not working.[12] That Purim is based on the only Jewish biblical book that omits any mention of God underscores this point. Its fundamentally secular nature facilitated the participation of non-Jews in its celebration. Still, the observance of the festivity in Suriname seems remarkable in that most non-Jewish revelers were the Jews' social inferiors.

Moreover, while previous works acknowledge the participation of enslaved Africans in Jewish religious life of the Atlantic World, these studies are largely unidirectional or dismissive. Jonathan Schorsch concludes that slaves experienced "general nonintegration" into the religious lives of their

Jewish masters and that Caribbean slaves participated in Jewish rituals and life cycles by and large peripherally and passively, as observers and enablers attending Jewish funerals and synagogue services, overhearing Hebrew elegies, and not working on Sabbath.[13] Within the context of the Jewish holiday of Passover, Natalie Zemon Davis has explicitly left the perspectives of Jewish-owned slaves open to conjecture.[14] The general preoccupation of these scholars with Jewish as opposed to African perspectives on the practice of Judaism in the Caribbean has left a gap. This chapter, then, seeks to discover whether archival sources indirectly capture the thoughts of bondpeople vis-à-vis the Jewish communities in which they lived. As such, this chapter is less aligned with Jonathan Schorsch's concern with Jewish identity, a particular focus of Jewish historiography, and more in consonance with Atlantic historians interested in the agency of slaves and their inner lives. I also join these scholars in their quest to overcome the limitation of the sources, almost always crafted by literate elites. My intention is to shine light on the Caribbean Purim as an unusual site for the public co-participation of bondpeople in Jewish leisure activities, an aspect of slave society Schorsch overlooks as a result of his focus on printed material and secondary sources (as opposed to archives).

The surviving Portuguese communal minutes, which date to the mid-eighteenth century, allow us to trace every mention of Purim, as well as its conspicuous absence, from the 1750s until 1825, the year authorities in the Dutch Republic abolished Jewish communal autonomy. The Jewish communal minutes also serve to anchor incidental Purim references scattered in wills, inventories, correspondence, governors' journals, colonial ordinances, ship records, and almanacs. Curaçao's Portuguese Jewish community, which also emerged in the 1650s, rivaled its Surinamese cohort in both longevity and real numbers, peaking at 1,100 official members in the late eighteenth century. Alas, its surviving communal minutes begin only in 1810, so the emergence of Purim as carnival on the island cannot be methodically traced. The minutes of other Jewish communities of British and other Dutch colonies in the New World and British Caribbean have generally not survived.[15] In part for these reasons, historical studies on Purim have ignored its observance in the Caribbean.[16] These factors make it expedient to focus on Suriname, which may serve as a possible guideline for understanding poorly documented Purims elsewhere in the Dutch and British Caribbean.[17]

The Primacy of Purim for Portuguese Jews

The political and cultural hegemony of Portuguese Jews over Atlantic Jewry is critical in understanding Purim's centrality among Jews in the Atlantic World. In the biblical narrative, Esther initially concealed her Jewish identity in order to marry the Persian king and then revealed her true origins to him in a plea to halt his planned genocide of her people. The collective experience of forced conversion and secret Judaism, initiated in the Iberian Peninsula in the late fourteenth through late fifteenth century, conditioned Portuguese Jews to identify with Esther, for, like them, she masqueraded as a non-Jew while never relinquishing her loyalty to her heritage and people. Miriam Bodian, author of a study of Portuguese Jews in early modern Amsterdam, attributes the "elevated status" of Purim among *conversos* in the Iberian Peninsula to their intense identification with Esther as an ancient crypto-Jew. For similar reasons, Cecil Roth argued almost a century ago that the Fast of Esther acquired among secret Jews an importance that "rivaled that of the Day of Atonement itself."[18] The popularity of Esther extended to the Iberian population as whole. Of all female figures in the Hebrew Bible, none received more attention in early modern Castilian texts than did Esther, particularly among *conversos*, while in Portugal she was considered the holiest of queens.[19]

This same heritage contributed to the enthusiasm for Purim in the open Jewish communities established by former crypto-Jews and their descendants in the Americas. A minor Jewish festival, Purim in Suriname rivaled all the major holidays of the Jewish calendar, including the hallowed Day of Atonement. While the Surinamese sources examined thus far include no mention of Purim fireworks, as witnessed in Curaçao, Suriname's Jews gave primacy to the festival in other ways, equally conspicuous. Devotion to Purim was first and foremost institutionally reinforced. The mandated recitation of the Book of Esther in synagogue was beautified by a high-quality "Meguila" with large letters and marble handles enclosed within a brass box, a costly relic that the Mahamad's regents specially ordered from Amsterdam in 1772, evidently to replace an older scroll that had worn out.[20] In the 1780s, more candles illuminated Suriname's two Portuguese synagogues on Purim than on an ordinary Friday night, and as many were lit as on a major holiday coinciding with Sabbath eve.[21] This brilliant display of light—forty-eight lamps and four tapers—was a significant investment considering the unreliability and expense of candle shipments from across the Atlantic.[22]

Although Purim was a minor holiday halakhically speaking (work, for example, was technically permitted), Surinamese Jews carefully safeguarded its unhindered observance and did not hesitate to protest its encroachment by non-Jewish authorities, just as they periodically protested the infringement by colonial officials of major Jewish holidays and Sabbaths.[23] In 1775, one concerned member of the Portuguese Jewish community asked the Mahamad to appeal to the commissioners of the Civil Court not to disturb "our individuals" by serving them sentences on the festival of Purim.[24] In fact, the minutes record several dispensations granted by the regents to Jews wishing to engage in secular matters and behaviors during biblically sanctioned holidays, such as Passover, but never during Purim.[25]

In the colony's annually published almanac, where every major Jewish holiday is listed from at least 1793, the Jewish community framed Purim as the colony's most important Jewish celebration.[26] Purim always occupies first place in the list of Jewish holidays, conveying the false impression that the Hebrew year began with that festival and that it reigned supreme over the Jewish New Year and Yom Kippur, the chronologically first and holiest festivals of the Jewish calendar.[27] "Haman's festival," as Purim was also known, along with the ninth of Av, which commemorates the destruction of the Jerusalem Temple in 70 C.E., are the only minor holidays consistently mentioned in these almanacs. Noticeably absent from more than half of the editions are the eight days of Hanukkah (the so-called "Feast of the Maccabees"), even though the congregation's leaders distributed candles to individuals and families for that holiday's domestic observance and many Surinamese Jews owned Hanukkah lamps.[28]

Devotion to Purim is also evident on a lay level. Suriname's earliest Jewish settlers showed a characteristic proclivity for Esther as a given name. In the colony's oldest Jewish cemetery, founded in 1666 and located at the Suriname River's Cassipora Creek, Esther is the second most popular name appearing on surviving epitaphs,[29] a naming tradition observed even more emphatically among Jews of British North America.[30] In a 1793 issue of Suriname's weekly newspaper, Purim masks were advertised for sale four months in advance of the holiday, an invitation to anticipation directed at Jewish and Christian readers alike.[31] Privately owned biblical scrolls were almost invariably Torah scrolls,[32] and Scrolls of Esther were the only known exceptions. For example, Sarah de Miranda (1750–1803), wife of Emanuel d'Anavia, on her deathbed legated her daughter Rachel a Scroll of Esther (*meguila off de Histoire van Ahasverus*).[33]

The Scroll of Esther also had special meaning for enslaved and manumitted members of the Portuguese Jewish community. Roza Mendes Meza,
a wealthy Eurafrican Jewess who was born a slave, listed in her 1771 inventory a Scroll of Esther (*Histoire van Hester*), alongside Hebrew books and a
Spanish-language prayer book.[34] In 1759, an unnamed "Jewish negro"
belonging to a Jew by the last name "La Parra" ran away from his master
to a Maroon settlement, carrying a "so-called History of Esther in Hebrew."
The scroll was found in one of the Maroon huts by a government military
expedition charged with capturing runaway slaves.[35] The owner of both the
fugitive and the scroll may have been the lieutenant of the Jewish military
division, Joseph de Abraham de la Parra, who periodically reported the
flight and recapture of runaway slaves.[36] The runaway's religious identity
or formal belonging in the Jewish community is ambiguous—he is referred
to as the "Joode Neeger van La Parra." Was he a "Jewish Negro" because
he was owned by a Jew? Or had he undergone a circumcision and perhaps,
too, an immersion ritual that would have accorded him full Jewish status
in the local community? Furthermore, what motivated him to abscond with
a Megillah? A biblical scroll was not a practical object to steal or to ensure
survival in the rainforest. Conceivably, he regarded the roll of parchment
as a talisman to protect him from capture. Such use of Jewish sacred objects
for protection was not unusual. Decades later, one observer noted that the
African-descended populations of both Suriname and Curaçao were accustomed to protecting their children against the evil eye by tying a talisman
containing Hebrew letters around their little necks. In the 1820s, these
charms sold for three guilders in Suriname and for five in Curaçao.[37]

Or perhaps, understanding the monetary and sentimental value of such
a scroll, a precious relic passed down through the generations, the slave's
intention was to inflict financial and emotional damage on his master. If
he was fully aware of the text's religious and historical message, he would
have seen that message as resonant with his own predicament as an unfree
person in a brutal slave society. The appeal of Esther for diasporic Jews, a
subordinate minority in a foreign culture, was often transferrable to
African-born slaves and their descendants, who formed a majority in many
Caribbean societies and some states of the U.S. South.[38] If this interpretation is correct, it would tie in well with Nell Painter's observation that
Sojourner Truth, among other enslaved and manumitted peoples of African
origins in the mid-nineteenth-century United States, also cherished the tri-
umphant story of Esther.[39] Like Sojourner Truth, the Parra fugitive may

have been "speaking in biblical code" when he stole the Scroll of Esther, reminding his owner of the vengeful outcome of the sacred narrative.[40]

To support this hypothesis one can point to the vindictive undercurrent that fundamentally informed the dynamics between runaway slaves and Jewish plantation owners. Emmanuel Pereyra and David Rodrigues Monsanto, the aforementioned Portuguese Jews who were murdered on the savanna in the 1730s during slave uprisings, were memorialized on their epitaphs with prayers calling for divine retribution against the rebels, disparaged on Monsanto's gravestone as "cruel uprising negroes" (crueys negros alevantados). Both epitaphs open with a Hebrew verse from the Book of Psalms reading: "O Lord God, to whom vengeance belongs; O God, to whom vengeance belongs, shine forth!"[41] We have also seen that a communal record book noting the murder of Jacob, son of Abraham Meijer, in a Maroon attack in 1789 concluded with the curse "may his blood be avenged."[42] In the culture of violent vindictiveness shared among slave owners and the enslaved alike, it is easy to imagine that unfree people—particularly those who took the unusual step of fleeing—not only identified with the narrative in the Book of Esther but also inverted the ethnoreligious identities of the story's heroes and villains.

We find another connection between slaves and the Scroll of Esther in Jewish naming traditions across the Caribbean. Now and again, whether in Barbados, Suriname, or St. Thomas, one comes across references to slaves named Purim. The archival and secondary source evidence thus far examined suggests that this name is found only among slaves owned by Portuguese Jewish masters.[43] All eight of these Purims are either explicitly or implicitly classified as "black" (negros). By contrast, slaves belonging to Portuguese Jews and bearing Portuguese Jewish names, such as Simha, Ismael, or Roza, tend to be Eurafrican in origin (they are classified under the various permutations of the word mulat).[44]

Slave names denoting religious holidays are not very common in Atlantic slave societies. Christian owners sometimes named their human property after the holidays of Easter or Christmas.[45] But a parallel practice is almost never noted among Jews living in slave societies. The one exception pertains to the holiday of Purim. Jewish-owned slaves in Suriname sometimes bore the name Vashti (King Ahasuerus's rebellious and wicked queen), Harbona (the eunuch in the Book of Esther who suggested Haman be hanged on his own gallows), or Haman himself.[46] Purim—applied only to enslaved males—is the only known example of a Jewish holiday qua slave name. As a distinctly Jewish name that is also unambiguously a slave name, "Purim" set the slave apart even as it tied him to the Jewish community. Although Purim can be observed as the last name of Jews elsewhere in the diaspora,[47] Jews never named their children after this holiday, even if they did sometimes select the names of heroic personages in the Purim narrative (notably Esther and Mordecai). As an "ironically inappropriate name," the moniker "Purim" also served to mock, similar to the practice of assigning a slave name like Caesar or Pompey to facetiously highlight subservience and, as Vincent Carretta has noted, to reinforce a slave's degradation.[48] Purim, a holiday of untrammeled joy, as a slave's name pokes fun at the inevitable misery of slavery and is an unmistakably deprecatory name.

The selection of Purim as a slave name could also be an indirect reference to the mishnaic law that stipulates a Hebrew slave be pierced with an awl during that Jewish holiday in order to signal his decision to remain with his Hebrew master rather than be manumitted, and to thereby accept perpetual subservience.[49] This is not to say that all slaves named Purim were viewed by local secular and rabbinical authorities as Jews (the opposite seems to be the case) but rather that Portuguese Jews living in Caribbean slave societies may have been aware of the rabbinical association between Purim and slavery.

Of the Surinamese slaves named Purim, the most visible first appears in the communal minutes of the 1770s. He is identified as creole, an indication of his native-born status, and as a sawyer with some knowledge of carpentry.[50] His mistress Ribca (born Ribca Nunes Forte), living at Jodensavanne, was the widow of Abraham Mendes Vais. Purim caused a ruckus by attacking both fellow slaves and members of the ruling elite. His first recorded offense was the murder on the eve of Yom Kippur, in September 1771, of a slave belonging to the synagogue and entrusted with keeping slaves quiet during the synagogue service.[51] Then, in March 1772, Jacob, son of Samuel Cohen Nassy, complained that Purim behaved outrageously and insolently against him, even physically approaching Nassy in the presence of witnesses. For the violation of his honor and physical space, one of several such occurrences, Nassy appealed to the regents of the Mahamad to mandate that Purim be punished according to Nassy's satisfaction. The regents ordered Ribca Mendes Vais to carry out the punishment on penalty of having Purim forever banished within eight days from the savanna.[52] The holiday of Purim that year began on March 19, and it is likely that the slave's riotous behavior, registered five days later, occurred during the weeklong festivities.

In October 1772, Purim was again causing commotion, this time explicitly on the eve of Yom Kippur itself. A combination of repetitive offenses and the fact that his latest rebellion occurred once again on the holiest day of the Jewish calendar probably convinced the Mahamad to banish him from the savanna. His owner was ordered to carry out this expulsion, and if she refused, Purim would be handed over to the colonial prosecutor.[53] If Purim was ever expelled, it was only a temporary relocation, for he appears again in the savanna in 1782. By this time, his owner, Ribca Vais, had been dead for just over a year and had left her slaves in the charge of one of her executors, who was mandated to put them to work to benefit her estate.[54]

Purim seems to have been as keenly aware of the significance of his name as he was of the Jewish calendar. Applying informed speculation, we may surmise that his rebellious behavior intensified during the holiday after which he was ironically named, as well as during Yom Kippur, a word that rabbinical thinkers since antiquity read as "like [ki] Pur[im]," understanding the austere Day of Atonement to be a mirror image of the festive Purim during the diasporic period and its very embodiment in messianic times.[55] There is some evidence that Suriname's Portuguese community also saw the Day of Atonement in close relationship to Purim. In September 1817, the regents resolved to make a public announcement during Sabbaths preceding both holidays restricting loud socializing in synagogue on both Yom Kippur and Purim. In that decree, worshippers were forbidden "to applaud or beat with hands or feet in the synagogues on any occasion, including the beating of Aman [Haman] the night and day of Purim."[56] It is possible that Suriname's Portuguese Jewish community, like that of Amsterdam, practiced *malkot* on the day before Yom Kippur, a ritual of self-flagellation that would have been very noisy.[57]

Purim's specific birthplace will never be known, since the native provenance of the vast majority of Africans taken away to slavery in the Americas was not recorded. If Purim was born around the mid-eighteenth century, there is some chance (41 percent) that he traced his origins to the Kormantin ethnic group (in what is today Ghana), and a one in four possibility that he came from either the Mandingo or Loango cultures (also located in West Africa).[58] Purim's awareness of the holiday after which he was called is not surprising given the importance West Africans attached to the literal and ontological meanings of their given names. Many West Africans and their diasporic descendants preserved a tradition of naming a child after his or her birth day in the week. Moreover, a name could signify a person's spiritual attributes or his parents' mundane events at the time of birth.[59]

Just as Purim had an African birth name and probably at least one byname, it is also clear that he maintained some of the spiritual traditions of his native West Africa. In 1782, David de Jacob R. de Meza discovered "the negro Purim" slaughtering a goat later discovered to be the property of the Portuguese Jew Isaac Lopes Nunes. When Meza tried to intervene, Purim forcibly resisted.[60] If Purim was not merely seeking a food source or to inflict financial damage on the owner, he may have been sacrificing the animal to a god, or in veneration of one of his ancestors, a practice common to many communities in Angola and other regions of West Africa.[61] On paper, Purim's act also seems similar to the animal sacrifices found among slaves held captive in Brazil, where local healers played a central role not only in curing diseases but also in linking living people with ancestral spirits, securing physical or spiritual bulwark, and carrying out purification and divinatory rituals.[62]

Purim would have had numerous occasions to appeal to his ancestors for intervention or protection. When chastised by the Mahamad for Purim's behavior, David de la Parra, an executor of widow Ribca Vais's estate, assured the regents that he was well aware of Purim's crime and "was still exhausted from administering him a severe beating." By that time, most of the savanna's free residents, including Meza, had complained about Purim's insolence "infinite times" and the Mahamad had passed numerous resolutions to have widow Ribca or her executors banish Purim from the countryside. Once again, the regents ordered Parra to expel Purim. If he did not obey, he would be required to bring Purim to the colonial prosecutor.[63] Purim had witnessed several slaves, owned by his late mistress, promised manumission after her death and probably realized how slim his own chances were for release from slavery, the "cherished gift of freedom" that was reserved mainly for a highly select group of mostly Eurafrican women and children.[64] Purim must have understood the inevitability of severe physical punishment, as well as a banishment that might catapult him out of the frying pan and into the fire. Yet did not the holiday of Purim teach one to hope for precipitous salvation?

Even in absence of an official policy that imposed the ruling society's spiritual traditions on unfree residents, enslaved populations in Suriname shared to varying degrees the religious heritage of their owners. Much research has been devoted to the participation of British Caribbean and

U.S. slaves in the Christmas holiday, which sometimes offered an opportunity for slaves to experience momentary upward social mobility. In early nineteenth-century Jamaica, for example, slaves celebrating Christmas appeared "an altered race of beings. They show themselves off to the greatest advantage, by fine clothes and a profusion of trinkets; they affect a more polished behavior and mode of speech; they address the whites with greater familiarity; they come into their masters' houses, and drink with them; the distance between them appears to be annihilated for the moment."[65]

In Suriname, slaves also lived according to the religious rhythms of their masters and mistresses, whether Jewish or Christian. As early as 1698, the colonial government issued an ordinance prohibiting slaves in and around Paramaribo from gathering in public to drum and play on Sundays and Christian holidays.[66] In 1711, a similar placard was issued banning negers on the savanna from gathering in large numbers on Jewish holidays and other occasions to drum, dance, and play without express permission of the Jewish regents.[67] The placard was reissued periodically over the course of the century in reference to Sundays and other "holy days," often explicitly underscoring the 1711 ordinance dealing with Jewish holidays.[68] Worthy of note are the several words referring to dance. The Dutch dansen implies a Christian European provenance, while the watermamadans is a clear allusion to the African water spirit and spiritual tradition common to certain regions of western Africa.[69] The term baljaaren, meanwhile, is a creolized Dutchification of the Portuguese and Spanish infinitive "to dance" (bailar). The placards first mentioned baljaaren in 1741, and the watermama dance in 1776, an indication that the colonial authorities had begun by then to perceive cultural distinctions between the leisurely activities of slaves and to assign to them separate Dutch, West African, and possibly Portuguese Jewish attributes.[70]

Slave participation in Jewish religious life in the colony was probably a constant during the period of slavery. A communal ordinance whose earliest extant version dates to 1748 includes a prohibition against the synagogue attendance of "Negras, Mulatas ou Indias," with or without children, and indicates the responsibility of their masters to remove them. In 1817, the First Parnas proposed the renewal of an interdiction against the disruption in synagogues by free and manumitted slaves (negrerias) entering with or without children in both the men's and women's section of the building. These individuals formed a disruptive group that attended synagogue under the pretext of rendering services to their owners or offering holiday greetings (felicitaçoems) to free or enslaved "blacks" (negros).[71] The successive reissue of such regulations reveals the tensions inherent in a society whose ruling elite wished to exclude slaves from its ranks even as it necessarily incorporated them into its communal rhythms and religious outlook.

The foregoing examples of Purim as a holiday and as a personal name transmit a general message about how ethnic groups interacted in Suriname. Most previous studies of Caribbean Jewry have either largely ignored the enslaved element or have sought to find Jewish "influences" among slaves and their free descendants.[72] But it is not, as most scholars have argued or implied, that these individuals were passive, unwitting recipients of a rich Jewish heritage that was so compelling or dominant it overwhelmed their own. Culture and its performance were a much more active process, particularly in the Dutch Caribbean. Jewish masters and mistresses habitually related their human property to the fiber of Jewish life. Unfree people of African origins, for their part, seemed to have fully understood the Jewish heritage of their immediate surroundings. Slaves owned by Jews sometimes incorporated a Portuguese Jewish cultural worldview into their own, as suggested by the actions of Purim the slave, the unnamed fugitive who absconded into the wilderness with a Scroll of Esther, or by the *baljaaren* of Jewish holidays, which are possibly of Portuguese Jewish provenience. But Jewish-owned slaves, particularly those who worked in the field with little direct contact with the owner and his or her extended family, also had sufficient cultural autonomy, in absence of an official colonial religion and language imposed on all residents, to preserve or cultivate their own traditions. The *watermama* dances, often performed during Jewish holidays but clearly West African in origin, are a prime example. Any discussion of cultural transformation demands a consideration of how both groups were affected in their encounter with each other. Substituting the idea of "influence" with a more mutual and active paradigm of cultural expression is much more than a semantic distinction. It allows us to see that rigid racial barriers and violence did not preclude cultural convergence.[73] Such confluence is only hinted at in the aforementioned individual expressions of Purim. It finds fuller expression in Purim as a pan-ethnic Caribbean festival.

Purim Pandemonium

In hemispheric American colonies where Judaism was a licit religion, Purim was the most public of Jewish holidays. This was partly because the festival's main attractions (costuming, masquerade, and fireworks displays) occurred outside of the synagogue. Rowdiness also characterized the holiday as practiced behind closed doors. The activity entirely confined to the house of worship—the public reading of the Megillah—entailed a riotous call-and-response component in which the congregation sometimes reacted violently. Purim celebrations became a pressing issue for Suriname's Jews and the colonial government only during the fifty years that bracketed the turn of the nineteenth century. The concern fell into two distinct categories: noise level within the synagogue with the accompanying destruction of synagogue property, and boisterous behavior on the streets of Paramaribo. We shall first deal with the former category, which was registered only internally and never reached the governor's desk.

The Sabbath of Remembrance, immediately preceding Purim and known in Portuguese-inflected Hebrew as Sabat Zahor, signaled the onset of Purim in the Dutch colonies. On that day, in keeping with ancient Jewish tradition, a special concluding Torah reading (*maftir*) was recited from the Book of Deuteronomy recalling the iconic villain Amalek, who attacked the ancient Israelites after their flight from Egyptian slavery. Jewish communities throughout the world have traditionally associated Amalek with Haman of the Purim story and have understood the Amalekites as a symbol of the evil that arises in each generation and must be stamped out.[74] A longstanding diasporic tradition, which Surinamese Jews also followed, was to produce a cacophony of noise every time the cantor uttered the name of Haman from the lectern during the reading of the Megillah, a custom inferred from the biblical verse "For I will utterly blot out the remembrance of Amalek from under the Heavens" (Exodus 17:14).[75]

Upholding the authority of the regents, especially by regulating behavior within the synagogue, was the Mahamad's main task. The vast majority of cases the regents dealt with, as a diachronic perusal of the communal minutes from the mid-eighteenth century onward shows, involved scrutinizing what went on in the synagogue and ascertaining that violators of proper decorum were swiftly disciplined. The six separate incidents of commotion during the reading of the Megillah registered in the communal minutes date from 1772 to 1819. Two involved a conflict between named individuals. On Purim day 1772, David de Jacob Raphael de Meza was reciting aloud the Scroll of Esther in synagogue and hammering the lectern, perhaps to quiet the congregation.[76] Abruptly, Meza descended from the reader's lectern and slapped Joseph Haim Pintto across the face.[77] Similarly, on Purim eve in 1808, Jacob Miranda asked David Souza Britto to cease making a commotion so that the cantor's recitation of the Scroll of Esther could be audible. When Britto refused, Miranda called him a "drunk and lowly sailor."[78] These two conflicts were resolved by a public request by the offenders for forgiveness at the synagogue lectern and a monetary fine.[79]

Most recorded cases of synagogue disruption during Purim, however, concerned crowd behavior. A few days after Purim in 1777, the regents convened to discuss the pandemonium that had ensued during the recitation of the Scroll of Esther in both the Beraha VeSalom synagogue in Jodensavanne and the Sedek VeSalom house of worship in Paramaribo. Worshippers had struck the benches with hammers, clubs, and other hard objects, preventing others from hearing the Megillah recitation by the cantor as mandated by Jewish law and damaging the synagogue furniture, to the burden of the charity chest. The regents therefore outlawed the "beating of Haman," permitting only self-striking instruments such as clappers, and appointed fathers, teachers, and children's tutors responsible for preventing raucous conduct.[80] In March 1797, worshippers again hammered the benches during the Megillah reading, rendering "ridiculous a ceremony practiced in all the congregations of Israel." The striking of synagogue furniture also disrupted "the precious moment of prayer" and invited the disdain of other religious groups for "our divine cult and its august ceremonies." The regents imposed a fine of 500 guilders on any *jahid* or *congregante* who struck any object with a hammer or made noise outside of the appropriate times. Moreover, informers would receive anonymity and a reward of 200 guilders. The resolution would be read aloud each year in synagogue, both on the eve of Purim and the following day, before the recitation of the Megillah, in both the Jodensavanne synagogue and Paramaribo's Sedek VeSalom house of prayer.[81] In 1819, the regents entirely forbade the worshippers from striking during any mention of "Haman." Only the *hazan* reading the Megillah was permitted to strike, and even he was directed to do so only with his foot, and with only three blows.[82] Even though the congregation had for the previous several years exhibited good behavior (*boa comportaçao*), the Mahamad reiterated the ruling in 1826 as a preventative measure.[83] This gradual imposition of somber and orderly worship, which virtually eliminated the congregation's audible participation, generally characterizes the process of ritual reform in Suriname and elsewhere in the Portuguese Jewish Caribbean beginning in the early nineteenth century. There, innovation in synagogue services was typically introduced gradually with none of the ideological warfare instigated by the Jewish

Emancipation decrees of western and central Europe during the late eighteenth and throughout the nineteenth centuries.[84] These episodes in Suriname rather suggest the self-consciousness of practicing Jews living in a Christian-dominated society and witnessed among Portuguese Jews in Europe since at least the seventeenth century.

Before 1772, neither surviving government placards nor extant records of the Surinamese Mahamad express specific complaints about the ways in which Jews celebrated Purim. This silence should not mislead us into assuming that all previous behavior in synagogue during Purim was docile, especially given prior patterns in Amsterdam, where the "mother community" of the Portuguese Jewish diaspora held court. Two weeks before Purim in 1640, Amsterdam's Portuguese Mahamad resolved to outlaw hammering in the synagogue during the reading of the Scroll of Esther, considering the custom more appropriate to barbarians than to civilized individuals. Three decades later, the decree was repeated and the fine increased twentyfold.[85] Such "barbaric" comportment was also habitual among the Portuguese Jews of London.[86] When an English non-Jew called John Greenhalgh visited the city's Portuguese congregation in 1662, he observed that during the synagogue service of Purim "they use great knocking and stamping when Haman is named."[87] The earliest recorded attempt to reduce the disruption dates to around the turn of the seventeenth century, when the congregation's Mahamad forbade any worshipper, regardless of sex or age, to "beat, or make a noise in Synagogue with a hammer, or any other instrument, since, independently of the scandal such a bad custom would give rise to, it may prevent many devout persons of our congregation from going to Synagogue on these occasions."[88] The diachronic reaction of Curaçao's Mahamad to "beating Haman" is unknown, since communal minutes predating 1810 have not survived, but the anti-Jewish remarks of the Jesuit Miguel Alexias Schabel, a Bohemian who lived on the island during the first decade of the seventeenth century, concerning the loud music emanating from the synagogue offer the possibility that Jews there also had cause for self-consciousness.[89]

The apparent lack of complaints from among Suriname's regents between the 1750s (the date of the earliest surviving minutes) and 1770s may have a great deal to do with the steady relocation of most Jewish planters and Mahamad meetings from the remote village of Jodensavanne to Paramaribo. As we have seen, the earliest known placard complaining about the Jewish festive days, dating to 1711, refers only to the ruckus caused by enslaved celebrants. Colonial legislators complained that great numbers of slaves (*negers*) in the savanna gathered on Jewish holidays and other days in order to "drum, dance, and play, and that on these occasions there, many disorders occur." They forbade these activities without prior permission of the regents, on pain of a whipping.[90] While absence of evidence is not necessarily evidence of absence, Purim as celebrated by Jews may have only come under public scrutiny when significant numbers of inland planters relocated to Paramaribo over the course of the last quarter of the eighteenth century. Living in a bustling urban environment inhabited by whites and an ever-growing class of free people of color may have given rise to a Jewish self-consciousness as witnessed earlier in Amsterdam, London, and possibly Curaçao.[91]

Moreover, increasing Jewish squeamishness with ritual rowdiness could reflect the implicit internalization of Christian behavioral norms in houses of worship. In contrast to Jodensavanne, the synagogue in Paramaribo would have received more Christian visitors who arrived out of curiosity, to reinforce social or business ties, or to negotiate political relations. In fact, Jews often extended these invitations themselves. One example dates to the Friday evening after Purim when the Ashkenazi community invited the governor and gentlemen of the Council of Policy to attend Sabbath evening services. To mark the occasion, the entrance to the synagogue was decorated with orange, the Dutch national color, and a musical concert was performed.[92] There is ample evidence that successive governors and other dignitaries also visited the synagogue in Jodensavanne, starting in the late seventeenth century.[93] But unlike the remote hinterland, in Paramaribo the synagogue was vulnerable to the prying eyes and straining ears of non-Jewish neighbors, whose unwelcome attention sometimes caused the congregation extreme embarrassment. One such incident involved a wedding ceremony turned sour in 1821, when passersby gravitated to the doorway of Sedek VeSalom to hear the "scandalous shouts and insults" coming from within.[94]

The Mahamad's paramount duty to enforce proper behavior became much more complicated anytime transgressions were carried out beyond the synagogue walls, where individuals outside of the community were inevitably implicated and the jurisdictional domain of the Mahamad was compromised. Once again, absence of evidence does not necessarily constitute evidence of absence. But it is likely that Purim took to the streets only with the mass migration of the colony's inland Jewish population to Paramaribo. In 1775, the Council of Policy and Criminal Justice issued the earliest surviving Surinamese placard specifically referring to the holiday of Purim. Colonial leaders complained that men in groups, masked, costumed, and walking with weapons, created a ruckus while deeply inebriated, hurling insults at other men and inciting violence on the Heerenstraat.[95] Adult males were consequently forbidden from appearing masked on these streets, much less from carrying out any "wantonness or molestation," under any pretext whatsoever under pain of arbitrary punishment.[96] It is noteworthy that the assembly of men and their costumes, weapons, drunkenness, noise level, and insults seemed to be of secondary importance. Masquerade was deemed the main culprit, ostensibly because facial disguise prevented accountability and punishment and, perhaps more than any other factor, encouraged uninhibited behavior.

The insults hurled may have been religious in nature, given events two decades later in Suriname, and considering the diasporic record of Purim's villain Haman morphing into a Christian symbol.[97] In March 1792, a band of masked Portuguese and Ashkenazi youth winding their way through Paramaribo's streets engaged in "various forbidden actions" that were "against the general peace [sossego] and against Catholics in this colony." Portuguese Jewish leaders worried that such actions would harm "the credit of the nation" and could incite the "displeasure and indignation" of the colonial magistrate against the entire Jewish community.[98] The impulse of these Portuguese and Ashkenazi Jews to scapegoat Catholics (perhaps with an effigy of Christ qua Haman) is telling, given the social position of Catholics in a nominally Dutch Reformed Protestant colony. Although Catholics were "tolerated" in the colony, as the Portuguese communal minutes explicitly note, Jews enjoyed a much longer-lived and generally securer status than these nonconforming Christians. Jewish autonomy was rooted in privileges granted under the English in the 1650s and reconfirmed and expanded after the Dutch takeover in 1667. Jews were immediately accorded the liberty of public worship of their religion, while the first Roman Catholic congregational building in Suriname was established only in 1785.[99] Targeting Catholics may have been a safer way to vent a general anti-Christian animus. But Portuguese Jews (and perhaps their Ashkenazi sympathizers) harbored a specific and enduring resentment for the religion they identified with the forced conversion of hundreds of thousands of Jews in centuries past. There is evidence in the communal records that Suriname's Portuguese Jews kept these bitter memories alive, especially in contexts where they praised the Dutch Republic for its tolerance of Jews.[100]

Denigration of Christianity did not deter some non-Jews (both white Christians and people of African descent) from sharing in the Purim pandemonium. In 1793, the Mahamad learned that "various people outside of the Judaic nation" masked themselves during the evening of Sabat Zahor and Purim with the possible intention of launching attacks. The communal minutes, which typically do not distinguish between Christian denominations, do not tell us whether these Christians were Dutch Reformed, who might have shared a disdain for Catholicism. The regents also noted that slaves of unspecified spiritual traditions (*negros*) invariably accompanied their masters in the annual costumed parades. The leaders made an announcement from the synagogue podium prohibiting all Portuguese Jews, whether *jehidim* or *congregantes*, from costuming themselves or wearing masks on those evenings, allowing children to do so only during the day. Furthermore, children were to remain in their homes from six in the evening onward to avoid the "insolence and commotion" that invariably characterized the hilarity.[101] The explicit inclusion of *congregantes*, typically Jews of Eurafrican descent, is not so much a reference to their sudden participation in Purim as to their exponential growth in the latter half of the eighteenth century.[102] During that period, communal minutes for the first time begin to habitually reference *jehidim* and *congregantes* in one breath.

Anxiety over Purim among the colony's Christian and Jewish leaders peaked during the British Interregnum (1799–1802, 1804–16). Shortly after Suriname capitulated in August 1799, British authorities issued a document of the Dutch surrender, whose second article stipulated that the "inhabitants of the colony shall enjoy full security to their persons and the free exercise of their religion,"[103] an implicit sanctioning of Purim and other holidays. But Purim was becoming an ever more fraught holiday given the colony's increasing militarization under British rule. The authorities not only regrouped existing Dutch battalions but also added over 3,500 rank-and-file soldiers, including "Germans of the Walloon guards, as well as some Hungarians and Austrians," and also augmented the local naval force.[104] At no time in Suriname's history had so many governors with a military background reigned.[105]

Five months before capitulation and nine days before Purim, the regents noted "the critical circumstances of this colony" caused by the Quasi-War between France and the United States. The regents feared that under the pretense of masquerading through the streets during the festival of Purim, opposing parties would commit aggressive acts that would give Jews a bad name. Jewish leaders were particularly nervous given that they had received notice about various "Christians" who had already purchased masks, a rumor probably based in truth if we consider the aforementioned newspaper advertisement from 1793 announcing Purim masks for sale.[106] The regents appealed to the governor to publicize a placard forbidding under heavy penalties men and children from walking in the streets masqueraded, as well as any medium of transportation that pulled domestic slaves and other people behind it.[107]

The regents issued similar ordinances from 1800 through 1819, and all of them expressed similar concerns: Purim celebrations, primarily outside the synagogue, would incite suspicion and ridicule among Christians, and it was indecent, insolent, and a threat to public order for slaves to run shouting and singing through the streets. The reaction of Governor Juriaan François Friderici (1790–1802) confirms the powerful threat of Purim to colonial stability. In February 1800, thirteen days before Purim, he issued a new ordinance forbidding any adult or child from donning a costume or mask.[108] But by 1807, his Purim edict had entirely lost its efficacy and the disruption was worse than ever. Not only had the revelers walked through the streets "very indecently with masks," but they had also paraded in decorated military costumes, to the beat of drums, sounding an alarm, an act forbidden by a colonial placard. Moreover, some male Jews donned "inappropriate and indecent costumes," parading "almost naked and in the form of Indians and Bush Negroes" through the streets. Among them were "even women disguised in the costumes of men," which inevitably led *mulatas* and *negras* to assume male dress and join in the revelry.[109]

Even if others took part, it is clear from these reports that Jews were the initial instigators of rowdy behavior on Purim. Their choice of disguises (sailor, soldier, Maroon, and Indian costumes, as well as female cross-dressing) and the earlier "drunk and lowly sailor" insult in the 1808 synagogue dispute therefore merit remark. Whereas Christians could select from both the Old and New Testaments, in addition to the lives of saints, for models of emulation, Jews limited themselves to some twenty biblical episodes and legends. This observation, offered by Nahma Sandrow in her study of Purim dramaturgy among modern Ashkenazim, helps explain why Jews in Suriname reached outside of the Bible into everyday life to express their boisterous selves.[110] But because these are the only costumes mentioned in the sources, we must seek another explanation.

Sailors, soldiers, Maroons, and Indians were all low-status groups in the colonial hierarchy. Between the 1750s and early nineteenth century, sailors were increasingly visible on Suriname's waterfront and rivers. In response to market demands, they were frequently hired as rowers of barges, previously typical slave work.[111] In the colony as elsewhere in the Atlantic World, sailors received brutal corporal punishment from their superiors and most had short lives.[112] Soldiers were often impressed into service, and those who had served under Dutch rule were extremely reluctant to continue their duties under British military authority.[113] In the Portuguese communal minutes, both sailors and soldiers are often associated with chronic inebriation.[114] As non-whites, Maroons and Indians occupied the lowest rungs of the colony's racial ladder (one notch above slaves), and their daily clothing, skimpy by white standards, was a symbol of denigration.

On the other hand, each of these groups exacted fear, if not respect. Sailors and soldiers and other "white ruffians" were hired as white officers (*blankofficiers*) on Surinamese plantations, a disposable workforce estate owners used to shield themselves from the wrath of their slaves.[115] At various times of the year besides Purim, some Portuguese Jews disguised themselves as soldiers in order to exact vengeance on their Jewish enemies incognito, an apparently well-known ruse in the colony. One Sabbath night in 1768, Imanuel de Abraham Jessurun and other Jews, including an Ashkenazi, walked through the streets of Paramaribo, disguised as drunken soldiers and armed with spades and other weapons, and attacked two Portuguese men, wounding one. Jessurun's repeat offense resulted in his repatriation out of the colony within two months, but he clearly had sympathizers beyond his accomplices.[116] Other Jews dealt with their opponents by hiring sailors as thugs. In 1796, a Portuguese Jew banned from attending a coreligionist's funeral fetched four sailors from his tavern and returned to harass those who physically barred him from entering the house of mourning.[117] Periodically, Portuguese Jewish regents called on non-Jewish soldiers as guards to protect the synagogue during the High Holy Days or as law enforcers if Jews did not behave themselves in the house of worship.[118]

Moreover, a Jewish soldier was not an ontological contradiction: Suriname's Jews, like those of Curaçao and in certain periods in Jamaica, had their own separate civil guard.[119] Jewish officers served in full military regalia, as we can see from the inventory of David Haim del Monte, a lieutenant of Suriname's Jewish militia, who owned houses in both Paramaribo and Jodensavanne and died in 1824.[120] But a separate militia enhanced a Jewish man's status only so far, for it also highlighted his exclusion from the society's mainstream military forces, which even free Christian men of African ancestry could join by the late eighteenth century.[121] The only way Jews could serve in the mainstream forces, it would seem, would be to secretly renounce their Jewishness and pass themselves off as white Christians, as a handful of Portuguese Jews did in Suriname around the turn of the nineteenth century.[122]

An awareness of this same derision, alternately doused with fear and respect, may have motivated males living in other Portuguese Jewish communities to don masks and sailor or soldier disguises during Purim. As a young man, boxing champion Daniel Mendoza, born in London's Jewish community in 1764, attended a Purim festival with his friends, all of them disguised as a party of sailors, with him playing the part of lieutenant. After encountering a press gang, the party was thrown in jail. Upon their release two days later, they decided to perform as sailors in a traditional Purim play, a performance that created "uproar and tumult."[123] In 1690, Amsterdam's Mahamad resolved that neither community members nor their children and servants be allowed to appear in the streets during Purim, as was customary, in costumes or masks, "since some of our enemies use this [custom of] masquerading to demonstrate their ill intent toward us."[124] A similar ordinance appeared in London in 1732.[125] In 1695, the Amsterdam regents outlawed public Purim celebrations after spotting children in the street dressed up as sailors or in masks. Daniel Swetschinski notes a general fear among the regents that "large and unruly crowds" as well as the public exuberance of various Jewish holidays would draw unwelcome attention from Christians who viewed Portuguese Jewish traditions with "suspicion or ridicule." Such public displays of euphoria vitiated the tranquility (*quietação*) the Mahamad sought to enforce.[126] These concerns echo those of the Mahamad in Suriname a century later. The regents there were likewise worried about Jews creating public spectacles and endangering the community's reputation or status. In 1772, they had explicitly asserted their right to seek the colonial government's intervention in the public scandals occasioned by Purim the slave on the savanna. According to the privileges conferred on Suriname's Portuguese Jews, they noted, the Mahamad had a right to assure the "good governance and tranquility" of the village.[127]

This anxiety about public disorder throws new light on the parallel obsession among Reformed Protestants in seventeenth-century New Amsterdam/New York, which Dennis Sullivan attributes to concern that disruptive behavior would cause economic loss.[128] But valuing civic peace need not be linked to anything beyond itself; it is possible that authorities strove for order simply to ensure their authority and ability to rule. In this context, it is also worthwhile to reconsider Yosef Kaplan's analysis of the concept of "bom judesmo" among Portuguese Jews. Kaplan explains that good Judaism was not understood as a strict adherence to Jewish law (*halakha*) but rather as "obedience and restraint," control of one's instincts, and "maximal consideration for the taste and inclinations of the surrounding society."[129] Kaplan contends that this understanding of Judaism was influenced by Iberian values of civility and that it was emphasized because in a community with a wide range of religious observance it was much more effective than exhorting the population to comply with the minutiae of Jewish law.[130] However, the cases heretofore discussed of Purim as celebrated in the public eye suggest that the ideals of self-containment did not emanate from any set of values imported from Portugal or Spain, nor were they a reaction to the Jewish community's recent return to and struggles with rabbinical Judaism. Rather, the principles of *bom judesmo*, like *quietação*, were a factor of Jewish existence as a tolerated minority at the whims of a dominant group. Public order was a value rhetorically upheld in every segment of free Dutch society, including the political elite. Among groups whose presence was tied to privileges that could be arbitrarily withdrawn, there were urgent reasons to embrace it.

Consideration of more extreme Purim costumes brings us to Maroons and Indians. As the only non-white groups in the colony that had successfully negotiated their political autonomy, these two also exacted respect. Both received annual tribute from the government, a method of pacification. Alexander Salonthay van Salontha, a plantation owner and colonial leader who lived in Suriname for nine years before returning to Europe, rightly noted in 1778 that such gifts were "in essence nothing more than openly recognizing their [the Maroons'] superiority."[131]

Finally, one must consider the mundaneness of soldier, sailor, Maroon, and Indian costumes, at least in a Surinamese context. All were commonly known groups in local society and as such an obvious choice for imitation. Soldiers became ever more omnipresent under British occupation, and sailors, who worked on the urban docks and along Suriname's rivers, were also very visible. Maroons and Indians, even if geographically marginalized to the colony's rainforest interior, did periodically visit the capital city, and they possessed political clout, whether under British occupation or otherwise.

There is also scattered evidence that Portuguese Jews living in the hinterland had close contact with both groups. Indians are sometimes mentioned in the communal minutes as trading partners of Jews or as their slaves.[132] In 1791, the regents deferred the hour of prayer so they could attend the funeral of an Indian.[133] In the savanna, Indians were sometimes hired to maintain the Jodensavanne and Cassipora cemeteries.[134] Abraham, son of Moses Bueno de Mesquita, was living and trading, not always harmoniously, among the Saramakka Maroons in 1802.[135] Aaron J. da Costa evidently also traded with a Maroon tribe. When he died on the savanna in 1820, his possessions included five "Bush Negro" plates (*Bosch Neeger Borden*).[136] In a sense, the Purim costumes with which Surinamese Jews clad themselves and their children attest to a lack of imagination, if not provincialism.[137]

The social position of Jews during the British Interregnum was far too complex to point to costuming as a means of performing a status lower or higher than their own. The historically elite status of Jews in the colony had been on the decline since the economic crisis began in the 1770s and the concurrent ascendance of the free Christian population of African descent, many of whom had by then risen above Jews, in many respects. This precipitous decline of Jewish status was evident even to foreigners. Shortly after capitulation, a senior British official reported that although Jews were "the first settlers of Surinam" and settled there "with their own laws and privileges granted them by the Sovereign," they were now "considered as the very lowest class of the white people."[138] In Suriname, an intensely multiethnic population and politically complex society, each group had a multivalent image. A Purim costume representing another social or ethnic group would therefore have communicated multiple messages. In cladding themselves as soldiers, sailors, Maroons, and Indians, Jews were simply expressing their rambunctious selves through a limited repertoire of costuming, also available to other revelers of various backgrounds.

Purim's public manifestations should attract our attention for a different reason. Particularly if we consider the enthusiastic participation of the enslaved, it is clear that Purim in Suriname from the second quarter of the eighteenth century had become an Afro-Creole festival, akin in many ways to what scholars and several contemporary observers in the Caribbean have understood as a local variety of Carnival.[139] Within the synagogue, Purim retained its characteristics as a classical Jewish holiday celebrated by Jews. But once it took to the streets, its ethnic applicability broadened. Its masquerade, cross-dressing, the relaxation of social boundaries, and dancing and singing through the streets invited the participation of others, just as did carnivals and other festivals imported to the Americas from Europe and Africa and transformed there in slave societies. We are not told the details of the dancing and singing during Suriname's Purim that would mark these cultural expressions as typical of the Dutch Protestant, Portuguese Jewish, or African diasporas, or that would allow us to develop a creolization hypothesis. But the countenanced participation of white Christians and slaves and the reactive objections of the Jewish and colonial authorities indicate that the holiday by the early 1800s had become a joint cultural production with strong West African overtones. In fact, the musical and animated slave assemblies, alternately referred to as *dansen*, *watermamadans*, and *bajlaaren*, and outlawed in Suriname by successive ordinances since the late seventeenth century, can all be seen as precursors, if not manifestations, of Suriname's carnivalesque festivities.[140] Their official proscription by the colonial and Jewish authorities is in itself diagnostic of carnival, which has a long history in the circum-Caribbean of interrelation with the law.[141]

Carnivals (with a lowercase "c") developed in diverse slave societies throughout the Caribbean and are not necessarily linked to a Catholic provenance and its associated period of abstinence preceded by frenetic crapulence. Carnivals also developed in colonies lacking substantial Catholic populations and whose official religion was Protestantism. Carnival-like celebrations in the Caribbean as observed among the enslaved and their free descendants have many origins.[142] Some strands of the tradition can be traced directly to Europe, while others show remarkable consistency with West African traditions.[143] In some cases a theory of parallel evolution is applicable, whereby "similar cultural artifacts can emerge independently in diverse regions." Perhaps more compelling is the creolization paradigm, whereby European traditions blended with imported African culture "to produce a distinctive form of expression,"[144] with no single aspect traceable to an ethnoreligious precedent. Determining the ancestry of Afro-Creole carnival is at best tentative, but the term rightly recognizes that people of African origins formed the majority of the Caribbean population. As such, the Afro-Creole carnival implicitly acknowledges the wealth of African derivatives and, more importantly, the worldviews of slaves and their free descendants.

What, then, did Purim celebrations mean to Suriname's multiethnic enslaved population? If masquerades and communal dances constituted for the African-descendant population crucial life-cycle rituals, including initiations, as they did in early modern West Africa, taking part in masked

Purim celebrations may have been a means by which slaves could inculcate ancestral values to their immediate community and transmit these to their descendants.[145] If most African-born slaves in Suriname spoke mutually unintelligible languages, dance may have functioned as a "performative literacy" and their bodies as a depository of "kinesthetic memory."[146] As we have seen, communal dances of slaves in Suriname were repeatedly outlawed by colonial ordinances since the late seventeenth century. Until it too was outlawed, Purim carousing may have served as a sanctioned outlet through which slaves could invoke or refashion their ancestral masquerade and communal dance traditions or to preserve or create social institutions.

Exuberant Purim celebrations only came under broad public scrutiny in Paramaribo, where the enslaved were among the most enthusiastic participants, circling the Jewish revelers and shouting and singing through the city streets. We may surmise that slaves had more freedom for public displays of animation in Jodensavanne, where violations of colonial ordinances were not as closely scrutinized. There is scattered evidence that some regents there tended to be lax or ineffectual enforcers of festal behavior among slaves and that some Jews and Christian officials even encouraged slave celebrations. The earliest example is from 1780, when the regents of the Mahamad complained about the *bailes de negros* in the savanna that caused inebriation among slaves, some of whom hurled insults at whites, just as Paramaribo's Purim revelers would affront Christians later in the century. To the regents' astonishment, some white Jews had actually encouraged the slaves to celebrate (*festejar*) and on other occasions had incited them to make a racket during slave funerals.[147] The regents resolved to reinforce the aforementioned 1711 colonial ordinance proscribing slave dances during Jewish holidays. Moreover, slaves were permitted to gather only during the nights of their funerals, and only if the decedent's master had received permission from the regents. Dancing and musical instruments were strictly forbidden.[148] The communal minutes do not speak of costumes or masquerade, and Purim is not at all mentioned in the discussion. However, the complaint was lodged on February 21, which in 1780 coincided with the fifteenth of Adar—the day after Purim.

The abolition of Jewish communal autonomy in the Dutch Caribbean colonies in 1825 had an unexpected effect on the unruly, ecumenical celebration of Purim. This decree, legislated throughout the Dutch Caribbean, aimed to make Jews socially equal to other free people by taking away their legal privileges and disabilities, as had already been legislated for the Dutch Republic (but not its colonies) in 1795. Jews in Suriname would no longer belong to an officially recognized ethnonational group but simply be considered followers of a religion, and the colonial government, rather than the Mahamad, would have direct authority over Jews. Given the Mahamad's long tradition of reining Purim in, it is not surprising that its first official response to the retraction of its power related to Hamansfeest, the most common term for Purim in Surinamese almanacs published between 1819 and 1955.[149] The regents decided to repeal all decrees against disorderly Purim behavior, including the ban on masks and "beating Haman" in synagogue. Such decrees not only trespassed their authority (since the dissolution of communal autonomy, "the Collegio must not intervene in what occurs in the neighborhood") but also were unnecessary. The regents noted with contentment the "good behavior of our individuals in the house of God," particularly on the eves of Sabat Zahor and the eve and day of Purim during the Megillah reading. The congregation had apparently internalized the values of "decorum, silence and decency," and the Mahamad was now merely a "church" council, not a corporate group exercising absolute authority over its constituents and their human property.[150] The reign of reining in Purim had ended.

Yet there is a hint in the communal minutes of wishful thinking. As an afterthought, the regents resolved that they would issue a reminder to worshippers of all ages, in both synagogues, on the eves of Sabat Zahor and on Purim before the reading of the Megillah, to uphold decorum and silence and to refrain from striking objects during the recitation of the Megillah and other prayers. Only the *hazan* would be permitted to strike, and even then solely with his foot, and just during the words "Haman the evil, cursed be Haman, cursed be Zeresh, and cursed be the evildoers" (*Amana [sic] rang arur aman, arura zeres & arurim a reshaim*). Violators would be considered as disobedient and disturbers of the holy place and punished accordingly.[151] Although the regents in their statement did not proscribe behavior outside the synagogue, it is tempting to imagine that they would have had ample cause to do just that. By 1825, Purim in Suriname had in fact become the patrimony of Suriname's multiethnic population. The detractors of its pandemonium could do little more than reissue ordinances that had been ineffectual since the late seventeenth century, when the joyful celebrations of Jews and African-origin slaves first began to coincide.

Conclusion

This chapter has argued that the Jewish festival of Purim is a prism through which to understand how precisely the cultural domains of enslaved people and Portuguese Jews in Surinamese society became imbricated. Jews extended their ethnoreligious heritage to unfree people by naming some of their slaves Purim, Harbona, Vashti, or Haman and by allowing their bondmen and women not only their own leisure but also participation in the holiday merrymaking. In their rebellious behavior, whether by challenging masters or mistresses on Jewish holidays, absconding into the wilderness with a Megillah, or synchronizing their outlawed communal celebrations with Jewish festive days, slaves owned by Jews demonstrated an awareness and active understanding of Jewish heritage.[152]

Jonathan Schorsch has perceptively observed that in Suriname and Curaçao, where Jewish institutional life was both highly autonomous and centralized, "slavery was more an affair of the collective community" than it was anywhere else in the Americas.[153] In Suriname in particular, most Portuguese Jewish plantations were clustered in the vicinity of Jodensavanne and Jews "exercised authority over the slaves . . . with a high degree of autonomy" that was recognized and legally reinforced by colonial authorities. Slaves owned by individual Jews were often pooled together to meet the exigencies of harvest time or to tame the ever-encroaching wilderness around the village's public square.[154] In this setting, the "communalism of the masters created and overlapped with a parallel communalism among the slaves."[155] Since their days of rest tended to follow the Hebrew calendar, Africans owned by Jews in the rainforest interior made the celebration of their spiritual traditions, particularly the *watermama* dance, coincide with Jewish holidays. The official, repetitive proscription of these celebratory dances since the late seventeenth century resonates with carnival, which in the circum-Caribbean was often subject to legal bans. Thus the musical and animated slave assemblies in Suriname, prohibited in the colony's placards, were precursors to, if not manifestations of, Surinamese carnivalesque festivities.

Public celebration of Purim reached a new zenith in the early 1800s and, with the participation of Christians and slaves, shows strong signs of having become the colony's carnival, an ecumenical festivity with strong Afro-Creole attributes. The sacred traditions of people of African origins, particularly those relocated from the rainforest interior, perhaps found an outlet

in the raucous celebration of Purim. While there are precedents elsewhere
to Purims that lasted up to fourteen days, notably in Jerusalem, Padua, and
central Europe, it is likely that the prolonging of the holiday in Suriname
was due at least in part to the negotiation of slaves for extended festive
days, particularly those associated with their *banyas*, or Afro-Creole
dances.[156] There are hints, discussed at the beginning of this chapter, that
something similar emerged on Curaçao, the other Dutch Caribbean colony
where Jews officially formed one-third of the white population and exercised a similarly high degree of communal autonomy. As such, Purim as
celebrated in Suriname (and perhaps in Curaçao) is a detailed example of
what Toby Green, in the context of West Africa, has described as "mutual
receptivity."[157] That such reciprocity occurred reminds us that the brutality
of slave society and the general rigidity of its racial categories did not preclude cultural convergence.

The model of social confluence Purim exemplifies, akin to concentric
circles, is an especially useful paradigm for Suriname, where by the early
nineteenth century, as we have seen, several religions and ethnic groups
were often represented within one nuclear family or household, and where
it was not unusual for a single testator to leave legacies to the five or six
major religious groups of the colony.[158] Purim, more than any other Jewish
holiday, presents an opportunity to closely consider a rarely treated aspect
of Caribbean society. This small corner of the social fabric, manifested in
shared cultural performance, more approximates latticework than the separate spheres, ordered upon hierarchy and violence, that most obviously
undergirded daily life in Caribbean slave societies.

At the same time, the public prominence of Purim tells us something
quintessential about the largest Jewish communities of the Dutch Caribbean and their extensive impact on the colonial ethnic landscape as
prestige-bearing minorities. Purim as celebrated in Suriname and Curaçao
is a manifestation, in concentrated form, of the three essential conditions
that characterized local Jews: by the second half of the eighteenth century,
they formed one-third to one-half of the white population, lived in a society
where most residents were both enslaved and of African origin, and enjoyed
an autonomy rooted in legal privileges unparalleled among Jews elsewhere
in the Atlantic World.[159] That it was possible to celebrate Purim ecumeni-
cally and publicly is at least as interesting as the restraints both the colonial
government and local Jewish authorities imposed to rein the Jewish holiday

in. A close examination of Purim, then, allows us to gauge the paradoxical unease with which both parties experienced the liberal treatment accorded Jews.

Much of the historiography of Jews in Christian Europe focuses on Jewish acculturation to the heritage of their Christian neighbors. Works on Jews in the Caribbean often speak of Jewish resistance or vulnerability to acculturation, while other publications seek to find Jewish provenience in Afro-Creole religious systems, implying that Jewish heritage was a powerful force on African-derived cultures.[160] Rather than arguing that Jews or Africans in the Americas were impacted by or, in turn, influenced the heritage of the other, the foregoing exploration of Purim in Suriname encourages us to instead concentrate on religious culture and spiritual traditions as a shared site of leisure activity. Examining such ritual or social activities as sites of "cultures in contact" may avoid the unnuanced cultural-resistance paradigm that seeks to portray Jews or Africans as triumphantly prevailing, against all odds, over assimilatory forces. More importantly, the "cultures in contact" approach is truer to the historical processes themselves and also upholds what decades of sociological and anthropological research have demonstrated.[161] Culture is dynamic and borders between groups are permeable. Focusing on how this cultural confluence took place could challenge a fundamental problem in the interdisciplinary field of Jewish studies, what one reviewer calls "the simplification of insider-outsider divides and relationships."[162]

The observance of the Purim holiday highlights the public prominence of Jews in the Dutch colony and the tensions increased visibility caused after the plantation community relocated from the savanna to the colony's capital city of Paramaribo and attempted to give full expression to their ethnoreligious heritage. The diachronicity of the Surinamese sources allows us to gauge the public nature of Purim as observed in the Dutch colony and successive efforts to contain its attendant unruliness. The behavior associated with this holiday sheds light on the tension inherent in the position Jews occupied in the colony as a white, non-Christian minority: highly privileged while at the same time disdained; apart from other sectors of society, while at the same time overlapping with them. Even though we lack testimony as to the inner thoughts and motivations of those who engaged in Purim festivities, there are hints that the non-Jewish population gave the holiday their own meaning. The enthusiastic participation of slaves suggests

that these individuals used the holiday's rowdier rituals to reenact or refashion their own African-derived traditions of masquerade and communal
dancing.

Finally, Purim as celebrated in the public sphere is an ideal opportunity
to consider what Stephanie Camp, in her study of bondmen in the antebellum South, calls "geographies of containment," referring to spatial and
temporal restrictions on slave mobility.[163] Purim created a rare occasion
after-hours for slaves to venture licitly out of their cabins or shacks, off
their plantations or back alleys, and into the streets. Even as we consider
what appears to be the enthusiastic participation of bondmen in this holiday, we must remember that such scenarios often involved coercion, as
when Christian slaveholders forced Christmas and Easter celebrations upon
their slaves or closely surveilled their revelry in order to contain and control
them, a phenomenon Camp refers to as "paternalistic plantation parties."[164]

But public Purim festivities seem to have diverged from this type of
authoritarian control in that masters engaged in the merriment alongside
their slaves. In this co-participation, neither slaves nor Jews were spectators.
Whereas in some other plantation societies slaves covertly mimicked their
masters and mistresses when it was safe to do so, and owners contemplated,
at a distance, their slaves' festive gatherings, observance of Suriname's
Purim did not involve the gaze of the "other." In this sense, Purim carousing more closely approximates the "illicit dance" or "outlaw gatherings"
that antebellum slaves engaged in to flout authority.[165] Suriname's Purim
created an illusory shared space in which every participant seemed to be an
invited guest. This flattening of social hierarchy helps explain why Purim
was the only Jewish holiday straitjacketed by colonial legislation, its co-
participants to be immediately apprehended, their mobility contained, and
their purses and bodies subject to the "arbitrary correction" of the law.

CHAPTER 7

The Abolition of Communal Autonomy

In July 1825, the Portuguese Jewish communal authorities of Suriname received momentous news. The Dutch monarch Willem I (r. 1815–40) had signed a resolution in early April repealing the special status of the colony's Jews.[1] All the "privileges, licenses, and exceptions" enjoyed by the "adherents of the Israelite religion" in the Dutch West Indian settlements were declared null and void. The decree, at least in stated intent, thereby conferred upon Jews a status equal to that of other settlers (*ingezeten*) in the colonies.[2] Only the ban against marriage with Christians remained in effect.[3] By August, the local newspaper the *Surinaamsche Courant* carried the news for all to see.[4]

The handful of scholars who have examined the abolition of Jewish communal autonomy in Suriname have come to contradictory conclusions. Julien Wolbers argued in 1861 that the special privileges defining Jewish status in the colony were by 1825 no longer necessary, as Jews were already equal to other religious groups.[5] Wieke Vink easily refutes this assertion by focusing on Jewish political disabilities and de facto discrimination by Christians, maintaining that the colony's Jews, and particularly their leaders, "were reluctant to renounce their privileges in exchange for civil rights."[6] Most other scholars who have addressed the abolition of Jewish communal autonomy in the Caribbean have focused on the British sphere. A number have observed that enfranchisement, simultaneously extended to Jews and free people of African descent, pitted the former group against the latter, whose status was raised above that of the Jews by virtue of their Christianity.[7] Although enfranchisement of Jews and free people of slave origins was not as closely linked in Suriname (their respective equalizing laws were not issued at the same time), similar competition arose between them, as Vink has shown. Yet no scholar thus far has considered whether the corporatism of Dutch Caribbean Jewry, ensconced in age-old privileges ratified by consecutive colonial governments, made the Jewish acquisition of equality distinctive in Suriname.

In this chapter, we will focus on the heretofore unexamined minutes of the Portuguese Jewish community for insights into this question, focusing on the social and political status of Portuguese Jews vis-à-vis Ashkenazim, slaves, free people of slave origins, and white Christians in the decade leading up to the pivotal year 1825. We will also explore internal attitudes about the abolition of Jewish autonomy from among the leadership and the laity. Lastly, since Jodensavanne functioned in some ways as a social and political reflection of the colony's Portuguese Jewish community, we will consider the effects of the age of enfranchisement on the Jewish village. Contrary to Wolbers's conclusions, the repeal of the special position of Jews came about not as a result of legal superfluity but because of an overseas mandate that sought to reform colonial society on the basis of social and political equality, ideals that had already been unevenly embraced in the metropole and to some extent, as we have seen, already in Suriname. By 1825, these ideals and their political expression had already manifested in much of western and central Europe, and it is there that we begin.

Jewish Emancipation

"Emancipation" is the widely accepted term for the attainment by Jews of civic and political equality. The designation, first applied in public European discourse to Jews only in 1828, is particularly incongruous when used in a Caribbean context.[8] Comprised of the Latin words meaning "out of ownership," Emancipation in a Jewish framework had nothing to do with slavery. Rather, Jewish Emancipation as it first emerged in Europe in the late eighteenth century involved in principle the removal of both privileges and disabilities, in order to place Jews legally on par with their fellow citizens.[9] Specifically, this meant abolishing Jewish corporatism and, more crucially, extending entitlements hitherto refused.[10] Undergirded by Enlightenment ideologies, and ushered in by the age of revolutions and the emergence of nation-states, Emancipation is considered the most important movement of modern Jewish history.[11] In France, which in 1790 became the first European nation to extend legal equality to Jews, and in many other western European lands, the goal of Jewish Emancipation was to achieve the "civil amelioration" and "regeneration" of Jews and to make them "happier and more useful" to society as a whole.[12]

Viewed in broad strokes, Jewish Emancipation arrived in western Europe in the eighteenth century, in central Europe the following century, and the century thereafter in eastern Europe and Turkey.[13] Traditionally, historical writing on Jewish Emancipation has focused on Europe, and particularly on France, Germany, and Britain.[14] Despite the status of Caribbean colonies as extensions of Europe, very few scholars have considered Jewish Emancipation as it manifested in the region.[15] As more historians broaden their inquiry to Jews living in Europe's overseas possessions and in post-colonial states, it becomes ever more apparent that Jewish Emancipation found highly distinctive expressions in different parts of the globe, highly dependent on the immediate political, social, and historical contexts.[16]

The introduction of Jewish legal parity in the Caribbean was limited to locations where Jews formed an economically significant community, namely Curaçao, Suriname, Barbados, and Jamaica. Decrees similar to the 1825 Dutch enactment had already been issued in the British Caribbean, or soon would be.[17] In Barbados in 1802 and 1820, the local government and Parliament, respectively, attempted to abolish all political disabilities pertaining to Jews, while the "Act for the Relief of His Majesty's Subjects . . . who profess the Hebrew Religion" removed remaining "restraints and disabilities" in 1831.[18] Reforms in Jamaica also began piecemeal, with the repeal in 1826 of an act first issued in 1711 prohibiting the "employment in the several Public Offices . . . of any Jew, Mulatto, Indian, or Negro."[19] As in Barbados, Catholics, Jews, and "free persons of colour" in Jamaica were relieved of their remaining disabilities with the passing in 1831 of the so-called Toleration Laws.[20] In contrast to Europe, the bestowal of legal parity on free persons living in the Caribbean colonies had a marked racial, rather than solely a religious or ethnic, dimension.

The very wording of the Dutch colonial decree of 1825 indicates that Suriname and Curaçao diverged considerably from both Europe and the British overseas possessions. In the Dutch colonies, Jewish Emancipation did not constitute the bestowal of rights hitherto denied, or the relief of restraints and disabilities, but rather the removal of long-standing privileges. As a document of legal demotion, the Surinamese decree was also the polar opposite of Jewish Emancipation as promulgated in the Batavian Republic, which forbade the exclusion of Dutch Jews from all "rights or advantages." Similarly, legislation in Britain and its colonies constituted "relief" or "enfranchisement" rather than a repeal of favors.[21] In Suriname, the necessity of stripping Jews of their special benefits foregrounds the fact that by 1825 their accumulated privileges far outnumbered their legal disabilities. The decree was promulgated during an era of heightened anti-Jewish sentiment in the Dutch colony, which increasingly exposed Jewish corporatism as a disability.

The Ordeal of Jewish Corporatism in Suriname

Scholars have maintained that the mass relocation of Portuguese Jewish planters from the countryside was largely responsible for loosening the hold of the Mahamad over its constituents.[22] They also argue that the collapse of the Jewish plantation heartland helped open the doors to "continual scorn and open dislike" of Jews, with no differentiation drawn between Ashkenazi and Portuguese Jews, who were now both disparaged as kikes (*smousen*), a term once limited to the former group.[23] As Marten Douwes Teenstra noted in 1842, Jews in Suriname were scoffed at not only by Christians but also by slaves. At least rhetorically, the latter regarded Jews as something other than white. If two "Christians" and one Jew walked by a group of slaves, these unfree observers would remark, "Two whites and one Jew."[24]

However, the relocation of rural Jews to the city was just one factor in the transformation of Jewish status, since by the mid-eighteenth century Jews had already lived dispersed in roughly half of Suriname's districts. As we have seen, at least a decade before the economic crisis, most Portuguese Jews in Suriname did not live in Jodensavanne or its riverside surroundings.[25] Arguably more crucial was the fact that in the 1770s, white Christians began to emigrate from Suriname en masse, leaving a gap that was filled by free men of color, many of whom streamed into the upper echelons of colonial society, creating a small but influential elite, most recently examined by Ellen Neslo.[26] The high status of Suriname's Jews began to deflate and incidents of anti-Jewish behavior became more common. Government or private employers often preferred to hire Dutch-educated Afro-Christian men over Jews or Germans.[27]

A few major incidents illustrate how the social descent of Jews was inversely linked to the rise of free people of African descent. During the funeral of Governor Bernard Texier (r. 1779–83), which due to its duration unexpectedly conflicted with the onset of the Jewish Sabbath, a scuffle broke out among Portuguese Jewish and Ashkenazi men. These individuals were attending the ceremony in an official capacity, in their separate companies as members of their respective Jewish civil guards. The Ashkenazim wished to leave the procession to avoid violating the sanctity of Sabbath, while Portuguese Jews insisted on remaining. The conflict resulted in severe blows mutually exchanged. Later, when the Council of Policy convened to discuss an appropriate sanction, officials specifically underscored the "discontent felt by a great many Christian citizens concerning the many privileges given to Jews." The tribunal ruled that Jews were no longer permitted to participate in their capacity as civil guards in any formal functions held in Paramaribo. While the ruling was reversed in response to Jewish protest, problems continued during the inauguration of interim governor Wolphert Jacob Beeldsnijder Matroos (r. 1783–84) later that year. Ashkenazi Jews complained that their company, although permitted to attend, had been placed separately from the other guards, behind the Christians. Implicitly, these Christians included people of African descent.[28] When Jews were once again threatened with exclusion, this time during the inauguration of Governor Jan Gerhard Wichers (r. 1784–90), the leaders of the two Jewish communities noted with horror that their rejection symbolically placed them below people of slave origins, for the militia comprised of free people of African descent would indeed be present. The forced absence of the Jewish companies, they complained, would cause the derision of Jews among the enslaved population.[29]

The plummeting status of Jews was clearly evident to newcomers, as we have seen, including a British official serving in Suriname in 1800 who reported that these pioneering settlers of Suriname were now considered "as the very lowest class of the white people."[30] This remarkable statement implies that Jewishness, regardless of class, bore a heavier stigma than being a poor white Christian.[31] Indeed, Henry Bolingbroke, an Englishman who relocated to Suriname in 1807, noted that the Dutch there failed to regard Jews "with a liberal benevolence." The two groups did not mingle socially and governors routinely snubbed the "wives of the richest Jews" by refusing to invite them to official festivals and balls, a phenomenon also observed in contemporaneous Jamaica.[32] In such an environment, corporate status invited negative discrimination of Jews both as individuals and as a body.

Under British intermediary rule (1799–1802, 1804–16), existing laws could not adequately regulate the access of Jews to civil and political society. Aside from the Jewish privileges, painstakingly preserved and copied by

generations of Surinamese Jews, colonial laws preceding the British Interregnum had never been systematically registered. Suriname's humid climate led to the disintegration of both archival and printed records. The
municipal officials who had been in charge of these legal documents before
1799 rapidly turned over and were either uninterested in or incapable of
overseeing the documents. Nor did the situation improve under British
rule. During the Interregnum, the governorship of Suriname was over-
turned eight times and no major laws were introduced into the colony, save
those hinging on the treatment of slaves.[33]

When Dutch rule was restored to Suriname in 1816, the monarchy
issued the "Government Regulations of Suriname" (*Regeerings-reglement
van Suriname*). These ordinances broadened the powers of the governor
and significantly weakened the influence of the Council of Policy, traditionally composed of wealthy Christian planters. The ordinances introduced a new Council of Civil Justice, comprised of officials from the
Netherlands who could make little sense of existing legislation. Part of
the problem was that Surinamese law, with its layers of Roman, old
Dutch, and colonial legislation, constituted a "veritable labyrinth" and,
in fact, a "veritable pool of injustice."[34] No compendium of Surinamese
law was ever published prior to 1869.[35] This state of affairs made Jews
extremely vulnerable to arbitrary discrimination, which intensified as
soon as Dutch rule was restored.

In 1816, the director of a local public school, C. A. Batenburg,
informed the Jewish communities that their children could not attend
without special permission from the school's commission. The regents of
the respective Jewish congregations presented an allied petition to the
governor, which he approved.[36] However, Batenburg and his successors
repeatedly violated it, first in 1819 then again in 1827.[37] Breaches during the
latter year came just after the First Parnas of the Portuguese synagogue
suggested that widowed mothers dependent on the communal charity
chest and too poor to provide their children with an education had "the
same right to enroll their children in the colony's public school [*staat
school*] as children of other religious persuasions."[38] But when these indigent women approached the school commissioner, Mr. Klint, he tried
to discourage them by insisting they file a formal request.[39] Whether
Klint's aversion was reactionary against Jews or poverty, or a mixture of
both, cannot be gauged from the account, but the Mahamad immediately sensed that the rights of these individuals had been violated and

appointed Moses Cohen Nassy, one of their leaders, to intercede. When confronted, Klint apologized for what he claimed was the ladies' misunderstanding of his earlier statement and agreed to dispatch a letter to the school with instructions to admit the orphaned children immediately.[40] The chilly reception accorded to Jews also extended to the teaching staff. When the Surinamese Portuguese regents received an invitation from Batenburg in 1818 to attend the distribution of school prizes, they unanimously declined, given that there were no "teachers of our nation there [in the schools] and considering the insults received various times."[41]

Nor were such slights limited to the schools. During the formal procession in 1818 celebrating the forty-fifth birthday of Willem I, Jewish leaders were called up last among the representatives of the different religions and were also the final group summoned among the most minor clerks or servants of public offices. The Portuguese regents found such frequent and public affronts humiliating to their Mahamad and to every Jew. Portuguese and Ashkenazi Jewish leaders, they recalled, had together approached the governor with their complaint in 1816, gesturing toward the Dutch constitution of 1814, which guaranteed dignity to leaders of all officially recognized religions. In their petition, the regents noted that since Jews constituted two-thirds of the white population of the colony, were "very ancient" (as pioneers in the colony), and were always "co-citizens," they therefore merited a place directly after representatives of the Reformed Protestant religion.[42] These assertions of entitlement are redolent of the confidence Surinamese Jews had enjoyed during the ancien regime, when their privileges had indeed elevated them in many respects above Lutherans and Catholics.

To the surprise of the regents, the governor remained unimpressed by these arguments. As the Portuguese Jewish minutes taker noted, he replied noncommittally that he hoped the "nation" (i.e., Jews) would be better treated, a choice of words which, if faithfully recounted, would suggest that the highest authority of the land continued to conceive of Jews as a state-within-a-state, vulnerable to negative discrimination, rather than as members of a religious group entitled to equal rights.[43]

The Jewish regents of both communities were not only concerned with symbolic relegation. The "Government Regulations of Suriname," introduced in 1816, contained an ordinance that implicitly disenfranchised Jews. Article 26 stipulated that members of the Court of Justice, the second most powerful office in the land, be nominated "no matter which *Christian* faith they have" (italics added). Local Jews engaged their coreligionists in Amsterdam to intervene before King Willem I, after which a mixed delegation of Ashkenazi and Portuguese Jews in Suriname and the fatherland presented him with a joint petition.[44] The king affirmed that the clause should be interpreted as "no matter which *faith* they have" (italics added).[45] The result of that negotiation clearly illustrates the wide gap between de jure and de facto discrimination. The Jewish communities had to wait fourteen years before article 26 lived up to its implicit promise. In 1836, Solomon de la Parra became the first Jew to be elected to the colonial court.[46] Parra, scion of a Portuguese Jewish planter family that had first settled in Suriname in the seventeenth century, was in the 1820s by some accounts the largest landholder of the colony.[47] In collaboration with his brother Samuel Haim de la Parra, he owned five sugar manors, four coffee and cotton plantations, and two timber estates.[48] As we shall see, Parra was also a symbol of the gradual breakdown of boundaries between the two Jewish communities.

Portuguese Jews and Ashkenazim

The corporatism of Surinamese Jews was also affected by changes to the Jewish community in the fatherland. Jews in the Batavian Republic, 45,000 to 50,000 strong, were emancipated in 1796. The vast majority had opposed Emancipation, fearing the end of their communal autonomy and religious freedom. The introduction of parity for the republic's Jews brought no improvement in their socioeconomic position, largely because of backlash from the non-Jewish population, which included the de facto barring of Jews from most occupations.[49] On February 26, 1814, Willem I (then prince of Orange-Nassau) effectively restored Jewish communal autonomy to the Ashkenazi and Portuguese congregations in the United Netherlands after a brief imposition of the French imperial Central Consistory system.[50] He also resolved to reorganize Dutch Jewry by dividing it into twelve major synagogues. Each synagogue was appointed its own chief rabbi, and a Chief Commission of Israelite Affairs, operating under the authority of the Ministry of Religious Affairs, and installed to supervise internal Jewish governance and the implementation of governmental decrees. The commission, which included two delegates from Suriname, was organized to support the acculturation and assimilation of Dutch Jews.[51] This structural reorganization radically diminished the authority and independence of Surinamese Jewish leaders.[52]

One of the first ordinances the Chief Commission of Israelite Affairs promulgated directed Jews in Suriname and Curaçao to drop the "Jewish" and "communal" aspects of their identities. They were to discard their traditional congregational names "High German Jewish Community" (Hoogduitsche Joodsche Gemeente te Suriname) and "Portuguese Jewish Community" (Portugeesche Joodsche Gemeente te Suriname). Henceforth the Portuguese Jewish nation would be the "Netherlands Portuguese Israelite Head Synagogue" (Nederlandsch Portugeesche Israelitische Hoofdsynagoge te Suriname), while the High German Jewish nation would be called the "Netherlands Israelite Head Synagogue" (Nederlandsche Israelitische Hoofdsynagoge te Suriname).[53] The label "Israelite" in place of "Jew" was a carryover from the annexation of the Netherlands by France, which ruled the land from 1795 to 1813.[54] The change from ethnonational to religious identity represents a concession to the ideological program of Jewish Emancipation whereby Jewishness was confined to the status of a religion and to the realm of the synagogue and its "ethnic" dimension eliminated.

The "nationalization" of both Surinamese communities as "Netherlandic" communicates subtle differences. By making a Netherlandic identity the norm, the reform erased the Jewish ethnic distinction from the Ashkenazim but retained it for the Portuguese Jews. If the former "High German Jews" were now "Netherlands Israelites," Portuguese Jews still preserved their ethnonational differentiator as "Netherlands *Portuguese* Israelites" (italics added). The name changes unwittingly gave the impression that Ashkenazi Jews were more Dutch, more socially integrated into the polity than their Portuguese coreligionists, a reality that was truer for Suriname than for the fatherland, where most Jews were economically marginal through the nineteenth century and spoke primarily Yiddish. By contrast, Ashkenazi Jews in the colony had always passed their wills in Dutch, kept their communal minutes in that language, and never required an interpreter.[55] Whereas in the 1780s, David Nassy sneered at the "ridiculous manners," "superstitions," and "bigotry" of his Ashkenazi coreligionists, by the early 1800s the "High German Jewish" community had gained considerable influence and esteem in the colony and outnumbered Portuguese Jews.[56] By the 1840s, Portuguese Jews constituted under 40 percent of Surinamese Jews who expressed an ethnic affiliation.[57]

Despite their corporate separation, the boundaries between the two communities were never rigidly reinforced. Over the course of the eighteenth century, Ashkenazim were permitted by the Portuguese Jewish bylaws to request that Portuguese cantors officiate in their synagogue.[58] Marriage between the two Jewish groups was never forbidden in Suriname, only disincentivized, and by the last quarter of the eighteenth century was clearly on the rise. The Portuguese community had since 1754 lowered their constituents to the status of *congregantes* should they marry Ashkenazim, while the latter had reciprocated since at least 1772.[59] Intramarriage between the two groups, however, remained relatively rare. In his sample of marriages contracted in the Portuguese Jewish community between 1788 and 1818, Robert Cohen found only five Portuguese men who married *tudescas*, and three Portuguese women who wed Ashkenazi men. All of these unions were forged in the last decade of his study.[60] The relatively small incidence of documented intramarriage remained the dominant pattern in subsequent generations. A book of Jewish marriage contracts dating from 1853 to 1870 and 1896 to 1905 indicates that 22 percent of unions were cross-communal.[61] Yet a census report suggests that the binary division of Suriname's Jewish community was becoming less meaningful to a significant percentage of members, a possible outgrowth, as discussed in Chapter 4, of the intraethnic Jewish mobility of Eurafrican Jews. In 1845, for example, 1,365 persons were registered as belonging to either the Ashkenazi or the Portuguese Jewish community. Of these, 145 (or almost 11 percent) were listed simply as "Israelites."[62]

One consequence of Ashkenazi numerical ascendance in Suriname, and the economic rise of a few of their families, was the increasing tendency of the two communities to ally politically before the colonial authorities. Previously, Portuguese *parnassim* had rebuffed any overtures of Ashkenazi leaders to join forces. In 1784, during the aforementioned inauguration ceremony of Governor Jan Gerhard Wichers, some Jews appearing with their civil guard began to argue with military personnel about proper placement in the procession. The colonial authorities ordered their slaves to beat the Jews and banned the latter from participating in the event. Two days later, the Ashkenazi *parnassim* asked their Portuguese counterparts to jointly protest this humiliating treatment. The Portuguese regents demurred, gesturing to the privileges that *their* ancestors had secured for all Jews and warning that such a coalition could give the Council of Policy the impression that Jews were colluding against it.[63]

The political instability introduced by the British Interregnum made intraethnic cooperation an increasingly compelling option. In May 1805, to mark the birthday of King George III, Lieutenant Governor William Carlyon Hughes ordered all burghers to appear in arms to celebrate the event. However, the occasion coincided with the Jewish Festival of Weeks (Sebuoth) and attendance would therefore have been a violation of Jewish law.[64] Whereas in a previous era Portuguese Jews typically reacted to the infringement of their privileges independently, now they joined together with their Ashkenazi coreligionists in deliberations. The two Mahamadot agreed to present a joint remonstration, accompanied by a copy of the Jewish privileges, both translated into the English language.[65] The two communities again collaborated in 1819, after a number of Ashkenazi *parnassim* overheard two Christian butchers using the anti-Jewish slur *smous* among themselves. Rather than interpreting the insult as directed solely at Ashkenazim, which they might have done given the historic specificity of the term, the Portuguese regents resolved to suspend these two employees.[66]

Arguably more far-reaching than political and religious collaboration and occasional intramarriage was a cultural blending that was as pervasive as it was subtle. This mingling is clearly seen in the realm of Hebrew pronunciation. Portuguese Jews and Ashkenazim possessed two distinct traditions of intoning the ancient language. While Portuguese Jews tended to emphasize the last syllable of the word, Ashkenazim stressed the penultimate. Certain consonants, notably the *sin/shin* and *sadik/tsadik*, were also intoned differently, while Portuguese Jews never aspirated the fifth letter of the Hebrew alphabet, *heh*. Thus, as mentioned in the "Notes on Usage" section of this book, Portuguese Jews pronounced the names of Suriname's Jewish places of worship as Berahá VeSalóm, Sedék VeSalóm, Nevé Salóm, and Darhé Jesarím, rather than Berácha VeShálom, Tsédek VeShálom, Néveh Shálom, and Dárhe Jeshárim (accent marks added). They intoned the family name of a Palestinian emissary who visited Suriname in 1773 as aCohén, rather than HaCóhen, and the Festival of Weeks as Sebuóth, rather than Shavú'os, and the Jewish Sabbath as Sabát and not Shábbos.

Before the turn of the nineteenth century, the infiltration of the Ashkenazi pronunciation manifested only occasionally. In 1776, for example, the minutes taker who recorded Rabbi Aron ACohen's request for provisions for the road wrote down "Tseda-Ladereh" rather than Seda-Ladereh (provisions for the road).[67] The Ashkenazi rendition increased steadily over time. At the turn of the eighteenth century, *misva*, the Portuguese-inflected Hebrew word for "commandment," was often rendered as *mitsva*.[68] Rather than a conscious process of outside influence, the subtle transformation in Hebrew pronunciation among Portuguese Jews resulted in confusion about what constituted the "authentic" inflection of the Hebrew language.

In 1812 and again in 1816, a serious upset developed over the proper pronunciation of particular words recited during the cantillation of the Torah,
the Five Books of Moses handwritten in the form of a scroll.[69] Confusion
arose because the Torah scroll never includes *ta'amim,* the diacritical and
subcritical marks that indicate both the melody and the correct syllable on
which to place the emphasis in a word. Although these marks were present
in some printed Bibles, nineteenth-century Jewish cantors, like their predecessors, learned the *ta'amim* largely through oral traditions that had been
passed down over the course of two thousand years.[70] While this oral tradition is now standardized, in the past it could vary, sometimes unintentionally
producing an alternative meaning of a word (parallel to the pronunciations
of the noun "desert" and the verb "to desert" in the English language).

Beginning in the 1810s, Portuguese cantors and regents became deeply
concerned about the emphasis of certain syllables. Their initial preoccupation with the preservation of the congregation's "ancient custom" soon
morphed into an anxiety about correct grammar.[71] Were the biblical
phrases supposed to be pronounced as "Béne Israel, Pérre Betneha, and
Débar Echad," or with the emphasis on the ultimate syllable, as in "Bené
Israel, Perré Betneha, and Debár Echad" ("sons of Israel," "the fruit of her
womb," "one word")?[72] The tumult resulted in the dismissal of cantors
Joseph Haim Baruh Louzada Junior and Joseph de Isaac Bueno de Mesquita, both of whom were accused of introducing "innovations." Their dis-
grace followed a flurry of correspondence on both sides of the Atlantic
Ocean, including an opinion from the *haham* of Amsterdam's Portuguese
Jewish community, and sworn testimony by Ashkenazi and Portuguese
cantors in Suriname.[73] As an aggregate, the depositions recorded by the
Mahamad suggest that there was no standard pronunciation of Hebrew in
the Surinamese Jewish community by the 1810s and that some cantors and
teachers, long deceased at the time of the controversy, had used both traditions interchangeably.

Although the polemic was consistently couched in terms of the sanctity
of established custom and, ultimately, correct grammar, it bears all the
markings of divergent Portuguese and Ashkenazi pronunciations of
Hebrew. As Surinamese Jews were themselves aware, the differences centered on the grammatical rules of *milhel* (מלעל) and *milrang* (מלרע), according to which the emphasis is placed on the penultimate or ultimate syllable,
respectively. While Ashkenazi Jews favored the former (i.e., the Jewish holiday of "Púrim"), Iberian-origin Jews favored the latter (i.e., "Purím").

Unbeknownst to Surinamese Jews, the linguistic dispute between the two Jewish groups first emerged in the early 1800s as an internal disagreement among central European Jewish Enlighteners (*maskilim*), who argued that the Hebrew pronunciation used by "Sephardim," as Ashkenazi Jews called Portuguese and Spanish Jews, was not only correct but also cultured. The polemic soon migrated to eastern Europe and Palestine, where the so-called "Sephardic" pronunciation ultimately triumphed as the Hebrew vernacular.[74]

The solicitation by the Portuguese regents of potentially authoritative opinions from the Ashkenazi community was entirely new in the Surinamese minutes. Although the regents were intent on determining the correct mode of pronunciation on the weight of "ancient practice" or correct Hebrew grammar, they had unwittingly stumbled upon the incremental result of cultural exchanges between two ethnic Jewish groups over the previous century and a half. The gradual attrition of the Portuguese language and the steady rise of Dutch and Sranan in both Jewish communities had made Portuguese Jews especially sensitive to, if not threatened by, variations in Hebrew pronunciation.

When the regents voted by a margin of 5 to 1 to irrevocably suppress the *milhel* intonation (which in fact represents the correct cantillation in the words they offered as examples), they did so with the intention of maintaining "every purity of pronunciation, according to the dictates of grammar." Violators would be banned from the reader's lectern and considered as "disruptors of the decency required in a holy congregation."[75] It is especially ironic that Portuguese Jewish leaders chose to displace their linguistic panic onto Hebrew, a language of which they (like most Portuguese Jews) were notoriously ignorant.[76] Nor did any of the regents seem to note the irony that the Ashkenazi accent had by then widely permeated the Portuguese Jewish inflection of Hebrew. The word *misva* ("commandment") was routinely pronounced as *mitsva*, and the very names of the congregations had shifted from the historic Portuguese pronunciation (Beraha VeSalom, Sedek VeSalom, and Neveh Salom) to the Ashkenazi inflection (Beracha VeShalom, Tzedek VeShalom, and Neveh Shalom).[77]

Around the same time, similar hysteria over proper articulation emerged in the Portuguese Jewish community of Curaçao. Amsterdam-born Jeosuah Piza, who began serving as the community's cantor in 1815, was accused of cantorial innovations, including the pronunciation of the blessing over the wine as *boré peri haga*fen ("He who created the fruit of the vine"), instead of *boré peri hague*fen, a clear reflection of the divergent Ashkenazi and Portuguese pronunciations.[78] Like Louzada, Piza was suspended from his post in December 1818 on the charge of introducing forbidden innovations. Historian Marten Douwes Teenstra, who attributed Piza's dismissal to not pronouncing "a certain comma very well,"[79] failed to appreciate the symbolic significance of language and inflection as the cultural boundaries between Ashkenazi and Portuguese Jews melted away.

Gradually, the de facto blurring of intraethnic boundaries found reinforcement in law. In 1813, in the waning years of the British Interregnum, Semuel Haim de Mordehai de la Parra married an Ashkenazi Jewess named Hanna Marcus Samson. In accordance with communal regulations regarding intramarriages, Parra was demoted to *congregante* status. After the Portuguese regents rejected his appeal to be restored to his original position, Parra turned to Governor Bonham, who not only ordered Parra restored to his *jahid* status but also mandated the abolition of the demotion decree among Portuguese Jews.[80] For the sake of "peace and quiet," Ashkenazi Jews then asked the governor to abolish the parallel decree in their own community as well.[81] However, the ordinances lost their validity after the restoration of Dutch sovereignty in the colony in 1816. A resolution passed by Governor Abraham de Veer in 1822 again formally abolished the distinctions between the two congregations. The Portuguese Mahamad did not heed them until 1828, when Judit Meyers, widow of Eliao da Fonseca, petitioned the General Procurator for permission to return to her native congregation, the Netherlandic Israelites in Suriname. The Portuguese regents had no choice but to obey the official's demand.[82] Surinamese Jews thus continued to enjoy a high level of de facto autonomy, but lay Jews were ever more at liberty to bring their complaints to the colonial government and thereby reinforce Jewish communal conformity to new colonial laws, however arbitrarily these laws manifested.

The formal dissolution of Portuguese Jewish corporatism in 1825 further tested the borderlines between the two communities. In 1827, Egbert van Emden, a Jew from the "Israelites of the Netherlands," lost his wife, Gracia, who had been born into the "Israelite Portuguese" community of the Batavian Republic. He requested not only that she be buried in the Jodensavanne Cemetery but also that he and his son, both Ashkenazim, be interred at her side.[83] This practice violated the age-old Surinamese Jewish tradition whereby the child of a legitimate union inherited the subethnic identity of his or her father. The status of Gracia as the daughter of the wealthy Solomon de la

Parra no doubt had much to do with the granting of Emden's request. Foreign birth may also have played in Emden's favor. He had arrived in the colony in 1818 at the age of nineteen. Whereas in a previous era, status as a native-born "child of the land" (*filho da terra*) afforded certain privileges over the recently arrived, Emden's Dutch birth may have now elevated his position in the colony.[84] During a formal meeting, the *parnassim* could find no explicit impediment to Emden's request in the existing Jewish communal regulations of the Batavian Republic.[85] Tellingly, practice in the metropole now held primacy over Creole Jewish tradition, at least in this case.

Only after the funeral did the Ashkenazi community voice any protest, not to dispute Gracia's final resting place but to claim the freewill offerings raised on her behalf. The Portuguese Mahamad assented to this claim without recorded friction, suggesting a deference to local tradition after all.[86] Ostensibly, an ideological change informed the regents' meek reaction to the request for burial. They found that "even though both congregations are divided and separate one from the other, . . . in the [Jewish] religion there does not exist the least minimal difference; rather, the ancient disagreements between the two Israelite congregations over the course of time, the animus and discord, are disintegrating."[87] Yet the leaders were willing to go only so far, declaring their resolution to be "without consequence for the future."[88] Whereas burial reform, as introduced by Jewish leaders on behalf of their African-origin coreligionists beginning in 1802, unequivocally introduced racial equality in law among all Jews, its ethnic counterpart remained a privilege of the wealthy.

The integration of Ashkenazim into the Portuguese community was also manifest in the synagogue. In 1826, the Portuguese Mahamad resolved to designate six central benches in Paramaribo's Sedek VeSalom for various "distinguished persons," including officials of the Ashkenazi synagogue Neveh Salom, each of whom were to be given the title of "the exalted magnate" (*agebir anehela*).[89] In December 1827, the Portuguese Mahamad decided to reserve a seat for Egbert van Emden in the center of the six benches between the columns that were appointed for former regents (*adjuntos*) and other "distinguished persons," for his use whenever he came to congregate in either of the Portuguese Jewish synagogues. The gesture was to show gratitude for the "continual services and assistance Emden had given the congregation, with no demand for payment and without being asked, and for frequenting the Portuguese synagogues since his arrival in the colony."[90] The placement of Emden in an honorary seat signaled the political primacy *tudescos* were gaining over their coreligionists. Much of this prestige rested upon their political activism in the fatherland on behalf of the Jewish community.

The Repeal of Jewish Privileges

As we have seen, even before the repeal of Jewish privileges, the legal status of Jews in Suriname during the first decades of the nineteenth century was uncertain. The abolition of Jewish communal autonomy, looming on the horizon by the 1810s, would mean that Jews would have no legal precedence protecting their new status. Whereas previously Jews had petitioned government officials, usually successfully, on the strength of legal traditions that stretched back to the 1660s, now neither Jews nor colonial officials had any legal antecedents to fall back on, and it was unclear what the consequences would be if the governor or his subordinates failed to reinforce laws of equality newly promulgated in the fatherland or in the colonies.

This ambiguity helps explain why, as Wieke Vink notes, Surinamese Jewish leaders "did not embrace emancipation wholeheartedly." When Dutch rule was restored to Suriname in 1816, and the abolition of Jewish communal autonomy became a distinct possibility, Jews "held back, fearing a discrepancy between theoretical emancipation in the law books, and daily practice in Suriname."[91] When the royal intention became clear, the regents of the two Jewish communities penned a joint petition to Governor Van Panhuys, asking him to retain their privileges. The governor indicated that the old favors enjoyed by Jews were "a hindrance to the maintenance of order and proper administration of justice in the colony" and that new privileges should be drafted and dispatched to the king for approval. The leaders of the respective communities then arranged several meetings among their members to discuss the Jewish privileges and dispatched letters to "their brothers in Europe," requesting intervention.[92]

As we have seen, article 26 of the "Government Regulations of Suriname," promulgated in 1816, allowed Jews to serve on the Council of Justice for the first time in the colony's history. The colonial government used the law to pressure Jews into relinquishing their communal autonomy. In December 1816, Governor Cornelis Reinhard Vaillant invited the *parnassim* of both Surinamese congregations to a meeting in his mansion during which he asked them, as a token of their gratitude for article 26, to forfeit their collective privileges.[93] As reported in the Portuguese minutes, the Jewish leaders diplomatically responded that they were not in a position to concede without first notifying the members and *adjuntos* of each "nation," and furthermore, that without the authority of the Dutch monarch (who had restored independence to the Netherlands in 1813), they could not break their oaths concerning a privilege that had been granted to the Jewish community with His Majesty's approval through the communal ordinances.[94] Rather than deal with the controversy head-on, Portuguese Jewish governance completely broke down after the First Parnas refused to convene a meeting and a few lower-ranking *parnassim* who were present during a subsequent meeting blocked the issue from the agenda.[95] Finally, in 1819, leaders from the two communities agreed in principle to the king's request, but only in order to remove the "vain and false pretext" among Christians that corporate status disqualified Jews from elective office.[96]

The debilitation of Jewish privileges had already begun with the onset of British rule in 1799, which introduced even more legal uncertainty than the usual inauguration of a new Dutch colonial governor. At the installment of each British intermediary governor, Surinamese Jewish leaders dispatched a congratulatory epistle with appeals that their privileges be continued.[97] At the reception honoring inaugural Governor Green in 1804, he and his entourage were led into the judicial chamber of the Mahamad, where a formal meeting was held. The regents presented the governor with a copy of their "ecclesiastic and political privileges," ratified by the Dutch sovereign and the States General. They explained the historical origins of these privileges and institutions and spoke of their attachment to Jodensavanne, "where they founded their synagogue and cemetery, where the bones of their ancestors" rested. They then asked the governor to preserve their privileges, promising to contribute to the well-being of the colony. According to the Portuguese minutes, the governor and his police commissioners responded "energetically," communicating their satisfaction with the Jews and promising to recommend to the monarch "the retention of Jewish privileges and immunities."[98] Six different British governors ruled Suriname over the course of the Interregnum, two of them for less than a year, and the colony's Jews had to repeat the protocol multiple times.[99]

After the departure of Governor Green in 1805, no additional state visits to Jodensavanne were recorded until 1822.[100] At this final meeting, the precarious status of Jewish communal autonomy was never more discernible. As if to scrutinize the advisability of the privileges, Governor Abraham de

Veer required leaders to have ready for his perusal all documents concerning their status as ratified in the fatherland. Finally, Governor De Veer made the purpose of the meeting clear: Did the Jews wish to maintain their privileges?[101] The Jewish leaders replied in the affirmative. They and the governor then engaged in a lengthy deliberation over amending the *ascamot*. The new ordinances were finally approved in February 1823, the last time a colonial power would affirm the communal privileges of Suriname's Jews.[102]

Wieke Vink calls the British Interregnum a "temporary reprieve" for the inevitable emancipation of Suriname's Jews, given that Jews in the Batavian Republic had already received civil and political equality in 1796.[103] The inexorable advance of Jewish Emancipation helps explain why the immediate reaction of the Portuguese Jewish regents was one not of protest, like that of the *parnassim* in the Batavian Republic, but of resignation to a foregone conclusion. Their first written response to the Emancipation decree of 1825 was to lend their "total, complete obedience" to the monarch.[104]

In the weeks that followed, the recording secretary of Suriname's Portuguese Jewish community registered no explicit shock, disappointment, or disagreement, only confusion. All of the questions pertained to the loss of privileges. Would a Jew previously appointed as treasurer of the Portuguese Jewish Orphan Chamber be automatically dismissed from his post? What of the Jewish jurators, the sworn officials who since the late seventeenth century were empowered to translate and draw up legal documents for Portuguese Jews?[105] How should Portuguese Jewish leaders record the legal transfer of property in Jodensavanne between Jewish parties?[106] To what degree, if at all, should the Mahamad continue to follow the communal bylaws (*ascamot*)? The colonial government was as uncertain as the Jews themselves, and no response was forthcoming. Lacking specific instructions, Portuguese Jewish leaders decided to assume the continuing validity of their communal ordinances, including the assessment and collection of taxes.[107]

Although scholars often employ the term "autonomy" synonymously with Jewish corporatism, there is a legal difference between the two conditions, as became clear after 1825. A community need not have formal corporate status to experience autonomy. The decree of Emancipation in Suriname abolished Jewish corporatism, but it did not deprive Jews of their de facto license to self-rule, a phenomenon paralleled in the fatherland after 1796.[108] The abolition of Jewish corporatism in Suriname, therefore, did not bring significant structural changes. The ordinance of 1825 explicitly preserved for Jews the privilege of administering their own communities as religious organizations. Colonial authorities appointed a committee from among the *parnassim* already in office to implement the changes regulating the community's religious functions. Solomon de la Parra, reputedly the colony's largest landowner, David Bueno de Mesquita, Abraham de Leon (soon replaced at his request by Samuel Fernandes and Moses Nahar), and Abraham Monsanto Fils continued on as the community's heads.[109] In the Ashkenazi community, Joel Gomperts, Urij Meyer Arons, D. M. Sanches, and M. A. Keyzer were tasked with announcing the royal decree in their synagogue and in the colonial newspapers.[110] In late 1826, the Portuguese Jewish community received orders from the governor that the existing *parnassim* remain in place and follow communal regulations until new ones were approved.[111] A year after the promulgation of Jewish Emancipation, Portuguese Jewry was still basically functioning as if it maintained all of its former privileges.[112]

New regulations were finally approved by the Minister of Colonies and the Minister of Religious Affairs in 1842 and 1843, respectively, but they were never enforced in Suriname due to "their incompatibility with local conditions." The ensuing disputes among the various authorities in Suriname and the fatherland, and the sheer distance between the Dutch Republic and its colony, postponed the promulgation of new communal regulations for another half century. In effect, Surinamese Jews prevailed in safeguarding their communal autonomy, so long as their behavior did not contravene local colonial policy.[113] The effective retention of communal autonomy also meant that Jewish laypersons would continue to subvert their leaders and appeal to the governor for more favorable rulings.

Integration from the Bottom

While the corporate functioning of Jews remained largely intact, the integration of Jews into broader, Creole society continued apace. Integration into the white Christian population, however, remained rare. Jewish conversion to Christianity was unusual in Suriname. In 1817, rumors circulated that David and Ester Vieira, Portuguese Jews resident in the colony, had been baptized under the auspices of the Christian minister R. Austin.[114] The regents' initial ignorance of the conversion and the attention the case received in the communal minutes are both indications that leaving the

Jewish fold was a highly unusual and perhaps also covert act in the colony.[115] Meanwhile, the adoption of Judaism by whites was almost unheard of. The only exception registered in the communal minutes pertains to Rebekah Lynch Purdy, a white Methodist who had married a Surinamese Portuguese Jew in New York and in 1820 converted to Judaism in Suriname, becoming Ester Ribca Purdy. The couple later returned to New York where they reentered the Christian community and died as Christians.[116]

While integration into the white Christian community signified a one-way street directed toward the abandonment of Judaism, absorption of Jews into the majority, African-origin population had a better chance of resulting in the retention of Jewish identity, as we have seen. This phenomenon highlights the divergence of the Jewish integration process in Suriname, in comparison to the experience of most European Jews. The mandate for Jewish integration into European societies after 1790 embodied a narrative of ascent.[117] Emancipation would render Jews economically productive, gradually lift them out of their systemic poverty, and foster their assimilation into the Christian middle class. In Suriname, however, Jewish integration to a certain extent followed a narrative of descent. Rather than convert en masse to Christianity, intermarry with white Christians, or, as was the case in Germany over the course of the nineteenth century, enter the middle class, Jews of the Caribbean displayed their ability to integrate by continuing to produce progeny with the majority African-origin population, in some ways a social demotion.

The steady improvement of the legal status of African descendants in Suriname increased the likelihood that these unions would be formalized. Since the seventeenth century, free people of slave origins faced successive ordinances restricting their lives, including restraints on freedom of movement, exclusion from the purchase and sale of dram, and mandates to distinguish their sartorial and leisure habits from those of slaves. In 1775, free *negers* were stripped of their right to nominate members to the Council of Policy, while freeborn persons of slave origins who possessed an institutionalized religion retained it.[118] The ordinance of 1761 instructing manumitted persons to show respect for whites and banning them from slave dances (*baljaaren*) explicitly noted that these parvenus in other respects enjoyed equal rights to the freeborn.[119] In 1828, just three years after the abolition of Jewish communal autonomy, the metropolitan authorities passed a law stating that all manumitted people (*vrije lieden*) who were burghers of Suriname, regardless of religion or color, would be considered equal according to civil law.[120] The decree also made manumitted people eligible for government positions and (at least by the letter of the law) confirmed the extension of this right to Jews. For the manumitted, this meant entrance into the new administrative elite, joining the white-dominated Dutch Reformed and Lutheran churches, and the possibility of marrying into the white elite without causing a sensation.[121]

Manumitted and freeborn children who were brought into the Jewish fold experienced enfranchisement through two intersecting streams: the bestowal of civic and political equality upon the colony's Jews as a whole and the gradual repeal of communal laws that discriminated against Jews of known slave origins. The first, legislation culminating in the abolition of communal autonomy in 1825, did not theoretically distinguish between Jews of divergent ancestries. The second stream accomplished the gradual but complete legal integration of free, African-origin Jews into the Jewish community. Changes began in 1802, as we have seen, when the Portuguese Jewish regents decided to repeal all distinctions in burial rites between *jehidim* and *congregantes*.[122] In 1820, these rulers applied the principle of equality to location of interment, proclaiming that all ritually immersed *congregantes* would be buried throughout the Portuguese Jewish cemeteries "without stipulation of the place of their graves."[123] In May 1841, all remaining legal distinctions between *congregantes* and *jehidim* were eliminated in both the Portuguese and Ashkenazi communities "in accordance with the spirit of times of the present age."[124] Surinamese Jews persisted as a community apart, maintaining their social position just below that of other whites. But manumissions and the progressive enfranchisement of free people of color also meant that the status of emancipated Jews more closely approximated that of former slaves than ever before.

This tension provides context for the case of the mysterious Abigail de Oro. On August 30, 1825, Benjamin ACohen, then serving as First Parnas of the Portuguese Jewish community, and his wife, Ribca Abarbanel, wrote a formal letter to the Mahamad announcing the birth of their daughter thirteen and a half years previously, on January 28, 1812. The couple explained that they had simply forgotten to register Abigail's birth and hoped now to do so, and be relieved of the late penalty.[125] A week later, the regents received two additional letters containing a competing narrative of what had actually transpired. In the first letter, Ribca's stepfather, Daniel Jessurun Lobo, claimed that the child in question was a foundling procreated by a mulattress (*mulattin*) named Lizie van Fernandes, who was by implication free. The

second letter, submitted by Ribca's brother Menaseh Abarbanel and her
stepbrother Benjamin Jessurun Lobo, offered sworn testimony that Ribca
had never been pregnant in her life.[126]

Ultimately, the regents determined that the allegations against ACohen
and his wife were true, unanimously suspended him from his position as
First Parnas, and banned him from reciting the Cohens' blessing in synagogue. Governor Abraham de Veer enforced the resolution.[127] On September 23, three weeks after his original appeal, ACohen and his wife, Ribca,
admitted in a letter addressed to the regents that they had lied about Abigail's provenience in order to protect her from the smirch (*vlek*) of being a
foundling. Abigail, they stated, was an "innocent creature" whose "lovely
qualities" showed her "to be worthy of a better birth." The Mahamad
resolved to ignore the letter and refused to restore ACohen to his leadership
position.[128]

But the case reopened in 1826, when Abigail passed away. A woman
named Esperança, the widow of Isaac Cohen Lobatto (née Sarucco), came
forward to recognize Abigail as her daughter. In her testimony, Esperança
declared that she had been compelled to desert her child many years previously and decided to give her to Benjamin ACohen and his wife. She
explained that she was moved to come forward only now because according
to Jewish law Abigail could not be buried in a Jewish graveyard unless her
Jewish birth mother recognized her. During the proceedings, a former *parnas* intervened to argue against Esperança's testimony and to prevent the
burial of Abigail in the Jewish cemetery. After consultation with the colonial
prosecutor, the regents agreed not to admit the testimony of the *adjunto*,
who considered Abigail de Oro a non-Jewish foundling of Eurafrican origins. Instead, they proceeded to fine Esperança twenty-five guilders for her
tardiness in registering the birth of her alleged child, thus countenancing
this latest origin myth. Abigail was thereby recognized as the daughter of a
Jewish woman and ultimately laid to rest in the Jewish cemetery.[129]

The willingness of the Mahamad to deliberate whether Abigail's birth
mother was a Portuguese Jewess or a non-Jewish woman of Eurafrican
descent and the audacity of the plaintiffs to bring forth their case in the
first place suggest the willingness of many Surinamese Jews to affect the
total erasure of the communal boundaries that separated Portuguese Jews
from non-Jews of slave origins. The case of Abigail de Oro is remarkably
similar to that of Salomâ Mèller, also known as Sally Miller, a young
enslaved woman born around 1815 and discovered in 1843 working in a

cabaret in New Orleans. A member of the local German community spotted Miller at work and perceived a remarkable resemblance to a co-immigrant who had perished during the transatlantic crossing over two decades earlier, who was allegedly the mother of the enslaved Miller. The immigrant community rallied around Miller, claiming that this young woman had been unjustly separated from her family at age three when they had arrived in New Orleans as indentured servants in 1818. Conversely, the slave girl's masters and former owners all claimed Miller to be a "quadroon" who had been legitimately purchased. John Bailey, the historian who recounts the narrative of the "lost German slave girl," concludes that her true identity can never be known with certainty.[130] The case can be read as the subtle recognition by German immigrants of the commonalities between people of European and Eurafrican origins within the context of dislocation and various states of unfreedom.

As in the case of Sally Miller, it impossible to verify who Abigail's true biological mother was, a white Portuguese Jew or a *mulatinha*, but it hardly matters. With the connivance of the colonial authorities, Surinamese Jews, like the roughly contemporaneous German immigrant community of New Orleans, were engaging in what Karen Morrison calls "creole kinship" forms.[131] The purpose of these forms was to transcend racial categories and, presuming that Sally and Abigail were both born in bondage, slavery itself. The confusion that slavery wrought within the social order facilitated the presentation of fiction as truth, or truth as fiction. By asserting their relationship to an individual, persons not related by blood could forge a perpetual relationship with someone of their choosing, formally connecting "the past and the future of both individuals and families."[132]

Jodensavanne in the Age of Jewish Emancipation

As noted in Chapter 1, Jodensavanne functioned as a barometer of the viability of Suriname's agrarian Jewish community and, by extension, of the strength of Portuguese Jewish political autonomy. By the early 1800s, the business occupations of most regents were now connected to shipping to and from Paramaribo.[133] With the foreclosure or sale of most Jewish-owned plantations, or their conversion into less lucrative timber estates, it was these urban professionals who now supported the village's poor.[134] Residents who could not earn their livelihood in Paramaribo remained in Jodensavanne, where they could continue gleaning from the charity coffers.[135]

The population shift directly affected communal governance, which until the 1780s had been executed at Jodensavanne. Since then, the regents met to deliberate in Jodensavanne only when they had the means to rent a boat and enslaved rowers and to undertake the long, ten-hour journey from the capital city.[136] Several sessions in the 1810s were canceled because of transportation problems.[137] Eventually, meetings at Jodensavanne ceased altogether. By 1818, meetings that were supposed to take place in Jodensavanne were routinely held in Paramaribo.[138] Meanwhile, at the Beraha VeSalom synagogue, worshippers could barely form a *minyan*, the quorum of adult males necessary for formal prayer, who according to communal regulations had to be white, and few had the means for freewill offerings.[139] These details provide an understanding of what the shrinking village must have looked like on a daily basis to Jewish residents of the savanna. Gone was the link between personal wealth and ritual prestige, gone was the internal mechanism for the upkeep of the synagogue and community. A centuries-old cultural heritage was waning before their very eyes.

The threat of requisition of the village by non-Jewish parties was also a concern. In 1820, communal leaders expressed their fear that someone "ill intentioned" might request from the government plots that actually belonged to the Portuguese Jewish community. Concerns also arose that the historic Beraha VeSalom synagogue could be sold by executors, passed on to "pagans," and consecrated to "idol worshippers," an oblique allusion to the Eurafricans and Maroons who resided there and in the environs.[140]

Humans were not the only threat to the village. Cow breeding and raising was an important source of subsistence for the indigent residents, who allowed their cattle to forage where they might.[141] While this had been a problem since at least the 1760s, it became uncontrollable in the 1780s. One *parnas* complained in 1784 "how improper and indecent" it was to allow cattle to wander in the central block of the savanna, turning the site around the synagogue square into an "indecorous dunghill."[142] On their visit to Jodensavanne during the Festival of Weeks in 1818, the *parnassim* were again shocked to find cattle grazing in the synagogue courtyard.[143] A decade later, even the vermin of Jodensavanne seemed to sense the village's gradual atrophy. Aron da Costa, the overseer of the village, reported in 1828 that the *copi* insect had burrowed its way through all the shrouds reserved for burials, rendering them useless.[144]

By the late 1810s, Surinamese almanacs characterized Jodensavanne as abandoned.[145] But is this characterization accurate? Scattered evidence raises some doubts. In the first place, Jodensavanne remained a religious pilgrimage site, just as in days of old. As David Nassy attested in 1788, the Feast of Tabernacles (*sukkot*) continued to attract some two hundred residents from Paramaribo and the plantations, Jews as well as Christians. Jews threw "little parties for dancing and merrymaking," and the place was milling with people during the entire month of September. During this time, Christians treated Jodensavanne as a tourist attraction, where they could explore the unusual village and take walks on the cordon path.[146] Eyewitness accounts from the 1820s still noted that Jodensavanne was kept lively through its use as a retreat by non-residents and especially as a place to celebrate the Jewish High Holy Days.[147] When John Lance, a British barrister who served as the colony's Commissioner of Arbitration, visited the Jewish village in June 1823 he gave no indication that it was deserted. He described it as "a very pretty place built upon a prominence about 40 or 50 feet high above the river" and contrasted the village with the nearby plantations he and his travel companion surveyed, all in ruins.[148]

The calamitous fire of 1821, which leveled the city of Paramaribo, stimulated a modest but significant reverse migration to the Jewish village and its surroundings. Abraham Tama, for example, moved there with his three minor children after the house he had been living in was destroyed. Slaves who formed a part of Jewish households relocated to Jodensavanne along with their masters. In December 1821, Tama, now serving as clerk of Jodensavanne, noted that the roofs of the village's houses and kitchens were covered with pine, and homeowners needed time to deck them with more fireproof shingles. He also asked the Mahamad for shingles to cover his slave house, a strong indication of an intention to remain.[149] Isaac Fernandez Junior and his family, who once lived in their own home on the Keizerstraat, relocated to a plantation, probably in Jodensavanne's environs.[150] So, too, the sixty-year-old Samuel Haim Cohen Nassy and his wife, Ribca de la Parra, age forty-seven, who had once lived in their own house on Paramaribo's Maagdestraat.[151]

The alternative homes Paramaribo's disaster refugees found in Jodensavanne and its environs in 1821 help explain an organized effort in the 1830s to revive the village as a place of residence for the working poor. In 1838, leaders of the poor and sick aid society known as the Hozer Holim Brotherhood launched a campaign to construct buildings for impoverished residents whose original homes had become uninhabitable and for prospective artisans who planned to establish themselves in the village with steady jobs.

A fundraising effort was also to be launched to assist new migrants wishing to set themselves up for business in the village.[152]

Residents of the village supplemented their meager income by providing lodging for visitors. The German soldier August Kappler, who was housed in Jodensavanne for six days sometime between 1836 and 1841, reported that all its Jewish residents were octogenarians who owned cows but not much else. He observed that Jews there worked largely as messengers, notes slated for delivery lining their pockets.[153] The impoverishment of the place was also evident to botanist F. W. Hostmann, when he traveled to the Upper Suriname River to gather specimens in 1842. Among his sojourns was the military barrack Gelderland, situated at a corner of Jodensavanne. Distracted as he was by the Catasetum and Lysianthius samples he cut and dried, Hostmann could not help but comment on the "Jew-Savanha," a place that once "prospered . . . by the industry of these fugitives [of the Inquisition]." Now, he noted, Jodensavanne was a "dismal place" from which "every vestige of wealth" had long since disappeared. The only exception was the "brick-built synagogue" that had resisted the ravages of time and formed "an ill contrast with the miserable huts by which it is surrounded, bespeaking the deepest poverty." Hostmann stayed at "a nicely erected barrack" reserved for "impoverished Israelites,"[154] possibly financed by the Hozer Holim Brotherhood.

The synagogue, which continued to be operational until the 1860s, is also evidence of an uninterrupted local Jewish presence.[155] Long after most of the village's residents departed for Paramaribo, the building's costly accoutrements remained in place. When David Nassy wrote his *Essai historique* in 1788, he included a detailed description of the synagogue interior, complete with "crowns of silver with which the Scrolls of the Law are decorated, and other necessary furnishings of the same metal, large candlesticks of yellow copper with several branches, and chandeliers of several kinds, which cost the individuals who donated them a considerable sum."[156]

Similar objects, of the kind one would hardly leave behind if the village were indeed abandoned, were still present in the 1820s. An inventory taken in 1827 listed ten Torah scrolls, some topped with ornamental silver pomegranates, as well as silver and gold crowns, silver pointers (an embellished implement that helps the reader follow the text), and sacramental cups.[157] A visitor in 1833 described the synagogue as "the principal jewel of this currently very impoverished village" and noted "copper crowns which are illumined at the evening service with wax candles."[158] A synagogue inventory from 1848 listed ten functional Torah scrolls, some enrobed in silken textiles. For their embellishment were a few pairs of silver pomegranates, some with dangling bells, and multipronged copper crowns engraved with the names of donors. The interior was illuminated with dozens of large and small copper and silver chandeliers, a few bearing engraved names, and silver memorial lamps. Wooden calendars for ritually counting the Omer (the forty-nine days between the second day of Passover and the first day of Pentecost) and two copper charity boxes adorned the walls. Sacred objects, also suggesting the active use of the congregation, included a silver cup, a spice box to observe the departure of Sabbath and holidays, a copper candelabrum for Hanukkah (described as a "Maccabean lamp"), and silver pointers for the reading of the Torah.[159] During the 1850s and 1860s, the colony's almanac listed J. J. Fernandes as the cantor of the Jewish village, another indication that the synagogue was still intact and in operation.[160]

Arguably, the most significant change had not to do with Jodensavanne itself but with its image in the popular mind. We have already noted how David Nassy, writing in 1788, was the first to idealize the Jewish village for its built and natural landscape, remoteness, tranquility, and religious freedom. Later generations began to cast Jodensavanne as a symbolic Promised Land. An article in the 1821 Surinamese almanac described Jodensavanne during the months of September and October as "another Jerusalem."[161] Similarly, an anonymous Christian who visited Jodensavanne in 1823 testified that as soon as she stepped into her host's house, she was overcome with the sense that she had been suddenly transported to Palestine. Her host, known only as "Mr. P.," accompanied by his wife, two daughters, and a crowd of slaves decked out in gold holiday jewelry, served her generous rounds of tea, pastries, and fruit preserves. Everything had an "Oriental" feel to it, so that the only thing missing was the proverbial footbath to wash away the desert dust.[162]

But Jodensavanne had never served as a substitute Zion, not even writ small. As David Nassy remarked in 1798, Jews lacked a homeland (*Patrie*) and if given one "would love it, moved not by a servile self-interest mixed with fear, but by that passion of the soul that inspires man with a determined affection supported by reason, honor, glory, and ambition."[163] Despite the Orientalist fantasies of Christian visitors, the dominant culture of Jodensavanne was not Semitic but rather Creole. Although seldom evoked in descriptions of the village, and even then only as shadowy figures, enslaved and free people of African descent, some of whom were also Jewish, constituted the majority of the village's population and the backbone of its continued existence. We know this thanks to a separate burial ground in Jodensavanne locally known before the 1970s as the "negro cemetery." This so-called *nengre ber'pe*, as it was called in Sranan Tongo, was located about one hundred meters east of the Jewish cemetery. Now known as the Creole Cemetery, this sacred ground preserves 141 grave markers, of which 36 are identifiable. These markers show that the earliest legible birth occurred in 1810 and the earliest and last determinable burials in 1860 and 1959, respectively. Twelve of the identifiable decedents were born during the period of slavery, which ended in 1863, followed by a ten-year period of mandatory contract labor. Some of these decedents lived across the Suriname River on the Carolina and Ayo plantations. Long after the synagogue's roof collapsed in 1873, these individuals continued to lay their dead to rest in the Creole Cemetery. If possession is nine-tenths of the law, as legal theory would have it, the descendants of Jodensavanne's slaves were the last proprietors of the historic Jewish village.

Many of the decedents had direct connections to local Jewish families. The names "van la Parra" and "Wijngaarde," a Dutch translation of the prominent "de la Parra" clan name, are clearly visible on various stakes and plaques. Other markers inscribed with "Lobles" and "Cotin" are obvious transformations of the Portuguese Jewish family names Robles and Cotiño. These family names indicate former ownership by or direct descent from Jews. The former hints at the pronunciation common to the colony's Afro-Creole population, who tended to transpose or substitute the consonants "l" and "r." Marten Douwes Teenstra, commenting on this distinctive inflection, noted in 1842 that in the mouths of "Creoles" and "negroes," the name of the Jewish clan de la Parra became *de ra Palla*.[164] It is evident that local Jews shared this manner of speech. A census dating to 1867, taken by Samuel Baruh Louzada, who at the time headed one of the two Jewish households of Jodensavanne, manifests this distinctive Afro-Creole transposition. The column indicating "religion" is headed by the word *lerigie* instead of *religie* (that is, "lerigion" instead of "religion"). Similarly, *gereformeerd*, the Dutch term denoting the religious denomination Dutch "Reformed" Protestant, is rendered as *gervolmelde*.[165]

This same census, and an additional one dating to the following year, indicate that the vast majority of Jodensavanne's residents were freeborn

FIGURE 14. Ruins of the Beraha VeSalom synagogue, Jodensavanne. Courtesy of Stephen Fokké, 2014.

Reformed Protestant or Roman Catholics married to Moravians (Protestant missionaries), or themselves Moravians, all of them likely of Eurafrican origins. Some of these individuals bore family names of Portuguese Jewish origin, including de Meza and Mezade (the latter a typical transposition imposed on the family names of former slaves), as well as variations of Wijngaarde. The two remaining Jewish householders in Jodensavanne were both married to Moravians, members of an evangelical movement highly successful in attracting slaves and their free descendants. Several other Moravians were emancipated slaves being leased as woodchoppers and house servants by the Reformed Protestant Abraham Garcia Wyngard and the Jewish Jacob Samuel de Meza.[166]

Most remarkably, five of the residents appearing in a similar census from around the same time and identified as employees were Maroons (*bosch negers*).[167] Their presence points to perhaps the most significant

FIGURE 15. Wooden grave markers at the Afro-Surinamese Cemetery of Jodensavanne. Courtesy of Stichting Jodensavanne (Jodensavanne Foundation),
2008.

transformation of Jodensavanne, underway since the turn of the nineteenth
century: the frontier zone where the Jewish village was situated was gradually disappearing. Members of the Auka and Saramakka tribes of the rainforest interior were surely shedding their role as self-emancipated rebels for
a quiet life partly based on trade of fish, timber, and other wares with
residents of Jodensavanne and its riverine environs, undertaken since the
1760s.[168] A hint of this vigorous trade is detectable in an 1820 inventory
of the belongings of Aaron J. da Costa, the aforementioned overseer of
Jodensavanne. Among his possessions were five "Bush Negro plates" (*Bosch
Neeger Borden*).[169] Alas, the account does not provide details that would
link these artifacts to the exquisite carvings for which Maroons have been
famous among scholars since at least the mid-twentieth century.[170] Whether
utilitarian or intended for decorative enjoyment (or both), these relics
reflect the Jewish community's receptivity to Afro-Surinamese influences.
They also provide a clue as to how Suriname's Jewish landscapes acquired
their Creole features.

Although Jodensavanne's demise is often linked to the collapse of the
plantation economy, or the abolition of communal autonomy in 1825, the

Jewish village did not so much die as transform over the course of the nineteenth century. The ancien regime, predicated on a brutally capitalistic sugar economy, the enslavement of most of the colony's residents, military incursions by and against Maroons, and the demographic prominence of a largely rural Jewish population, began to unravel during the last quarter of the eighteenth century. This transformation, which drained Jodensavanne of its already modest population and deprived its indigent residents of a predictable source of charitable support, gave rise to the mythification of Jodensavanne as a place of unparalleled freedom and privilege for the world's Jews. When Marten Douwes Teenstra traveled to the Jewish village in 1828 he found there "only a few senile decrepit Israelites" in dilapidated houses, surrounded by decayed ruins. The residents with whom he interacted, all septo- and octogenarians, continually emphasized "the original and early privileges which they enjoyed here, while they complained without exception about the loss of their private jurisdiction."[171] For the rest of Surinamese Jewry, though, life went on.

Conclusion

When news of the abolition of communal autonomy arrived in Suriname in July 1825, the heads of both Jewish communities endeavored to forestall the loss of their privileges. For them, loss of these freedoms spelled social demotion, particularly as it helped close the status gap between Jews and Christians of slave origins. Nor was there any guarantee that equality on paper would be enforced on the ground. But the regents also accepted Jewish Emancipation as a foregone conclusion, cognizant of the fact that parallel legislation had already arrived nearly thirty years earlier in the Batavian Republic.

There is no evidence, however, that laypersons lamented the loss of Jewish communal autonomy. On the contrary, the laity continued to contravene the orders of the Mahamad, as they had since time immemorial, by submitting appeals before the colonial governor. Some of these petitions caused the governor to eliminate the legal boundaries and hierarchies that perpetuated distinctions between Ashkenazi and Portuguese Jews, white and Eurafrican Jews, and, in the case of Abigail de Oro, the Jewish community and non-Jews of slave origins.

Despite their trepidation about the loss of communal autonomy, Jewish leaders were well poised at the dawn of the nineteenth century to meet the contradictory challenges of new civic and political equality for Jews. Generations of corporate status and accommodation to a slave society made them experts in negotiating their social and political position within the colony. One hundred and fifty years of diplomatic relations also gave them excellent preparation for confronting structural anti-Jewish discrimination, which, paradoxically, coincided with the era of Jewish Emancipation, both in Suriname and in Europe.

The departure from the colony of a substantial portion of the white Christian population beginning in the last quarter of the eighteenth century gave Suriname's Jews an unprecedented demographic prominence. According to their own calculations, they comprised two-thirds of the white population by the 1810s. The vacuum left by white Christians was filled by Paramaribo's rapidly expanding free population of African descent, placing Jews in competition with these parvenus for economic resources and social prestige. The public derision of Jews in the eyes of white Christians, partly associated with the collapse of the Jewish plantation heartland beginning in the 1770s, also became generalized among slaves and their manumitted descendants. True civic and political equality, such as the right of Jews to enter the public schools and serve in the colonial court, was legislation observed in the breach for several years. Yet, the de facto denial of full civic and political rights to Jews was milder than what transpired in the fatherland, where Jews were systematically barred from the public schools throughout the nineteenth century and experienced concomitant economic disabilities.[172]

Ironically, the leaders who were so reluctant to support Jewish Emancipation benefited most by the decree, since for the first time they were permitted to serve in the colonial court. This possibility finally became a reality in 1836, when Solomon de la Parra was elected as the first Jew on the court's council. Robert Cohen also notes that those who had most to lose from the abolition of communal autonomy were the elites, and they therefore objected the most. But they used existing communal regulations or created new ones that would "buttress their status and maintain, or even increase, their power."[173] Although Jews faced illegal discrimination in Suriname during the first decades of the nineteenth century, and Jewish influence in Suriname "was at its lowest ebb" during the British Interregnum (1799–1802, 1804–16), both Portuguese and the Ashkenazi Jews made a "comeback" over the course of the nineteenth century. As their prestige grew, so did their political influence. By 1865, four of the thirteen members of the newly appointed colonial council were Jews.[174]

By the time Jewish Emancipation was promulgated in Suriname in 1825, both Jewries were heading in the direction of integration into the majority society. Conversion to Christianity and intermarriage with white Christians remained rare, and Surinamese Jewry continued to constitute a community apart from white Christians. On the other hand, a process of amalgamation from below was firmly in place. By the late eighteenth century, the Portuguese Jewish community had absorbed a small but critical sector of the majority African-descended population, who either converted to Judaism or were themselves born Jews after generations of accommodation to slave society. For people of African origins, association with or incorporation into a Jewish community constituted upward social (if not economic) mobility. For them, formal adoption of Judaism was not just the acquisition of a religion but also the attainment of an ethnic identity. The ultimate abolition of all legal distinctions between *jehidim* and *congregantes* in 1841, preceded by piecemeal legislation first introduced in 1802, formally countenanced a process well underway. Formal integration between Ashkenazim and Portuguese Jews, on the other hand, had to be mandated from without, when the colonial government intervened in 1814 to legally dissolve all distinctions between the two groups. As with so many laws passed in Suriname, the de facto distinctions between Portuguese Jews and Ashkenazim continued and intermarriage remained relatively rare.

At least from the perspective of leaders, Jewish Emancipation had a greater impact on Portuguese than on Ashkenazi Jewry. The 1825 decree leveled their special relationship with the governor, who had granted privileges directly to the Portuguese Jewish community since the seventeenth century. It eroded the superior social status Portuguese Jews had enjoyed vis-à-vis their Ashkenazi coreligionists since that time. Another setback for their high status was the progressive enfranchisement of free people of African descent. Because of this process, Jews experienced their Emancipation as a relegation to a lower status in both the Dutch and British Caribbean. But Jewish Emancipation was much more of a demotion in the Dutch colonies than in the British West Indies, where Jews *received* a franchise. In Suriname and Curaçao, by contrast, the privileges Jews had enjoyed for a century and a half were declared null and void and Jewish corporatism abolished. For Portuguese Jewish leaders, advocating on behalf of the Jews meant preserving a social status just below that of Reformed Protestants, not the advocacy of a new order.

Despite the abolition of communal autonomy in 1825, internal governance changed little, structurally speaking, over the course of the nineteenth century. The fracturing of colonial and metropolitan power, the long distance that separated Suriname from the fatherland, and the willingness of the colonial government to leave Jews largely to their own affairs meant that the abolition of communal autonomy was in some respects a legal fiction. At the same time, Jewish Emancipation brought to the fore the legal distinction between autonomy and corporatism. After the abolition of Jewish corporatism, Jews continued to recognize their religious leaders and to live in accordance with traditional Jewish rules and institutions. Now, however, the governor reserved an unmitigated right to impose rulings on the Jewish community. The abolition of distinctions between Ashkenazim and Portuguese Jews, for example, came from Governor Bonham, rather than from either of the two communities.[175] In this sense, the abolition of communal autonomy made Jews less autonomous as a body but increased their self-determination as individuals.

The steady attrition of Jodensavanne's Jewish population starting in the 1770s gave rise to the mythology that the village was once the colony's Jewish heartland. The abolition of communal autonomy in 1825 helped recast Jodensavanne as a once-thriving economic center and seat of supreme Jewish political power, an image perpetuated by contemporaneous Jewish leaders and generations of scholars. A close reading of travel accounts, communal minutes, and censuses, however, demonstrates that Jodensavanne, as in days of yore, simply mirrored a larger process underway in the colony at large: the ever-growing influence of enslaved and free people of African descent in developing the colony's languages and cultures, and the collapse of an old order predicated on slavery and sanctioned violence. The coalescence and attenuation of Suriname's Jewish community was directly linked to that order.

True Settlers in a Slave Society

Often, the first glimpse we inherit of the distant past is an idealization created by later generations. In the case of the Portuguese Jews of Suriname, we are heirs to a number of myths that have depicted this community as affluent, largely endogamous, unsurpassed in its civic and political liberties, and predominantly residing within Jodensavanne, a Jewish village that for nearly a century and a half supposedly served as a miniature Jerusalem. Fortunately, the chroniclers of the past who originated these legends also transmitted the primary sources with which to decode them. This book has delved into that prodigious archival record in an effort to challenge or nuance long-standing impressions. It has combined the approach of Jewish history with the newer methods of Atlantic history, creating a paradigm for Jewish Atlantic history that combines comparison, connection, and localism, and highlights four elements: the demographic and economic primacy of Caribbean Jewry among hemispheric American Jewries; Portuguese Jewish ascendancy; the age of slavery; and the triad of privileges, disabilities, and Jewish Emancipation. The results of this inquest further advance our understanding of Suriname's Jewish community and its Atlantic context in the following ways.

Jodensavanne, which secondary literature regards as emblematic of Surinamese Jews, was no proto-Zionist settlement. The laws Jewish leaders created, ratified, and amplified in the Jewish village to govern their community over the course of eight generations were composed not with the creation of a new Jerusalem in mind but rather to coerce, control, and ensure the physical and economic survival and Portuguese Jewish character of the community. Jodensavanne was never an influential village, a bustling commercial center, or even a full-time residential center for most of the colony's Jews. Most of the individuals who resided in the Jewish village year-round

FIGURE 16. Jacob Marius Adriaan Martini van Geffen, *Gezicht op de Jodensa-vanne aan de Suriname rivier* (*View of Jodensavanne on the Suriname River*), 1850. Courtesy of Rijksmuseum, Amsterdam.

were indigents surviving on a subsistence economy augmented by communal taxes, charitable contributions from riverside plantations, donations from relatives, or, after the 1770s, the urban wealthy. Wealthy planters generally occupied their Jodensavanne houses on Sabbaths and holidays but tended to live on their agrarian estates on secular days. Nor did Jodensavanne's location along the rainforest periphery present the possibility of export crop production, for the village's soil was sandy and infertile. Instead, small-scale commerce, such as the manufacture and sale of bread, timber harvested from the surrounding rainforest, a contraband market, particularly in rum products, and petty trade with soldiers serving on the cordon path, afforded the main opportunities for income-generating labor. Poorly paid clerics serving the synagogue routinely shirked their duties in order to tend to their plantations or to seek supplementary income or business prospects in the capital city.

Jodensavanne, held up as a paragon of freedom by authors such as David Nassy, embodied the ultimate paradox, reminiscent of the one first noted by Edmund Morgan for British North America's white settlers.[1] The freedom to live as Jews in Jodensavanne existed side by side with the Jewish enslavement of Africans who served their owners in the village and on nearby plantations. As a frontier settlement menaced by outlaw Maroons residing in the surrounding rainforest, Jodensavanne was heavily militarized and formally became synonymous with a paramilitary outpost in the 1770s, after the creation of the cordon path, a defense line dotted with fortifications and running from the rainforest interior to the Atlantic coastline. Like the capital city of Paramaribo, where the corners of particular neighborhood blocks were reserved for physical punishment, the Jewish village had its own dedicated space for the routine physical discipline of slaves—the synagogue square. The architecture of the village's synagogue, the layout of its plaza, and the very name of the congregation all imply a messianic design intent on the part of Jodensavanne's founders. But there are no textual indications that eschatological fervor buoyed the spirits of the village's pioneering residents or of their multigenerational successors. While the founders of Jodensavanne seem to have been inspired by traditional Jewish ideas on spiritual and national redemption, the Jewish village was a fledgling outpost with an uncertain existence, where deprivation and violence were ongoing realities. Nor is there any evidence that contemporaneous residents regarded the village as a "Jerusalem on the Riverside." This moniker is a later interpolation of modern-day scholars inspired by the visitors and writers who, beginning in the nineteenth century, characterized Jodensavanne as a resurrected Jerusalem, or even as a State of Israel avant la lettre.

Yet these factors do not diminish the importance of Jodensavanne, for the village functioned as a barometer of the agrarian nature of Suriname's Portuguese Jewish community, the significant role of Jewish planters in the colony's export economy, and the village's strategic role for colonial authorities. The perfunctory hospitality and impromptu synagogue services Jodensavanne's leaders organized for political and military visitors over the generations underscore the fact that the village was in the service of the Dutch Empire. For metropolitan and colonial authorities, the establishment of a marginal territory on the edge of a frontier was a method to contain and dominate Jews, who as non-Christians could never be fully integrated into white society until the gradual introduction of legal parity starting in the nineteenth century. This very containment allowed the government to use Jews to police the border between colonized settlements and the wilderness.

As a village reserved for the residence of Jews, Jodensavanne evokes comparisons to the Italian ghetto. Yet, unlike the early modern ghettos that proliferated in the Italian principalities in the mid-sixteenth century, Jodensavanne was not the site of compulsory residence for all Jews and where only Jews could live, nor did it possess a walled perimeter opened at dawn and hermetically sealed at night. Instead, Jodensavanne was a village allowed to exist autonomously, but for utilitarian rather than idealistic purposes. Like the Italian ghettos, Jodensavanne served in part to separate Jews from the Christian population but aimed to conserve Jewish life and governance rather than to subject Jews to conversionary pressure, and certainly not to delimit their economic activities.

James Ron argues in *Frontiers and Ghettos* that states have just two methods of controlling populations that cannot be incorporated: subjecting people on the other side of the border to dispossession and massacre, or bringing them under state regulation by shuttling them onto reservations where they can be policed and oppressed but spared from massacre.[2] History proves the paradigms of this political scientist too simple, for the Jews of Suriname conform to neither of Ron's described methods. Instead, Jodensavanne aligns more closely with Mikkel Thorup's archetype whereby colonizing governments established a "storage facility" for those who could not be fully incorporated into the state but could protect the frontier from violent incursions.[3] The goal of Suriname's government was actually three-pronged: to contain and regulate the Jewish population without oppression, to keep it separate from white Christian settlements, and to create a human shield against unsubjugated people, namely Indians and Maroons who lived in the wilderness that abutted territory inhabited by whites. In time, this function expanded to include alliances between Jodensavanne's Jews and officially recognized Indian and Maroon groups, with whom Jews carried out trade or captured runaway slaves. In sanctioning Jodensavanne as an autonomous Jewish settlement peopled by an ethnoreligious collectivity whose privileges were ratified by successive regimes, Suriname's colonial government achieved a type of inclusion through exclusion unparalleled in the Christian world.

If, then, Jodensavanne was exceptional—although in a different sense from what has been assumed—was the same true for the political status of Suriname's Portuguese Jews? If the litmus tests are Europe and other parts of the Americas, it is difficult to dispute the status of Portuguese Jews in Suriname as unmatched. Surinamese Jews were wholly integrated into the local economy, were spatially unrestricted, possessed their own tribunal and village, and could even vote for members of the Council of Policy. In their access to governance, and to the colony's system of production, distribution, and consumption, and in their freedom to publicly practice their religion, even on secular days that coincided with Christian holy days, Jews approached or even exceeded the legal status of white Protestants. Their territorial and judicial autonomy, on the other hand, brought them closer in status to Indians and subjugated Maroon groups. This resemblance is in consonance with Marten Schalkwijk's political analysis of early modern Suriname as comprised of "multiple states." Suriname's Jewry, too, must be understood as one of the numerous states that existed in the Dutch colony until the year of Emancipation in 1863, when the colonial government finally deemed Maroons, Indians, and all people of African descent as integral parts of the colony.[4] Because of its corporate autonomy, and because of the Dutch government's policy of non-interference in the linguistic and religious lives of its subordinates, the Surinamese Jewish community was structurally closer to Maroon and Indian tribes, and in some respects slaves, than to other white groups.

Yet neither unparalleled privileges nor legal parity, achieved de jure in 1825, translated into generalized wealth. As communal records indicate, many Portuguese Jews were unaccounted-for transients, while the majority of documented residents barely eked out a living or lived at the expense of the community's charity coffers. Financially speaking, the privileges granted to Jews in Suriname only indirectly benefited the Jewish underclass, by helping to create plantation-generated wealth that was partly used for eleemosynary purposes.

To dwell on these exceptional liberties, as contemporaries and historians have done, is to ignore the fact that Jewish privileges were contested both within and without. Some governors concluded that the latitude accorded Portuguese Jewry went too far, while Christian clergymen periodically opposed it for the sake of preserving the religious nature of Sundays. But arguably the greatest threat to Jewish autonomy came from within. Jewish laymen frequently contested the validity of bylaws and the authority of the Jewish leaders who upheld them. Why these underlings protested is difficult to say, since most did not leave behind first-person testimony. Perhaps they felt harnessed by the sheer number of bylaws, or perhaps they were motived by personal grudges. It is also possible that the laity was engaging in the early modern "judicial shopping" common to religious minorities, who tended to resort to the majority court of the land, which they perceived (often correctly) as more just or reliable than their own.[5] More than any factor, the contested nature of authority within the Portuguese Jewish community is a reflection of the judicial pluralism that complicated daily administration, with the Mahamad competing against legislative powers both within the colony and the fatherland and contending with the time lag resulting from the vast Atlantic Ocean, unpredictable weather, and sluggish seafaring vessels. This negotiated authority, to borrow Jack Greene's concept, also disrupted daily life in the sister community of the island of Curaçao.[6] In Suriname, the existence of competing authorities in the colony and fatherland meant that individual Jews, whether leaders or laypersons, could capitalize on their pluralistic legal situation to jockey for a better position, allying themselves with different power-holders as the situation allowed. This was possible in part because the municipal government of Amsterdam exercised an invasive approach to the religious affairs of its subjects, a tendency that to a degree carried over to the colonies. Jews who were sufficiently resourceful and affluent could lobby their cases in the fatherland, thus undermining Surinamese Jewish autonomy.

A comparison to the situation in the British Caribbean and in Anglophone North America permits a better understanding of what it meant to be a Jew in the Dutch colony of Suriname. Surinamese Jews, in contrast to the situation of their coreligionists farther north, were not only permitted to live according to their community's dictates but obliged to do so. This coercive dimension finds its parallel in the Jewish community of Leghorn, where leaders had the authority to admit or bar fellow Jews from inclusion in the privileges of the Livornina, a sine qua non of economic survival. There, as in Suriname, the "mandate to be different," that is, the obligation of every Jew to formally belong to the Jewish community and to live Jewishly, was enforced by their leaders and reinforced by the local government. The authority Jewish leaders exercised over the behavioral conformity of their constituents helps explain the profusion of paper generated and preserved by Suriname's Mahamad and why Jewish records from Suriname are so much more abundant than those from the sister communities of North America and the British Caribbean.

At least within the confines of the Dutch Atlantic World, Suriname also stood out as the quintessential example of Jewish rootedness, since both Amsterdam and Curaçao functioned as transit points rather than as stable destinations. As transient as a significant portion of Atlantic Jewry was, the settling of Suriname by Jews beginning in the mid-seventeenth century was a dramatic departure from the previous century, when most European Jewish families had resided in the same city for just one generation.[7] Suriname received more migrants from Amsterdam than it returned and constituted the primary destination of the fatherland's *despachados*. Through their uninterrupted longevity in the colony, significant size (one- to two-thirds of the white population), resistance to intermarriage with white Christians, reliance on a slave-based economy, and engagement with the local African-origin population, the Portuguese Jews of Suriname rendered Jewishness nearly synonymous with settler society, acquiring what scholars of other historical contexts have variably qualified as a status as "local others" or "Creole indigeneity."[8] Jewish entrenchment in the colony was thus the combined result of regularized transience, lofty privilege, and extreme coercion.

This paradoxical non-indigenous indigeneity owed much to a trajectory increasingly intertwined with people of sub-Saharan descent. Suriname was the only place in the Atlantic World where Eurafrican Jews, converted by their masters, emerged as a distinct and separate class. The presence of Eurafrican groups in other parts of the Atlantic was always short-lived and never resulted in cultural or institutional autonomy. The emergence of Suriname's Eurafrican Jews was due to the suppression by the colony's Portuguese Jewish settlers of a key legacy of rabbinical Judaism: matrilineal descent. Ultimately, however, the matrilineal principle of Judaism resurfaced, with Jewishness transmitted through Eurafrican women born as Jews. By this time, in the last quarter of the eighteenth century, Eurafrican Jews began to challenge their subordination within the Jewish community, in a period that saw many similar Eurafrican protests against discriminatory laws outside the Jewish fold across the Caribbean. The remonstrations of Suriname's Eurafrican Jews failed to immediately obtain for them an equal status, but their cultural autonomy manifested in the preservation of their own brotherhood and house of worship. The demise of this Eurafrican Jewish institution in 1817 (rather than in the 1790s, as scholars previously argued) was not the result of the Mahamad's efforts to dismantle it, contrary to earlier studies, but rather the grassroots blurring of communal boundaries and the gradual introduction of legal equality in the Jewish community and colony at large, which removed many of the disabilities regulating the lives of free people with slave origins.

The Eurafricans were by no means a fringe group among Suriname's Jews, most of whom were probably of African descent by the turn of the nineteenth century. Nor was the "Africanization" of the colony's Jewry merely a demographic phenomenon. By the last quarter of the eighteenth century, the Jewish holiday of Purim had transformed into an Afro-Creole festival that had much in common with carnival, marked as it was—at least outside the synagogue—by masquerading, cross-dressing, and the relaxation of social boundaries. Africans and their descendants did not simply join in the festivities but made the holiday their own, expressing cultural traditions often denied other outlets.

The communal autonomy enjoyed by the Jews of Suriname was abolished in 1825, constituting a demotion in the legal status of the colony's Jews, largely because it did away with the cumulative privileges that had informed Jewish standing in the colony since Dutch rule began in 1667. The social status of Surinamese Jews had steadily fallen beginning in the 1780s, triggered by the colony-wide economic crisis and reinforced by the mass relocation of inland Jews to the capital city of Paramaribo and the concomitant emergence of a burgeoning, recently manumitted community (nearly one-third of the city's total population), as well as the interrelated return migration of European-origin people to their respective fatherlands.[9] The progressive enfranchisement of free people of African descent outside the Jewish community over the course of the nineteenth century underscored the social demotion of Surinamese Jews, just as it did in Curaçao and the British Caribbean. But Jewish Emancipation was much more a relegation in the Dutch colonies, for while in the British Caribbean Jews *received* a franchise, in Curaçao and especially in Suriname Jews *lost* their corporate status, special privileges, and exemptions. The loss of communal autonomy seems to have been of greater concern to the leaders of the Portuguese and Ashkenazi communities than to their lay members. In the years leading up to 1825, Jewish leaders attempted to forestall the loss of autonomy since the colonial government offered them no guarantee that equality on paper would be enforced on the ground. But they also accepted Jewish Emancipation as a foregone conclusion, cognizant of the fact that parallel legislation had already arrived nearly thirty years earlier in the Batavian Republic.

Lay Jews, on the other hand, seem not to have lamented the loss of their community's autonomy. They continued to contravene the instructions of the Mahamad, as they had since the colony's founding, by submitting appeals before the colonial governor and, when possible, the metropolitan authorities. Nor did they object, unlike Jews in the Netherlands, to integration into the majority society. Jewish conversion to Christianity and intermarriage with white Christians, however, were virtually unheard of, and Surinamese Jewry continued to constitute a community apart from white Christians. Likewise, de facto distinctions between Portuguese Jews and Ashkenazim continued and intramarriage remained relatively rare, even after the colonial government dissolved all legal distinctions between the two groups in 1814. When intramarriage occurred, it did not weaken the institutional boundaries between the two communities, who worshipped apart until the late twentieth century. Unlike the proposed trajectory of Jewish Emancipation in Europe, which called for adaptation to a secularized Christian society, Jewish integration in Suriname followed a narrative of descent, with Jews seldom forging marital alliances with Christians but continuing to create families with people of African descent.

Suriname shared some features with other Jewish communities in the Atlantic World. As in Suriname, Portuguese Jewry in the Caribbean and in North America wielded demographic, political, and cultural hegemony over Ashkenazim until the early 1800s. Most Jews in these regions existed in and were economically imbricated with slave societies. Everywhere, Jews were barred from government office. Suriname's exceptions predominated, however. The Jews' territorial autonomy, political influence, significant investment in the land, and rootedness, as well as the emergence of an autonomous Eurafrican Jewish contingent, were all factors that made Suriname an unparalleled social setting. But by no means does unparalleled mean marginal, since the beneficiaries of this environment represented about one-quarter of all Jews living in the Americas by the late eighteenth century. One of the most exploitative slave societies was therefore likewise the place where vast numbers of Jews, more Jews than in the entire mainland of British North America, found a stable abode.[10] For over two centuries, the close link between opportunity and coercion, conspicuous as it was around the Atlantic World, was also a distinguishing mark of Suriname.

Jewish Population of Suriname by Ethnicity

Jewish Population of Hemispheric America,
    ca. Late Eighteenth Century

Enslaved People of African Descent, Suriname

Table 2. Jewish Population of Suriname by Ethnicity

Year	Portuguese Jews	Ashkenazi Jews	Other	Total	Source
1684	160	3[1]	69 (children)[2]	163	NAN, Sociëteit van Suriname, inv. nr. 213, pp. 231, 233; Schnurmann, *Atlantische Welten*, 382.
1690		40–50			Nassy, *Essai historique*, part 1, 83.
1695	475	75		550	Kruijtzer, "European Migration," 119.
1788	834	447	100 "free Jewish Mulattos" of both communities	1,411	Nassy, *Essai historique*, part 1, 39.
1791	870	460	—	1,330	*Surinaamsche staatkundige almanach voor den jaare 1793*, 7.
1845	485	733	145 "Israelites"	1,363	Vink, *Creole Jews*, 27.

Note: This census lists all persons from the Jewish nation who owed capitation and land tax to the Society of Suriname in 1684. As such, it does not take into account the Jewish poor and transient, not all of whom would have been lodging with taxpaying Jewish families.
1. Categorized as Ashkenazi by author based on Ashkenazi last names (Alexander Moses and Jacob Benjamin, with one unnamed woman). This census pertains only to plantations on the Suriname River; it does not include Paramaribo.
2. I could not find this data in the archival source that Schnurmann (*Atlantische Welten*) cites (NAN, Sociëteit van Suriname, inv. nr. 213, pp. 226–33). She does not distinguish by ethnicity.

Table 3. Jewish Population of Hemispheric America, ca. Late Eighteenth Century

Place	Date	Population	Source	Share of total hemispheric American Jewish population
United States	1790	1,500	Ira Rosenswaike, "An Estimate and Analysis of the Jewish Population of the United States in 1790," *PAJHS* 50: 1 (1960): 23–67, 25–26, 34 (1,300–3,000 according to Sarna, *American Judaism*, 375).	28.7%
Suriname	1791	1,350–1,430	Nassy, *Essai historique*, part 2, 39 (1,411, including 100 free "Mulatres Juifs libres")	26.6%
Curaçao	1789	1,095	Klooster, "Subordinate but Proud," 289.	20.9%
Jamaica	1776	800–900	Faber, *Jews, Slaves, and the Slave Trade*, 58.	16.2%
Barbados	Late eighteenth century	175	LMA/4521/D/01/01/08, pp. 22 (1820: "the aggregate of our nation . . . 35 individuals"), 57 (1820: "former times when our congregation was five times as numerous").	3.3%
St. Eustatius	1790	170	Cohen, *Through the Sands of Time*, 11.	3.2%
St. Thomas	1789	ca. 30	Rolf Berger, *Die Inseln St. Thomas und St. Croix: Eine vergleichende wirtschaftsgeographische Untersuchung auf landschaftskundlicher Grundlage* (Hamburg: J. G. Bitter & Sohn, 1934), 115 (estimate is based on "9 families")[1]	0.6%
St. Croix	—	Unknown but comparable to St. Thomas [ca. 30][2]	—	0.6%
Total:		Low estimate: 5,150 High estimate: 5,330		

Note: To calculate the percentages, the average of high and low estimates was chosen for Suriname and Jamaica. No data are available for St. Croix, but its Jewish population probably did not exceed two dozen. Many Caribbean Jewish communities, such as in Nevis, were transient and their population size unknown. Natalie Zacek, "'A People So Subtle': Sephardic Jewish Pioneers of the English West Indies," in Caroline A. Williams, ed., *Bridging the Early Modern Atlantic World: People, Products, and Practices on the Move* (Surrey, England: Ashgate, 2009), 97–112, 111; Marcus, *The Colonial American Jew*, 1:95–140.

1. After 1795, there was a surge in St. Thomas's Jewish population owing to the commercial collapse of Curaçao and St. Eustatius. This helps to explain why, in 1802, there were 160 Jews on the island according to Cohen, *Through the Sands of Time*, in the West Indies. Lower figures for 1801, 1803, and 1824 are in Johan Peter Nissen, *Reminiscences of a 46 Years' Residence in the Island of St. Thomas, in the West Indies* (Nazareth, Pa.: Senseman & Co., 1838), 138–39.

2. In 1835, the Jewish population of St. Thomas and St. Croix, respectively, was 425 and 42. Hall, *Slave Society in the Danish West Indies*, 200.

Table 4. Enslaved People of African Descent, Suriname

Year	Number	Percentage of population (excluding Indians and Maroons)	Source
1667	2,000	50%	Arends, "Demographic Factors in the Formation of Sranan," 233–85, 259; cf. Suze Zijlstra, "Anglo-Dutch Suriname: Ethnic Interaction and Colonial Transition in the Caribbean, 1651–1682" (Ph.D. diss., Universiteit van Amsterdam, 2015), 89 (half of population enslaved ca. 1663), 90 (2,500 or 62.5% in 1665)
1671	2,500	75.8%	Zijlstra, "Anglo-Dutch Suriname," 1–2.
1684	3,877	81.5% or 83.9%	Zijlstra, "Anglo-Dutch Suriname," 161, 90; Victor Enthoven, "Dutch Crossings: Migration Between the Netherlands and the New World, 1600–1800," Atlantic Studies 2 (October 2005): 153–76, 160; Van Stipriaan, Surinaams contrast, 311, 314.
1690	4,000		Jacques Arends, "The Development of Complementation in Saramaccan," in Bernard Caron, ed., Proceedings of the 16th International Congress of Linguists (CD-ROM, Paper no. 0386, Oxford: Pergamon, 1998).
1697	4,915	91.7%	Zijlstra, "Anglo-Dutch Suriname," 161.
1752	37,835	94.8%	Enthoven, "Dutch Crossings," 160; Van Stipriaan, Surinaams contrast, 311, 314.
1775	60,000	—	Zijlstra, "Anglo-Dutch Suriname," 161.
1791	53,000 (of which 8,000 in Paramaribo)[1]	91.2%	Surinaamsche staatkundige almanach voor den jaare 1793, 7 (note: pagination repeats several times in this volume).
1829	40,000 (on plantations)	—	NAN, Collectie 241, A. F. Lammers, inv. nr. 11, part 16 [1], Bylagen A–Z (pp. 1–322), petition of Surinamese plantation owners and directors to the king of the Netherlands, ca. 1831, p. 134.

1. Whites: 3,360; free "mulattoes and negroes": 1,760.

ABBREVIATIONS

Archives and Collections

AJA	American Jewish Archives, Cincinnati, Ohio
BAC	Bibliothèque et Archives Canada, Toronto
BEH	Bibliotheek Ets Haim, Livraria Montezinos, Amsterdam
CBG	Centraal Bureau voor Genealogie, The Hague
CJA	Canadian Jewish Archives
CO	Colonial Office (housed in TNAUK)
DC	Director's Correspondence (housed in RBGL)
GMIE	Archieven van Gemeente Mikvé Israel-Emanuel (housed in MMB)
HCA	High Court Admiralty (housed in TNAUK)
HO	Home Office (housed in TNAUK)
JCBL	John Carter Brown Library, Providence, Rhode Island
JHM	Joods Historisch Museum, Amsterdam
LMA	London Metropolitan Archives
MMB	Mongui Maduro Bibliotheek, Curaçao
NAN	Nationaal Archief Nederland/National Archives of the Netherlands, The Hague
NPIGS	Nederlandse Portugees Israelitische Gemeente in Suriname (housed in NAN)
	inv. nrs. 1–6: Minuut-notulen van vergaderingen van de Senhores do Mahamad
	inv. nrs. 7–9: Minuut-notulen van vergaderingen van de Junta
	inv. nrs. 10–14: Minuut-notulen van vergaderingen van de Senhores de Mahamad (Parnassijns) en van de Junta (Parnassijns en ouderlingen)
	inv. nrs. 75–82: Ingekomen rekesten en memories
	inv. nr. 416, Alfabetische staten van geborenen over 1662–1723 en 1723–77)
	inv. nr. 423, Register van begravenen op de kerkhoven van de Savanne
NYHSL	New-York Historical Society Library
RBGK	Library, Art & Archive, Royal Botanic Gardens, Kew
RvP	Raad van Politie Suriname (housed in NAN)
SAA	Stadsarchief Amsterdam/Municipal Archives, Amsterdam
SONA	Suriname: Oud Notarieel Archief (housed in NAN)
SPSM	Spanish and Portuguese Synagogue, Montreal (Canada)
T	Treasury (housed in TNAUK)
TNAUK	The National Archives of the United Kingdom, Kew
UBLBC	Universitaire Bibliotheken Leiden, Bijzondere Collecties, the Netherlands

WO   War Office (housed in TNAUK)
YUL   Yale University Library (New Haven, Connecticut)

Journals

PAJHS   *Publications of the American Jewish Historical Society*
TJHSE   *Transactions of the Jewish Historical Society of England*

NOTES

Introduction

1. Voltaire, *Candide, ou l'Optimiste* (Paris: La Sirène, 1759). All quotes are from the English edition, published as *Candide, or, All for the Best* (London: J. Nourse, 1759), 74–79. Observations about these facts of error are from Gert Oostindie, "Voltaire, Stedman and Suriname Slavery," *Slavery and Abolition* 14: 2 (August 1993): 1–34, 1–4. The full expression is "avoir la dent dure," or to be scathingly critical. Hervé Duchêne, *Candide* (Rosny: Bréal, 1999), 84. "Vanderdendur" also evokes the French word for merchant (*vendeur*), thus "the scathingly critical merchant."

2. The Historical Research Department of the Nation of Islam, *The Secret Relationship Between Blacks and Jews* (Chicago: Latimer Associates, 1991); Tony Martin, *The Jewish Onslaught: Despatches from the Wellesley Battlefront* (Dover, Mass.: Majority Press, 1993); Mary Lefkowitz, *History Lesson: A Race Odyssey* (New Haven, Conn.: Yale University Press, 2008).

3. For refutations based on a social justice agenda, see Harold David Brackman, *Farrakhan's Reign of Historical Error: The Truth Behind The Secret Relationship Between Blacks and Jews* (Los Angeles: Simon Wiesenthal Center, 1992) and *Ministry of Lies: The Truth Behind the Nation of Islam's The Secret Relationship Between Blacks and Jews* (New York: Four Walls Eight Windows, 1994), and Saul S. Friedman, *Jews and the American Slave Trade* (New Brunswick, N.J.: Transaction Publishers, 1998).

4. Eli Faber, *Jews, Slaves, and the Slave Trade: Setting the Record Straight* (New York: New York University Press, 1998).

5. Jonathan Schorsch, *Jews and Blacks in the Early Modern World* (New York: Cambridge University Press, 2004). This book also makes important contributions in the area of rabbinical responses to slavery.

6. Jonathan Schorsch, "American Jewish Historians, Colonial Jews and Blacks, and the Limits of *Wissenschaft*: A Critical Review," *Jewish Social Studies*, n.s., 6: 2 (Winter 2000): 102–32.

7. Wieke Vink, "Creole Jews: Negotiating Community in Colonial Suriname" (Ph.D. diss., Erasmus Universiteit Rotterdam, 2008), 32.

8. Frank Tannenbaum, *Slave and Citizen: The Negro in the Americas* (New York: Random House, 1946). For critiques, see Carl N. Degler, *Neither Black nor White: Slavery and Race Relations in Brazil and the United States* (New York: Macmillan, 1971); Leslie B. Rout, *The African Experience in Spanish America, 1502 to the Present Day* (Cambridge: Cambridge University Press, 1976); and Alejandro de la Fuente, "From Slaves to Citizens?: Tannenbaum and the Debates on Slavery, Emancipation, and Race Relations in Latin America," *International Labor and Working-Class History* 77: 1 (Spring 2010): 154–73.

9. For one such ahistorical interpretation, see Shai Cherry, *Torah Through Time: Understanding Bible Commentary from the Rabbinic Period to Modern Times* (Philadelphia: Jewish Publication Society, 2007), chap. 4, "The Hebrew Slave."

10. Mary L. Gordon, "The Nationality of Slaves Under the Early Roman Empire," *Journal of Roman Studies* 14 (1924): 93–111, 110.

11. Wim Klooster, *The Dutch Moment: War, Trade, and Settlement in the Seventeenth-Century Atlantic World* (Ithaca, N.Y.: Cornell University Press, 2016); Wim Klooster and Gert Oostindie, *Realm Between Empires: The Second Dutch Atlantic, 1680–1815* (Ithaca, N.Y.: Cornell University Press, 2018), 250 (for quote).

12. Klooster and Oostindie, *Realm Between Empires*, 8, 251.

13. Ibid., 70.

14. Johannes Menne Postma, *The Dutch in the Atlantic Slave Trade, 1600–1815* (Cambridge: Cambridge University Press, 1990), 112–15, 121–24, and, for an explanation of the toponyms, 56–57.

15. Cornelis Christiaan Goslinga, *The Dutch in the Caribbean and in the Guianas, 1680–1791* (Assen: Van Gorcum, 1985), 309. This percentage, reflecting colonial record-keeping practices, does not account for Maroons or Indigenous people.

16. Justin Roberts, *Slavery and the Enlightenment in the British Atlantic, 1750–1807* (New York: Cambridge University Press, 2013), 132, 171–72; Larry Gragg, "West Indies," in Junius P. Rodriguez, ed., *The Historical Encyclopedia of World Slavery*, 2 vols. (Santa Barbara, Calif.: ABC-Clio, 1997), 1:690–92, 691.

17. In most sugar colonies, at least 80 percent of the population was enslaved. By contrast, in the trade colony of Dutch Curaçao, one-half of the population was enslaved in the eighteenth century. Among sugar colonies, other exceptions include nineteenth-century Cuba and Puerto Rico, which never attained an absolute majority. Francisco A. Scarano, "Spanish Caribbean," 137–142, 141 and Pieter Emmer, "Dutch Caribbean," 142–46, 144, both in Seymour Drescher and Stanley L. Engerman, eds., *A Historical Guide to World Slavery* (New York: Oxford University Press, 1998).

18. Alex van Stipriaan, "The Suriname Rat Race: Labour and Technology on Sugar Plantations, 1750–1900," *New West Indian Guide* 63: 1/2 (1989): 94–117, 95, 98, 100, 107; Gert Oostindie and Alex van Stipriaan, "Slavery and Slave Cultures in a Hydraulic Society," in Stephan Palmié, ed., *Slave Cultures and the Cultures of Slavery* (Knoxville: University of Tennessee Press, 1995), 78–99, 81–87; NAN, Raad van Politie, inv. nr. 827, trial against Barend Hendrik Beekman, Director of the La Jalousie plantation on the River Commewijne, February 27, 1775, pp. 127–134 (scans 267–82). Throughout this book, scans refer to digitized archives available since January 2017 via the Nationaal Archief Nederland website (http://www.gahetna.nl/).

19. Van Stipriaan, "The Suriname Rat Race," 94–117, 95; Klooster and Oostindie, *Realm Between Empires*, 70.

20. The distinction between the two concepts appears in Ira Berlin, *Many Thousands Gone: The First Two Centuries of Slavery in North America* (Cambridge, Mass.: Harvard University Press, 1998), 8–13. For critiques, see Herman L. Bennett, *Africans in Colonial Mexico: Absolutism, Christianity, and Afro-Creole Consciousness, 1570–1640* (Bloomington: Indiana University Press, 2003), 14–15 and Sherwin K. Bryant, "Enslaved Rebels, Fugitives, and Litigants: The Resistance Continuum in Colonial Quito," *Colonial Latin American Review* 13: 1 (2004): 36–7n11.

21. B. W. Higman, *A Concise History of the Caribbean* (Cambridge: Cambridge University Press, 2011), 138.

22. Michel-Rolph Trouillot, *Silencing the Past: Power and the Production of History* (Boston: Beacon Press, 1995), 18.

23. References to the distinctive "complexion" of Jews in legal sources of colonial Virginia served to prevent Jews from owning Christians but did not result in the enslavement of Jews. See Bryon Curti Martyn, "Racism in the U.S.: A History of the Anti-Miscegenation Legislation and Litigation" (Ph.D. diss., University of Southern California, 1979), 111–14.

24. Alexander de Lavaux, *Generale Caart van de Provintie Suriname*, 1737.

25. "Autonomy" first emerged in the late nineteenth century to denote not political sovereignty or semi-sovereignty but something akin to "national-cultural determination." It was first applied by supporters of the Jewish autonomist movement in eastern Europe. Salo Wittmayer Baron, *A Social and Religious History of the Jews*, 18 vols. (New York: Columbia University Press, 1952–83), 11:315.

26. Yosef Hayim Yerushalmi, *Diener von Königen und nicht Diener von Dienern: Einige Aspekte der politischen Geschichte der Juden* (Munich: C. F. von Siemens Stiftung, 1995); Anna Sapir Abulafia, *Christian-Jewish Relations, 1000–1300: Jews in the Service of Medieval Christendom* (New York: Pearson Education, 2011).

27. In addition to secondary sources, these conclusions are based largely on CJA, Shearit Israel Spanish & Portuguese Synagogue, Congregational Chronology, boxes 1–2 (box 2: for what became Canada); "The Earliest Extant Minute Books of the Spanish and Portuguese Congregation Shearith Israel in New York, 1728–1786," *PAJHS* 21 (1913): 1–82, 33 (for New York); and LMA/4521/D/01/01 (for Barbados). Moreover, when Jews in Barbados and Jamaica did experience a corporate existence, it often manifested in onerous taxation or economic restrictions, as discussed in Chapter 2.

28. This point, the basis for all academic Jewish studies, has also been specifically applied to the Surinamese context. See Wieke Vink, *Creole Jews: Negotiating Community in Colonial Suriname* (Leiden: KITLV, 2010), 256.

29. David de Sola Pool, *Portraits Etched in Stone: Early Jewish Settlers, 1682–1831* (New York: Columbia University Press, 1952), 167 ("Spaniolic mixture") and "The Use of Portuguese and Spanish in the Historic Shearith Israel Congregation in New York," in Izaak A. Langnas and Barton Sholod, eds., *Studies in Honor of M. J. Benardete (Essays in Hispanic and Sephardic Culture)* (New York: Las Américas Publishing Company, 1965), 360; Maurice Fishberg, *The Jews: A Study of Race and Environment London* (New York: Walter Scott Publishing and Charles Scribner's Sons, 1911), 382; Isaac S. Emmanuel, "El Portugues [*sic*] en la Sinagoga 'Mikve Israel' de Curaçao," *Otsar yehudei sefarad: Leheker toledot yehudei sefarad vetarbutam* 1 (1959): 31; Linda Rupert, *Creolization and Contraband: Curaçao in the Early Modern Atlantic World* (Athens: University of Georgia Press, 2012), 231; Gérard Nahon, "Inscriptions Funéraires Hébraiques et Juives a Bidache Labastide-Clairence (Basses-Pyrénées) et Peyrehorade (Landes): Rapport de Mission," *Revue des Études Juives* 127 (October/December 1968): 347–65, 351; Ben Teensma, "Take Florida: Or the Unattended Project of a Dutch Sephardi Phantast," *Itinerario* 21: 3 (1997): 142–50, 144 (for quote) and 22: 1 (1998): 131–42.

30. Robert Cohen, "Jewish Demography in the Eighteenth Century: A Study of London, the West Indies, and Early America" (Ph.D. diss., Brandeis University, 1976), 9.

31. Klooster and Oostindie, *Realm Between Empires*, 133. Jamaica's Ashkenazi congregation was founded only in 1787. Schorsch, *Jews and Blacks in the Early Modern World*, 5.

32. *Surinaamsche staatkundige almanach voor den jaare 1793* (Paramaribo: W. P. Wilken, 1793), 7 (second section); Gijs Kruijtzer, "European Migration," in Gert Oostindie, ed., *Dutch Colonialism, Migration, and Cultural Heritage* (Leiden: KITLV, 2008), 119. For the Ashkenazi population of 1690, see David Nassy, *Essai historique sur la colonie de Surinam* (Paramaribo [Amsterdam]: n.p., 1788), part 1, 83.

33. Vink, *Creole Jews*, 196–97; SAA, 334, Archief van de Portugees-Israëlietische Gemeente, inv. nr. 1029, "Extracte uijt het Register der Resolutien van de Ed. Agthb. Heeren directeuren van de Societeijt van Suriname," January 6, 1734, pp. 890–94.

34. Alex van Stipriaan, "An Unusual Parallel: Jews and Africans in Suriname in the 18th and 19th Centuries," *Studia Rosenthaliana* 31: 1/2 (1997): 74–93, 76 (in 1788).

35. Robert Cohen, *Jews in Another Environment: Surinam in the Second Half of the Eighteenth Century* (Leiden: Brill, 1991), 126.

36. NAN, NPIGS, inv. nr. 2, June 24, 1790.

37. Nassy, *Essai historique*, part 1, 83–84; NAN, NPIGS, inv. nr. 11, December 7, 1824.

38. AJA, MS-581, Box X-416, folder 4, Escamoth of the Ashkenazi community, 1734–1821, Photostat.

39. Klooster and Oostindie, *Realm Between Empires*, 136; Jacob Adriaan Schiltkamp, *De geschiedenis van het notariaat in het octrooigebied van de West-Indische Compagnie* (voor Suriname en de Nederlandse Antillen tot het jaar 1964) ('s-Gravenhage: N. V. de Ned. Boek- en Steendrukkerij v/h H. L. Smits, 1964), 181–83; P. M. Netscher, *Geschiedenis van de Koloniën Essequebo, Demerary en Berbice, van de vestiging der Nederlanders aldaar tot op onzen tijd* ('s Gravenhage: Martinus Nijhoff, 1888), 185; Paul Koulen, "Slavenhouders en geldschieters: Nederlandse belangen in Berbice, Demerara en Essequebo, 1815–1819," *Gen. Magazine* 21: 1 (2015): 46–52, 50–51; NAN, 1.05.05.439, Lijste van het Manschap het geene met het Schip de Vrouwe Leonora Capt Pieter Cornelis Booz near de Colonie de Berbice in May 1721 staen te vertrekken, 1721, pp. 11–12. I thank Marjoleine Kars for the latter source.

40. Klooster and Oostindie, *Realm Between Empires*, 10. For Suriname, the first attempt to do so was scholarly. J. A. Schiltkamp and J. Th. de Smidt, eds., *Placaten, ordonnantiën, en andere wetten, uitgevaardigd in Suriname, 1667–1816*, 2 vols. (Amsterdam: S. Emmering, 1973).

41. Judith Kalik, *Scepter of Judah: The Jewish Autonomy in the Eighteenth-Century Crown Poland* (Leiden: Brill, 2009), 1; Francesca Bregoli, *Mediterranean Enlightenment: Livornese Jews, Tuscan Culture, and Eighteenth-Century Reform* (Stanford, Calif.: Stanford University Press, 2014), 2, 22, 208, 242.

42. Klooster and Oostindie, *Realm Between Empires*, 10 (for "cultural autonomy").

43. Ibid., 6, 251.

44. For examples of Jews viewed primarily or exclusively through their economic functions, see Bernard Bailyn, *Atlantic History: Concept and Contours* (Cambridge, Mass.: Harvard University Press, 2005), 86; Daviken Studnicki-Gizbert, *A Nation upon the Ocean Sea: Portugal's Atlantic Diaspora and the Crisis of the Spanish Empire, 1492–1640* (Oxford: Oxford University Press, 2007); and Jessica Vance Roitman, *The Same but Different?: Inter-cultural Trade and the Sephardim, 1595–1640* (Leiden: Brill, 2011). For the Jewish historiographical approach, see Robert Cohen, "Early Caribbean Jewry: A Demographic Perspective," *Jewish Social Studies* 45: 2 (Spring 1983): 123–34, 126; Jacob R. Marcus, *The Colonial American Jew, 1492–1776*, 3 vols. (Detroit: Wayne State University Press, 1970); Jonathan D. Sarna, *American Judaism: A History* (New Haven, Conn.: Yale University Press, 2004) and its bibliography; Laura Arnold Leibman,

Messianism, Secrecy and Mysticism: A New Interpretation of Early American Jewish Life (Portland, Ore.: Vallentine Mitchell, 2012); and Sina Rauschenbach and Jonathan Schorsch, eds., *The Sephardic Atlantic: Colonial Histories and Postcolonial Perspectives* (Cham, Switzerland: Palgrave Macmillan, 2018). For the parallel outside of Jewish historiography, see Bernard Bailyn, "Introduction: Reflections on Some Major Themes," in Bernard Bailyn and Patricia L. Denault, eds., *Soundings in Atlantic History: Latent Structures and Intellectual Currents, 1500–1830* (Cambridge, Mass.: Harvard University Press, 2009), 2.

45. For the application of the Atlantic history method to the Jewish past, see Holly Snyder, "Navigating the Jewish Atlantic: The State of the Field and Opportunities for New Research," in D'Maris Coffman, Adrian Leonard, and William O'Reilly, eds., *The Atlantic World* (New York: Routledge, 2015), 417; Arthur Kiron, "An Atlantic Jewish Republic of Letters?" *Jewish History* 20: 2 (2006): 171–211; Noah L. Gelfand, "A Transatlantic Approach to Understanding the Formation of a Jewish Community in New Netherland and New York," *New York History* 89: 4 (Fall 2008): 375–95; James Homer Williams, "An Atlantic Perspective on the Jewish Struggle for Rights and Opportunities in Brazil, New Netherland, and New York," in Paolo Bernardini and Norman Fiering, eds., *The Jews and the Expansion of Europe to the West, 1450–1800* (New York: Berghahn Books, 2001), 369–93; Peter Mark and José da Silva Horta, *The Forgotten Diaspora: Jewish Communities in West Africa and the Making of the Atlantic World* (Cambridge: Cambridge University Press, 2011); and the works of Jessica Vance Roitman. For the Atlantic Jewish World conceived as a geographical space, see Barry Stiefel, *Jewish Sanctuary in the Atlantic World: A Social and Architectural History* (Columbia: University of South Carolina Press, 2014); Leibman, *Messianism, Secrecy and Mysticism* and Laura Leibman, "Jewish Atlantic World," Reed Digital Collections, http://cdm.reed.edu/cdm4/jewishatlanticworld/intro.php.

46. The term "disability" is a historiographical term denoting civil and political constraints enshrined in law.

47. This framework was first developed in Aviva Ben-Ur, "Atlantic Jewish History: A Conceptual Reorientation," in Arthur Kiron, ed., *Constellations of Atlantic Jewish History, 1555–1890: The Arnold and Deanne Kaplan Collection of Early American Judaica* (Philadelphia: University of Pennsylvania Press, 2014), 25–46.

48. Nassy, *Essai historique*, part 1, xii.

49. Jan Jacob Hartsinck, *Beschryving van Guiana, of de wilde kust in Zuid-America*, 2 vols. (Amsterdam: Gerrit Tielenburg, 1770), 2:649.

50. Marten Schalkwijk, *The Colonial State in the Caribbean: Structural Analysis and Changing Elite Networks in Suriname, 1650–1920* (The Hague: Amrit/Ninsee, 2011), 219.

51. Victor Enthoven, "Suriname and Zeeland: Fifteen Years of Dutch Misery on the Wild Coast, 1667–1682," in J. Everaert and J. Parmentier, eds., *International Conference on Shipping, Factories and Colonization* (Brussels: Koninklijke Academie voor Overzeese Wetenschappen, 1996), 249–60, 256; Hartsinck, *Beschryving van Guiana*, 2:649.

52. Lodewijk Augustinus Henri Christiaan Hulsman, "Nederlands Amazonia: Handel met indianen tussen 1580 en 1680" (Ph.D. diss., Universiteit van Amsterdam, 2009), 179.

53. NAN, Oud Archief Suriname, Raad van Politie, inv. nr. 1, Minuut-notulen, discussion of letter of Samuel C. Nassy, October 7, 1689, p. 41; Jessica Vance Roitman, "Portuguese Jews, Amerindians, and the Frontiers of Encounter in Colonial Suriname," *New West Indian Guide* 88 (2014): 18–52.

54. Upon the initial arrival of European individuals in the first half of the seventeenth century, Caribs, together with Arawaks and Waraus, constituted a population of perhaps 100,000 individuals in Suriname, clustered along the coastline. Colonization gradually pushed them inland. Just Wekker, "Indiaanse woon- en leefgebieden in Suriname," *Oso* 13: 1 (April 1994): 6–13, 6.

55. For the economic adaptability of exilic Huguenots, see Jon Butler, *The Huguenots in America: A Refugee People in New World Society* (Cambridge, Mass.: Harvard University Press, 1983).

56. Alex van Stipriaan, *Surinaams contrast: Roofbouw en overleven in een Caraibische plantage-kolonie, 1750–1863* (Leiden: KITLV, 1993).

57. Klooster and Oostindie, *Realm Between Empires*, 138. For a discussion of the "kindness of Jewish masters," see Schorsch, *Jews and Blacks in the Early Modern World*, 300–303.

58. See, for example, Katherine Freedman, "Sustaining Faith: Quakers and Slavery in the Early Anglo-Atlantic, 1655–1679," *Journal of Global Slavery* 3: 3–4 (Fall 2018): 211–33; John M. Chenoweth, *Simplicity, Equality, and Slavery: An Archaeology of Quakerism in the British Virgin Islands, 1740–1780* (Gainesville: University of Florida Press, 2017), 18 (Quakers were not "'kinder' masters who practiced a 'more humane' brand of slavery").

59. Julien Wolbers, *Geschiedenis van Suriname* (Amsterdam: De Hoogh, 1861), 125–26. "Saltwater slaves" refers to people born in Africa and transported to the Americas.

60. NAN, Sociëteit van Suriname, inv. nr. 113, Octrooi verleend door de Staten-Generaal bij de overdracht van Suriname door de Staten van Zeeland aan de West-Indische Compagnie, September 23, 1682, [p. 2] (article 6: *swarte slaven ofte negros*).

61. Van Stipriaan, *Surinaams contrast*, 311 (table 44); Henk den Heijer, *Goud, Ivoor en slaven: Scheepvaart en handel van de Tweede West-Indische Compagnie op Afrika, 1674–1740* (Zutphen: Walburg, 1997), 366.

62. Oostindie, "Voltaire, Stedman and Suriname Slavery," 4.

63. Van Stipriaan, *Surinaamscontrast*, 314; den Heijer, *Goud, ivoor en slaven*, 366; Kofi Yakpo, Margot van den Berg, and Robert Borges, "On the Linguistic Consequences of Language Contact in Suriname: The Case of Convergence," in Eithne B. Carlin et al., eds., *In and Out of Suriname: Language, Mobility and Identity* (Leiden: Brill, 2014), 164–95; 171.

64. NAN, A. F. Lammens, Collectie 241, inv. nr. 7, part XII, 1, nrs. 1–27 (paginated 1–86), p. 29, "Aanwysing der plaatsen waar de slaven gewoon waren met de zogenaamde Spaansebok gestraft waren op seven hoeken van Paramaribo, zoals het oud tyds was."

65. Richard Price, *Alabi's World* (Baltimore: Johns Hopkins University Press, 1990), 175, 177.

66. The earliest surviving legislation explicitly prohibiting plantation managers and owners from implementing the *Spaansche bok* dates to 1784. Schiltkamp and De Smidt, eds., *Placaten, ordonnantiën, en andere wetten, uitgevaardigd in Suriname*, 2:1066–75, 1071 (entry #876, August 31, 1784). However, allusions to earlier interdictions in various archival sources point to earlier laws. Cornelis van Aerssen Van Sommelsdijck, Suriname's first governor, was apparently the first to introduce a law forbidding planters from maiming or beating their slaves to death and obliging them to hand over their slaves to the Council of Justice if they deemed severe punishment warranted. Wolbers, *Geschiedenis van Suriname*, 62. Similar laws are mentioned in NAN, Raad van Politie, inv. nr. 827, trial against Barend Hendrik Beekman, Director of the La Jalousie plantation on the River Commewijne, February 27, 1775, pp. 127–34 (scans 267–82) and NPIGS, inv. nr. 2, May 24, 1781.

67. NYHSL, John Greenwood, Diaries, 1752–1758, 1763–1765, Original Memorandum Book No. 2 (1752–58), 34–35.

68. NAN, NPIGS, inv. nr. 2, date blotted out (between June 19 and June 29, 1781); Gouvernementssecretarie der Kolonie Suriname, (1684) 1722–1828, inv. nr. 113, p. 496a–b (scans 383–87).

69. NAN, Raad van Politie, inv. nr. 827, trial against Barend Hendrik Beekman, Director of the La Jalousie plantation on the River Commewijne, February 27, 1775, pp. 127–34, 128 verso, scans 267–82, 270; N. Govers, *Vijf en Veertig Jaren Onder de Tropenzon: Leven van den eerbiedwaardigen Petrus Donders C.ss.R: Apostel der Indianen en melaatsen in Suriname* (Heerlen: Joh. Roosenbom, 1946), 134.

70. On this point, see Schalkwijk, *The Colonial State in the Caribbean*, 238, 238n40.

71. Cohen, "Jewish Demography in the Eighteenth Century" and *Jews in Another Environment*.

72. Natalie Zemon Davis, "David Nassy's 'Furlough' and the Slave Mattheus," in Pamela S. Nadell, Jonathan D. Sarna, and Lance J. Sussman, eds., *New Essays in American Jewish History: To Commemorate the 60th Anniversary of the American Jewish Archives Journal and the 10th Anniversary of the American Jewish Archives Under the Direction of Dr. Gary P. Zola* (Cincinnati: American Jewish Archives of Hebrew Union College-Jewish Institute of Religion, 2010), 79–93, nn. 508–11 and "Regaining Jerusalem: Eschatology and Slavery in Jewish Colonization in Seventeenth-Century Suriname," *Cambridge Journal of Postcolonial Literary Inquiry* 3: 1 (December 2015): 1–28; Vink, *Creole Jews*.

73. Van Stipriaan, *Surinaams contrast* and "The Suriname Rat Race"; Oostindie and Van Stipriaan, "Slavery and Slave Cultures in a Hydraulic Society"; Oostindie, "Voltaire, Stedman and Suriname Slavery."

74. Price, *Alabi's World*, 9, 383 and *First-Time: The Historical Vision of an Afro-American People* (Baltimore: Johns Hopkins University Press, 1983).

75. See, in particular, Schalkwijk, *The Colonial State in the Caribbean*.

76. Erik R. Seeman, "Jews in the Early Modern Atlantic: Crossing Boundaries, Keeping Faith," in Jorge Cañizares-Esguerra and Erik R. Seeman, eds., *The Atlantic in Global History, 1599–1800* (New York: Routledge, 2016 [2007]), 39–59, 40.

77. Van Stipriaan, "An Unusual Parallel," 86.

78. Ibid.; Nassy, *Essai historique*, part 1, vii–viii; Van Stipriaan, *Surinaams contrast*, 419.

79. Wolbers, *Geschiedenis van Suriname*, 442, 565.

80. Ellen Brigitte Aurelia Neslo, "The Formation of a Free Non-white Elite in Paramaribo, 1800–1863," *Caribbean Studies* 43: 2 (July–December 2015): 177–210, 183.

81. Ibid., 186.

82. "Notifikatie: Beperking van de Bewegingsvrijheid van Slaven," August 17, 1799 (#935), April 27, 1804 (#968), in Schiltkamp and De Smidt, eds., *Placaten, ordonnantiën, en andere wetten, uitgevaardigd in Suriname*, 2:1190, 1230.

83. Neslo, "The Formation of a Free, Non-white Elite in Paramaribo," 187.

84. "Notifikatie: Beperking van de Bewegingsvrijheid van Slaven," August 17, 1799 (#935), in Schiltkamp and De Smidt, eds., *Placaten, ordonnantiën, en andere wetten, uitgevaardigd in Suriname*, 2:1190. According to the editors, the restriction was withdrawn on August 30, 1799, and there is no record of its reissue after April 27, 1804.

85. Ellen Brigitte Aurelia Neslo, *Een ongekende elite: De opkomst van een gekleurde elite in koloniaal Suriname 1800–1863* (De Bilt, the Netherlands: HaEs Producties, 2016), 198.

86. Neslo, "The Formation of a Free, Non-White Elite in Paramaribo," 187, 195.

87. Ibid., 188.

88. Neslo, *Een ongekende elite*, 230–33; Cohen, *Jews in Another Environment*, 162.

89. NAN, NPIGS, inv. nr. 437, [p. 4]; NAN, NPIGS, inv. nr. 11, p. 13; Vink, *Creole Jews*, 174.

90. Vink, *Creole Jews*, 191–92.

91. Holly Snyder, " 'Customs of an Unruly Race': The Political Context of Jamaican Jewry, 1670–1831," and Kay Dian Kriz, "Belisario's 'Kingston Cries' and the Refinement of Jewish Identity in the Late 1830s," both in Tim Barringer, Gillian Forrester, and Barbaro Martinez-Ruiz, eds., *Art and Emancipation in Jamaica: Isaac Mendes Belisario and His Worlds* (New Haven, Conn.: Yale University Press, 2007), 151–62, 163–78.

92. Van Stipriaan, "An Unusual Parallel," 89.

93. For examples of the traditional scholarly view, see ibid., 87 and Cohen, *Jews in Another Environment*.

94. The only surviving communal bylaws ("askamoth") of the two united congregations of Brazil, which constitute the first Jewish institutions in the Americas, refer only to "K. K. de Sur Israel" and "K. K. de Maguen Abraham." SAA, Archief van de Portugees-Israëlitische Gemeente, inv. nr. 334, Portugees-Israëlitische Gemeente Sur Israel te Brazilië, 1304. Members of Montreal's congregation initially referred to themselves as "Israelites of the Town of Montreal," probably because most were of Ashkenazi origin. BAC, H-985, minutes, 11 Kislev 5539 [November 30, 1778].

95. Miriam Bodian, *Hebrews of the Portuguese Nation: Conversos and Community in Early Modern Amsterdam* (Bloomington: Indiana University Press, 1997), 92, 103–6.

96. Bodian, *Hebrews of the Portuguese Nation*, 72. Another historian notes that the term "Sephardim" was used "in the later period," with no further elaboration. Zosa Szajkowski, "Population Problems of Marranos and Sephardim in France, from the 16th to the 20th Centuries," *Proceedings of the American Academy for Jewish Research* 27 (1958): 83–105, 87.

97. Bodian, *Hebrews of the Portuguese Nation*, 72. For the indiscriminate application, see Gérard Nahon, *Métropoles et périphéries séfarades d'Occident: Kairouan, Amsterdam, Bayonne, Bordeaux, Jérusalem* (Paris: Cerf, 1993); Michael Studemund-Halévy, *Biographisches Lexikon der Hamburger Sefarden: Die Grabinschriften des Portugiesenfriedhofs an der Königstraße in Hamburg-Altona* (Hamburg: Christians, 2000); Yosef Kaplan, Paloma Díaz-Mas, and Harm den Boer, "Presentación: Fronteras e interculturalidad entre los sefardíes occidentales," in Paloma Díaz-Mas and Harm den Boer, eds., *Fronteras e interculturalidad entre los sefardíes occidentales* (Amsterdam: Rodopi, 2006), 8; Holly Snyder, "A Tree with Two Different Fruits: The Jewish Encounter with German Pietists in the Eighteenth-Century Atlantic World," *William and Mary Quarterly* 58: 4 (October 2001): 855–82; Bodian, *Hebrews of the Portuguese Nation*; and my own early work, including *Sephardim in Twentieth Century America: A Diasporic History* (New York: New York University Press, 2009); Aviva Ben-Ur and Rachel Frankel, *Remnant Stones: The Jewish Cemeteries of Suriname: Epitaphs* (Cincinnati: Hebrew Union College Press, 2009); and Aviva Ben-Ur with Rachel Frankel, *Remnant Stones: The Jewish Cemeteries and Synagogues of Suriname: Essays* (Cincinnati: Hebrew Union College Press, 2012).

98. Daniel M. Swetschinski, *Reluctant Cosmopolitans: The Portuguese Jews of Seventeenth-Century Amsterdam* (London: Littman Library of Jewish Civilization, 2000), xii; Tirtsah Levie

Bernfeld, *Poverty and Welfare Among the Portuguese Jews in Early Modern Amsterdam* (Oxford: Littman Library of Jewish Civilization, 2012), 5, and the various works of Mordehay Arbell.

99. NAN, SONA, inv. nr. 6, will of Isaac de Vries de jonge, August 1, 1723, p. 75 verso (*hoogde duitse Joodse gemeente*); NAN, Sociëteit van Suriname, May 31, 1743 (*Hoog duitsche Joodsche Natie*); AJA, MS-581, Box 7, folder 7/14, Parnassim of the High German Jewish community in Amsterdam to their counterparts in Suriname, September 20, 1786 (*Hoogde Joodsche synagogue*); NAN, NPIGS, inv. nr. 135, "Notificasaõ," October 12, 1766 (*Asquenazim*); NAN, NPIGS, inv. nr. 2, May 8, 1785 (*asquenzim*); inv. nr. 1, June 14, 1780 (*asquenas*) and June 14, 1780 (*tudescos*).

100. Alex van Stipriaan, " 'Een verre verwijderd trommelen . . .': Ontwikkeling van Afro-Surinaamse muziek en dans in de slavernij," in Ton Bevers, Antoon Van den Braembussche, and Berend Jan Langenberg, eds., *De Kunstwereld: Produktie, distributie en receptie in de wereld van kunst en cultuur* (Hilversum: Verloren, 1993), 143–73, 145.

101. The Trans-Atlantic Slave Trade Database has thus far identified the names and personal information of 91,491 Africans seized from captured slave ships or taken from African trading sites after 1807 in efforts to suppress the slave trade. The cultural origins of these names are now undergoing analysis. See https://archive.slavevoyages.org/about/origins.

102. Rosemary Brana-Shute, "The Manumission of Slaves in Suriname, 1760–1828" (Ph.D. diss., University of Florida, 1985), 227. For the latter term, see Plakaat 902, "Voorzorgsmaatregelen tegen melaatsheid," in Schiltkamp and De Smidt, eds. *Placaten, ordonnantiën, en andere wetten, uitgevaardigd in Suriname*, 1:1144; for *vrije volkeren*, see NAN, Sociëteit van Suriname, inv. nr. 308, "Leijst van het Opneemen . . . ," May 19, 1762, p. 80.

103. Brana-Shute, "The Manumission of Slaves in Suriname," xvi; Cynthia McLeod, "En celebración de la extraordinaria vida de Elisabeth Samson," *Encuentros: Centro Cultural del BID* [Banco Interamericano de Desarrollo] 27 (August 1998): 2.

104. Margot van den Berg, " 'Mi no sal tron tongo': Early Sranan in Court Records, 1667–1767" (master's thesis, University of Nijmegen, 2000), 14n12.

105. Neslo, *Een ongekende elite* and "The Formation of a Free Non-white Elite in Paramaribo."

106. McLeod, "En celebración," 2; Brana-Shute, "The Manumission of Slaves in Suriname," xvi. For terminology considerations within a U.S. context, see Michael P. Johnson and James L. Roark, *Black Masters: A Free Family of Color in the Old South* (New York: W. W. Norton, 1984), xvi and Margo Jefferson, *Negroland: A Memoir* (New York: Pantheon, 2015).

107. George E. Brooks, *Eurafricans in Western Africa: Commerce, Social Status, Gender, and Religious Observance from the Sixteenth to the Eighteenth Century* (Athens: Ohio University Press/Oxford: James Currey, 2003).

108. Similarly, Jean Jacques Vrij calls the former group *bevredigden*. Jean Jacques Vrij, "Bosheren en konkelaars: Aukaners in Paramaribo 1760–1780," in Peter Meel and Hans Ramsoedh, eds., *Ik ben een haan met een kroon op mijn hoofd: Pacificatie en verzet in koloniaal en postkoloniaal Suriname* (Amsterdam: Berk Bakker, 2007), 19–34, 25.

109. In Suriname today, there are nine indigenous languages, belonging to one of two language families, Cariban and Arawakan, and spoken by eight ethnic groups. See Eithne B. Carlin (text) and Diederik van Goethem (photography), *In the Shadow of the Tiger: The Amerindians of Suriname* (Amsterdam: KIT Publishers, 2009), 9.

110. George Lakoff, *Women, Fire, and Dangerous Things: What Categories Reveal About the Mind* (Chicago: University of Chicago Press, 1987).

111. See, for example, Jacob Rader Marcus, "The West India and South American Expedition of the American Jewish Archives," *American Jewish Archives* 5 (1953): 5–21; Menasseh ben Israel, *Sefer Mikveh Israel* (Vilna, 1835/1836), 2b (מערב הודו). Ben Israel's book first appeared in Latin and, almost simultaneously, in Spanish editions as Menasseh ben Israel, מקוה ישראל: *Hoc est, Spes Israelis* (Amsterdam: n.p., 1650) and מקוה ישראל: *Esto es, Esperança de Israel* (Amsterdam: Semuel ben Israel Soeiro, 1649–50).

112. On this point, see Robert Carl-Heinz Shell, *Children of Bondage: A Social History of the Slave Society at the Cape of Good Hope, 1652–1838* (Hanover, N.H.: University Press of New England, 1994), 217–18.

113. NAN, Gouvernementssecretarie der Kolonie Suriname, inv. nr. 4, January 8, 1747, inv. nr. 7, January 26, 1755 (*Vaderlande; vaderland*); NPIGS, inv. nr. 46, *Gouvernements-Blad* 6 (1834); H. C. Focke, *Neger-Engelsch Woordenboek* (Leiden: Ph. H. van den Heuvell, 1855), v (*Moederland*).

114. Bailyn, "Introduction," 2; Patrick O'Brien, "Historiographical Traditions and Modern Imperatives for the Restoration of Global History," *Journal of Global History* 1 (2006): 3–39, 23 (for the end year as 1825); Kevin H. O'Rourke and Jeffrey G. Williamson, "When Did Globalization Begin?" (National Bureau of Economic Research [NBER] Working Paper Series, Working Paper 7632, Cambridge, Mass., April 2000), 22.

115. A. G. van Wieringen, *Geschiedenis der Belastingen in de Kolonie Suriname* (The Hague: Algemeene Landsdrukkerij, 1912), 8 (Gouverneur-Generaal). Schalkwijk (*The Colonial State in the Caribbean*) translates *raad fiscaal*, literally the "council of the colonial prosecutor," as "attorney general." In the archival sources, the term is often shortened to *fiscaal* or *fiscael*.

116. For the translation error, see, for example, Paul Hollanders, "'Animus Revertendi' Versus 'Animus Manendi': The Will to Return Versus the Will to Stay in Dutch Colonial Literature Applied to Colonists in Late Eighteenth-Century Suriname," in Jeroen Dewulf, Olf Praamstra, and Michiel van Kempen, eds., *Shifting the Compass: Pluricontinental Connections in Dutch Colonial and Postcolonial Literature* (Newcastle upon Tyne: Cambridge Scholars Publishing, 2013), 248–60 and Wieke Vink, *Creole Jews: Negotiating Community in Colonial Suriname* (Leiden: KITLV, 2010), 13. For the function of the Council of Policy and the post-Emancipation police force, see Schalkwijk, *The Colonial State in the Caribbean*, 253, 284.

117. In the early years of Dutch rule, the Raad van Politie was called the Politycquen Raet. Its duties included voting on, promulgating, and reinforcing legislation, as well as serving as the highest court in the land. On this point, see Schalkwijk, *The Colonial State in the Caribbean*, 252.

118. For a critique of the term, see Patricia Nelson Limerick, *The Legacy of Conquest: The Unbroken Past of the American West* (New York: W. W. Norton, 2011), especially 23–25, 259. For the continued use of "frontier" in Dutch Atlantic historiography, see Benjamin Kaplan, Marybeth Carlson, and Laura Cruz, eds., *Boundaries and Their Meanings in the History of the Netherlands* (Leiden: Brill, 2009).

119. NAN, NPIGS, inv. nr. 135, contract signed by Sarah de Semuel Ha. De Meza et al., July 10, 1798, p. 131 (*fronteira*); NAN, Sociëteit van Suriname, inv. nr. 213, Jewish community to Governor Cornelis van Sommelsdijck, undated (probably 1684 or 1685), 375–76, 376 (*frontier plaetsen*).

120. See, for example, TNAUK, HCA 30/223, Samuel Nassi to Paulo Jacome Pinto, September 8, 1672; Abigail de Britto to Francisco de Medina, September 10, 1672; Samuel Velho to Ribca Velho, September 15, 1672.

121. Davis, "David Nassy's 'Furlough,'" 79–93, 508–11, 79.

122. NAN, NPIGS, inv. nr. 2, June 26, 1787, p. 430 and inv. nr. 1666, Aanwinsten, David Cohen Nassy, "Memoire sur les Moyens d'ameliorer la colonie de Surinam," Philadelphia, 1795, [pp. 56, 58] (*mon Essai Historique de Surinam; mon ouvrage Essai Historique sur Surinam*); *Surinaamsche almanak voor het Jaar 1820* (Paramaribo: E. Beijer & C. G. Sulpke, 1819), 44–45 (*voornamelijk aan eenen Nassy toegeschreven*); Marten Douwes Teenstra, *De negerslaven in de colonie Suriname en de uitbreiding van het Christendom onder de heidensche bevolking* (Dordrecht: H. Lagerweij, 1842), 321 (*hoofdzakelijk aan de pen van . . . Nassy toegeschreven*), 321. See also Sigmund Seeligman, "David Nassy of Surinam and His 'Lettre Politico-Theologico-Morale sur les Juifs,'" *PAJHS* 22 (1914): 25–38, 27.

Chapter 1

1. NAN, Gouvernementssecretarie der Kolonie Suriname, inv. nr. 3, Journaal, March 14–18, 1743 (scans 64–68); NAN, NPIGS, inv. nr. 11, September 20, 1821, p. 135 (*Nassy landing plaats*); John Gabriel Stedman, *Narrative of a Five Years Expedition Against the Revolted Negroes of Surinam: Transcribed for the First Time from the Original 1790 Manuscript*, ed. Richard Price and Sally Price (Baltimore: Johns Hopkins University Press, 1988), 364 (for the lavish meals of Surinamese planters). His name appears variously in archival and printed sources as Joan Jacob Mauritius, Joan Jacob Mauricius, Joan Jakob Mauricius, Johan Jacob Mauricius, and Joan Jacob v. Mauricius.

2. Joan [*sic*] Jacob Mauritius [*sic*] to the Estates General, September 28, 1748, in *Recueil van egte stukken en bewijzen door Salomon du Plessis en door andere tegens Mr. Jan Jacob Mauricius, als mede de Societeit van Suriname en den selven Gouverneur Mauricius tegen den gemelde du Plessis en andere ingedient en overgelevert*, 5 vols. (1752–54), 3:79 ('*t eenige Steedje in de Waereld, daar niet dan Jooden woonen*).

3. *History of the Corporation of Spanish and Portuguese Jews "Shearith Israel" of Montreal, Canada* (Montreal: n.p., 1918), 9 ("one of the idyls of Jewish history").

4. Adam Rovner, *In the Shadow of Zion: Promised Lands Before Israel* (New York: New York University Press, 2014), 193 (literally, "promised land"); Diederik Samwel, *Suriname* (Haarlem: J. H. Gottmer, 2015), 160 (*hun eigen beloofde land in het tropische regenwoud*).

5. Stiefel, *Jewish Sanctuary in the Atlantic World*, 128; Joseph Adler, *Restoring the Jews to Their Homeland: Nineteen Centuries in the Quest for Zion* (Northvale, N.J.: J. Aronson, 1997), 215.

6. Daniel J. Elazar, review of Robert Cohen, *Jews in Another Environment*, in *Jewish Political Studies Review* 4: 1 (Spring 1992): 135–37, 136.

7. Cohen, *Jews in Another Environment*, 301n6 and (following Cohen) Davis, "Regaining Jerusalem," 24.

8. Davis, "Regaining Jerusalem," 23, 26.

9. I. Harold Sharfman, *Jews on the Frontier: An Account of Jewish Pioneers and Settlers in Early America* (Chicago: H. Regnery, 1977), 212. I have found no evidence in Noah's writing to support this assertion, nor was he apparently aware of the existence of the "Arrarat" plantation, co-owned in the 1730s by the brothers Selomoh, David, Abraham, and Imanuel Pereyra. NAN, NPIGS, inv. nr. 75, petition of Selomoh Pereyra, August 3, 1733.

10. Samwel, *Suriname*, 159 (*Joodse handelscentrum*); Stiefel, *Jewish Sanctuary in the Atlantic World*, 124; Abram Leon Sachar, *The Jew in the Contemporary World: Sufferance Is the Badge*

(New York: A. A. Knopf, 1939), 380 ("strange city of the jungle"); Faber, *Jews, Slaves, and the Slave Trade*, 65 ("urban real estate ownership by Jews").

11. Klooster, *The Dutch Moment*, 228–31.

12. Ibid., 224.

13. Bernfeld, *Poverty and Welfare*, 32, 41, 64–65, 165 (on the poor of Amsterdam's Jewish community and efforts to relocate them).

14. A. J. F. van Laer, *Van Rensselaer Bowier Manuscripts: Being the Letters of Kiliaen van Rensselaer, 1630–1643, and Other Documents Relating of the Colony of Rensselaerswyck* (Albany: University of the State of New York, 1908), 136–52; Wim Klooster, "Networks of Colonial Entrepreneurs: The Founders of the Jewish Settlements in Dutch America, 1650s and 1660s," in Richard L. Kagan and Philip D. Morgan, eds., *Atlantic Diasporas: Jews, Conversos, and Crypto-Jews in the Age of Mercantilism, 1500–1800* (Baltimore: Johns Hopkins University Press, 2009), 36.

15. Bastiaan D. van der Velden, *Ik lach met Grotius, en alle die prullen van boeken: Een rechtsgeschiedenis van Curaçao* (Amsterdam: SWP, 2011), 217 (100 guilders); Nicolaas Jansz van Wassenaar and Barend Lampe, *Historisch verhael alder ghedenck-weerdichste geschiedenisse* (Amstelredam: Bij Ian Evertss, Cloppenburgh en Jan Janssen, 1622–35), 98 (50 guilders). Both cite paragraph 20 of *Vrijheden en exemptiën voor de Patronen, Meesters en Particulieren, die op Nieuw-Nederlandt eenige Colonien of Vee zullen planten* (1630).

16. Jaap Jacobs, "Dutch Proprietary Manors in America: The Patroonships in New Netherland," in L. H. Roper and B. Van Ruymbeke, eds., *Constructing Early Modern Empires: Proprietary Ventures in the Atlantic World, 1500–1750* (Leiden: Brill, 2007), 301–26, especially 301–7.

17. George Edmundson, "The Dutch in Western Guiana," *English Historical Review* 16: 64 (October 1901): 640–75, 650; Wim Klooster, "The Essequibo Liberties: The Link Between Jewish Brazil and Jewish Suriname," *Studia Rosenthaliana* 44 (2011): 77–82, 77.

18. Klooster, "The Essequibo Liberties," 78.

19. Leo Lucassen, "To Amsterdam: Migrations Past and Present," in Nancy Foner et al., eds., *New York and Amsterdam: Immigration and the New Urban Landscape* (New York: New York University Press, 2014), 52–82, 58–59; Erika Kuijpers, *Migrantenstad: Immigratie en social verhoudingen in zeventiende-eeuws Amsterdam* (Hilversum: Verloren, 2005), 63; Bernfeld, *Poverty and Welfare*, 41–42.

20. Cohen, *Jews in Another Environment*, 20 and SAA, 334, Archief van de Portugees-Israëlietische Gemeente, inv. nr. 87, October 30, 1750 (for guilds); Isaac Pinto, *Reflexoens politicas tocante a constituiçaõ da naçao judaica* (Amsterdam, 5508 [1747/1748]), 6 (for the four trades).

21. Klooster, "Networks of Colonial Entrepreneurs," 42; David J. Halperin, trans., *Sabbatai Zevi: Testimonies to a Fallen Messiah* (Oxford: Littman Library of Jewish Civilization, 2007).

22. Klooster, "Networks of Colonial Entrepreneurs," 41.

23. Isaac Samuel Emmanuel and Suzanne A. Emmanuel, *History of the Jews of the Netherlands Antilles*, 2 vols. (Cincinnati: American Jewish Archives, 1970), 1:46.

24. Ibid., 46, 51.

25. Menasseh Ben Israel, מקוה ישראל: *Hoc est, Spes Israelis* (Amsterdam: n.p., 1650) and מקוה ישראל: *Esto es, Esperança de Israel* (Amsterdam: Semuel Ben Israel Soeiro, 1649–50).

26. Egon Wolff and Frieda Wolff, *Dicionário Biográfico: Judaizantes e Judeus no Brasil, 1500–1808*, 2 vols. (Rio de Janeiro: Cemitério Comunal Israelita, 1986), 1:138; Egon Wolff and

Frieda Wolff, *Quantos Judeus Estiveram no Brasil Holandês* (Rio de Janeiro: n.p., 1991), 65; Emmanuel and Emmanuel, *History of the Jews of the Netherlands Antilles*, 1:42–43.

27. Mark Ponte to Aviva Ben-Ur, June 9, 2017 (the map indicates "S. Carlis," the document "S. Carlo"; both are housed in SAA). Karwan Fatah-Black (*White Lies and Black Markets: Evading Metropolitan Authority in Colonial Suriname, 1650–1800* [Leiden: Brill, 2015], 76) also identifies Nassi as Brazilian born.

28. Jane S. Gerber, "Pride and Pedigree: The Development of the Myth of Sephardic Aristocratic Lineage," in Brian Smollett and Christian Wiese, eds., *Reappraisals and New Studies of the Modern Jewish Experience: Essays in Honor of Robert M. Seltzer* (Leiden: Brill, 2015), 85–103, 88; David Graizbord, "Religion and Ethnicity Among 'Men of the Nation': Toward a Realistic Interpretation," *Jewish Social Studies* 15: 1 (Fall 2008): 32–65, 47–48; Heinrich Graetz, *History of the Jews* (Philadelphia: Jewish Publication Society of America, 1893), 2:509 (for the tradition of Davidic ancestry among the Babylonian Resh Galuta, or Prince of the Exile).

29. Daniel Swetschinski, "Waardige kooplieden, ijverige bankiers, loyale hovelingen; de Suasso's en het Huis van Oranje/Worthy merchants, keen bankers, loyal courtiers: The Suassos and the House of Orange," in Daniel Swetschinski and Loeki Schönduve, *De familie Lopes Suasso: Financiers van Willem III/The Lopes Suasso family, bankers to William III* (Amsterdam: Waanders Zwolle/Joods Historisch Museum Amsterdam, 1988), 9–64, 195. The Abravanels also claimed Davidic descent. See Carl Cohen, "Martin Luther and His Jewish Contemporaries," *Jewish Social Studies* 25: 3 (July 1963): 195–204, 199.

30. Esther Cohen, introduction to Esther Cohen and Mayke B. de Jong, eds., *Medieval Transformations: Texts, Power, and Gifts in Context* (Brill: Leiden, 2001), 1–10, 3. Alternatively, they claimed descent from Aeneas, the mythological Trojan hero and ancestor of the Romans.

31. Steven Weitzman, "Rabbinic Revelations," in John Efron et al., *The Jews: A History* (Upper Saddle River, N.J.: Pearson Prentice Hall, 2009), 92–115; 105; Nina Caputo, "Regional History, Jewish Memory: The Purim of Narbonne," *Jewish History* 22: 1/2 (2008): 97–114, 105; Michael Brenner, *A Short History of the Jews* (Princeton, N.J.: Princeton University Press, 2010), 64; Salo Wittmayer Baron, *A Social and Religious History of the Jews*, 3 vols. (New York: Columbia University Press, 1937), 1:333.

32. Jeremy Cohen, "The Nasi of Narbonne: A Problem in Medieval Historiography," *AJS Review* 2 (1977): 45–76, 53–54, 57, 65.

33. Abraham A. Neuman, *Jews in Spain: Their Social Political, and Cultural Life During the Middle Ages*, 2 vols. (Philadelphia: Jewish Publication Society of America, 1942), 2:224.

34. David Nirenberg, "Mass Conversion and Genealogical Mentalities: Jews and Christians in Fifteenth-Century Spain," *Past and Present* 174: 1 (2002): 3–41, 4–7.

35. Andrée Aelion Brooks, *The Woman Who Defied Kings: The Life and Times of Doña Gracia Nasi—A Jewish Leader During the Renaissance* (St. Paul, Minn.: Paragon Books, 2002), 318–20.

36. Davis, "Regaining Jerusalem," 2.

37. Robert Cohen, "The Egerton Manuscript," *American Jewish Historical Quarterly* 62: 4 (June 1973): 333–47, 340. A transcription of the Dutch version appears in Samuel Oppenheim, "An Early Jewish Colony in Western Guiana: Supplemental Data," *PAJHS* 17 (1909): 53–70.

38. NAN, Staten-Generaal, no. 5767, letter by J. Rijckaert and David van Baerle, West India Company, Chamber of Amsterdam, to the States General, Amsterdam, February 21, 1664; Nassy, *Essai historique*, part 1, 13, part 2, 113–22; Emmanuel and Emmanuel, *History of the Jews of the Netherlands Antilles*, 1:44.

39. Nassy, *Essai historique*, part 2, 114.

40. Ibid., part 1, 13.

41. Klooster, "Networks of Colonial Entrepreneurs," 46.

42. Ibid.; Klooster, "The Essequibo Liberties"; Nassy, *Essai historique*, part 1, 13.

43. Justin Roberts, "Surrendering Surinam: The Barbadian Diaspora and the Expansion of the English Sugar Frontier, 1650–75," *William and Mary Quarterly* 73: 2 (April 2016): 225–26; Alison Games, "Cohabitation, Suriname-Style: English Inhabitants in Dutch Suriname After 1667," *William and Mary Quarterly* 72: 2 (April 2015): 195–242, 202.

44. Games, "Cohabitation, Suriname-Style," 205.

45. Klooster, "Colonial Entrepreneurs," 33.

46. Ibid., 49.

47. Ibid., 48–49.

48. Klooster and Oostindie, *Realm Between Empires*, 127.

49. Here were the estates of Sara da Silva, E. R. R. de Prado, Abraham de la Parra, the widow I. Marques, an individual identified only as "Pardo," and the Ashkenazi Jew Gerrit Jacobs. A. de Lavaux, Algemeene Kaart van de Colonie of Provintie van Suriname, ca. 1770, map 13 in Ir. F. C. Bubberman et al., *Links with the Past: The History of the Cartography of Suriname, 1500–1971* (Amsterdam: Theatrum Orbis Terrarum B.V., 1973). Jacob de Meza and Jacob Nunes de Castro received plots of land on the same creek in 1685. NAN, Sociëteit van Suriname, inv. nr. 213, Warrants van Landen, p. 402.

50. NAN, NPIGS, inv. nr. 539, untitled list of land grants; NAN, NPIGS, inv. nr. 10, September 13, 1819.

51. NAN, NPIGS, inv. nr. 98 (1677–78).

52. NAN, Oud Archief Suriname, Raad van Politie, inv. nr. 210, January 10, 1671, p. 36.

53. NAN, NPIGS, inv. nr. 416, pp. 45, 46, 51.

54. *A discription of the Coleny of Surranam in Guiana*, 1667, map 7 in Bubberman et al., *Links with the Past*; John Carter Brown Library, map of the Surinam and Commewijne rivers, 1667 or later.

55. Jacob Selwood, "Left Behind: Subjecthood, Nationality, and the Status of Jews After the Loss of English Surinam," *Journal of British Studies* 54: 3 (July 2015): 578–601, 589.

56. Ibid., 590.

57. TNAUK, CO, 1/35, A list of such persons of ye Hebrew nation willing to depart & transport themselves & estates to Jamaica, pp. 175–76.

58. Selwood, "Left Behind," 590–95; Nassy, *Essai historique*, part 1, 27–28; Games, "Cohabitation, Suriname-Style," 230–31. William Byam, then governor of Antigua, remarked to William Lord Willoughby in 1670 that Suriname's Jews "seem now highly dissatisfied with the country." W. Noël Sainsbury, ed., *Calendar of State Papers, Colonial Series, 1574–1660, Preserved in the State Paper Department of Her Majesty's Public Record Office* (London: Longman, Green, Longman, & Roberts, 1860), 204.

59. Nassy, *Essai historique*, part 1, 30; Selwood, "Left Behind," 598n101; Lucien Leo Eduard Rens, "Analysis of Annals Relation to Early Jewish Settlement in Surinam," in Robert Cohen, ed., *The Jewish Nation in Surinam: Historical Essays* (Amsterdam: S. Emmering, 1982), 29–46, 41–43; Games, "Cohabitation, Suriname-Style," 231n81. Selwood and Rens do not think any of these families departed; however, Games notes that some Portuguese Jewish men from Suriname turn up in Barbados in 1675 and thereafter. On the other hand, maps dating to the

early Dutch period still indicate the estates of leading Jewish planters, such as de Solis and Pereira, who were supposedly among the evacuees in 1677.

60. Selwood, "Left Behind," 598.

61. M. Walraven, MS. copy after the so-called "Labadisten-map" of the year 1686, map 9 in Bubberman et al., *Links with the Past.* In the 1760s, a handful of Jewish-owned plantations still operated near Thorarica Stadt on the left bank of the Suriname River, the only estates at that time remaining in the former capital city. Philippe Fermin, *Description Générale, Historique, Géographique et Physique de la Colonie de Surinam,* 2 vols. (Amsterdam: E. van Harrevelt, 1769), 1:10.

62. Ben-Ur with Frankel, *Remnant Stones: The Jewish Cemeteries and Synagogues of Suriname,* 44.

63. Ibid., 13; G. W. C. Voorduin, *Gezigten uit Nederland's West-Indien, naar de natuur geteekend, en Beschreven door G.W.C. Voorduin, Luitenant ter zee: Op steen gebragt door JHr. J. E. van Heemskerck van Beest, oud Luitenant ter Zee* (Amsterdam: Frans Buffa en Zonen, 1860), plaat VI; Joan [*sic*] Jacob Mauritius [*sic*] to the Estates General, September 28, 1748, in *Recueil van egte stukken en bewijzen door Salomon du Plessis,* 3:79.

64. Venezuelan Boundary Commission, *Report and Accompanying Papers of the Commission Appointed by the President of the United States "To Investigate and Report Upon the True Divisional Line Between the Republic of Venezuela and British Guiana"* (Washington, D.C.: United States of America, 1897), 4:43 ("Jews' town"); TNAUK, War Office 1/148, report of Floris Visscher van Heshuysen, [1804], pp. 533–607, 572 (*village connu sous le nom de la Savane des Juifs*); UBLBC, "Ontwerp tot een Beschryving van Surinaamen," transcript of manuscript dating between 1739 and 1748, 2 (Jooden Savane); NYHSL, Original Memorandum Book No. 2 of John Greenwood, p. 19 ("Jews' Savannah"); NAN, Gouvernementssecretarie der Kolonie Suriname, inv. nr. 318, December 22, 1755 (*het Jooden Dorp*) and inv. nr. 319, February 29, 1756 (Jooden Savana).

65. J. S. Roos, "Joodesavane of Joodsch Dorp," in H. D. Benjamins and Joh. F. Snelleman, eds., *Encyclopaedia van Nederlandsch West-Indië* (Amsterdam: S. Emmering, 1981 ['s Gravenhage: Martinus Nijhoff, 1914–17]), 392–93; N. H. Swellengrebel and E. Van Der Kuyp, *Health of White Settlers in Surinam* (Amsterdam: Colonial Institute at Amsterdam, 1940). These authors are probably confusing the relocation with the exodus from the town of Torarica during the plague.

66. Games, "Cohabitation, Suriname-Style," 241.

67. Joseph Sutherland Wood, *The New England Village* (Baltimore: Johns Hopkins University Press, 1997), 142.

68. For a general argument concerning the quest for more fertile lands, see Van Stipriaan, *Surinaams contrast,* 50.

69. Nassy, *Essai historique,* part 1, 23, 40, part 2, 49–50.

70. Ibid., part 2, 50. The governor's name appears in contemporaneous sources variously as Joan or Johan van Scharphuysen, Scharphuizen, or Jan van Scherpenhuizen.

71. Bernfeld, *Poverty and Welfare,* 350n201; Fatah-Black, *White Lies and Black Markets,* 76–77 (for quote), 82.

72. Wolbers, *Geschiedenis van Suriname,* 82.

73. Ibid., 61, 78–79; Schalkwijk, *The Colonial State in the Caribbean,* 207–8; Gerard Willem van der Meiden, *Betwist bestuur: Een eeuw strijd om de macht in Suriname, 1651–1753* (Amsterdam: De Bataafsche Leeuw, 1986).

74. Bernfeld, *Poverty and Welfare*, 4 (on poverty's subjectivity); Ruud Beeldsnijder, "Op de onderste trede: Over vrije negers en arme blanken in Suriname, 1730–1750," *Oso: Tijdschrift voor Surinaamse Taalkunde, Letterkunde en Geshiedenis* 10: 1 (1991): 7–30, 20–21 (on the difficulty of defining poverty in early modernity); NAN, NPIGS, inv. nr. 1, August 25, 1774, petition of Lea, widow of Ishac Messias, and inv. nr. 79, Ingekomen rekesten en memories, petition of Ishak de Britto, May 29, 1757 (for examples of being slave-poor).

75. Bernfeld, *Poverty and Welfare* and "Financing Poor Relief in the Spanish-Portuguese Jewish Community in Amsterdam in the Seventeenth and Eighteenth Centuries," in Jonathan I. Israel and R. Salverda, eds., *Dutch Jewry: Its History and Secular Culture (1500–2000)* (Leiden: Brill, 2002), 63–102, 67 (her observation of Amsterdam applies broadly).

76. Swetchinski, *Reluctant Cosmopolitans*, 176, 186; Bernfeld, "Financing Poor Relief," 72–73 and *Poverty and Welfare*, 52; Frances Malino, *The Sephardic Jews of Bordeaux: Assimilation and Emancipation in Revolutionary and Napoleonic France* (Tuscaloosa: University of Alabama Press, 1978), 10; Miriam Bodian, "The 'Escamot' of the Spanish-Portuguese Jewish Community of London, 1664," *Michael* (1985): 9–26, 13.

77. Emmanuel and Emmanuel, *History of the Jews of the Netherlands Antilles*, 2:775, 779; Robert Cohen, "Passage to a New World: The Sephardi Poor of Eighteenth-Century Amsterdam," in Lea Dasberg and Jonathan N. Cohen, eds., *Neve Ya'akov: Jubilee Volume Presented to Dr. Jaap Meyer on the Occasion of His Seventieth Birthday* (Assen: Van Gorcum, 1982), 31–40, 34.

78. Bernfeld, *Poverty and Welfare*, 38.

79. Beeldsnijder, "Op de onderste trede," 18.

80. See, for example, NAN, NPIGS, inv. nr. 3, May 29, 1794, June 28, 1796; inv. nr. 4, March 17, 1812 (want of clothing); inv. nr. 3, August 25, 1790, December 27, 1792, May 28, 1793, June 28, 1796 (illness as a poverty exacerbator).

81. NAN, NPIGS, inv. nr. 82, September 4 and 16, 1760; inv. nr. 1, April 23, 1772, March 22, 1775, September 19, 1779, October 5, 1780, October 8, 1780; inv. nr. 2, March 21, 1786, March 22, 1786, July 6, 1783, September 3, 1783; inv. nr. 4, September 15, 1808, September 27, 1808, December 6, 1810.

82. Ruud Beeldsnijder, *"Om werk van jullie te hebben": Plantageslaven in Suriname, 1730–1750* (Utrecht: Vakgroep Culturele Antropologie, 1994), 42–43 and "Op de onderste trede," 7; Postma, *The Dutch in the Atlantic Slave Trade*, 182–83; NAN, Sociëteit van Suriname, inv. nr. 213, Notulen gehouden bij den heeren Gouverneur en Raaden van Politie en Justitie, May 9, 1685, p. 393 (*schaersheijt*).

83. NAN, Sociëteit van Suriname, 1.05.03, inv. nr. 213, Marcus Broen to Governor Cornelis van Sommelsdijck, May 22, 1685, pp. 429–30, 429; inv. nr. 239, Lijste de debiteuren van de Joodse Natie, welke aan de Ede. Societijt ujt hoofe van den slaven Handel nog verschuldigh zijn, pp. 229–30.

84. NAN, Sociëteit van Suriname, inv. nr. 213, Sentença dada por os sette adjuntos com os Ssres do Mahamad, October 14, 1670, p. 385; Lista das sommas com que foraõ fintados os Sres jehidim, September 25, 1680, p. 390 (50,000 Surinamese guilders). My assumption that the operating budget remained stable during this ten-year period is based on similar patterns in the eighteenth and early nineteenth centuries. Their identification as *jehidim* who owed (with one exception) no less than 50 guilders makes it likely that they were estate owners.

85. TNAUK, HCA 30/223, Francisco Henriques Pereyra, Suriname, to Pedro Henriquez Pereyra, Amsterdam, November 7, 1672; JHM, David Hisqo. Baruh Louzada et al., "Livro de

Ascaboth & Meseberah," Suriname, various dates from 1789 and after, p. 25 (for his position as *haham*).

86. TNAUK, HCA 30/227, Part 1, Ishac Arias, Suriname, to Pedro Henriques Pereira, Amsterdam, December 12, 1671.

87. NAN, Sociëteit van Suriname, inv. nr. 213, Aenwijsinge van alle de namen der personen die hooft en ackergeldt betaelt hebben of nogh betaelen moeten voor de jaeren 1681 en 1682, pp. 195–99.

88. NAN, Sociëteit van Suriname, inv. nr. 213, Governor Cornelis van Sommelsdijck to Philip van Hulten, May 18, 1685, pp. 409–12, 411. For these challenges, see Jan Marinus van der Linde, *Surinaamse suikerheren en hun kerk: Plantagekolonie en handelskerk ten tijde van Johannes Basseliers, predikant en planter in Suriname, 1667–1689* (Wageningen: H. Veenman, 1966), 76–77.

89. On the function of reputed wealth and benevolence in attracting the indigent to Amsterdam's Portuguese Jewish community, see Bernfeld, *Poverty and Welfare*. For exaggeration of Jewish wealth among scholars and amateur chroniclers, see Wolbers, *Geschiedenis van Suriname*, 173, 314–15; Cohen, "Jewish Demography in the Eighteenth Century;" Marilyn Delevante and Anthony Alberga, *The Land of One People: An Account of the History of the Jews of Jamaica* (Kingston, Jamaica: Ian Randle, 2008).

90. Cohen, *Jews in Another Environment*, 88.

91. Vink, *Creole Jews*, 26.

92. NAN, Sociëteit van Suriname, inv. nr. 213, Suriname Lijste tot den 31en decembr 1684, pp. 223–24, 224; Claudia Schnurmann, *Atlantische Welten: Engländer und Niederländer im amerikanisch-atlantischen Raum 1648–1714* (Köln: Böhlau Verlag GmbH & Cie, 1998), 382.

93. Nassy, *Essai historique*, part 1, 48; NAN, Sociëteit van Suriname, inv. nr. 213, Suriname Lijste tot den 31en decembr 1684, pp. 223–24, 224.

94. NAN, Sociëteit van Suriname, inv. nr. 213, Suriname Lijste tot den 31en decembr 1684, pp. 223–24, 224.

95. NAN, Sociëteit van Suriname, inv. nr. 318, Op de Joode Savane, p. 105 (*Jos. Prado, vrij mulat van 10 jaeren*). Robert Cohen's reference to a Jodensavanne 1762 census listing 27 people of African descent is a misattribution; it is in fact a head count of Paramaribo's Jewish community. Cohen, *Jews in Another Environment*, 159; NAN, Sociëteit van Suriname, inv. nr. 318, Lijst van de Blanken die sig alhier aan Parambo. bevinden, May 19, 1762, pp. 82–83.

96. NAN, Sociëteit van Suriname, inv. nr. 318, various dates, 1762, pp. 80–115.

97. NAN, NPIGS, inv. nr. 75, November 13, 1708.

98. Vink, *Creole Jews*, 196–97; SAA, 334, Archief van de Portugees-Israëlietische Gemeente, inv. nr. 1029, "Extracte uijt het Register der Resolutien van de Ed. Aght. Heeren directeuren van de Societeijt van Suriname," January 6, 1734, pp. 890–94.

99. M. S. Polak of the Para Division may have been Jewish.

100. NAN, Sociëteit van Suriname, inv. nr. 318, various dates, July 9, 1762, pp. 82–83; NAN, Sociëteit van Suriname, inv. nr. 213, Lijste van alle de Blancke, negros, ende Indiaanse kinderen onder de 12 jaaren in Comewine, Cottica, Cometuana, Pirica, Mood Creeck, oock aen Parimaribo, December 31, 1684, p. 240 verso. The only Jew in 1684 was Jacob Nunes Henriques, father to two "negro" children.

101. NAN, NPIGS, inv. nr. 75, petition of Jahacob Valenssy, October 4, 1703.

102. Ibid.; petition of Avraham Arias, April 28, 1705; petition of Ishac de Ja. De Meza, April 25, 1707.

103. For the principle of frontage, see A. J. A. Quintus Bosz, *Drie eeuwen grondpolities in Suriname: Een historische studie van de achtergrond en de ontwikkeling van de Surinaamse rechten op de grond* (Paramaribo: Universiteit van Suriname, 1980), 46.

104. NAN, NPIGS, inv. nr. 75, petition of Moseh Henriquez Cotino, 15 Tamuz 5456 (July 15, 1696).

105. Ibid., petition of Mosseh de Ribas, 5 Sivan 5470 (June 3, 1710). The name of the creek is spelled "Caxuina."

106. Ibid., petition of Moseh Henriquez Cotino, 15 Tamuz 5456 (July 15, 1696).

107. Ibid., petition of Ester, widow of Joseph Cohen Nassy, April 3, 1719.

108. Ibid., David Judeu, 5694 [1704].

109. SAA, inv. nr. 334, Archief van de Portugees-Israëlietische Gemeente, 1029, Abraham Gabay Izidro to the Parnassim and Gabay of the Talmud Tora, Amsterdam, 1735, pp. 9–12, 12.

110. NYHSL, John Greenwood, Diaries, 1752–1758, 1763–1765, Original Memorandum Book No. 2 (1752–58), 101–2.

111. Ibid., 102–3.

112. NAN, NPIGS, inv. nr. 75, petition of Jacob de Casseres Brabo to the Mahamad, January 29, 1698.

113. NAN, NPIGS, inv. nr. 25, folder marked "1703, " Memoria de las faltas que hizo el Rabi Jahacob de Casseres brabo [*sic*]," 1703.

114. Ibid., testimony of Isaac de Abraham Israel, 5463 [1703], p. 438.

115. Van der Linde, *Surinaamse suikerheren*, 63.

116. NAN, NPIGS, inv. nr. 1, August 18, 1775; inv. nr. 2, September 4, 1787, June 30, 1790; inv. nr. 3, November 29, 1790, January 14, 1798; inv. nr. 4, February 21, 1803.

117. Cecil Roth, "The Remarkable Career of Haham Abraham Gabay Yzidro," *TJHSE* (1974): 211–13, 211; SAA, inv. nr. 334, Archief van de Portugees-Israëlietische Gemeente, inv. nr. 1029, folder 9, Gabay Izidro to Amsterdam Mahamad, 1735; NAN, SONA, inv. nr. 55, will of Ribca de Britto, widow of the late Abraham Gabay Izidro (also identified as Abraham Gabay Isidro), November 23, 1785, pp. 17–22. Izidro described the soil's infertility using the words *terra . . . incomodo* [*sic*], which can also be rendered as "inconvenient land."

118. NAN, NPIGS, inv. nr. 138, Contracten, gesloten door de gemeente B.V.S., 1699–1776; Ben-Ur and Frankel, *Remnant Stones: The Jewish Cemeteries of Suriname*, 208 (epitaph 264).

119. NAN, NPIGS, inv. nr. 7, June 23, 1764, August 25, 1764, December 7, 1764.

120. Ibid., October 6, 1766.

121. NAN, NPIGS, inv. nr. 82, petition of David Pereira Brandon, 1760, p. 9 (*venda pubica de vette warij como tambeijn amasar pam* [*sic*]).

122. Ibid., inv. nr. 2, July 8, 1781.

123. Ibid., inv. nr. 1, undated entry, ca. 1779; inv. nr. 5, June 29, 1813.

124. See, for example, Stiefel, *Jewish Sanctuary in the Atlantic World*, 124; Leibman, *Messianism, Secrecy and Mysticism*, 27.

125. NAN, NPIGS, inv. nr. 75, 25 Tisry 5488 [October 10, 1727].

126. Ibid., inv. nr. 101, Askamoth voor de gemeente B.V.S., vastegesteld 1754, treatise 6, article 11 (*incomodidades desta colonia*; scan 10).

127. Ibid., inv. nr. 2, March 26, 1788, December 23, 1800; inv. nr. 4, January 1, 1801.

128. Roos, "Joodesavane of Joodsch Dorp," 392; Marten Douwes Teenstra, *De Landbouw in de Colonie Suriname*, 2 vols. (Groningen: H. Eekhoff, Hz., 1835), 2:133.

129. NAN, NPIGS, inv. nr. 3, December 24, 1795.

130. Ibid., inv. nr. 5, March 22, 1816; inv. nr. 6, February 25, 1818 (for quote), March 12, 1818, March 15, 1818, December 10, 1818.

131. One tax list, for example, lists the charity plantations Waicoribo, Quapibo, Mamre, Gelderland, Amsterdam, and Dotan but no privately occupied plots in Jodensavanne. NAN, NPIGS, inv. nr. 1, June 26, 1770.

132. Ibid., inv. nr. 25, taxation for the synagogue chest, 29 Elul 5483 [September 29, 1723], p. 268.

133. Ibid., inv. nr. 7, June 23, 1761.

134. See, for example, ibid., inv. nr. 1, May 6, 1779 (Rephael del Castilho as administrator of unnamed charity plantation); August 24, 1779 (Nieuwe Rust plantation, charity estate administered by Jacob Henriquez).

135. Okke ten Hove, Heinrich E. Helstone, and Wim Hoogbergen, *Surinaamse Emancipatie 1863: Familienamen en Plantages* (Amsterdam: Rozenberg Publishers, 2003), 52.

136. NAN, NPIGS, inv. nr. 1, June 26, 1770 (the Waicoribo, Quapibo, Mamre, Gelderland, Amsterdam, and Dotan plantations).

137. Adriaan van Berkel, *Amerikaansche Voyagien, behelzende een Reis na Rio de Berbice, gelegen op het vaste Land van Guiana, aan de wilde-kust van America, mitsgaders een andere na de Colonie van Suriname, gelegen in het noorder deel van het gemelde landschap Guiana* (Amsterdam: Johan ten Hoorn, 1695), 109 (Joodenquartier).

138. Alexander de Lavaux, *Generale Caart van de Provintie Suriname*, 1737; Van Stipriaan, *Surinaams contrast*, 32.

139. However, one archaeologist argues that Jodensavanne proper covered 20.6 hectares (less than 8.25 acres). Benjamin S. Mitrasingh, "Een voorbeschouwing van het archeologisch onderzoek in Joden Savanne," *Mededelingen van het Surinaams Museum* 41 (December 1983): 4–18, 6.

140. *Algemeene Kaart van de Colonie of Provintie Suriname* (Amsterdam: Covens en Mortier, 1758).

141. NAN, Klapper op de namen van Plantages in Suriname ca. 1740–1780 uit het Oud-notarieel archief van Suriname, four notebooks.

142. UBLBC, "Ontwerp tot een beschrijvinge van Surinaamen," Amsterdam, 1788 (type-script copy made in Paramaribo, 1911), 32; Hartsinck, *Beschryving van Guyana* (500 acres for cacao and coffee estates), 1:269; Jan Christiaan Lindeman, *The Vegetation of the Coastal Region of Suriname*, vol. 1, part 1 (Amsterdam: Van Eedenfonds, 1953), 89; Nassy, *Essai historique*, part 2, 52 (*sable*, meaning sand in French); RBGK, DC/69/128–133, F. W. Hostmann to William Jackson Hooker, October 8, 1842 ("very barren white sand [mica?]").

143. NAN, NPIGS, inv. nr. 75, petition of Abraham de Quiros y Costa, 8 Iyar 5491, copy made August 17, 1731 (a few entries are effaced); Wolbers, *Geschiedenis van Suriname*, 106.

144. NAN, NPIGS, inv. nr. 75, petition of Abraham de Quiros y Costa, June 28, 1734. The unit of land measurement feet (*pes* in Portuguese) probably refers to Rhineland feet used during this period in Suriname. Each "ketting" equaled 66 Rhineland feet; a plot measuring one by ten kettings in dimension equaled one acre. UBLBC, "Ontwerp tot een beschrijvinge van Surinaamen," p. 32. For explicit reference to Rhineland (*rijnlandsch*) feet in Jodensavanne, see NAN, NPIGS, inv. nr. 135, p. 136.

145. UBLBC, "Ontwerp tot een beschrijvinge van Surinaamen," p. 32 (300–500 acres); Hartsinck, *Beschryving van Guyana*, 1:269 (500 acres for cacao and coffee estates).

146. NAN, NPIGS, inv. nr. 75, petition of Abraham Raphael Arrias, 22 Sebat 5483 [January 28, 1723].

147. Nassy, *Essai historique*, part 2, 50.

148. For David Nassy's definition, see ibid., 49.

149. Bernard Moitt, "In the Shadow of the Plantation: Women of Color and the *Libres de fait* of Martinique and Guadeloupe, 1685–1848," in David Barry Gaspar and Darlene Clark Hine, eds., *Beyond Bondage: Free Women of Color in the Americas* (Urbana: University of Illinois Press, 2004), 37–59, 39. I thank Rebecca J. Scott for introducing me to this concept.

150. Ben-Ur with Frankel, *The Jewish Cemeteries and Synagogues of Suriname*, 32.

151. NAN, NPIGS, inv. nr. 75, petition of Ishac Pinto, 15 Av 5470 [August 15, 1710].

152. Ibid., petition of Ishac Pinto, May 29, 1721.

153. NAN, SONA, inv. nr. 5, will of Ishac Pinto, June 23, 1721.

154. Michael North, "Towards a Global Material Culture: Domestic Interiors in the Atlantic and Other Worlds," in Veronika Hyden-Hanscho et al., eds. *Cultural Exchange and Consumption Patterns in the Age of Enlightenment: Europe and the Atlantic World* (Bochum: Verlag Dr. Dieter Winkler, 2013), 81–96; Thera Wijsenbeek-Olthuis, "Vreemd en eigen: Ontwikkelingen in de woon- en leefcultuur binnen Hollandse steden van de zestiende tot de negentiende eeuw," in P. te Boekhorst, P. Burke, and W. Frijhoff, *Cultuur en Maatschappij in Nederland, 1500–1850: Een historisch-antropologisch perspectief* (Amsterdam: Boom, 1992), 79–107, 91–95.

155. NAN, NPIGS, inv. nr. 75, Imanuel de Solis to the regents, January 22, 1708; Mosseh de Riba to the regents, April 23, 1715 (for his status as an *adjunto*).

156. NAN, NPIGS, inv. nr. 75, petition of Samuel and Baruh Cohen Nassi (spelled "Semuel C. Nassy"), May 21, 1706.

157. Nassy, *Essai historique*, part 2, 50.

158. NAN, NPIGS, inv. nr. 75, petition of Imanuel Mussaphia, September 15, 1721; petition of Samuel Abenacar, September 15, 1721.

159. SAA, inv. nr. 334, Archief van de Portugees-Israëlietische Gemeente, inv. nr. 1029, "Manifesto" of Abraham Gabay Izidro to the Parnassim and Adjuntos of Kahal Kodes Beraha VeSalom, "48 dias del Homer del ano de 4 Sivan 5495" [May 25, 1734], section 31, p. 46.

160. NAN, NPIGS, inv. nr. 75, petition of Imanuel de Soliz, October 4, 1703; inv. nr. 210, Register van plakkaten, ordonnantiën, resoluties van de Raad van Politie, placard of Governor Philips Julius Lichtenburghs [*sic*] mandating the placement of shingles on roofs in Thorarica [*sic*], p. 9 verso, April 6, 1669 (*singles*; scan 26).

161. NAN, NPIGS, inv. nr. 75, petition of Abraham Ysrael, 25 Tebet 5452 [January 14, 1692].

162. NAN, NPIGS, inv. nr. 25, tax reform edict, 4 Tisry 5493 [September 23, 1732].

163. NAN, NPIGS, inv. nr. 75, petition of Abraham Ysrael, 25 Tebet 5452 [January 14, 1692].

164. Alice Morse Earle, *The Sabbath in Puritan New England* (New York: Charles Scribner's Sons, 1891), 34 (for New England).

165. NAN, Stadhouderlijke Secretarie, inv. nr. 1264, *Redres der Reglamenten, Institutien, en Instellingen van de H. Gemeente B.V.S.*, November 9, 1752, p. 18 (treatise 15, Portuguese section); NAN, NPIGS, inv. nr. 1, ca. February 1, 1779 (this page is out of chronological order on the microfilm) and inv. nr. 136, contract signed by A. M. Robles, Simon Cohen Lobato, and J. Fernandes Jr., July 18, 1823 (referencing treatise 10, articles 1 and 3).

166. NAN, NPIGS, inv. nr. 117, article 155; TNAUK, War Office 1/148, report of Floris Visscher van Heshuysen, [1804], pp. 533–607, 573; "Verhaal van een Togtje in Suriname," *Vaderlandsche Letteroefeningen* (Amsterdam: G. S. Leeneman van der Kroe en J. W. IJntema, 1823), 178–88, 183.

167. NAN, NPIGS, inv. nr. 76, petition of Mordecai [name appears only in Hebrew letters], February 12, 1754.

168. Ibid., inv. nr. 11, December 7, 1824.

169. Ibid., inv. nr. 94, *Recueil der Privilegien vergunt aan die van de Portugeesche Joodsche Natie in de Colonie van Suriname*, 1746, p. 52.

170. Vink, *Creole Jews*, 198; NAN, NPIGS, inv. nr. 1, August 10, 1773, April 15, 1777, August 12, 1778, February 20, 1779; inv. nr. 2, June 14, 1780, June 1, 1782, May 8, 1785, June 26, 1787, January 3, 1790, April 21, 1790, May 24, 1790.

171. NAN, NPIGS, inv. nr. 75, petition of Dr. Abraham Pinto and Ishac Pinto, April 25, 1707.

172. Ibid., petition of Imanuel Solis, January 22, 1708.

173. Norbert Elias and John L. Scotson, *The Established and the Outsiders: A Sociological Enquiry into Community Problems* (London: Sage, 1994 [1965]), xxxii.

174. Bernfeld, *Poverty and Welfare*, 47–50, 56.

175. Ibid., 38.

176. Cohen, *Jews in Another Environment*, 24. Elsewhere, however, Cohen remarks that "fully a quarter of the Jews despatched to Surinam or their listed family members, found their last resting place there." Cohen, "Passage to a New World," 36.

177. NAN, NPIGS, inv. nr. 75, petition of Simha Peregrino (signed "sinha pelegrion"), November 16, 1728.

178. Ibid., petition of David Judeu, 5464 [1703–4]; NAN, NPIGS, inv. nr. 416, p. 47.

179. NAN, NPIGS, inv. nr. 75, petition of Jacob Pelengrino, October 1732.

180. Rachel Frankel, "Antecedents and Remnants of Jodensavanne: The Synagogues and Cemeteries of the First Permanent Plantation Settlement of New World Jews," in Paolo Bernardini and Norman Fiering, eds., *The Jews and the Expansion of Europe to the West, 1450–1800* (New York: Berghahn Books, 2001), 394–436; Ben-Ur with Frankel, *Remnant Stones: The Jewish Cemeteries and Synagogues of Suriname*, chap. 4; Davis, "Regaining Jerusalem"; Leibman, *Messianism, Secrecy and Mysticism*, chap. 1. By contrast, Barry Stiefel (*Jewish Sanctuary in the Atlantic World*, 126) suggests the dimensions of the synagogue plaza are of colonial Spanish provenience.

181. On the observation of the shape, see Stiefel, *Jewish Sanctuary in the Atlantic World*, 126.

182. Ben-Ur with Frankel, *Remnant Stones: The Jewish Cemeteries and Synagogues of Suriname*, 115.

183. Ibid., 123 and "Architecture of Autonomy: The Blessing and Peace Synagogue of Suriname," in Jonathan Sarna et al., *New Essays in American Jewish History: To Commemorate the 60th Anniversary of the American Jewish Archives Journal and the 10th* Anniversary of the American Jewish Archives Under the Direction of Dr. Gary P. Zola (New York: Ktav Press, 2010), 51–77; Midrash Hane'elam, Bereshit, Parshat Hayei Sarah, in *Sefer HaZohar* (Vilna: Wdowa I Bracia Romm [the widow and brothers Romm], 1923), 125a. I thank Jonathan D. Sarna for suggesting a possible link to the *Zohar* citation.

184. Schorsch, *Jews and Blacks in the Early Modern World*, 252 (for the phrase); NAN, NPIGS, inv. nr. 1, September 17, 1771, December 15, 1771, October 21, 1772, October 19, 1778; ibid., inv. nr. 2, December 10, 1786, March 27, 1790 (for the so-called *negros da sedaca*).

185. Ben-Ur with Frankel, *Remnant Stones: The Jewish Cemeteries and Synagogues of Suriname*, 114–15.

186. Critique of Robert Cohen's book *Jews in Another Environment* in Davis, "Regaining Jerusalem," 2; Cohen, *Jews in Another Environment*, passim.

187. Beeldsnijder, *"Om werk van jullie te hebben,"* appendix 4, 264–66; Van Stipriaan, *Surinaams contrast*, 311 (table 44); den Heijer, *Goud, ivoor en slaven*, 366.

188. The estimate and percentage are derived from Van Stipriaan, *Surinaams contrast*, 314; Postma, *The Dutch in the Atlantic Slave Trade*, 213; Goslinga, *The Dutch in the Caribbean and in the Guianas*, 279, 291, 309, 341, 519; and Kofi Yakpo, Margot van den Berg, and Robert Borges, "On the Linguistic Consequences of Language Contact in Suriname: The Case of Convergence," in Eithne B. Carlin et al., *In and Out of Suriname: Language, Mobility and Identity* (Leiden: Brill, 2014), 164–95, 171 (for the period 1651–1826). The total number of Africans transported to Suriname from 1651 through the abolition of slavery in 1863 has not yet been tabulated. The information assembled in the *Slave Voyages* database (https://www .slavevoyages.org) requires painstaking computation of the passengers aboard thousands of individual ships, which often reached multiple destinations. Additionally, illegal transport continued after the abolition of the slave trade imposed on Suriname in 1807 during the British Interregnum and not all of these voyages have been accounted for.

189. NAN, Sociëteit van Suriname, inv. nr. 213, list marked "no. 5," "Joodsche natie: Lyste van alle de persoonen der Joodsche natie aen d Ede. Societeit voor de Colonies van Suriname schuldigh over hooft en ackergeldt tot den 31en decembr 1684," pp. 226–33, 233. The figures are as follows: 972 Africans (nearly 84 percent), 163 whites (slightly over 14 percent); 23 Indians (nearly 2 percent). However, this census only includes Jews indebted to the Sociëteit van Suriname, which possibly excludes the landless. Note that the citation for this census in Enthoven, "Suriname and Zeeland," 255 (Sociëteit van Suriname, inv. nr. 213, p. 204, "Alle personen die hooft-en ackergeld betaald hebben, 1684"), is incorrect.

190. Nassy, *Essai historique*, part 2, 55.

191. NAN, NPIGS, inv. nr. 2, July 6, 1783, p. 117.

192. Nassy, *Essai historique*, part 2, 55.

193. Ibid.; NAN, NPIGS, inv. nr. 75, passim.

194. NAN, NPIGS, inv. nr. 75, petition of Ishac de Ja. de Meza, April 25, 1707; petition of Dr. Abraham Pinto and Ishac Pinto, April 25, 1707; petition of Semuel Cohen Nassy, October 8, 1715 (requesting a total of five years to build); petition of Jahacob Henriquez Ferreyra, August 2, 1734 (requesting three years to build).

195. Ibid., petition of Imanuel de Soliz, October 4, 1703 (for quote).

196. Ibid., January 22, 1708.

197. Ibid., inv. nr. 99, treatise 1, article 7.

198. Ibid., inv. nr. 8, December 22, 1772 (*fazer manter qeitasao aos escravos em quanto se esta rezando*); inv. nr. 1, October 12, 1778 (*negros da sedaka*).

199. Ibid., inv. nr. 1, September 19, 1779.

200. Ibid., inv. nr. 2, January 29, 1784.

201. Ibid., inv. nr. 1, October 3, 1774.

202. Ibid., October 5, 1774.

203. Schorsch, *Jews and Blacks in the Early Modern World*, 262.

204. "Beknopte beschrijving van de joden-savanah," *Surinaamsche almanac voor het jaar 1833* (Amsterdam: C. G. Sulpke, 1832), 285–91, 289 (*vertrouwde Slaven*); NAN, NPIGS, inv. nr. 141, Inventarissen van gewijde voorwerpen, August 7, 1827, and inventory dated Jodensavanne, December 12, 1848.

205. On this observation for slaves of Surinamese plantations in general, see Oostindie and Van Stipriaan, "Slavery and Slave Cultures in a Hydraulic Society," 87; Van Stipriaan, "An Unusual Parallel," 86 and *Surinaams contrast*, 419.

206. NAN, Sociëteit van Suriname, inv. nr. 213, Jewish community to Governor Cornelis van Sommelsdijck, undated (probably 1684 or 1685), pp. 375–76, 375 verso.

207. Martijn van den Bel, Lodewijk Hulsman, and Lodewijk Wagenaar, eds., *De reizen van Adriaan van Berkel naar Guiana: Indianen en planters in de 17de eeuw* (Leiden: Sidestone Press, 2014), 35.

208. Schalkwijk, *The Colonial State in the Caribbean*, 209, 226 (for ten rural militias, eighteenth century); NAN, Oud Archief Suriname, Raad van Politie, inv. nr. 210, January 10, 1671, p. 18 verso (for six rural militias, including a Jewish one).

209. John Gabriel Stedman, *Narrative of a Five Years' Expedition Against the Revolted Negroes of Surinam, in Guiana, on the Wild Coast of South America, from the Year 1772, to 1777* (London: J. Johnson, 1813), 2:35, 200.

210. Marten Schalkwijk, "Durkheim and Marx in the Caribbean: Slavery, Laws, and Marronage in Suriname, 1650–1863," *Academic Journal of Suriname* 1 (2010): 67–74, 68; Hugo A. M. Essed, *De binnenlandse oorlog in Suriname, 1613–1793* (Paramaribo: Anton de Kom Universiteit, 1984), 27–29; Price, *Alabi's World*, 9; Wolbers, *Geschiedenis van Suriname*, 137.

211. Price, *Alabi's World*; Nassy, *Essai historique*, part 1, 76.

212. Nassy, *Essai historique*, part 1, 76; Price, *Alabi's World*, 383.

213. Emmanuel, son of Aron Pereyra (epitaph 325, d. 1738); David Rodrigues Monsanto (epitaph 348, d. 1739), in Ben-Ur and Frankel, *Remnant Stones: The Jewish Cemeteries of Suriname*, 230, 237.

214. Nassy, *Essai historique*, part 1, 91–92 ("Sarua"); Goslinga, *The Dutch in the Caribbean and in the Guianas*, 387–88.

215. Emmanuel, son of Aron Pereyra (epitaph 325, d. 1738); David Rodrigues Monsanto (epitaph 348, d. 1739), in Ben-Ur and Frankel, *Remnant Stones: The Jewish Cemeteries of Suriname*, 230, 237. Verse 2 continues, "Lift up yourself, you judge of the earth: render to the proud their recompense."

216. The name of the village in which Meijer perished is effaced (Aldea de P[ ]nij). NAN, NPIGS, inv. nr. 423, 15.

217. David Cohen Nassy (C73, d. 1743), in Ben-Ur and Frankel, *Remnant Stones: The Jewish Cemeteries of Suriname*, 61.

218. Nassy, *Essai historique*, part 1, 95.

219. Goslinga, *The Dutch in the Caribbean and in the Guianas*, 384.

220. Nassy, *Essai historique*, part 1, 75, 91–92; Price, *Alabi's World*, 9, 383 and *First-Time*, 70–71.

221. NAN, NPIGS, inv. nr. 7, October 10, 1753. The tax was demanded only of *jehidim*, not *congregantes*. There was a general understanding that *congregantes* did not pay capitation

taxes to the Portuguese Jewish community, though in practice the policy varied. See ibid., inv. nr. 1, December 16, 1783.

222. Schalkwijk, "Durkheim and Marx in the Caribbean," 68; Wolbers, *Geschiedenis van Suriname*, 549.

223. Silvia W. de Groot, "The Boni Maroon War, 1765–1793, Surinam and French Guyana," *Boletín de Estudios Latinoamericanos y del Caribe* 18 (June 1975): 30–48, 31, 36.

224. NAN, Sociëteit van Suriname, inv. nr. 370, testimony of the *Negerinnen* Diana van Isak Mesias en Lucretia van Pinto, pp. 332–34.

225. NAN, NPIGS, inv. nr. 2, July 29, 1782.

226. Ibid., inv. nr. 1, September 26, 1773, February 5, 1774, October 14, 1776, October 27, 1777, September 19, 1779, October 17, 1783.

227. Wim Hoogbergen, *The Boni Maroon Wars in Suriname* (Leiden: Brill, 1990), 129–31.

228. NAN, NPIGS, inv. nr. 2, June 17, 1789.

229. Ibid., inv. nr. 1, December 15, 1774, July 28, 1777.

230. De Groot, "The Boni Maroon War," 42; NAN, NPIGS, inv. nr. 4, September 30 and October 1, 1805.

231. NAN, Sociëteit van Suriname, inv. nr. 370, Ses Maandelijkse Rapport van de werken van forteficatie der binnen landsen defencie in de colonie van Surinamen, p. 533.

232. Bubberman et al., *Links with the Past*, 64.

233. Zvi Loker and Robert Cohen, "An Eighteenth-Century Prayer of the Jews of Surinam," in Robert Cohen, ed., *The Jewish Nation in Surinam: Historical Essays* (Amsterdam: S. Emmering, 1982), 75–87. The original manuscript, housed at the American Jewish Historical Society, is undated. Based on informed conjecture (p. 76), Loker and Cohen erroneously dated it to 1789–90, coinciding with Boni Maroon attacks on plantations near Jodensavanne. The actual date is recorded in an inventory of books formerly housed in the Beraha VeSalom synagogue. The entry reads: "Hum Livrinho d'oraça'o, & implorar o Triúmpho pelas Armadas detta Nossa Colonia, depechados Contra os Nossos Enemigos, os rebeldes Negros aurentados. Comporta C. ordem dos muy Dignos Sres. do M. M. desta Nossa Sta. Kehila pelo Referido Primo. Hazan Louzada, no Ao. 5566." NAN, NPIGS, inv. nr. 131, [p. 3]."

234. Schalkwijk, *The Colonial State in the Caribbean*, 229–30; Wolbers, *Geschiedenis van Suriname*, 547–51.

235. Schalkwijk, *The Colonial State in the Caribbean*, 229.

236. NAN, NPIGS, inv. nr. 4, November 20 and December 4, 1804.

237. August Kappler, *Zes Jaren in Suriname: Schetsen en tafereelen uit het maatschappelijke en militaire leven in deze kolonie* (Utrecht: W. F. Dannenfelser, 1853), 90.

238. Nassy, *Essai historique*, part 2, 57. Nassy's assertion is correct. See, for example, Van Berkel, *Amerikaansche Voyagien*, 109; Hartsinck, *Beschryving van Guiana*, 2:875–76; Fermin, *Description Générale*, 1:10.

239. The book first appeared in French and soon after was translated to Dutch. Nassy, *Essai historique* and *Geschiedenis der Kolonie van Suriname* (Amsterdam: Allart and van der Plaats, 1791).

240. Nassy, *Essai historique*, part 2, 50–54.

241. Ibid., 56, 53.

242. NAN, NPIGS, inv. nr. 36, [David Nassy], "Prospectus van een Seminarium of kweekschool . . . op de Joode Savane zal opgerigt worden," [1796], 8.

243. Nassy, *Essai historique*, part 2, 56.

244. Alex van Stipriaan, "Debunking Debts: Image and Reality of a Colonial Crisis: Suriname at the End of the 18th Century," *Itinerario* 19: 1 (1995): 69–84; Nassy, *Essai historique*, part 1, 55, 78, part 2, 27.

245. Nassy, *Essai historique*, part 1, 72–73, part 2, 10.

246. Goslinga, *The Dutch in the Caribbean and in the Guianas*, 309.

247. Nassy, *Essai historique*, part 1, 154–56.

248. NAN, NPIGS, inv. nr. 1, July 28, 1777, June 12, 1780.

249. David Lowenthal, "Nostalgia Tells It Like It Wasn't," in Christopher Shaw and Malcolm Chase, eds., *The Imagined Past: History and Nostalgia* (Manchester: Manchester University Press, 1989), 18–32, 24.

250. On the *Essai historique* as apologia, see Vink, *Creole Jews*, 193 and Cohen, *Jews in Another Environment*, 73.

251. For this erroneous claim, aside from Robert Cohen (*Jews in Another Environment*, 301n6) and Davis, "Regaining Jerusalem," 24, see also M. F. Abbenhuis, *Suriname: Verhalen en schetsen uit de Surinaamse Geschiedenis*, part II, installment 3 (Paramaribo: Drukkerij Leo-Victor, 1944), 51; Rovner, *In the Shadow of Zion*, 192; and Yosef Kaplan, "'Jerusalem on the Banks of the River Suriname': The Golden Age of Jewish Settlement in Suriname Jerusalem," in *Tzedek ve-Shalom: A Synagogue from Suriname in the Israel Museum, Jerusalem* (Jerusalem: Israel Museum, 2010), 97–109, 102 and "'Yerushalayim She-al Gedot Nahar Surinam': Tur HaZahav shel HaHityashvut HaYehudim BeSurinam," in Tania Coen-Uzzielli, ed., *Mi-Surinam Li-Yerushalayim: Beit-HaKenesset "Tsedek VeShalom" BeMuzeon Israel* (Jerusalem: Israel Museum, 2011), 89–99, 94 (in Hebrew).

252. Tuvia Preschel, "BeChol Makom SheGalu . . . Galta 'Yerushalayim' Immahem," *Or ha-Mizrah* 28: 3–4 (1979/1980): 279–93, 291 (in Hebrew). For other examples of the cognitive error, see Baron, *A Social and Religious History of the Jews*, 15:3–73 (chap. 63: "Dutch Jerusalem") and Yosef Hayim Yerushalmi, "Between Amsterdam and New Amsterdam: The Place of Curaçao and the Caribbean in Early Modern Jewish History," *American Jewish History* 72: 2 (December 1982): 172–92, 179.

253. Neil Asher Silberman, *Digging for God and Country* (New York: Alfred A. Knopf, 1982), 8–9, 30–31 and "'If I Forget Thee, O Jerusalem': Archaeology, Religious Commemoration, and Nationalism in a Disputed City, 1801–2001," *Nations and Nationalism* 7: 4 (2001): 487–504, 492.

254. Note that this spelling represents the Judeo-Portuguese dialect of Suriname, as reflected in archival sources. On the vibrancy of Jodensavanne during the holidays, see Nassy, *Essai historique*, part 2, 56.

255. For a survey and historical analysis of these cemeteries, see Ben-Ur and Frankel, *Remnant Stones: The Jewish Cemeteries of Suriname: Epitaphs* and Ben-Ur with Frankel, *Remnant Stones: The Jewish Cemeteries and Synagogues of Suriname*.

Chapter 2

1. David Sorkin, "Is American Jewry Exceptional?: Comparing Jewish Emancipation in Europe and America," *American Jewish History* 96: 3 (September 2010): 175–200, 200; Bernfeld, *Poverty and Welfare*, 14 ("We are enjoying here more freedom than elsewhere in the Jewish world," citing Portuguese Jewish leaders of Amsterdam, 1630).

2. NAN, NPIGS, inv. nr. 5, January 10, 1815.

3. Nassy, *Essai historique*, part 2, 27.

4. Ibid., part 1, 78.

5. Joan [*sic*] Jacob Mauritius [*sic*] to the Estates General, September 28, 1748, in *Recueil van egte stukken en bewijzen door Salomon du* Plessis, 3:79.

6. Van der Meiden, *Betwist bestuur*, 118.

7. John Gabriel Stedman, *Narrative, of a five years' expedition, against the Revolted Negroes of Suriname, in Guiana on the Wild Coast of South America: From the year 1772 to 1777*, 2 vols. (London: J. Johnson, 1796), 2:292; see also 1:290 (Jews "enjoy extraordinary privileges in this colony").

8. V. P. Malouet, *Collection de Mémoires et correspondances officielles sur l'administration des colonies, et notammentsur la Guiane française et hollandaise*, 4 vols. (Paris: Baudouin, 1806), 3:191. "Intendant" is the title of a high-ranking official or administrator, especially in France, Spain, Portugal, or one of their colonies.

9. Robert Cohen, "Surinam Jews Under British Rule: A Contemporary's Report," 39–48, 47 (without archival page numbers); TNAUK, WO 1/148, report of Floris Visscher Heshuysen, [1804], 533–607, 573 (*c'est peutetre* [*sic*] *le seul en son genre sur toute la surface de la terre*); Frederick Oudschans Dentz, "De Geschiedenis van een Boek," *De West-Indische Gids* (1925/ 1926): 571–82, 571.

10. Guillaume-Thomas Raynal, *Histoire philosophique et politique des établissements et du commerce des Européens dans les deux Indes*, 6 vols. (Amsterdam, 1770), 4:255 and (Amsterdam, 1772), 4:257. The quote also appears in Jacques Accarias de Sérionne, *La richesse de la Hollande: Ouvrage dans lequel on expose l'origine du commerce & de la puissance des hollandois*, 2 vols. (London: Aux dépens de la Compagnie, 1778), 1:280–81.

11. Wieke Vink, "Jews in Suriname," in Mark Avrum Ehrlich, ed., *Encyclopedia of the Jewish Diaspora: Origins, Experiences, and Culture*, 3 vols. (Santa Barbara, Calif.: ABC-CLIO, 2009), 1:738–40, 738.

12. Jacob Rader Marcus, foreword, in David Nassy (Jacob Rader Marcus and Stanley F. Chyet, eds., Simon Cohen, trans.), *Historical Essay on the Colony of Surinam* (Cincinnati: American Jewish Archives, 1974 [1788]), ix–x; Marcus, *The Colonial American Jew*, 1:152.

13. Ben-Ur with Frankel, *Remnant Stones: The Jewish Cemeteries and Synagogues of Suriname*, 31; Ben-Ur and Frankel, *Remnant Stones: The Jewish Cemeteries of Suriname*, 8; Aviva Ben-Ur, "Een joods dorp in een slavenmaatschappij: Jodensavanne in de Nederlandse kolonie Suriname," in Julie-Marthe Cohen, ed., *Joden in de Cariben* (Amsterdam: Joods Historisch Museum, 2015), 131–54 and "'Jerusalem on the Riverside': Jewish Political Autonomy in the Caribbean," revised keynote lecture, in Michael Studemund-Halevy, ed., *Mapping the Western Diaspora in the Caribbean* (Barcelona: Tirocinio, 2016), 30–54.

14. NAN, NPIGS, inv. nr. 416; NAN, Sociëteit van Suriname, inv. nr. 500, Jacob Henriques Barrios Jessurun, David Nunes Monsanto, and Samuel Hoheb Brandon, Regents of the Portuguese Jewish nation in Suriname, to J. G. Wichers, January 5, 1785; Robert Cohen, "The Misdated Ketubah: A Note on the Beginnings of the Suriname Jewish Community," *American Jewish Archives* (April 1984): 13–15, 14–15; Rens, "Analysis of Annals," 29–30.

15. Enthoven, "Suriname and Zeeland," 250; Van der Meiden, *Betwist Bestuur*, 19–20.

16. NAN, Stadhouderlijke Secretarie, inv. nr. 1264, *Redres der Reglamenten, Institutien, en Instellingen van de H. Gemeente B.V.S.*, p. 1 (in both the Dutch and Portuguese sections; Hebrew year 5422); SAA, 334, Archief van de Portugees-Israëlietische Gemeente, inv. nr. 1029, pp. 428–29 (Hebrew year 5423).

17. British Library, Egerton 2395, fols. 46–47v.

18. NAN, Sociëteit van Suriname, inv. nr. 213, David Nassi et al. to Governor Philip Julius Lichtenbergh, October 1, 1669, pp. 377–79.

19. Enthoven, "Suriname and Zeeland," 249–50.

20. Nassy, *Essai historique*, part 2, 125; NAN, Sociëteit van Suriname, inv. nr. 213, David Nassi et al. to Governor Philip Julius Lichtenbergh, October 1, 1669, pp. 377–79, 388 verso.

21. S. E. Barber, "Power in the English Caribbean: The Proprietorship of Lord Willoughby of Parham," in L. H. Roper and B. Van Ruymbeke, eds., *Constructing Early Modern Empires: Proprietary Ventures in the Atlantic World, 1500–1750* (Brill: Leiden, 2007), 204.

22. Vink, *Creole Jews*, 70.

23. Nassy, *Essai historique*, part 1, 30; Selwood, "Left Behind," 598, 598n101; Rens, "Analysis of Annals," 41–43; Games, "Cohabitation, Suriname-Style," 231n81.

24. Marcus, *The Colonial American Jew*, 1:26; TNAUK, CO 1/35, p. 173 (Versterre claimed his policy was mandated by the States General and the States of Zealand).

25. Nassy, *Essai historique*, part 1, 27–28; Games, "Cohabitation, Suriname-Style," 230–31.

26. Nassy, *Essai historique*, part 2, 131–35; NAN, Sociëteit van Suriname, inv. nr. 213, David Nassi et al. to Governor Philip Julius Lichtenbergh, October 1, 1669, pp. 377–79.

27. Nassy, *Essai historique*, part 2, 131–35; NAN, Sociëteit van Suriname, inv. nr. 213, David Nassi et al. to Governor Philip Julius Lichtenbergh (*sic*; his name in some archival sources also appears as "Lichtenberg"), October 1, 1669, pp. 377–79.

28. NAN, Sociëteit van Suriname, inv. nr. 213, David Nassi et al. to Governor Philip Julius Lichtenbergh, October 1, 1669, pp. 377–79.

29. The Portuguese translation of the document refers to this status as *verdadayramente vasalhos da Republica de Hollanda* and *Burgezes*. NAN, NPIGS, inv. nr. 177, Introducçao, askamot, April 27, 1755.

30. Nassy, *Essai historique*, part 2, 131–35; NAN, Sociëteit van Suriname, inv. nr. 213, David Nassi et al. to Governor Philip Julius Lichtenbergh, October 1, 1669, pp. 377–79.

31. Nassy, *Essai historique*, part 2, 122 (for extreme need); 131; NAN, Sociëteit van Suriname, inv. nr. 213, David Nassi et al. to Governor Philip Julius Lichtenbergh, October 1, 1669, pp. 377–79, 377.

32. Nassy, *Essai historique*, part 2, 133.

33. Ibid.

34. Ibid., 135.

35. See, for example, Cohen, *Jews in Another Environment*, 300 ("privileges and regulations") and Vink, *Creole Jews*, 73.

36. See, for example, NAN, NPIGS, inv. nr. 116, Ascamoth of algemeene politique, aeconomische, kerkelyke & civiele institutien van de Portugeesche Joodsche Natie deezer colonie van Surinam, p. 1.

37. NAN, NPIGS, inv. nr. 94, *Recueil en Privilegien vergunt aan der van de Portugesche Joodsche Natie in de Colonie van Suriname*, 1746, p. 13 (Jewish tribunal), pp. 37–44 (Jewish marriage); Schiltkamp and De Smidt, *Placaten, ordonnantiën, en andere wetten, uitgevaardigd in Suriname*, #393 (1741), #607 (1761), #849 (1781), pp. 469–70, 737, 1023–28 (Jewish marriage), p. 52 (Jodensavanne), p. 54 (Gabay's expulsion).

38. See, for example, NAN, Stadhouderlijke Secretarie, inv. nr. 1264, Westinidiën Kerkelyke Zaeken, I. Nassy c.s., commissie voor de Portugees-Joodse gemeente, 1752, treatises 5–6, pp. 13–19 (Dutch section).

39. Schiltkamp, *De geschiedenis van het notariaat*, 181 (for the spread of Dutch knowledge among Jews).

40. NAN, NPIGS, inv. nr. 94, *Recueil en Privilegien vergunt aan der van de Portugeesche Joodsche Natie in de Colonie van Suriname*, 1746, 99–103, 106–7, 109–14, 116; NAN, Raad van Polities, inv. nr. 238; NAN, Stadhouderlijke Secretarie, inv. nr. 1264, Westinidiën Kerkelyke Zaeken, I. Nassy c.s., commissie voor de Portugees-Joodse gemeente, 1752 (for complete bylaws); NAN, NPIGS, inv. nr. 95–98, 108 (for bylaw fragments and list of typos); NAN, Raad van Politie, inv. nr. 239 (for privileges).

41. For the parallel in a Livornese context, see Bregoli, *Mediterranean Enlightenment*, 22.

42. Vink, *Creole Jews*, 136.

43. NAN, Sociëteit van Suriname, inv. nr. 213, Samuel Nassi to Governor Joseph Julius Lichtenberg, November 22, 1669, December 28, 1670, p. 383.

44. Van der Linde, *Surinaamsche suikerheeren*, 172.

45. NAN, Sociëteit van Suriname, inv. nr. 213, Lista das sommas com que forão fintados os Sres jehidim deste santo kahal pellos Sres do Mahamad, p. 390. The term *parata* (*executie*) refers to foreclosure, or the right to sell collateral without the involvement of a judge.

46. NAN, NPIGS, inv. nr. 94, *Recueil en Privilegien vergunt aan der van de Portugeesche Joodsche Natie in de Colonie van Suriname*, 1746.

47. Ibid., 49–52 (title 7); Van der Linde, *Surinaamsche suikerheeren*, 174–76.

48. Cohen, *Jews in Another Environment*, 126; Van der Linde, *Surinaamsche suikerheeren*, 172–73; Richard J. H. Gottheil, *The Belmont-Belmonte Family* (New York: privately printed, 1917), 92–102 (on Belmonte).

49. Schiltkamp and De Smidt, *Placaten, ordonnantiën, en andere wetten, uitgevaardigd in Suriname*, 1:323–24, 323 (#279, November 21, 1718).

50. Cohen, *Jews in Another Environment*, 126; Schiltkamp and De Smidt, *Placaten, ordonnantiën, en andere wetten, uitgevaardigd in Suriname*, 1:341–42, 342 (plakaat 291, January 20, 1721); NAN, NPIGS, inv. nr. 94, *Recueil en Privilegien vergunt aan der van de Portugeesche Joodsche Natie in de Colonie van Suriname*, 1746, pp. 51–52 (title 7). The 1721 ordinance suggests that Christians were also Sunday violators.

51. NAN, NPIGS, inv. nr. 1, March 28, 1771; inv. nr. 2, January 29, 1784. The privilege was penned by Governor van Sommelsdijck; the resolution had been issued by the Council of Policy in 1696.

52. Ibid., inv. nr. 2, January 29, 1784.

53. Ibid., inv. nr. 99, treatise 24, article 1 (1748).

54. Cohen, *Jews in Another Environment*, 143.

55. See entries listed under "verbanning" in J. Th. de Smidt and T. van der Lee, *West Indisch Plakaatboek: Publikaties en andere wetten betrekking hebbende op St. Marten St. Eustatius Saba, 1648/1681–1816* (Amsterdam: S. Emmering, 1979). For the banishment of a married woman and slaves (*negros*), see NAN, Gouvernementssecretarie der Kolonie Suriname, Gouverneurs Journaal, February 25, 1768.

56. Aviva Ben-Ur and Jessica Vance Roitman, "Adultery Here and There: Crossing Sexual Boundaries in the Dutch Jewish Atlantic," in Gert Oostindie and Jessica Roitman, eds., *Dutch Atlantic Connections, 1680–1800* (Leiden: Brill, 2014), 185–223, 190–91, 202.

57. Ibid., 202, 206 (for exile from Paramaribo and Jodensavanne); NAN, NPIGS, inv. nr. 7, November 1, 1769, March 17, 1770, April 19, 1770 (for banishment at governor's initiative to

Jodensavanne); inv. nr. 2, March 18, 1787 (for banishment to the *cordonpad*); de Groot, "The Boni Maroon War," 31 (for a white civil servant stationed as a spy among Maroons).

58. NAN, NPIGS, inv. nr. 1, October 8, 1772 (for the expulsion of the slave named Purim); inv. nr. 2, March 12, 1786 (for the free *negra* named Ase).

59. For some exceptions, see Goslinga, *The Dutch in the Caribbean and in the Guianas*, 359 (the expulsion of white Christian women and a Jewish woman accused of having sex with slaves and an Indian); Cohen, *Jews in Another Environment*, 128–29; NAN, NPIGS, inv. nr. 7, August 18, 1749 (the banishment of wealthy Jewish planter Ishac Carrilho, addressed later in the chapter).

60. NAN, NPIGS, inv. nr. 1, October 16, 1770.

61. Ibid., August 17, 1772.

62. Ibid., January 14, 1780.

63. Nassy, *Essai historique*, part 1, 188 (the translation is from Nassy, *Historical Essay*, 120).

64. Cohen, *Jews in Another Environment*, 294n9.

65. Ibid., 128–29; NAN, NPIGS, inv. nr. 7, August 18, 1749.

66. The privileges compiled in the mid-eighteenth century refer to the 1682 charter as a valid legal precedent for Jewish status in the colony.

67. Wolbers, *Geschiedenis van Suriname*, 173, 215–16, 229–31.

68. Cohen, *Jews in Another Environment*, 130.

69. Goslinga, *The Dutch in the Caribbean and in the Guianas*, 358 ("Surinam marriage" was "the informal but still permanent relationship concluded with some form of ceremony" between a woman of African origin and a white man, "ending with the death or departure of the white male"); R. A. J. van Lier, *Frontier Society: A Social Analysis of the History of Surinam* (The Hague: Martinus Nijhoff, 1971), 78 ("marriage Surinam-style").

70. NAN, NPIGS, inv. nr. 1, February 20, 1779.

71. Ibid., inv. nr. 7, November 24, 1756, December 15, 1760, April 7, 1761, June 23, 1761.

72. Ibid., June 1, 1761.

73. Cohen, *Jews in Another Environment*, 133. The Enlightenment figure identified in the 1780s only as "de Montel" is probably not, contrary to Cohen, Selomoh Montel. On the former Montel, see Nassy, *Historical Essay*, 163–64, 215, 218.

74. NAN, NPIGS, inv. nr. 7, November 24, 1753, February 14, 1753, March 9, 1753, April 17, 1753; inv. nr. 1, January 9, 1770 (for his return).

75. Ibid., inv. nr. 1, March 20, 1770 (for the explanation for his return).

76. Ibid., inv. nr. 3, October 15, 1793 (for his crime), November 6, 1793 (for his sentence), December 16, 1798 (for his return).

77. The 1784 *ascamot* contain a clause (treatise 4, chap. 1, art. 1) urging the governor to reinforce the Mahamad's authority: "And it will please his Excellency the Governor to protect the College and lend a strong hand, so that the same may be respected and obeyed." Cohen, *Jews in Another Environment*, 151. This clause traces back to the privileges of 1669. Nassy, *Essai historique*, part 2, 133. As demonstrated earlier in this chapter, the repetition of this clause through time speaks to the periodic flaunting of Portuguese Jewish authority from both within and without.

78. NAN, NPIGS, inv. nr. 1, October 16, 1772, October 21, 1772, October 26, 1772, September 5, 1774, March 22, 1775; inv. nr. 2, November 2, 1780.

79. Ibid., inv. nr. 1, October 16, 1772 (for the excommunication), October 26, 1772, September 5, 1774.

80. Fred. Oudschans Dentz, "Surinaamsche Almanakken," *De West-Indische Gids* 28: 1 (1947): 175–76, 175.

81. See, for example, *Surinaamsche almanach op het jaar onzes Heere Jesu Christi, anno 1798* (Paramaribo: W. W. Beeldsnyder, 1798), v; *Surinaamsche almanach op het jaar onzes Heere Jesu Christi, anno 1799* (Paramaribo: A. Soulage, 1799), 6; *Surinaamsche almanak voor het jaar 1821* (Paramaribo: E. Beijer & C. G. Sulpke, 1820), v. The lengthening of Jewish holidays is not mentioned here, another suggestion of the fragility of privileges.

82. NAN, NPIGS, inv. nr. 3, August 1, 1799.

83. Ibid., inv. nr. 5, December 28, 1815 (regarding the violation of Jewish sacred days).

84. Ibid., inv. nr. 11, March 27, 1825.

85. Ibid., inv. nr. 5, March 17, 1816.

86. Ibid., inv. nr. 7, September 28, 1757, and for another example, September 24, 1760.

87. Ibid., inv. nr. 3, August 1, 1799.

88. Ibid., inv. nr. 97, April 14, 1683 (18 Nissan 5443; referring to *escama* of 5441 [1680–81]).

89. Ibid., inv. nr. 99, (1748), [p. 79].

90. Ibid., p. 1 (*as mtas. confuzoems que de continuo causarao as Ascamoth & Instituisoems*).

91. Ibid., inv. nr. 116, Ascamoth of algemeene Politique Aconomische Kerkelyke & Civiele Institutien van de Portugeesche Joodsche Natie deezer Colonie van Surinam, pp.1–3 and inv. nrs. 109–14, Askamot under various titles.

92. Ibid., inv. nrs. 103 (1754; 59 bylaws), 114 (1787–1789), and 116 (nineteenth century; 26 bylaws).

93. See, for example, Zosa Szajkowski, "Internal Conflicts Within the Eighteenth Century Sephardic Communities of France," *Hebrew Union College Annual* 31 (1960): 167–80; Dean Phillip Bell, *Jewish Identity in Early Modern Germany: Memory, Power and Community* (Aldershot, England: Ashgate, 2007), 69–70; Matt Goldish, *Jewish Questions: Responsa on Sephardic Life in the Early Modern Period* (Princeton, N.J.: Princeton University Press, 2008), 51–52.

94. Jessica Vance Roitman, "'A Flock of Wolves Instead of Sheep': The Dutch West India Company, Conflict Resolution, and the Jewish Community of Curaçao in the Eighteenth Century," in Jane Gerber, ed., *The Jewish Diaspora in the Caribbean* (Oxford: Littman Library of Jewish Civilization, 2013), 85–105, 85–86, 99–101.

95. This mandate probably existed in all Atlantic Jewish communities. For New York, see "The Earliest Extant Minute Books of the Spanish and Portuguese Congregation Shearith Israel in New York," 33.

96. NAN, NPIGS, inv. nr. 7, September 24, 1760. The problem of recusal was common across the Atlantic. For London, see LMA/4521/A/01/01/004, Ascamot, 5492 [1731–32], bylaw 3 (unpaginated).

97. NAN, NPIGS, inv. nr. 1264, Stadhouderlijke Secretarie, I. Nassy c.s., commissie voor de Portugees-Joodse gemeente, treatise 3, articles 8–9, p. 5 (Portuguese section).

98. Ibid., inv. nr. 2, April 22, 1789.

99. Ibid., inv. nr. 3, December 23, 1794, February 3, 1795, April 3, 1796.

100. Ibid., January 22, 1798. The interpretation that Jojo was a slave's name is mine. See NAN, SONA, inv. nr. 49, Testamenten, codicillen en akten, February 28, 1783, will of "de vrije Alegre, alias Jojo van Mercado," 321–24.

101. Van der Meiden, *Betwist bestuur.*

102. On Brouwer, who had served on the Court of Civil Justice and as captain of the Civil Guard, see Fred. Oudschans Dentz, "De Fortuinlijke Loopbaan in Suriname van den Zweed C. G. Dahlberg," *New West Indian Guide* 1 (1940): 269–79.

103. NAN, Gouvernementssecretarie der Kolonie Suriname, inv. nr. 43, October 1750, scans 482–87.

104. NAN, Gouvernementssecretarie der Kolonie Suriname, inv. nr. 40, April 27, 1748. On de Ronde, see Wolbers, *Geschiedenis van Suriname,* 847.

105. ULBC, "Ontwerp tot een Beschryving van Surinaamen," transcript of manuscript dating between 1739 and 1748, p. 27. The name of the street appears as "Orange Tuyn."

106. Wolbers, *Geschiedenis van Suriname,* 402; NAN, Gouvernementssecretarie der Kolonie Suriname, inv. nr. 3, Journaal, October 29, 1742; NAN, NPIGS, inv. nr. 138; NAN, November 20, 1767 (alluding to the twenty-fifth anniversary of the Lutheran Church); JHM, David Hisqo. Baruh Louzada et al., "Livro de Ascaboth & Meseberah," 1789 and after, Suriname, [p. 25] (for planter Ishak Arrias as the congregation's first *haham*). The sum the Lutheran church had to pay was the equivalent of one-tenth of the governor's annual salary. ULBC, "Ontwerp tot een Beschryving van Surinaamen," transcript of manuscript dating between 1739 and 1748, p. 29.

107. Wolbers, *Geschiedenis van Suriname,* 407–8; Armando Lampe, *Mission or Submission?: Moravian and Catholic Missionaries in the Dutch Caribbean During the Nineteenth Century* (Göttingen: Vandenhoeck & Ruprecht, 2000), 32.

108. Wolbers, *Geschiedenis van Suriname,* 197, 358; Aaron Spencer Fogleman, *Two Troubled Souls: An Eighteenth-Century Couple's Spiritual Journey in the Atlantic World* (Chapel Hill: University of North Carolina Press, 2013), 142.

109. NAN, Microfilms Brieven J. H. Lance, John Henry Lance to Elizabeth Lance, June 8, 1823.

110. Karwan Fatah-Black, "A Swiss Village in the Dutch Tropics: The Limitations of Empire-Centered Approaches to the Early Modern Atlantic World," *BMGN-Low Countries Historical Review* 128: 1 (2013): 31–52, 39.

111. Trevor J. Saxby, *The Quest for the New Jerusalem: Jean de Labadie and the Labadists, 1610–1744* (Dordrecht: Martinus Nijhoff Publishers, 1987), 275–77; Goslinga, *The Dutch in the Caribbean and the Guianas,* 275 (who claims Governor van Sommelsdijck wanted them to live in or near Paramaribo, but they refused). Their plantation still served as a geographical marker in 1752. NAN, Stadhouderlijke Secretarie, inv. nr. 1264, *Redres der Reglamenten, Institutien, en Instellingen van de H. Gemeente B.V.S.,* November 9, 1752, p. 29 (treatise 34, article 3, Portuguese section: *do Plante do Sr. Saml. Uz. D'Avilar pa riba, the o Plante Labadista, pla pma Divisaõ*).

112. Fatah-Black, "A Swiss Village in the Dutch Tropics," 32, 48–51; Saxby, *The Quest for the New Jerusalem,* 273–88; Thomas David, Bouda Etemad, and Janick Marina Schaufelbuehl, *La Suisse et l'esclavage des Noirs* (Lausanne: Éditions Antipodes, 2005), 71–72.

113. NAN, inv. nr. 512, Sociëteit van Suriname, Voorstel (afkomstig van J. G. Wichers) om 20 á 25 families zich te laten vestigen tussen Paramaribo en de redoute Purmerend. Z.d. (dated to "after 1785").

114. Hartsinck, *Beschryving van Guiana,* 2:649.

115. Vrij, "Bosheren en konkelaars," 22; NAN, Microfilms Brieven J. H. Lance, John Henry Lance to Elizabeth Lance, August 2, 1826 ("an old treaty made between them [the

'Bush Negros in the River Marowina'] and the colonial govt."); NAN, Societëit de Suriname, Resolutien van de Directie van Suriname 1779, inv. nr. 69, October 6, 1779, 291; NAN, Societëit de Suriname, Resolutien van de Directie van Suriname 1779, October 20, 1779, 179 (for gifts to Indians).

116. NAN, NPIGS, inv. nr. 7, April 18, 1751; inv. nr. 1, December 20, 1779; inv. nr. 8, October 10, 1780.

117. Ibid., inv. nr. 7, April 18, 1751. His name appears variously in the sources, including "Spork," "Sporcke," and "Sporcken."

118. Ibid., October 30, 1750. The description is 6 boms pinus, which I assume to refer to pinus caribaea saplings (rather than full-grown trees).

119. NAN, Sociëteit van Suriname, inv. nr. 126, Prince of Orange and Nassau to Governor and Courts, July 15, 1750 (unpaginated); NAN, NPIGS, inv. nr. 7, April 18, 1751.

120. Charles H. Parker, "Paying for the Privilege: The Management of Public Order and Religious Pluralism in Two Early Modern Societies," Journal of World History 17: 3 (2006): 267–96.

121. Bregoli, Mediterranean Enlightenment, 19.

122. Ibid., 20–22.

123. Ibid., 26.

124. NAN, Staten-Generaal, inv. nr. 5764, Jewish petitioners to the Board of Directors of the West India Company, November [day of the month missing], 1653.

125. Bregoli, Mediterranean Enlightenment, 29–30.

126. Faber, Jews, Slaves, and the Slave Trade, 60.

127. TNAUK, T 1/488, Thomas Dicey to the Lords Commissioners of His Majesty's Treasury, May 1, 1772, pp. 285–86, 286 verso.

128. Faber, Jews, Slaves, and the Slave Trade, 47.

129. Stephen Alexander Fortune, Merchants and Jews: The Struggle for British West Indian Commerce, 1650–1750 (Gainesville: University Press of Florida, 1984), 45, 121; Herbert Friedenwald, "Material for the History of the Jews in the British West Indies," PAJHS 5 (1897): 45–101, 97–98; Allan D. Meyers, "Ethnic Distinctions and Wealth Among Colonial Jamaican Merchants, 1685–1716," Social Science History 22: 1 (Spring 1998): 47–81, 60.

130. Pedro L. V. Welch, Slave Society in the City: Bridgetown, Barbados, 1680–1834 (Kingston: Ian Randle, 2003), 122.

131. For the analytical error and the demographic data, see Meyers, "Ethnic Distinctions and Wealth," 56, 77. Although Meyers discusses a "Jewish merchant class," not the Jewish community in general, he also states that "the Jewish community was almost invariably a merchant class" (56).

132. Seeman, "Jews in the Early Modern Atlantic," 43.

133. AJA, MS-581, Box 7, folder 7/14, David Levin Salomons and Benamain Nathan de Jong, parnaslieden of the High German Jewish community, to the regents of the High German Jewish synagogue in Suriname, Amsterdam, September 20, 1786.

134. TNAUK, CO 278/1, "Memorandum of Suriname," June 6, 1800, pp. 51–55, 52. In the original, the word appears as "considerd."

135. Henry Bolingbroke, A voyage to the Demerary, containing a statistical account of the settlements there, and of those on the Essequebo, the Berbice, and other contiguous rivers of Guyana (London: Richard Phillips, 1807), 371.

136. NAN, NPIGS, inv. nr. 1, February 18, 1778; inv. nr. 2, April 23, 1789 (for the waning "custom" that Portuguese Jewish witnesses testify in Jodensavanne rather than in Paramaribo).

137. Ibid., inv. nr. 5, October 26, 1813.

138. Ibid., inv. nr. 11, November 20, 1822.

139. Ibid., November 27, 1822.

140. Ibid., January 9, 12, and 19, 1823, February 2, 16, and 24, 1823.

141. Bregoli, *Mediterranean Enlightenment*, 59 (for the tendency among European and Ottoman Jews); Najwa Al-Qattan, "Dhimmis in the Muslim Court: Legal Autonomy and Religious Discrimination," *International Journal of Middle East Studies* 31: 3 (August 1999): 429–44 (for the tendency among Jews and Christians in eighteenth- and nineteenth-century Ottoman Damascus).

142. For the concepts, see Paolo Sartori and Ido Shahar, "Legal Pluralism in Muslim-Majority Colonies: Mapping the Terrain," *Journal of Economic and Social History of the Orient* 55 (2012): 637–63.

143. Karina Sonnenberg-Stern, *Emancipation and Poverty: The Ashkenazi Jews of Amsterdam, 1796–1850* (New York: St. Martin's Press, 2000), 39–40; Menachem Eljakiem Bolle, *De Opheffing van de Autonomie der Kehillot in Nederland 1796* (Amsterdam: Systemen Keesing, 1960), 27.

144. Sonnenberg-Stern, *Emancipation and Poverty*, 40.

145. Kalik, *Scepter of Judah*, 20.

146. Kenneth Stow, *Theater of Acculturation: The Roman Ghetto in the Sixteenth Century* (Seattle: University of Washington Press, 2001), 32–38.

147. Herbert Friedenwald, "Notes," *PAJHS* 3 (1895): 149–50, 150 (for quote); Joseph R. Rosenbloom, *A Biographical Dictionary of Early American Jews* (Lexington: University Press of Kentucky, 1960), 147.

148. Eric Schlereth, "A Tale of Two Deists: John Fitch, Elihu Palmer, and the Boundary of Tolerable Religious Expression in Early National Philadelphia," *Pennsylvania Magazine of History and Biography* 132: 1 (January 2008): 5–31, 6–7.

149. "The Earliest Extant Minute Books of the Spanish and Portuguese Congregation Shearith Israel in New York," 73; *History of the Corporation of Spanish and Portuguese Jews*, 11; Stephen J. Whitfield, "The Braided Identity of Southern Jewry," in Mark K. Bauman, ed., *Dixie Diaspora: An Anthology of Southern Jewish History* (Tuscaloosa: University of Alabama Press, 2006), 427–51, 431; Leon Jick, *The Americanization of the Synagogue, 1820–1870* (Hanover, N.H.: University Press of New England, 1976), 54–55.

150. Jason Schulman, " 'The Law Knows No Heresy': Jewish Communal Autonomy and the American Court System," *Hindsight Graduate History Journal* 6 (Spring 2012): 52–80; Barry L. Stiefel, "In the Board We Trust: Jewish Communal Arbitration Cases in Antebellum Charleston, South Carolina," *Southern Jewish History* 19 (2016): 1–27; Sheldon Godfrey and Judith Godfrey, "The King vs. Moses Gomez et al.: Opening the Prosecutor's File, Over 200 Years Later," *American Jewish History* 80: 3 (Spring 1991): 397–407.

151. Bregoli, *Mediterranean Enlightenment*, 29–30.

152. On the concept of *libertas differendi*, see Simon Rawidowicz, "Em kol herut: Libertas Differendi," *Metzudah* III–IV (June 1945): 5–20. For an English translation, see Simon Rawidowicz (Benjamin C. I. Ravid, ed.), *Israel: The Ever-Dying People and Other Essays* (Rutherford, N.J.: Farleigh Dickinson University Press, 1986), 118–29, 118. The "mandate to be different" is my coinage.

153. See, for example, LMA/4521/A/01/03/02 through LMA/4521/A/01/03/009, Minutes of the London Mahamad (1751–1833); LMA/4521/D/01/01/001 through LMA/4521/D/01/01/001–11, Minutes of the Mahamad and Adjuntos, Barbados (1769–1838); "The Earliest Extant Minute Books of the Spanish and Portuguese Congregation Shearith Israel in New York," 1–82; AJA, MS-581, Box X-416, folder 4 (for Surinamese Ashkenazim).

Chapter 3

1. Goslinga, *The Dutch in the Caribbean and in the Guianas*, 353.

2. Cohen, "Jewish Demography in the Eighteenth Century," 62; Klooster and Oostindie, *Realm Between Empires*, 2.

3. Cohen, "Jewish Demography in the Eighteenth Century," 62.

4. Cohen, "Early Caribbean Jewry," 132.

5. Cohen, *Jews in Another Environment*, 20, and SAA, 334, Archief van de Portugees-Israëlietische Gemeente, inv. nr. 87, October 30, 1750 (for guilds); Pinto, *Reflexoens*, 6 (for the four trades).

6. Jonathan Israel, *The Dutch Republic: Its Rise, Greatness and Fall, 1477–1806* (Oxford: Oxford University Press, 1995), 658; Sonnenberg-Stern, *Emancipation and Poverty*, 33–34.

7. Scholars who have noted this remarkable mobility include Robert Cohen, "Patterns of Marriage and Remarriage Among the Sephardi Jews of Surinam, 1788–1818," in Robert Cohen, ed., *The Jewish Nation in Suriname: Historical Essays* (Amsterdam: S. Emmering, 1982), 89–100, 90–91; Marcus, *The Colonial American Jew*, 1:150; and Bernfeld, *Poverty and Welfare*.

8. Bernfeld, *Poverty and Welfare*, 41; Herbert Bloom, *Economic Activities of the Jews of Amsterdam in the Seventeenth and Eighteenth Centuries* (Williamsport, Pa.: Bayard Press, 1937), 150–51; Emmanuel and Emmanuel, *History of the Jews of the Netherlands Antilles*, 2:774–80.

9. Nassy, *Essai historique*, part 1, 164 (*vraiment les véritables citoyens & habitants de Surinam*).

10. NAN, Sociëteit Suriname, inv. nr. 213, Portuguese Jewish leaders to Governor van Sommelsdijck, pp. 375–76, undated (probably May 1685).

11. NAN, Sociëteit Suriname, inv. nr. 500, Jacob Henriques Barrios Jessurun, David Nunes Monsanto, and Samuel Hoheb Brandon, Regents of the Portuguese Jewish nation in Suriname, to J. G. Wichers, January 5, 1785.

12. Several of these documents are transcribed in Nassy, *Essai historique*, part 2, 113–73.

13. Cohen, "Patterns of Marriage," 91.

14. NAN, Doop-, Trouw- en Begraafboeken (DTB) van Suriname, 1662–1838, inv. nr. 5, passim.

15. Altona (at least 1680); Amsterdam (1781, 1809, 1796, 1776; another died as an adult in 1718); Leghorn (1697); Barbados (before 1762); Saint-Esprit, Bayonne (1784); Bordeaux (1775); London (1700, 1697); Fez (1683); and St. Eustatius (before 1782). Ben-Ur and Frankel, *Remnant Stones: The Jewish Cemeteries of Suriname*, 646.

16. Rosalind J. Beiler, "Searching for Prosperity: German Migration to the British American Colonies, 1680–1780," in Wim Klooster and Alfred Padula, eds., *The Atlantic World: Essays on Slavery, Migration, and Imagination* (Upper Saddle River, N.J.: Pearson/Prentice Hall, 2005), 91–106, 92.

17. Ben-Ur and Frankel, *Remnant Stones: The Jewish Cemeteries of Suriname*, 646.

18. In the seventeenth century, a small number of Ashkenazim were dispatched from Amsterdam by the city's Portuguese Jewish community; and British America's Jewish community, by the 1720s numerically dominated by Ashkenazim, also had recourse to the *despacho*

("dispatch;" "dispatching"). See, for example, Israel Bartal and Yosef Kaplan, "Immigration of Indigent Jews from Amsterdam to the Land of Israel at the Beginning of the Seventeenth Century," *Shalem* 6 (1991/1992): 175–193, 181, 189 (in Hebrew); "From the 2nd Volume of Minute Books of the Congn: Shearith Israel in New York," *PAJHS* 21 (1913): 83–171, 91, 99, 121, 128, 134, 139. But the *despacho* remained largely a method of controlling exilic Iberian Jewish populations.

19. J. D. Herlein, *Beschryvinge van de Volk-Plantinge Zuriname* (Leeuwarden: Meindert Injema, 1718), 48.

20. Of nearly 1,700 epitaphs, only seven mention a Surinamese nativity. Ben-Ur and Frankel, *Remnant Stones: The Jewish Cemeteries of Suriname*, Jodensavanne Cemetery: epitaph 174 (1758–1832); Old Sephardi Cemetery: epitaphs 202 (1791–1846), 560 (1824–1893), 581 (1820–1866); Old Ashkenazi Cemetery: epitaphs 288 (1781–1838), 313 (1753–1823), 314 (1864–1819).

21. Cohen, *Jews in Another Environment*, 23; Cohen, "Passage to a New World," 34–35; Vink, *Creole Jews*, 32. See also "Poor Sephardic Jews in Amsterdam," index prepared by Vibeke Sealtiel Olsen, http://www.sephardicgen.com/databases/AmsterdamPoorSrchFrm.html.

22. Daniel Strum, "A Colmeia e o Enxame: Manuel Severim de Faria, Isaac de Pinto e o Pensamento sobre a População em Língua Portuguesa," *Revista Portugesa de Filosofia* 65: 1/4 (January–December 2009): 463–501, 486.

23. Todd M. Endelman, *Broadening Jewish History: Towards a Social History of Ordinary Jews* (Oxford: Littman Library of Jewish Civilization, 2011), 242–43; A. S. Diamond, "Problems of the London Sephardi Community, 1720–1733," *TJHSE* 21 (1962–1967): 39–63, 60–61; Cohen, "Passage to a New World," 34–35.

24. Aviva Ben-Ur, "Jewish Savannah in Atlantic Perspective: A Reconsideration of the First Intentional Jewish Community of North America," in Sina Rauschenbach and Jonathan Schorsch, eds., *The Sephardic Atlantic: Colonial Histories and Postcolonial Perspectives* (Cham, Switzerland: Palgrave Macmillan, 2018), 183–214.

25. Bernfeld, "Financing Poor Relief," 75.

26. Augustus Hervey (David Erskine, ed.), *Augustus Hervey's Journal* (London: William Kimber, 1953), xxii–xxxii.

27. H. Huussen, "Legislation on the Position of the Jews in the Dutch Republic, c. 1590–1796," *Tijdschrift voor Rechtgeschiedenis/Legal History Review* 69 (2010): 43–56; Ineke Brasz, *De kille van Kuilenburg: Joods leven in Culemborg* (Culemborg: G. J. L. Koolhof, 1984).

28. Cohen, "Passage to a New World," 35; Gérard Nahon, "Les rapports des communautés judéo-portugaises de France avec celle d'Amsterdam au XVIIe et au XVIIIe siècle," *Studia Rosenthaliana* 10: 2 (1976): 151–88, 170–71 (for the original Portuguese).

29. Ben-Ur, "Jewish Savannah in Atlantic Perspective," 194–98, 204, 212.

30. SAA, 334, Archief van de Portugees-Israëlietische Gemeente, inv. nr. 1029, II, p. 778.

31. Yosef Kaplan, "Deviance and Excommunication in the Portuguese Community of 18th Century Amsterdam," in J. Michman, ed., *Dutch Jewish History* (Jerusalem: Institute for Research on Dutch Jewry, 1993), 3:103–15, 107.

32. SAA, 334, Archief van de Portugees-Israëlietische Gemeente, inv. nr. 1029, p. 794.

33. Ibid., 792.

34. Ibid. First Hazan, on behalf of the Parnassim and Gabay of the congregation and Talmud Torah of Amsterdam, to Haham Abraham Gabay Izidro, 6 Sivan 5494 [June 7, 1734], pp. 780–83.

35. John Archer, "Puritan Town Planning in New Haven," *Journal of the Society of Architectural Historians* 34 (1975): 140–49, 140.

36. SAA, 334, Archief van de Portugees-Israëlietische Gemeente, inv. nr. 1029, p. 832.

37. Pinto, *Reflexoens*, 14.

38. A. J. A. Quintus Bosz, "Geschiedenis van het Fort Nieuw Amsterdam in het verdedigingsstelsel van Suriname," in *Nieuwe West-Indische Gids* 43 (1963/64): 103–48, 113; Van der Meiden, *Betwist bestuur*, 81–82.

39. As suggested in SAA, 334, Archief van de Portugees-Israëlietische Gemeente, inv. nr. 1029, Portuguese Jewish regents of Amsterdam to Portuguese Jewish regents of Suriname, January 7, 1748, p. 810.

40. Fatah-Black, *White Lies and Black Markets*, xv (for list of governors); Goslinga, *The Dutch in the Caribbean and in the Guianas*, 338 (on the instability of the government in those years).

41. Bernfeld, *Poverty and Welfare*, 41.

42. Pinto, *Reflexoens*, 17.

43. On the People's Movement of 1747–48, quelled by Prince Willem IV, see Jozeph Michman, *The History of Dutch Jewry During the Emancipation Period, 1787–1815: Gothic Turrets on a Corinthian Building* (Amsterdam: Amsterdam University Press, 1995), 3.

44. Bernfeld, *Poverty and Welfare*, 123, 131.

45. SAA, 334, Archief van de Portugees-Israëlietische Gemeente, inv. nr. 1029, p. 710.

46. Ibid., 716, 709.

47. Ibid., 703.

48. Ibid., 712.

49. Ibid., 706, 708, 711.

50. Ibid., 706, 713, 717.

51. Bernfeld, "Financing Poor Relief," 89.

52. SAA, 334, Archief van de Portugees-Israëlietische Gemeente, p. 723.

53. Ibid., 724.

54. Ibid., 701.

55. Meaghan N. Duff, "Adventurers Across the Atlantic: English Migration to the New World, 1580–1780," in Wim Klooster and Alfred Padula, eds., *The Atlantic World: Essays on Slavery, Migration, and Imagination* (Upper Saddle River, N.J.: Pearson/Prentice Hall, 2005), 77–90, 85.

56. SAA, 334, Archief van de Portugees-Israëlietische Gemeente, inv. nr. 1029, letter to David de Pinto, pp. 835–37.

57. Ibid.; Pinto, *Reflexoens*, 23.

58. Schiltkamp, *De geschiedenis van het notariaat*, 183.

59. This is Robert Cohen's gloss on Pinto, *Reflexoens*, 21–22; Cohen, *Jews in Another Environment*, 22.

60. Seymour Drescher, "Jews and New Christians in the Atlantic Slave Trade," in Paolo Bernardini and Norman Fiering, eds., *The Jews and the Expansion of Europe to the West, 1450 to 1800* (New York: Berghahn Books, 2001), 439–70, 460. See also Cohen, *Jews in Another Environment*, 24.

61. Cohen, *Jews in Another Environment*, 22.

62. Ibid., 23.

63. Cohen, "Early Caribbean Jewry," 132.

64. NAN, SONA, Testamenten, codicillen en akten, passim; Holly Snyder, "A Sense of Place: Jews, identity, and social status in colonial British America, 1654–1831" (Ph.D. diss., Brandeis University, 2000), 237.

65. NAN, NPIGS, inv. nr. 2, June 14, 1785. See also the request from the foreign-born Abraham Touro for an annual charity allowance (ibid., January 6, 1789).

66. Ibid., December 31, 1788, January 19, 1789.

67. JHM, David Hisqo. Baruh Louzada et al., "Livro de Ascaboth & Meseberah," Suriname, various dates from 1789 and after.

68. For Philadelphia, see AJA, MS505, Box No. 1676a, folder titled "From 1 to 42," Minutes K. K. Mikve Israel, March 25, 1782 (unpaginated). Prayers for purchasers of the Philadelphia synagogue's cornerstones and the two stones supporting the doorposts in 1782 were to be recited annually "for Ever." For Curaçao, see Emmanuel and Emmanuel, *History of the Jews of the Netherlands Antilles*, 1:546 (*ascaba* for Haham Josiau Pardo), and for Montreal, see SPSM, Archive Notes (typescript), Minute Book I, October 13, 1863 (reference to "the list of perpetual Ascaboth for the Congregation").

69. JHM, David Hisqo. Baruh Louzada et al., "Livro de Ascaboth & Meseberah," Suriname, various dates from 1789 and after, [pp. 8, 9, 10]. For the bracketed first names, see NAN, SONA, Testamenten, codicillen en akten, inv. nr. 6, will of Isaac Meatob, September 23, 1723, p. 80.

70. JHM, David Hisqo. Baruh Louzada et al., "Livro de Ascaboth & Meseberah," Suriname, various dates from 1789 and after, [pp. 25–26]; TNAUK, HCA 30/223, Francisco Henriques Pereyra, Suriname, to Pedro Henriquez Pereyra, Amsterdam, November 7, 1672 (for his vocation as a planter).

71. JHM, David Hisqo. Baruh Louzada et al., "Livro de Ascaboth & Meseberah," Suriname, various dates from 1789 and after, p. 24. The annual *escava*, to be recited the second day of Passover, was instituted and financed by Semuel Haim Cohen Nassy "for his ancestor." NAN, NPIGS, inv. nr. 4, March 17, 1812.

72. NAN, NPIGS, inv. nr. 131, Inventarissen van papieren, berustend onder de 1e voorzanger B.V.S., D. B. Louzada, 1793–1812; Loker and Cohen, "An Eighteenth-Century Prayer of the Jews of Surinam"; Schalkwijk, *The Colonial State in the Caribbean*, 229–30; Wolbers, *Geschiedenis van Suriname*, 547–51.

73. Loker and Cohen, "An Eighteenth-Century Prayer of the Jews of Surinam," 78, 81 (for a slight variation of the phrase); "Miscellaneous Items Relating to Jews of North America," *PAJHS* 27 (1920): 223–24 (contains an English translation only). Note that Loker and Cohen incorrectly estimated the manuscript's date.

74. Ben-Ur and Frankel, *Remnant Stones: The Jewish Cemeteries of Suriname*, 61 (epitaph 73, d. 1743); Nassy, *Essai historique*, part 1, 95.

75. Loker and Cohen, "An Eighteenth-Century Prayer of the Jews of Surinam," 76.

76. Emmanuel, son of Aron Pereyra (epitaph 325, d. 1738), and David Rodrigues Monsanto (epitaph 348, d. 1739), in Ben-Ur and Frankel, *Remnant Stones: The Jewish Cemeteries of Suriname*, 230, 237.

77. The name of the village in which Meijer perished is effaced (Aldea de P[ ]nij). NAN, NPIGS, inv. nr. 423, 15.

78. Schorsch, *Jews and Blacks in the Early Modern World*, 67–71, 75.

79. Studemund-Halévy, *Biographisches Lexikon der Hamburger Sefarden*, 665.

80. Solomon Levy Maduro and Abraham Maduro, eds., *Sefer Berit Yitshak* (Amsterdam: Israel Mondwei, 5528 [1767–68]), 15v. This is apparently a reprint of the 1729 edition, cited in Moritz Steinschneider, *Catalogus Librorum Hebraerum in bibliotheca Bodleiana jussu curatorum digessit et notis instruxit M. Steinschneider* (Berlin, 1931), entry 3222. Copies consulted are located at JCBL and BEH. Many other versions of this prayer book exist, bearing the same title, but do not reference slaves. See, for example, Solomon Levy Maduro, ed., *Sefer Berith Yitschak* (Amsterdam, 5525 [1764–65]), at BEH, and the 1729 edition of the same title, held at YUL.

81. Monika Saelmaekers, "Can Halakhic Texts Talk History?: The Example of *Sefer Or Zarua* (Ms. Ros. 3, Ca. 1300 C.E.)," *Zutot* 6: 1 (2009): 17–23, 21.

82. Solomon Levy Maduro and Abraham Maduro, eds., *Sefer Berit Yitshak* (Amsterdam: Gerard Johan Jansen 1767–68), 7v.

83. *Sefer Berit Yitshak* (Amsterdam: Belinfante and de Vita, 1803/1804 [Amsterdam: Solomon Levy Maduro, 1764/1765]). I came upon this book during my trip to the island in 2004.

84. Benjamin J. Kaplan, "Fictions of Privacy: House Chapels and the Spatial Accommodation of Religious Dissent in Early Modern Europe," *American Historical Review* 107: 4 (October 2002): 1031–64, 1061.

85. P. A. Christiaans, ed., *Bronnenpublikaties van de Indische Genealogische Vereniging, deel 7: Het Evangelisch-Luthers Doopregister van Paramaribo, 1743–1809* ('s-Gravenhage: Indische Genealogische Vereniging, 1996); UBLBC, "Ontwerp tot een Beschryving van Surinaamen," transcript of manuscript dating between 1739 and 1748, p. 28. Lutherans built their first urban church in 1740.

86. Teenstra, *De Landbouw in de Colonie Suriname*, 2:138.

87. Wolbers, *Geschiedenis van Suriname*, 403 (for the Lutheran community).

88. NAN, SONA, inv. nr. 38, will of Joseph, son of Abraham de la Parra, June 21, 1767, p. 108, and inv. nr. 55, Abraham Gabay Izidro (also identified as Abraham Gabay Isidro), November 23, 1785, 21; Ten Hove, Helstone, and Hoogbergen, *Surinaamse emancipatie 1863*, 52.

89. NAN, NPIGS, inv. nr. 1, June 26, 1770.

90. Frederik Oudschans Dentz, "The Name of the Country Surinam as a Family-Name [*sic*]: The Biography of a Surinam Planter of the Eighteenth Century," *PAJHS* 48: 1 (September 1958): 19–27; "The Name of the Country Surinam as a Family Name: The Biography of a Surinam Planter in the Eighteenth Century [Supplement]," *PAJHS* 48: 4 (June 1959): 262–64; and "De naam van het land Suriname als geslachtsnaam: De levensgeschiedenis van een Surinaamse planter uit de 18de eeuw," *De West-Indische Gids* 36: 1 (July 1955): 65–71; NAN, Klapper op de namen van Plantages in Suriname ca. 1740–1780 uit het Oud-notarieel archief van Suriname, Section: G-M, Not. Archief Suriname inv. nr. 196, p. 345; Ben-Ur and Frankel, *Remnant Stones: The Jewish Cemeteries of Suriname*, 481 (epitaph 57).

91. Dentz, "The Name of the Country Surinam as a Family-Name," 22.

92. Arnold Wiznitzer, "O Livro de Atas das Congregações Judaicas 'Zur Israel' en Recife e 'Magen Abraham' en Mauricia, Brasil, 1648–1653," *Anais da Biblioteca Nacional* 74 (1953): 221–28, 223 (bylaw 10) and "The Merger Agreement and Regulations of Congregation Talmud Torah of Amsterdam (1638–1639)," *Historia Judaica* 20 (1958): 109–32, 113; NAN, NPIGS, inv. nr. 149, Reglamentos ou Escamot da Naçao Judaica Portugeza de C[uraçao] revistos e aprovados pelos Parnasim da nacao Judaica Portugeza d[e Ams]terdam, [p. 1]; LMA/4521/A/01/01/

001, Livro do K. K. Saar Asamaim, 5440 [1679/1680], p. 1 (bylaw 1); Gérard Nahon, "The Portuguese Jewish Nation of Amsterdam as Reflected in the Memoirs of Abraham Haim Lopes Arias, 1752," in Chaya Brasz and Yosef Kaplan, eds., *Dutch Jews as Perceived by Themselves and by Others: Proceedings of the Eighth International Symposium on the History of the Jews in the Netherlands* (Leiden: Brill, 2001), 59–78, 65–66; Bregoli, *Mediterranean Enlightenment*, 30.

93. NAN, NPIGS, inv. nr. 98 (undated); inv. nr. 102 (1755), treatise 25, article 1, pp. 48–49.

94. Ibid., inv. nr. 11, November 4, 1821.

95. Ibid., inv. nr. 102 (1755), treatise 26, pp. 49–50.

96. Ibid., inv. nr. 2, March 16, 1784.

97. Wieke Vink, *Creole Jews*, 6.

98. NAN, NPIGS, inv. nr. 75, petition to Mahamad, September 9, 1708; Nassy, *Essai historique*, part 1, 83–84 (50 Ashkenazim in 1690).

99. NAN, NPIGS, inv. nr. 102 (1755), treatise 1, article 3.

100. Ibid., inv. nr. 7, September 6, 1757; inv. nr. 1, August 12, 1778.

101. Ibid., inv. nr. 2, September 26, 1781.

102. Ibid., inv. nr. 99 (1748), treatise 26, article 5; AJA, MS-581, X-416, folder 5, Askamoth, 1754, p. 6.

103. Neville Laski, *The Laws and Charities of the Spanish and Portuguese Jews' Congregation of London* (London: Cresset Press, 1952), 1n1.

104. Ibid. ("admitted and assessed male member"); LMA/4521/D/01/01/08, p. 35.

105. Laski, *The Laws and Charities of the Spanish and Portuguese Jews' Congregation of London*, 34n203.

106. "From the 2nd Volume of Minute Books of the Congn: Shearith Israel in New York," *PAJHS* 21 (1913): 83–171, 104.

107. Ibid. In the original text, the word appears as "bonofit."

108. Howard B. Rock, *Haven of Liberty: New York Jews in the New World, 1654–1865* (New York: New York University Press, 2012), 46.

109. Swetschinski, *Reluctant Cosmopolitans*, 188–89; Tirtsah Levie Bernfeld to Aviva Ben-Ur, April 9, 2016.

110. NAN, NPIGS, inv. nr. 99 (1748), treatise 26, section 3.

111. MMB, GMIE, passim; NAN, NPIGS, inv. nr. 149, Reglamentos ou Escamot da Naçao Judaica Portugeza de C[uraçao] revistos e aprovados pelos Parnasim da nacao Judaica Portugeza d[e Ams]terdam, [p. 9].

112. Ibid., inv. nr. 99, treatise 26, article 1.

113. NAN, Gouverenmentsecretaris, inv. nr. 528, February 2, 1772 (unpaginated).

114. UBLBC, "Ontwerp tot Een Beschryving van Surinaamen," 303.

115. Beeldsnijder, *"Om werk van jullie te hebben,'"* 132.

116. Norval Smith, "The History of Surinamese Creoles II: Origin and Differentiation," in Eithne B. Carlin and Jacques Arends, eds., *Atlas of the Languages of Suriname* (Leiden: KITLV Press, 2002), 131–51, 135.

117. Davis, "Regaining Jerusalem," 21.

118. Beeldsnijder, *"Om werk van jullie te hebben,"* 132.

119. NAN, SONA, inv. nr. 788, October 21, 1779, section 26.

120. NAN, NPIGS, inv. nr. 1, April 29, 1769.

121. Ibid., inv. nr. 3, June 6, 1797.

122. NAN, SONA, inv. nr. 57, will of "de vrije mulatin Maria de Prado" [*sic*], June 12, 1787, pp. 460–65; inv. nr. 75, will of Simha Judia, May 10, 1790, section 39.

123. NAN, SONA, Testamenten, inv. nr. 57, will of Hana Pelengrino, February 23, 1786, pp. 145–48.

124. NAN, NPIGS, inv. nr. 1, October 17, 1773.

125. NAN, SONA, inv. nr. 58, will of Daniel Pelengrino, November 22, 1787, pp. 496–504.

126. Ibid., 500.

127. NAN, SONA, inv. nr. 61, will of Abraham Ismael Judeo, March 15, 1780 (opened June 5, 1789), 297–308, 306.

128. NAN, SONA, inv. nr. 234, inventory of Roza Judia, November 13 and 14, 1771, pp. 439–47, 441–42.

129. Schiltkamp, *De geschiedenis van het notariaat*, 181 (for the spread of Dutch among Surinamese Jews).

130. Vink, *Creole Jews*, 73.

131. Examples of family unification policy and the recognition of extralegal spousal relations among slaves in plantation Suriname are scattered throughout the sources. See, for example, NAN, NPIGS, inv. nr. 1, June 20, 1775; SONA, inv. nr. 5, will of Isaak Pinto da Fonseca, February 5, 1720, p. 63; inv. nr. 8, will of Joshua Hiskiahu Arias, November 5, 1728, p. 140; inv. nr. 29, will of Josias Pardo, February 12, 1759, p. 69; inv. nr. 12, will of Emmanuel de Soliz, January 8, 1733, p. 3; inv. nr. 10, will of Esther Arias (née da Fonseca), April 19, 1730, pp. 206–10, 207; inv. nr. 16, will of Benjamin Henriques de Granada, March 2, 1737, p. 66 and will of the vreije Neger Harder and de vreije Negerin Nannoe, March 23, 1737, pp. 71–73. The motivation for such recognition was usually pragmatic rather than sentimental.

132. Klooster and Oostindie, *Realm Between Empires*, 10–11, 111, 189; Jacques Arends, "Demographic Factors in the Formation of Sranan," in Jacques Arends, ed., *The Early Stages of Creolization* (Amsterdam: John Benjamins, 1995), 233–85, 238, 262 and "The History of the Surinamese Creoles I," 124.

133. Klooster and Oostindie, *Realm Between Empires*, 150.

134. Ibid.

135. Cees Fasseur, *The Politics of Colonial Exploitation: Java, the Dutch, and the Cultivation System* (Ithaca, N.Y.: Cornell University Press, 1992), 56.

136. Postma, *The Dutch in the Atlantic Slave Trade*, 114, 121, 133, 163.

137. Linda M. Heywood and John K. Thornton, *Central Africans, Atlantic Creoles, and the Foundation of the Americas, 1585–1660* (Cambridge: Cambridge University Press, 2007), 238; Davis, "Regaining Jerusalem," 21.

138. David Wheat, *Atlantic Africa and the Spanish Caribbean, 1570–1640* (Chapel Hill: University of North Carolina Press, 2016), 20, 216–18; Postma, *The Dutch Atlantic Slave Trade*, passim; Beeldsnijder, *"Om werk van jullie te hebben,"* 122.

139. *Surinaamsche Courant* 3 (January 9, 1824): [4]; NAN, Microfilms Brieven J. H. Lance, John Henry Lance to William Lance, April 19, 1825, John Henry Lance to Elizabeth Lance, June 12, 1827, p. 377.

140. Heliana Ribeiro de Mello, "Restructured Portuguese: From Africa to Brazil," in Magnus Huber and Mikael Parkvall, eds., *Spreading the Word: The Issue of Diffusion Among the Atlantic Creoles* (London: University of Westminster Press, 1999), 165–66.

141. Norval Smith, "The Genesis of the Creole Languages of Surinam" (Ph.D. diss., Universiteit van Amsterdam, 1987), 145–46.

142. Ibid.

143. Rupert, *Creolization and Contraband*, 221; Van den Berg, "'Mi no sal tron tongo,'" 6.

144. Arends, "The Origin of the Portuguese Element in the Surinam Creoles," in M. Huber and M. Parkvall, eds., *Spreading the Word: Papers on the Issue of Diffusion of Atlantic Creoles* (London: University of Westminster Press, 1999), 195–208, and "The History of the Surinamese Creoles I," 119.

145. Melville J. Herskovits, "On the Provenience of the Portuguese in Saramacca Tongo," *West India Guide* 12 (1930–31): 546–57, 557; Jan Voorhoeve, "Historical and Linguistic Evidence in Favour of the Relexification Theory in the Formation of Creoles," *Language in Society* 2 (1973): 133–45; Arends, "The Origin of the Portuguese Element," and "The History of the Surinamese Creoles I," 119. See also Joy Gleason Carew, "Language and Survival: Will Sranan Tongo, Suriname's Lingua Franca, Become the Official Language?" *Caribbean Quarterly* 28: 4 (December 1982): 1–16, 1.

146. John H. McWhorter, *The Power of Babel: A Natural History of Language* (London: William Heinemann, 2001), 14.

147. Thomas Edward Penard and Arthur Philip Penard, "European Influence on the Arawak Language of Guiana," *De West-Indische Gids* 8: 1 (1927): 165–76, 166–68. Note that the Penards confuse Portuguese with Spanish words, a common tendency in early linguistic studies.

148. On linguistic anastomosis see McWhorter, *Power of Babel*, 129.

149. Stedman, *Narrative, of a Five Years' Expedition* (London: J. Johnson, 1796), 2:264–65.

150. Teenstra, *De Landbouw in de Colonie Suriname*, 2:200; T. May, "De Lepra, Haar Voorkomen, Verspreiding en Bestrijding, in 't Bijzonder in Suriname," *De West-Indische Gids* 8: 1 (April 1927): 547–56, 550.

151. For an interpretation of "trefu" as used among Surinamese people of African descent, see Stephen Snelders, *Leprosy and Colonialism: Suriname Under Dutch Rule, 1750–1950* (Manchester: Manchester University Press, 2017), 84–88. For preexisting food taboos in Angola, see James Hoke Sweet, *Recreating Africa: Culture, Kinship, and Religion in the African-Portuguese World, 1441–1770* (Chapel Hill: University of North Carolina Press, 2003), 176.

152. Jonathan Ray, "Contested Community: The Problem of Political Organization in the Early Sephardic Diaspora," *Hispania Judaica Bulletin: Articles, Review, Bibliography, and Manuscripts on Sefarad* 11 (2015): 11–25, 16.

Chapter 4

1. NAN, Aanwinsten Eerste Afdeling, inv. nr. 1552, 1929 XIV, Livro de Varias Quetuboth, pp. 66, 67, 87, 107. The names of the brides do not appear in Latin letters and are rendered here and in the caption for Figure 10 according to Portuguese Jewish pronunciation.

2. Ibid., passim.

3. For the historiography, see Swellengrebel and Van Der Kuyp, *Health of White Settlers in Surinam*, 31; Frederik Oudschans Dentz, "Joodse Kleurlingen," *De West-Indische Gids* 35 (1955): 234; Schorsch, *Jews and Blacks in the Early Modern World*, 65, 223–24, 300; Snyder, "A Sense of Place," 328; Cohen, "Patterns of Marriage," 93–94; Vink, "Jews in Suriname," 739; and Rosemarijn Hoefte, "Free Blacks and Coloureds in Plantation Suriname: The Struggle to Rise," in Jane G. Landers, ed., *Against the Odds: Free Blacks in the Slave Societies of the Americas*

(New York: Routledge, 2013), 102–29, 129n103. For communal self-representation, see "Approximatieve staat der bevolking van de kolonie Suriname, 1817," in *Surinaamsche almanak voor het jaar 1821*, 30; Teenstra, *De Landbouw in de Colonie Suriname* (cited without page number) in Dentz, "Joodse Kleurlingen," 234; and TNAUK, CO 278/17, "Population Returns of White Inhabitants with their Families and their Slaves of all Description," census conducted per order of interim Governor P. Bonham, 1811, [p. 4]. This census cited in the *Surinaamsche almanak* indicates that 2.6 percent of Suriname's Jewish community was "colored." Bonham's census indicates that 2.9 percent and 10.6 percent of the Ashkenazi and Portuguese Jewish communities, respectively, consisted of "colored people."

4. Van Lier, *Frontier Society*, 110–11.

5. Vink, *Creole Jews*, 56.

6. Cohen, *Jews in Another Environment*, 163–72, 309n65.

7. Cohen, "Patterns of Marriage," 96. Cohen's evidence is a quote from David Nassy (*Essai historique*, part 2, 60) that "attributes the more moderate [sexual] behavior of the Jews to the 'constant care and . . . assiduous efforts'" of their parents.

8. Moses I. Finley, *Ancient Slavery and Modern Ideology* (New York: Viking Press, 1980), 68, 95, and for a critique, Orlando Patterson, *Slavery and Social Death: A Comparative Study* (Cambridge, Mass.: Harvard University Press, 1982), 24–26.

9. George Peter Murdock, *Social Structure* (New York: Free Press, 1949), 260 (for the quote).

10. Catherine Hezser, *Jewish Slavery in Antiquity* (Oxford: Oxford University Press, 2005); David Meldola, son of Raphael Ledolah, in *Peri Ets Hayyim* (Amsterdam, 5517 [1766–67]), 72 verso, section 44, p. 74 verso, section 45 (this responsum does not specify whether the child born to the slave was sired by her master, but I assume it was); Schorsch, *Jews and Blacks in the Early Modern World*, 271–72. While the medieval Iberian codifier Moses ben Maimon ruled that owners engaging in sexual relations with their slaves were obligated to send them away or free and marry them as converts to Judaism, this ruling was not honored in slaveholding societies where ownership of females was pervasive. See Yaron Ben-Naeh, "Blond, Tall, with Honey-Colored Eyes: Jewish Ownership of Slaves in the Ottoman Empire," *Jewish History* 20: 3/4 (2006): 315–32, 324. Ben-Naeh's observation for the Ottoman Empire also applies to the Atlantic World.

11. Cohen, "Patterns of Marriage," 93 ("all inhabitants were strictly forbidden to have dealings or sexual relations with Negro and Indian women"); Van Lier, *Frontier Society*, 76 ("All inhabitants").

12. The law appears variably as article 9 or 10 of the "Reglement voor de Plantagebedienden," sometimes called "Reglement voor de Plantagebedienden en de Ambachtslieden" or "Nieuw Reglement voor de Plantagebedienden." The penalty for all infringers of the "Reglement" is variably stipulated as 2,000 pounds of sugar, 100–200 guilders, and "further punishment depending on the circumstances." The clause is no longer mentioned by 1814, when the ordinance is called "Wijziging van het Reglement voor Plantagebedienden." The stated penalty steadily declined from 2,000 pounds of sugar in 1686 to 100–200 guilders thereafter. Schiltkamp and De Smidt, *Placaten, ordonnantiën, en andere wetten, uitgevaardigd in Suriname*, 1:168 (#134, article 10: 1686), 1:383 (#319, article 10: 1725), 1:669 (#556, article 9: 1759), 2:724 (#594, article 9: 1761), 21069–70 (#876, article 9: 1784), 2:1322 (#1037: 1814).

13. For a parallel, see Keri Leigh Merritt, *Masterless Men: Poor Whites and Slavery in the Antebellum South* (Cambridge: Cambridge University Press, 2017), 5. Cohen ("Patterns of Marriage," 93) calls the clause a "dead letter" by 1817 but probably meant 1814.

14. Enthoven, "Suriname and Zeeland," 255 (for 1667, 1671, and 1684); Postma, *The Dutch in the Atlantic Slave Trade*, 185 (for 1684–1754); Van Stipriaan, *Surinaams contrast*, 28, 33–34 (for the 1700s and the acme of 60,000 slaves).

15. Arends, "The History of the Surinamese Creoles I," 123–24. In 1791, the ratio in the plantation district was 33:1 and in Suriname as a whole 16:1. Vink, "Jews in Suriname," 738.

16. Calculations based on 1684 data in Enthoven, "Suriname and Zeeland" and Goslinga, *The Dutch in the Caribbean and in the Guianas*, 279, 291, 309, 341, 519.

17. Van Lier, *Frontier Society*, 8, 97, 100; Pierre Jacques Benoit, *Voyage à Surinam* (Brussels: Société des Beaux-Arts-Gérants: De Wasme et Laurent, 1839), 19–20; Brana-Shute, "The Manumission of Slaves in Suriname," 399–400.

18. Van der Linde, *Surinaamse suikerheren en hun kerk*, 75.

19. Wolbers, *Geschiedenis van Suriname*, 775.

20. Schnurmann, *Atlantische Welten*, 382.

21. Cohen, *Jews in Another Environment*, 54; Cohen, "Patterns of Marriage," 97. Cohen argues that Jews diverged from the pattern of white gender imbalance, but his evidence begins only in the late eighteenth century.

22. Van Lier, *Frontier Society*, 74.

23. Schiltkamp and De Smidt, *Placaten, ordonnantiën, en andere wetten, uitgevaardigd in Suriname*, 1:412.

24. Humphrey E. Lamur, "Slave Religion on the Vossenburg Plantation (Suriname) and Missionaries' Reactions," in Hilary Beckles and Verene Shepherd, eds., *Caribbean Slave Society and Economy: A Student Reader* (New York: New Press, 1991), 287–94, esp. 287. Another scholar argues that until the 1820s, Dutch colonial planters preferred that their slaves maintain their pagan religions, which of course provided the former with another justification for enslavement. Gert Oostindie, "The Enlightenment, Christianity and the Suriname Slave," *Journal of Caribbean History* 26 (1992): 154–55. Most of the evangelizing of the Moravians was carried out among the Saramakka Maroons after 1765, and their activities in the capital city did not proliferate until the 1820s. Arends, "The History of Surinamese Creoles I," 126–27; Fogleman, *Two Troubled Souls*, 142.

25. One Dutch eyewitness, for example, noted during his sojourn in 1680s Suriname that although most slaves had no religion, "various among them had been baptized" (*verscheyden onder haar Gedoopt zijn*). Van Berkel, *Amerikaansche voyagien*, 126.

26. Brana-Shute, "The Manumission of Slaves in Suriname," 261.

27. Van Lier, *Frontier Society*, 73.

28. Postma, *The Dutch in the Atlantic Slave Trade*, 70–71.

29. SAA, inv. nr. 334, Archief van de Portugees-Israëlietische Gemeente, inv. nr. 1029, pp. 428–29.

30. NAN, SONA, inv. nr. 230, petition of Joseph Pelegrino to Governor General Johan Coetier [Jean Coutier], Paramaribo, July 17, 1720, pp. 83–87; NAN, SONA, inv. nr. 13, will of Isaac da Costa, November 8, 1725, fol. 13, pp. 245–47.

31. Levy Maduro and Maduro, *Sefer Berit Yitshak*, 16.

32. NAN, Stadhouderlijke Secretarie, inv. nr. 1264, *Redres der Reglamenten, Institutien, en Instellingen van de H. Gemeente B.V.S.*, November 9, 1752, p. 24 (treatise 26, article 6, Portuguese section); responsum of David Meldola, son of Raphael Ledolah, in *Peri Ets Hayyim* (Amsterdam, 5517 [1766–1767]). Meldola refers to both the Talmud and Rabbi Moses Maimonides. The case (which, like most responsa literature, omits personal names and geographical markers) likely pertains to Curaçao.

33. Davis, "David Nassy's 'Furlough,'" 85; NAN, RvP, inv. nr. 417, February 23, 1777, pp. 64–65; RvP, inv. nr. 418, August 4, 1777, pp. 21–25.

34. NAN, Gouvernementssecretarie der Kolonie Suriname, inv. nr. 528, memorandum concerning the free mulatto congregantes, M. S. Hoheb Brandon, Semuel Ha. Dela Parra, and Abraham Bueno de Mesquita to Governor J. F. Friderici, March 7, 1794, [pp. 3–4].

35. Politieke Ordonnantie van de Staten van Holland, April 1, 1580, article 7 (*moghen niet trouwen de oomen met heure nichten . . . nochte insghelicx de moeyen met heuren neven, dat is met heuren broeders- ofte susterssoon*, http://www.republikanisme.nl/nederland/de-opstand/politieke-ordonantie.html); NAN, NPIGS, inv. nr. 96, Vertalingen in het Spaans en Portugees van de Gouverneurs-beschikking. Surinamese Jews had obtained a special privilege in the 1650s to arrange their own marriages under the jurisdiction of their religious leaders. After 1703, however, Dutch law required Jewish marriage contracts be approved by Dutch officials and registered with the state archives. On the repeal of exclusive autonomy in Jewish marital laws, see Ralph G. Bennett, "The Blacks and Jews of Surinam," *African Notes: Bulletin of the Institute of African Studies, University of Ibadan* 17: 1–2 (1993): 62–82, 69; P. A. Hilfman, "Some Further Notes on the Jews in Surinam," *PAJHS* 16 (1907): 10–13; and Marcus, *The Colonial American Jew*, 1:154.

36. For parallel use of the phrase "born in the same house" in The Cape, see Shell, *Children of Bondage*, 222.

37. NAN, SONA, inv. nr. 13, will of Ishac da Costa, November 8, 1725, fol. 13, pp. 245–47.

38. Ibid.

39. NAN, SONA, inv. nr. 230, petition of Joseph Pelegrino to Governor General Johan Coetier [Jean Coutier], Paramaribo, July 17, 1720, pp. 83–87.

40. Ben-Ur and Frankel, *Remnant Stones: The Jewish Cemeteries of Suriname*, 277 (epitaph 460); Jean Jacques Vrij to Aviva Ben-Ur, August 15, 2003, who notes that the word appears as *karboeger*.

41. NAN, SONA, inv. nr. 33, will of Benjamin Musaphia, April 16, 1764.

42. Kathleen J. Higgins, "Gender and the Manumission of Slaves in Colonial Brazil: The Prospects for Freedom in Sabará', Minas Gerais, 1710–1809," *Slavery and Abolition* 18: 2 (1997): 1–29, 12.

43. NAN, SONA, inv. nr. 783, will of Ishac Mesias, July 3, 1759, pp. 41–46, 41b. Mesias's undated tombstone, which he prepared during his lifetime, is transcribed in Ben-Ur and Frankel, *Remnant Stones: The Jewish Cemeteries of Suriname*, 224 (epitaph 309).

44. Harry Hoetink, "Race Relations in Curaçao and Surinam," in Laura Foner and Eugene D. Genovese, eds., *Slavery in the New World: A Reader in Comparative History* (Englewood Cliffs, N.J.: Prentice-Hall, 1969), 178–88, 184; Rosemary Brana-Shute, "Approaching Freedom: The Manumission of Slaves in Suriname, 1760–1828," *Slavery & Abolition* 10: 3 (December 1989): 40–63 and "The Manumission of Slaves in Suriname," 399–400.

45. Davis, "Regaining Jerusalem," 19.

46. Michael Goodich, ed., *Other Middle Ages: Witnesses at the Margins of Medieval Society* (Philadelphia: University of Pennsylvania Press, 1998), 14.

47. For "Pelegrino" as an adopted New Christian name, see Studemund-Halévy, *Biographisches Lexicon*, 357.

48. NAN, NPIGS, inv. nr. 80, petition of Mirian Pelengrina, January 26, 1758, p. 5.

49. The Portuguese translation of the Exodus quote would have been *não oprimirás o extrangiero*.

50. NAN, NPIGS, inv. nr. 76, undated petition of Jahacob Pelengrino (before 1750); Leviticus 24:22. His epitaph, dated April 11, 1750, is transcribed in Ben-Ur and Frankel, *Remnant Stones*, 277 (epitaph 460).

51. Leviticus 24:22; Cohen, *Jews in Another Environment*, 168; NAN, Gouvernementssecretarie der Kolonie Suriname, inv. nr. 528, Memorie gedaan maaken ende overgegeeven aan den Hoog Edele Gestrenge Heere J. F. Friderici (petition of the "couleurlingen" to the governor), September 2, 1793.

52. TNAUK, HCA 30/223, Jeosuah and Jacob Nasy to Jeosuah de Farro, September 15, 1672 (the word appears as *peregrinasao*, without the tilde). Leaders a century later gestured to their national exile (*prelongado cautiverio*). NAN, NPIGS, inv. nr. 8, June 24, 1777 (*neste prelongado cautiverio*).

53. NAN, Aanwinsten Eerste Afdeling, inv. nr. 1552, 1929 XIV, Livro de Varias Quetuboth, p. 107.

54. NAN, Doop-, Trouw- en Begraafboeken (DTB) van Suriname, inv. nr. 44, p. 47 (born 7 Hesvan 5424).

55. NAN, Sociëteit van Suriname, inv. nr. 229, Lyste van alle de manschap der Joodse natie wonende op de Revier van Suriname en Casewina, 1701, p. 31; NAN, NPIGS, inv. nr. 75, petition of David Judeu, 5464 [1703–1704].

56. Marcus, *The Colonial American Jew*, 3:1228–31, 1235; Sarna, *American Judaism*, 28; Stern, "The Function of Genealogy in American Jewish History," 94–97; Sheldon J. Godfrey and Judith C. Godfrey, *Search out the Land: The Jews and the Growth of Equality in British Colonial America* (Montreal: McGill-Queen's University Press, 1995), 294n14. For Judah's dates, see *PAJHS* 23:151; for Levy's dates, see de Sola Pool, *Portraits Etched in Stone*, 198–201.

57. LMA/4521/A/01/03/008, minutes for January 21, 1822, p.194; LMA/4521/A/01/03/009, minutes for June 16, 1825, p. 24 (for London); Florike Egmond, "Contours of Identity: Poor Ashkenazim in the Dutch Republic," in *Dutch Jewish History* 3 (1993): 205–25, 217–18.

58. NAN, NPIGS, inventories 416–23, birth and death registers, passim.

59. Michael Craton, "Reluctant Creoles: The Planters' World in the British West Indies," in Bernard Bailyn and Philip D. Morgan, eds., *Strangers Within the Realm: Cultural Margins of the First British Empire* (Chapel Hill: University of North Carolina Press, 1991), 314–62, 343.

60. Goslinga, *The Dutch in the Caribbean and in the Guianas*, 359; Harmannus Hoetink, *De gespleten samenleving in het Caraibisch gebied* (Assen: Van Gorcum, 1962), 71; Schiltkamp and De Smidt, *Placaten, ordonnantiën, en andere wetten, uitgevaardigd in Suriname*, 1:277 (plakaat 240); Van Lier, *Frontier Society*, 77.

61. Goslinga, *The Dutch in the Caribbean and in the Guianas*, 359; Hoetink, *De gespleten samenleving*, 71. This is probably Ganna Levy Hartog, the woman Ralph G. Bennett discovered was his wife's ancestor. She was expelled from the colony on January 25, 1731, "for having had sex with an Indian slave." Bennett, "The Blacks and Jews of Surinam," 70. Sexual liaisons between white women and slaves were also rare in The Cape but not as severely punished as in Suriname. Shell, *Children of Bondage*, 316–20.

62. Fermin, *Description Générale*, 121.

63. NAN, NPIGS, inv. nr. 101 (1754), treatise 26, article 3.

64. Ibid.

65. NAN, Sociëteit van Suriname, inv. nr. 229, Generaale Lyste van de Blancke Roode en Swarte slaaven, 1702, p. 169 and inv. nr. 318, Leysten van de Ingeseetenen deeser colonie,

February 9, 1763, pp. 77ff. Silva, like all estate owners in the list, appears in the column of whites (*blanken*), but the name Judeu indicates slave origins.

66. NAN, Gouvernementssecretarie der Kolonie Suriname, inv. nr. 528, Memorie gedaan maaken ende overgegeeven aan den Hoog Edele Gestrenge Heere J. F. Friderici (petition of the "couleurlingen" to the governor; the word appears as *carboegel*), September 2, 1793; Vink, *Creole Jews*, 271.

67. Ben-Ur and Frankel, *Remnant Stones: The Jewish Cemeteries of Suriname*, 277 (epitaphs 460–61). The grave of the third individual named in the petition, Gabriel de Mattos, was not found, however, his son (Joseph, son of Gabriel de Mattos) died in 1751 (epitaph 462).

68. Neither the term *congregante* nor racial designations appear in NAN, NPIGS, inv. nr. 416. The first mention of *congregantes* in the birth register dates to 1793. NAN, NPIGS, inv. nr. 417, p. 3. See also NAN, NPIGS, inv. nr. 418, Registro Mortuorio, 1777, p. 14; NAN, NPIGS, inv. nr. 423. For the earliest examples of references to *congregantes* in the minutes, see NAN, NPIGS, inv. nr. 7, June 23, 1761, October 6, 1766; inv. nr. 1, June 26, 1770, October 21, 1772. I have found no references to racial designations in the minutes before NAN, NPIGS, inv. nr. 1, January 23, 1776. For a reference to a 1662/1663 ordinance on *congregantes*, see SAA, inv. nr. 334, Archief van de Portugees-Israëlietische Gemeente, inv. nr. 1029, pp. 428–29.

69. Two of the *congregantes* were converts to Judaism (Hana de Gentillez, identified as a *guerá congreganta*, and Jahacob Bello Mesquita, a *congregante guer*). Another, Joseph, son of David Cohen Nassy, was a Eurafrican who, for reasons explained in the next chapter, was specifically designated as "not a *congregante*" but as a "mulatto." NAN, NPIGS, inv. nr. 418, entry for "Hana de Gentillez," 103 and entry for "Jahb. Bello Mesquita (*congregante*) (*gúer*)," 43.

70. See, for example, the case of Aron Bueno Bibas, who was stripped of his *jahid* status in 1773 for taking a dispute to the governor. After payment of a fine the following year, the Mahamad reversed their decree. NAN, NPIGS, inv. nr. 8, June 3, 1773, September 12, 1774.

71. NAN, Gouvernementssecretarie der Kolonie Suriname, inv. nr. 528, Memorie gedaan maaken ende overgegeeven aan den Hoog Edele Gestrenge Heere J. F. Friderici (petition of the "couleurlingen" to the governor), September 2, 1793. These examples come from the first signature page only.

72. NAN, NPIGS, inv. nr. 417, entry for "Mirjam Judia de Meza (Molata)," 74.

73. NAN, SONA, inv. nr. 64, will of Simcha Pinto, December 17, 1790, p. 375.

74. NAN, NPIGS, inv. nr. 3, October 2, 1797.

75. "Approximative staat der bevolking van de kolonie Suriname, 1817," in *Surinaamsche almanak voor het jaar 1821*, 30.

76. Ibid., 31.

77. Ibid., 30; NAN, NPIGS, inv. nr. 4, April 17, 1803.

78. Wolbers, *Geschiedenis van Suriname*, 442, 565.

79. For a parallel among the white population of The Cape, see Hans F. Heese, *Groep sonder Grense: Die rol en status van die gemengde bevolking aan die Kaap, 1652–1795* (Bellville: Wes-Kaaplandse Instituut vir Historiese Navorsing, Universiteit van Wes-Kaapland, 1984); Ansu Datta, *From Bengal to the Cape: Bengali Slaves in South Africa* (N.p.: Xlibris Corporation, 2013), 64–66.

80. Hezser, *Jewish Slavery in Antiquity*, 33.

81. He also referred to himself as Jahacob Abrahams. NAN, NPIGS, inv. nr. 75, petition of Jahacob Abrahams, April 11, 1724.

82. SAA, inv. nr. 334, file 1304, Ascamoth 5409 (Brazilië) [1648–1649], bylaw 32.

83. NAN, NPIGS, inv. nr. 99, treatise 26.

84. NAN, Stadhouderlijke Secretarie, inv. nr. 1264, *Redres der Reglamenten, Institutien, en Instellingen van de H. Gemeente B.V.S.*, November 9, 1752, treatise 26, article 1.

85. NAN, NPIGS, inv. nr. 101 (1754), treatise 26, article 1.

86. AJA, MS-581, X416/4, Haskamoth, Paramaribo, Suriname, 1734–1821, p. 3a (eighth bylaw).

87. Ibid., p. 15 (bylaw passed February 2, 1772); NAN, NPIGS, inv. nr. 99 (1748), treatise 26, article 1.

88. NAN, NPIGS, inv. nr. 4, April 17, 1803.

89. Ibid., inv. nr. 13, November 4, 1832.

90. Hannah Ruth London, *Miniatures of Early American Jews* (Rutland, Vt.: C. E. Tuttle [1953]), 34. The portrait is housed in the American Jewish Historical Society.

91. Karl Watson, "Shifting Identities: Religion, Race, and Creolization Among the Sephardi Jews of Barbados, 1654–1900," in Jane Gerber, ed., *The Jews in the Caribbean* (Oxford: Littman Library of Jewish Civilization, 2014), 195–22, 220.

92. James William Hagy, *This Happy Land: The Jews of Colonial and Antebellum Charleston* (Tuscaloosa: University of Alabama Press, 1993), 84, 183 (for the lack of ritual circumcisers in North America); LMA/4521/D/01/01/08, April 22, 1799, p. 126. Due to space constraints, Brandon's complicated experiences with the Barbados Jewish community have been summarized here but will be dealt with more extensively in a future publication.

93. NAN, NPIGS, inv. nr. 5, December 29, 1812; LMA/4521/D/01/01/008, Fair copies of petitions to the Speaker and General Assembly of Barbados, 1819–1920 (no exact date provided), p. 33. The assumption about Brandon's suspected Christianity as a factor is mine.

94. LMA/4521/D/01/01/003, March 7, 1819 (for Brandon's trip to North America and involvement in fundraising for a new Philadelphia synagogue); LMA/4521/D/01/01/008, p. 33 (for a bequest to the new Philadelphia synagogue), pp. 77, 106 (for "color'd connexions").

95. Laura Arnold Leibman and Sam May, "Making Jews: Race, Gender and Identity in Barbados in the Age of Emancipation," *American Jewish History* 99: 1 (January 2015): 1–26, 11 (for "conspiracy theory").

96. John Davies, "Taking Liberties: Saint Dominguan Slaves and the Formation of Community in Philadelphia, 1791–1805," in Jeff Forret and Christine E. Sears, eds., *New Directions in Slavery Studies: Commodification, Community, and Comparison* (Baton Rouge: Louisiana State University Press, 2015), 93–110, 94.

97. For one such family, see Harold Moïse, *The Moïse Family of South Carolina: An Account of the Life and Descendants of Abraham and Sarah Moise Who Settled in Charleston, South Carolina, in the Year 1791 A. D.* (Columbia, S.C.: R. L. Bryan Co, 1961), 2–3.

98. Hagy, *This Happy Land*, 85; Jacob Neusner, "The Role of English Jews in the Development of American Jewish Life, 1775–1850," *American Jewish History: The Colonial and Early National Periods, 1654–1840*, 2 vols. (New York: Routledge, 1998), 1:148; Ralph Melnick, "Billy Simons: The Black Jew of Charleston," *American Jewish Archives* (April 1980): 3–8, 6.

99. NAN, NPIGS, inv. nr. 14, March 11, 1841.

100. Ibid.

101. Vink, *Creole Jews*, 240.

102. NAN, NPIGS, inv. nr. 8, March 17, 1784. For another example, see inv. nr. 11, September 23, 1822.

103. Aviva Ben-Ur, "Peripheral Inclusion: Communal Belonging in Suriname's Sephardic Community," in Alexandra Cuffel and Brian Britt, eds., *Religion, Gender, and Culture in the Pre-modern World* (New York: Palgrave Macmillan, 2007), 185–210.

104. NAN, Stadhouderlijke Secretarie, inv. nr. 1264, *Redres der Reglamenten, Institutien, en Instellingen van de H. Gemeente B.V.S.*, November 9, 1752, p. 21 (treatise 19, article 4, Portuguese section); NAN, NPIGS, inv. nr. 102 (1754), treatise 19, articles 3 and 4, pp. 43–44.

105. Ben-Ur with Frankel, *Remnant Stones: The Jewish Cemeteries and Synagogues of Suriname*, 66.

106. Ibid.

107. NAN, NPIGS, inv. nr. 423, p. 19; AJA, microfilm reel 67a, n. 785, undated will of Joseph Gabay Farro.

108. NAN, NIPGS, inv. nr. 11, October 30, 1820, p. 13.

109. Ibid., inv. nr. 137, Grafboek van het kerkhof te Paramaribo (1849).

110. Vink, *Creole Jews*, 226.

111. AJA, unprocessed box, Ashkenazi community of Suriname, Cahier van Finta des Nederlandsch-Israëlitische Gemeente te Suriname over A. M. 5619 [1858/1859], [p. 6].

112. Vink, *Creole Jews*, 303–4.

113. Ibid., 209; Schorsch, *Jews and Blacks in the Early Modern World*, 237–38.

114. J. Hartog, *Curaçao: From Colonial Dependence to Autonomy* (Aruba: De Wit, 1968), 148; Emmanuel and Emmanuel, *History of the Jews of the Netherlands Antilles*, 1:146; Marcus, *The Colonial American Jew*, 1:200; all cited in Schorsch, *Jews and Blacks in the Early Modern World*, 222, 237–38.

115. NAN, NPIGS, inv. nr. 149, Reglamentos ou Escamot da Naçao Judaica Portugeza de C[uraçao] revistos e aprovados pelos Parnasim da nacao Judaica Portugeza d[e Ams]terdam, treatise titled "Tocante os Jehidim & Imposta," articles 2 and 5.

116. On the destruction of these archives, see Emmanuel and Emmanuel, *History of the Jews of the Netherlands Antilles*, 1:7–8, 2:1112; AJA, Manuscript Collection No. 99, Bertram W. Korn Papers, box 3, folder 3, "Blacks-Jewish Blacks in the Caribbean," Rabbi Leo M. Abrami to Bertrand Korn; Charles Gomes Casseres, "Lost and Found," in Jane Gomes Casseres, ed., *Generation to Generation: The Continuing Story of Congregation Mikvé Israel-Emanuel* (Curaçao: Congregation Mikvé Israel-Emanuel, 2003), 93–101, 101; will of Isaac Samuel Emmanuel, case number 1900298877, Probate Division, Court of Common Pleas, Cincinnati, undated and attached to a 1979 tax return, 4 pages.

117. For the latter point, see Wolbers, *Geschiedenis van Suriname*, 775; Harry (Harmannus) Hoetink, *Het patroon van de oude Curaçaose samenleving: Een sociologische studie* (Assen: Van Gorcum, 1958), 55.

118. Klooster and Oostindie, *Realm Between Empires*, 131 (for the relative instability of the two white populations of each colony).

119. Daniel Livesay, *Children of Uncertain Fortune: Mixed-Race Jamaicans in Britain and the Atlantic Family, 1733–1833* (Chapel Hill: University of North Carolina Press, 2018), 4.

Chapter 5

1. Israel Goldstein, *My World as a Jew: The Memoirs of Israel Goldstein*, 2 vols. (New York: Herzl Press, 1984), 1:308. For further discussion, see Aviva Ben-Ur and Julie-Marthe Cohen, "Unworthy of Their Ancestors: Representing Caribbean Jewry in 1954 and 2015," in David

Bunis, Corinna Deppner, and Ivana Vučina Simović, eds., *Jubilee Volume in Honor of Michael Studemund-Halévy* (Barcelona: Tirocinio, 2018), 52–84.

2. Livesay, *Children of an Uncertain Fortune*, 8–9, 399; John Garrigus, "Blue and Brown: Contraband Indigo and the Rise of a Free Colored Planter Class in French Saint-Domingue," *The Americas* 50: 2 (October 1993): 233–63, 257–61.

3. Garrigus, "Blue and Brown," 259.

4. Livesay, *Children of an Uncertain Fortune*, 10; Wim Klooster, "Subordinate but Proud: Curaçao's Free Blacks and Mulattoes in the Eighteenth Century," *New West Indian Guide* 68: 3/4 (1994): 283–300, 293–94.

5. Klooster, "Subordinate but Proud," 294.

6. Neville A. T. Hall, *Slave Society in the Danish West Indies: St. Thomas, St. John, and St. Croix* (Kingston, Jamaica: University of the West Indies Press, 1992), 152–53, 160–61.

7. NAN, Gouvernementssecretarie der Kolonie Suriname, inv. nr. 528, Memorie gedaan maaken ende overgegeeven aan den Hoog Edele Gestrenge Heere J. F. Friderici (petition of the "couleurlingen" to the governor), September 2, 1793; Vink, *Creole Jews*, 271; NAN, NPIGS, inv. nr. 101 (1754), treatise 26, article 1.

8. NAN, NPIGS, inv. nr. 102 (1754), treatise 19, articles 3 and 4, pp. 43–44.

9. Wim Klooster, "Comparative Perspectives on the Urban Black Atlantic on the Eve of Abolition," *International Review of Social History* 65 (2020); NAN, NPIGS, inv. nr. 99 (1748), treatise 26, article 1; Cohen, *Jews in Another Environment*, 161, 305n38.

10. NAN, NPIGS, inv. nr. 101 (1754), treatise 26, article 1 and inv. nr. 149, Reglamentos ou Escamot da Naçao Judaica Portugeza de C[uraçao] revistos e aprovados pelos Parnasim da nacao Judaica Portugeza d[e Ams]terdam, [p. 9]. There is no categorical evidence of a "congregante/jahid" divide in Amsterdam, although "negro" and "mulatto" Jews experienced a peripheral inclusion similar to that of Suriname. Yosef Kaplan, "Political Concepts in the World of the Portuguese Jews of Amsterdam During the Seventeenth Century: The Problem of Exclusion and the Boundaries of Self-Identity," in Yosef Kaplan, Henry Mechoulan, and Richard H. Popkin, eds., *Menasseh Ben Israel and His World* (Leiden: E. J. Brill, 1989), 45–62, 57–58. For Curaçao, see 127–28.

11. NAN, NPIGS, inv. nr. 101 (1754), treatise 19, article 4.

12. AJA, MS-581, Box X-416, folder 4, Escamoth of Instellinge gedaan, ende genomen door de oprigters van K. K. Askenazens Neve Salom, February 2, 1772 (unpaginated).

13. NAN, NPIGS, inv. nr. 1, April 18, 1770 (for Ribca as a fundraiser for the expansion of the overcrowded Sedek VeSalom synagogue); September 28, 1775 (for the trial).

14. Ibid., July 8, 1777, November 26, 1778; inv. nr. 135, September 29, 1775.

15. NAN, NPIGS, inv. nr. 423, entry for "Mosseh Rodrigues del Prado (congregante)," died October 3, 1797, p. 25; NAN, SONA, inv. nr. 57, will of "de vrije mulatin Maria de Prado" or Mariana del Prado, June 12, 1787, pp. 460ff.

16. NAN, NPIGS, inv. nr. 1, May 8, June 17, and June 25, 1777; inv. nr. 2, June 26 and October 9, 1782, June 25 and 26, 1782.

17. See, for example, ibid., inv. nr. 1, May 8, 1777; inv. nr. 2, June 25, June 26, and October 9, 1782.

18. Ibid., inv. nr. 1, December 7, 1778.

19. Ibid., December 8, 1778.

20. Ibid., December 8, 1778.

21. Ibid., February 1, 1779.

22. Ibid., February 20, 1779. The governor was likely Jan Nepveu.

23. In 1770, *congregantes* did not appear on the communal tax roll. For the requirement of wealth in legal self-defense, see NAN, NPIGS, inv. nr. 1, October 25, 1779.

24. Ibid., inv. nr. 435, Minuut-notulen van vergaderingen, November 20, 1787, p. 65[b]; inv. nr. 137, Grafboek van het kerhof te Paramaribo, listed under "linea Pa" (unpaginated).

25. NAN, Gouvernementssecretarie der Kolonie Suriname, inv. nr. 528, Memorie gedaan maaken ende overgegeeven aan den Hoog Edele Gestrenge Heere J. F. Friderici (petition of the "couleurlingen" to the governor), September 2, 1793.

26. NAN, NPIGS, inv. nr. 102 (1754), treatise 55, 1755.

27. Ibid., inv. nr. 420, Registro Mortuario, "Jos. de David Cohen Nassy (Molato & nao congregante)," April 17, 1790/3 Yiar 5550, p. 49. He does not appear in NAN, NPIGS, inv. nr. 137, Grafboek van het kerkhof te Paramaribo.

28. NAN, Gouvernementssecretarie der Kolonie Suriname, inv. nr. 528, Memorie gedaan maaken ende overgegeeven aan den Hoog Edele Gestrenge Heere J. F. Friderici (petition of the "couleurlingen" to the governor), September 2, 1793, [p. 5].

29. Ibid., March 7, 1794; Cohen, *Jews in Another Environment*, 163.

30. NAN, NPIGS, inv. nr. 420, Registro Mortuario, December 18, 1790 (11 Tebet 5551), p. 93; NAN, NPIGS, inv. nr. 435, December 21, 1790, p. 92 verso.

31. NAN, NPIGS, inv. nr. 435, December 21, 1790, p. 92 verso.

32. Ibid., 93.

33. NAN, Gouvernementssecretarie der Kolonie Suriname, inv. nr. 528, Memorie gedaan maaken ende overgegeeven aan den Hoog Edele Gestrenge Heere J. F. Friderici (petition of the "couleurlingen" to the governor), September 2, 1793. Robert Cohen dates the founding of the brotherhood to 1779, a misprint he borrows from previous authors. Cohen, "Patterns of Jewish Marriage," 93, citing Dentz, "Joodse Kleurlingen," 234; Van Lier, *Frontier Society*, 110–11.

34. NAN, NPIGS, inv. nr. 98, fragment of a compendium of *ascamot*, undated, but probably seventeenth century ("nao posse aver otra [Esnoga] no kaal, senao este que de prezente ha"); inv. nr. 101 (1754), bylaw 1 ("que naõ pode haver em toda a colonia mais que huma Esnoga, que he aque prezentemente ha na povoaçaõ da Savana . . . excepto a caza de oraçaõ intitulada Sedek VeSalom"); inv. nr. 109 (1787), scan 5 ("a synagoga fabricada na povoçao de Savana sera considerada como a igrezia may da Naçao em Surinam, sem estar sujeyta a nenhua outra em que lugar & debaixo de que poder ou governo possa estar sem ser permitido ter outra synagoga em toda a colonia que aquella que tem oijem a Naçao em Paramo. intitulada S.V.S. cuja ficará como o opresente debaixo das ordems & dependente da quella da Savana").

35. NAN, NPIGS, inv. nr. 2, June 26, 1787.

36. Wim Klooster, "The Rising Expectations of Free and Enslaved Blacks in the Greater Caribbean," in Wim Klooster and Gert Oostindie, eds., *Curaçao in the Age of Revolutions, 1795–1800* (Leiden: KITLV Press, 2011), 57–74.

37. NAN, NPIGS, inv. nr. 2, April 21, 1790.

38. NAN, SONA, inv. nr. 63, will of "de vreye mulat" Joseph Nassy, February 25, 1790, pp. 97ff.

39. NAN, NPIGS, inv. nr. 2, June 10, 1787, p. 421.

40. Ibid., inv. nr. 3, June 26, 1793.

41. Vink, *Creole Jews*, 281–82.

42. Elias and Scotson, *The Established and the Outsiders*, xxxii.

43. Cohen, *Jews in Another Environment*, 162–63.

44. NAN, NPIGS, inv. nr. 5, January 2, 1814.

45. William Wilberforce Bird, *State of the Cape of Good Hope in 1822* (London: John Murray, 1823), 348.

46. NAN, NPIGS, inv. nr. 417, p. 109; inv. nr. 420, p. 107. Her great-grandmother, Ribca Samson, may have been Eurafrican; the identity of her great-grandfather is unknown. See "Notes on Usage" in the Introduction for a full definition of these racial classifications.

47. Ibid., inv. nr. 2, April 28, 1790.

48. Ibid., inv. nr. 3, February 20, 1791.

49. Ibid., June 14, 1791, August 8, 1791.

50. Ibid., December 29, 1791.

51. Ibid., September 12, 1792 and November 26, 1792.

52. Ibid., September 19, 1792.

53. Ibid., December 2, 1792.

54. Ibid., December 27, 1792.

55. Ibid., December 2, 1792.

56. Cecil Roth, *The Great Synagogue: London, 1690–1940* (London: Edward Goldston & Son, 1950), 72 (cases from 1718 and the 1730s); Bernfeld, "Financing Poor Relief," 81 (for seventeenth-century Amsterdam).

57. Vink, *Creole Jews*, 136, 235.

58. For other suggestions of their social networks with Christians, see ibid., 169, 239.

59. NAN, NPIGS, inv. nr. 3, December 2, 1792.

60. See, for example, Cohen, *Jews in Another Environment*, 157.

61. NAN, Raad van Justitie, inv. nr. 535, petition of Isaac Gabay Fonseca, August 27, 1792, pp. 134–35.

62. NAN, NPIGS, inv. nr. 3, February 4, 1793.

63. Ibid., January 21, 1793.

64. Cohen, *Jews in Another Environment*, 172 (the governor confirmed the Mahamad's "decision to abolish the mulatto fraternity"); Vink, *Creole Jews*, 230 (following Cohen); Snyder, "A Sense of Place," 328; Stiefel, *Jewish Sanctuary in the Atlantic World*, 203 ("potential cult").

65. NAN, 1.05.10.01, Gouvernementssecretarie Suriname, inv. nr. 528, "Memorianten" to Governor J. F. Friderici, September 2, 1793, last page (unpaginated). He signed as "Moses del Prado."

66. NAN, NIPGS, inv. nr. 3, September 11, 1793, verbal communication from Roza Pereyra regarding her son Jacob Jessurun. Another *jesiba* they organized in Paramaribo was called Miscan Sello. NAN, NPIGS, inv. nr. 2, June 30, 1790.

67. Ibid., inv. nr. 3, June 6, 1797 (reference to a copy of the 1794 treatise authenticated by the governor); September 12, 1797 (problem still unresolved).

68. Ibid., September 28, 1797.

69. Ibid., inv. nr. 36, Pubricaçaõ, December 28, 1796, pp. 298–99, 337.

70. Ibid., inv. nr. 3, June 6, 1797.

71. Ibid., September 11, 1793, verbal communication from Roza Pereyra regarding her son Jahacob Jessurun.

72. Ibid., May 25, 1794, August 20, 1794.

73. Ibid., July 13, 1790 (10 guilders); September 16, 1794 (7.10 guilders).

74. Ibid., September 16, 1794.

75. Ibid., September 29, 1795.

76. Ibid., September 4, 1798.

77. Ibid., inv. nr. 4, December 29, 1807.

78. Ibid., June 29, 1810; inv. nr. 5, October 8 and 25, 1812, December 27, 1814.

79. Ibid., inv. nr. 3, August 30, 1791.

80. Ibid., October 7, 1794.

81. Ibid., inv. nr. 4, February 25, 1805.

82. See, for example, ibid., inv. nr. 5, January 20, 1816.

83. Ibid., inv. nr. 3, September 4, 1798.

84. Ibid., inv. nr. 5, April 13, 1815.

85. Ibid., July 29, 1816.

86. Ibid.

87. Ibid., September 29, 1816.

88. Ibid., November 27, 1816.

89. Ibid., December 23, 1816.

90. Ibid., March 25, 1817.

91. Ibid., inv. nr. 437, [p. 4].

92. Ibid., Extracto do Registro de Notulas & Rezolucoems do Collegio dos Sres ao MM & Deputados da Nacao do KKBVS, April 13, 1802.

93. Ibid., inv. nr. 11, p. 13.

94. Vink, *Creole Jews*, 174 and 241 (for quote).

95. NAN, NPIGS, inv. nr. 11, February 25, 1822 (as *sohet* and *bodek*), June 10, 1822 (for donation).

96. Ibid., inv. nr. 6, July 27, 1817.

97. Ibid., inv. nr. 11, July 6, 1823.

98. Nassy, *Essai historique*, part 2, 27.

99. Vink, *Creole Jews*, 87n39, 239 (for further examples); NAN, Gemeentebestuur van Suriname, inv. nr. 58, Register der vrye personen woonachtig in de wyk Litta. B opgenomen door wykmeesters in de maand July 1828, passim; TNAUK, CO 278/17, "Population Returns of White Inhabitants with their Families and their Slaves of all Description," census conducted per order of interim Governor P. Bonham, 1811, passim.

100. See, for example, NAN, SONA, inv. nr. 81, will of Johan Conrad Wilhelm Braunmuller, May 29, 1799, p. 33; will of Isak de Abraham Bueno de Mesquita, inv. nr. 821, will nr. 51; inv. nr. 822, will of Casparus Reyns, 1827, will nr. 10; will of Ludwich Esais Heinrich Forberger, September 29, 1827, will nr. 23.

101. Cohen, *Jews in Another Environment*, 172 (the governor confirmed the Mahamad's "decision to abolish the mulatto fraternity"); Vink, *Creole Jews*, 230 (following Cohen); Snyder, "A Sense of Place," 328; Stiefel, *Jewish Sanctuary in the Atlantic World*, 203 ("potential cult").

102. For examples of broader apathy in the broader Jewish community, see NAN, NPIGS, inv. nr. 4, September 9, 1804; inv. nr. 11, November 25, 1821. Eurafrican Jews spoke about this

broader apathy as well. See NAN, NPIGS, inv. nr. 5, April 13, 1815 (referring to "scandals and disorders" during prayer and "the little respect and attention that many individuals of both kehilot have . . . for the divine cult").

103. Phillip Troutman, "Grapevine in the Slave Market: African American Geopolitical Literacy and the 1841 *Creole* Revolt," in Walter Johnson, ed., *The Chattel Principle: Internal Slave Trades in the Americas* (New Haven, Conn.: Yale University Press, 2004), 20–33; Jessica Vance Roitman, "'A Mass of Mestiezen, Castiezen, and Mulatten': Contending with Color in the Netherlands Antilles, 1750–1850," *Atlantic Studies* 14: 3 (2017): 399–417, 407 (for the application of Troutman's principle to free people of African descent).

104. NAN, NPIGS, inv. nr. 111, chapter 1, article 2, 1787. "Tanto homen como mulheres" appears in superscript over the words "Todo Jahid."

105. Levy Maduro and Maduro, *Sefer Berit Yitshak*, 12a; Kaplan, "Political Concepts," 60–61; "The Earliest Extant Minute Books of the Spanish and Portuguese Congregation Shearith Israel in New York," 73; *History of the Corporation of Spanish and Portuguese Jews*, 11; Whitfield, "The Braided Identity of Southern Jewry," 431; Jick, *The Americanization of the Synagogue*, 54–55.

106. David B. Ruderman, *Early Modern Jewry: A New Cultural History* (Princeton, N.J.: Princeton University Press, 2011), 58–59.

107. Finley, *Ancient Slavery and Modern Ideology*, 68, 95.

108. On Judaism and Islam as religions of the Atlantic World, see Mark and da Silva Horta, *The Forgotten Diaspora*; Robin Law and Paul E. Lovejoy, eds., *The Biography of Mahommah Gardo Baquaqua: His Passage from Slavery to Freedom in Africa and America* (Princeton, N.J.: Markus Wiener, 2007); and Michael Gomez, *Exchanging Our Country Marks: The Transformation of African Identities in the Colonial and Antebellum South* (Chapel Hill: University of North Carolina Press, 1998), esp. chap. 4.

109. Because they are not archivally driven, such works rely on ancient rabbinical sources as representative of early modern practices. See, for example, Erik R. Seeman, "Crossing Boundaries, Keeping Faith: Jewish Deathways," in *Death in the New World: Cross-Cultural Encounters, 1492–1800* (Philadelphia: University of Pennsylvania Press, 2010), 232–62 and, to a lesser extent, Schorsch, *Jews and Blacks in the Early Modern World.*

110. Klooster, "Comparative Perspectives on the Urban Black Atlantic on the Eve of Abolition" (for the first quote); Olaudah Equiano, *The Interesting Narrative of the Life of Olaudah Equiano or Gustavus Vassa, the African, Written by Himself,* 9th ed. (London: self-published, 1794 [1789]), 263–64.

111. Dentz, "Joodse Kleurlingen," 234. The words in modern Israeli Hebrew would be rendered as *shiva* and *yeshiva*, respectively.

112. Advertisement published by B. M. Meza and Samuel de Robles, *Weeklyksche Surinaamsche Courant,* nr. 48 (May 29, 1794): 8; nr. 49 (June 5, 1794): 7; nr. 50 (June 12, 1794): 8. For sale advertisement by owner A. J. Koopman, see *Surinaamsche Courant,* nr. 66 (August 15, 1804): 4. I thank Paul van Capelleveen for his assistance in obtaining copies of these issues.

113. Ben-Ur with Frankel, *Remnant Stones: The Jewish Cemeteries and Synagogues of Suriname,* 128, 143.

Chapter 6

1. This chapter is a revised version of Aviva Ben-Ur, "Purim in the Public Eye: Leisure, Violence, and Cultural Convergence in the Dutch Atlantic," *Jewish Social Studies* 20: 1 (Fall 2014): 32–76.

2. This composite portrait of fin-de-siècle Purim as celebrated in Suriname is based on Schiltkamp and De Smidt, *Placaten, ordonnantiën, en andere wetten, uitgevaardigd in Suriname*, 2:883 (plakaat 757, "Notifikatie, Maatregelen tegen uitspattingen op Feestdagen," May 24, 1775, Paramaribo); NAN, NPIGS, inv. nr. 3, February 22, 1793, March 14, 1797, March 13, 1799; inv. nr. 4, February 27, 1800, March 27 and 28, 1807; inv. nr. 5, March 27, 1815, February 18, 1817; and inv. nr. 11, February 9, 1823. The terms I translate as "slaves" and "personal valets" are *negros* and *moleques*, respectively. The Anglo-Dutch term *voeteboy*, used in contexts extraneous to Purim, probably approximates "enslaved valets," which I understand to mean enslaved personal attendant. For the word as used in the 1830s, see Teenstra, *De negerslaven in de colonie Suriname*, 75 (*een jongen (voete boy) als lijfknecht*).

3. Emmanuel and Emmanuel, *History of the Jews of the Netherlands Antilles*, 1:235, 2:1088–89; CBG, Collectie Joshua Mozes Levy Maduro, inv. nr. 56, folder marked "viering Purim," handwritten note dated February 26, 1858 (unpaginated), and transcription of petition of Jews to the governor, Oud Archief van Curaçao, part 298, 1825 (in Dutch).

4. Emmanuel and Emmanuel, *History of the Jews of the Netherlands Antilles*, 1:235, 2:1088–89; CBG, Collectie Joshua Mozes Levy Maduro, inv. nr. 56, folder marked "viering Purim," handwritten note dated February 26, 1858 (unpaginated); B. de Gaay Fortman, "Curaçao en Onderhoorige Eilanden, 1816–1828," *Nieuwe West Indische Gids* 9: 1 (1928): 497–518, 516 (unattributed anecdote dated to both "each year" and 1818).

5. *Archives Israélites* (Paris, 1853), 91, cited in Emmanuel and Emmanuel, *History of the Jews of the Netherlands Antilles*, 1:371n10.

6. NAN, CBG, Collectie Joshua Mozes Levy Maduro, inv. nr. 56, folder marked "viering Purim"; "Purim Celebrations," *Home Journal, Published by the Young Men's Hebrew Association of Curaçao* 1: 10 (March 15, 1890): [5].

7. NAN, NPIGS, inv. nr. 4, February 28, 1800 (Paramaribo).

8. However, mostly due to vernacular practice, it was not unusual for Purim to last longer than the rabbinically prescribed one day of festivities in both the Land of Israel and in the diaspora. According to rabbinical law, in Jerusalem and all ancient walled cities, Purim continues through the next day. See Jean Baumgarten, "Prieres, rituels et pratiques dans la société juive ashkénaze," *Revue de l'histoire des religions* 218: 3 (2001): 369–403, 384. Some Jewish communities since late antiquity have observed a three-day Purim, which has generated some controversy through the ages. N. S. Doniach, *Purim, or, The Feast of Esther: An Historical Study* (Philadelphia: Jewish Publication Society of America, 1933), 3:67–68, 251–58n36. Padua's Jewish community, drawing on a variety of subethnic Jewish influences, observed Purim for eight days to two weeks. Roni Weinstein, *Marriage Rituals Italian Style: A Historical Anthropological Perspective on Early Modern Italian Jews*, trans. Batya Stein (Leiden: Brill, 2003), 384 (example from 1580). Similarly, the youth-centered Purim celebrations of early modern central Europe began weeks before the actual holiday. Juspa Schammes, *Minhagim de-qehila qadish Varmaisa*, 2 vols. (Jerusalem: Mifal torat hakhme Ashkenaz, 1988–1992), 1:258 (in Hebrew; the transliteration of the title and author's name varies).

9. Elliott Horowitz, *Reckless Rites: Purim and the Legacy of Jewish Violence* (Princeton, N.J.: Princeton University Press, 2006), 44.

10. This certainly applies to learned individuals. In the 1760s and 1770s, theologian and educator Ezra Stiles visited his local synagogue in Newport on at least two separate occasions to hear the Scroll of Esther read aloud; other times he simply noted the occurrence of Purim

in his diary. Ezra Stiles, *The Literary Diary of Ezra Stiles: Jan. 1, 1769–Mar. 13, 1776*, ed. Franklin Bowditch Dexter (New York: Charles Scribner's Sons, 1902), 1:7, 41, 354–55. For ecumenical Purim as celebrated in modern Iran and Yemen, see Shifra Epstein, "Purim: The Smiting of the Figures of Haman and Zeresh in Yemen," *Mankind Quarterly* 29: 4 (1989): 401–16.

11. Weinstein, *Marriage Rituals Italian Style*, 433.

12. For a parallel, consider cross-dressing, inebriation, and recreational firing of guns during holidays such as New Year's Day, May Day, Shrove Tuesday (Vastenavond, the Tuesday preceding Lent), and *kermis*, as celebrated in New Netherland. Dennis Sullivan, *The Punishment of Crime in Colonial New York: The Dutch Experience in Albany During the Seventeenth Century* (New York: Peter Lang, 1997), 53, 55.

13. Schorsch, *Jews and Blacks in the Early Modern World*, 14.

14. Davis, "Regaining Jerusalem," 28.

15. Klooster, "Subordinate but Proud," 289 (for Curaçao's Jewish population in 1789). The minutes of Nieuw Amsterdam's Jewish community do not survive, while those of English/ British New York commence only in 1728. "The Earliest Extant Minute Books of the Spanish and Portuguese Congregation Shearith Israel in New York," and "From the 2nd Volume of Minute Books of the Congn: Shearith Israel in New York." Available communal minutes of the Jewish community of Barbados begin in 1791 (minutes dating from 1775 are at risk and not open to the public). No records from the Nevis Jewish community have survived. In Jamaica, many Portuguese Jewish records were destroyed during the earthquake and fire of 1907. LMA/4521/D/01/01/001 and LMA/4521/D/01/01/002 (for Barbados); Michelle M. Terrell, *The Jewish Community of Early Colonial Nevis: A Historical Archaeological Study* (Gainesville: University Press of Florida, 2005), 13; "The Jewish of Jamaica: A Historical View," *Caribbean Quarterly* 13: 1 (March 1967): 46–53, 51.

16. Jonathan Schorsch briefly considers Purim the slave (*Jews and Blacks in the Early Modern World*, 264, 467n50), lists or discusses Purim as a slave name (243–44, 247, 305, 306, 309), and alludes to it as a holiday in Amsterdam (84, 465n18). The literature on Purim—none of it pertaining to Caribbean Jews—is vast. See Horowitz, *Reckless Rites* and "The Rite to Be Reckless: On the Perpetration and Interpretation of Purim Violence," *Poetics Today* 15: 1 (Spring 1994): 9–54; Doniach, *Purim*; Cecil Roth, "The Feast of Purim and the Origins of the Blood Accusation," *Speculum* 8: 4 (October 1933): 520–26; *Purim: The Face and the Mask: Essays and Catalogue of an Exhibition at the Yeshiva University Museum* (New York: Yeshiva University Museum, 1979); J. G. Krieger, "Pablo de Santa Maria, the Purim Letter, and *Siete edades del mundo*," *Mester* 17 (1988): 95–103; Epstein, "Purim: The Smiting of the Figures of Haman and Zeresh in Yemen," 401–16; Susan Gilson Miller, "Crisis and Community: The People of Tangier and the French Bombardment of 1844," *Middle Eastern Studies* 27: 4 (October 1991): 583–96; Jeffrey Rubenstein, "Purim, Liminality, and *Communitas*," *Association of Jewish Studies Review* 17: 2 (Autumn 1992): 247–77; Jean Baumgarten, *Introduction à la littérature yiddish ancienne* (Paris: Cerf, 1993), 443–73 and "Prieres, rituels et pratiques dans la société juive ashkénaze"; Ahuva Belkin, "The 'Low' Culture of the Purimshpil," in Joel Berkowitz, ed., *Yiddish Theater: New Approaches* (Oxford: Littman Library of Jewish Civilization, 2003), 29–43; Harvey E. Goldberg and Rosie Pinhas-Delpuech, "Les jeux de Pourim et leurs déclinaisons à Tripoli: Perspective comparative sur l'usage social des histoires bibliques," *Annales: Histoire, Sciences Sociales* 49: 5 (September–October 1994): 1183–95; Michael C. Steinlauf, "Fear of Purim: Y. L. Peretz and the Canonization of Yiddish Theater," *Jewish Social Studies*, n.s., 1:

3 (Spring 1995): 44–65; José Alberto Rodrigues da Silva Tavim, "Purim in Cochin," *Journal of Indo-Judaic Studies* 11 (2009): 13–14; and Jean R. Freedman, "The Masquerade of Ideas: The *Purimshpil* as Theatre of Conflict," in *Revisioning Ritual: Jewish Traditions in Transition* (Oxford: Littman Library of Jewish Civilization, 2011), 94–132.

17. For example, James Robertson discusses a proposed bill, purportedly written by the island's "negro slaves," that indicates a "wide awareness of the Jewish Purim holiday among white Christians in mid-eighteenth-century Kingston." We might wonder, in light of my findings, whether Jamaica's pseudonymous bill hints at an Afro-Creole expression of the island's Purim. James Robertson, "A 1748 'Petition of Negro Slaves' and the Local Politics of Slavery in Jamaica," *William and Mary Quarterly* 67: 2 (April 2010): 319–46, 322, 344.

18. Bodian, *Hebrews of the Portuguese Nation*, 10; Cecil Roth, "Religion of the Marranos," *Jewish Quarterly Review*, n.s., 22: 1 (July 1931): 1–33, 26.

19. Emily Colbert Cairns, *Esther in Early Modern Iberia and the Sephardic Diaspora: Queen of the Conversas* (Cham, Switzerland: Palgrave Macmillan, 2017), 5; António Vieira (1608–1697), *El V. P. Antonio de Vieyra de la Compañía de Jesús: Todos sus sermones, y obras diferentes, que de su original Portugués se han traducido en Castellano*, 4 vols. (Barcelona: Maria Marti, 1734), 3:135 ("en todas las Naciones no hallareis Reyna Santa, mas que unicamente à Esthèr").

20. NAN, NPIGS, inv. nr. 1, December 20, 1772.

21. Ibid., inv. nr. 3, December 29, 1791 (referring to a resolution of August 26, 1787); inv. nr. 11, March 26, 1822, p. 217.

22. Ibid., inv. nr. 2, August 16, 1787, p. 440 (for quantities, delayed shipments, and exorbitant prices); January 9, 1786, p. 326 (for the resignation of wax candle shipping agents in Amsterdam); Anthony Vieyra Transtagano, *A Dictionary of the Portuguese and English Languages, in two parts, Portuguese and English: and English and Portuguese* (London: J. Nourse, 1773), unpaginated (for translations of *candea* and *cirio*). The brilliant display of lights on Purim was also customary among Ashkenazi communities in Europe. Schammes, *Minhagim de-qehila qadish Varmaisa*, 1:258.

23. See, for example, NAN, NPIGS, inv. nr. 5, March 17, 1816 and inv. nr. 10, February 15, 1819; inv. nr. 11, March 27, 1825 (concerning privileges not to be served sentences three days before and after Passover); Van der Linde, *Surinaamse suikerheren*, 169–87.

24. NAN, NPIGS, inv. nr. 1, March 22, 1775.

25. Ibid., inv. nr. 3, April 24, 1791 (permission to shave on Passover intermediary days), March 27, 1798 (permission to serve sentences on Passover). Such dispensations were also accorded Jewish courtiers of medieval Spain to enable them "to meet the social demands of their exalted positions." Neuman, *The Jews of Spain*, 2:225.

26. Almanacs presently available and thus far examined date to 1789, 1793–96, 1798–99, 1804, 1818, 1820, 1821, 1828, 1833, 1855, and 1857.

27. *Surinaamsche staatkundige almanach voor den jaare 1793*, xxxii, xxxiii; *Surinaamsche staatkundige almanach voor den jaare 1794* (no publication data available); *Surinaamsche staatkundige almanach voor den jaare 1795* (Paramaribo: W. P. Wilkens, 1796), xlii; *Surinaamsche staatkundige almanach voor den jaare 1796* (Paramaribo: W. P. Wilkens, 1796), xxxi; *Surinaamsche almanach op het jaar onzes Heere Jesu Christi, Anno 1798*, iv; *Surinaamsche almanach op het jaar onzes Heere Jesu Christi, Anno 1799*, 6; *Surinaamsche staatkundige almanak voor den jaare 1818* (Paramaribo: J. M. Mulder, 1817), vi; *Surinaamsche almanak voor het jaar 1820* (Paramaribo: E. Beijer and C. G. Sulpke, 1819), v; *Surinaamsche almanak voor het jaar 1821*, v;

Surinaamsche almanak voor het jaar 1828 (Paramaribo: Tot Nut van 't Algemeen, 1827), xi; *Surinaamsche almanac voor het jaar 1833* (Paramaribo: Tot Nut van 't Algemeen), xiii; *Suriname: Jaarboekje voor het jaar 1856* (Den Haag: L. J. Verhoeven, 1856), ii; *Suriname: Jaarboekje voor het jaar 1857*, ii. Only one almanac thus far examined lists Tu BiShevat as the first Jewish holiday. *Surinaamsche almanach voor het schrikkeljaar, 1804* (Paramaribo: Engelbrecht en Comp., 1804), 8. Of course, part of this is happenstance, since, with the exception of the 10th of Tevet and Tu BiShevat, Purim would appear first on any calendar commencing with the month of January.

28. NAN, NPIGS, inv. nr. 3, December 29, 1791, March 13, 1792 (candle distribution); NAN, SONA, inv. nr. 234, inventory of Roza Judia, November 13 and 14, 1771, pp. 439–47, 441 (*een ganucas lamp*); inv. nr. 783, Minuut-akten, inventory of Ishak Messias, November 4, 5, 6, 7, 10, 11, 12, 13, and 14, 1760 (*hua Hanuquilha*), 71–82, 74v; inventory of Sallem Plantation on the Suriname River belonging to Jahacob Uriel Davilar, p. 41v (*twee macabeos lampe*); inventory and appraisal of Jacob Gabay Crasto, January(?), 1762 (*1 Hanukilha*); inv. nr. 788, Minuut-akten en geregistreerde akten, nr. 109, inventory of goods left by Ribca Mendes Vays, née Nunes Forte, November 24, 1780, p. 114 (*1 Hanuca lamp*), inventory and appraisal of estate and other goods left by Ribca, widow of Mosseh Naar, November 27, 1780 (*1 hanuquilha*), 146–50, 148; inv. nr. 789, Minuut-akten en geregistreerde akten, inventory of Abraham Gabay Fonseca, February 21, 1781 (*1 hanucas lamp*), 27–39, 36. For an example of an almanac that omits Hanukkah, see *Surinaamsche almanak voor het jaar 1820*, vi.

29. Aviva Ben-Ur, "The Cultural Heritage of Eurafrican Sephardi Jews in Suriname," in Jane S. Gerber, ed., *The Jewish Diaspora in the Caribbean* (Oxford: Littman Library of Jewish Civilization, 2013), 169–93.

30. Holly Snyder, "Queens of the Household: The Jewish Women of British America, 1700–1800," in Pamela S. Nadell and Jonathan D. Sarna, eds., *Women in American Judaism: Historical Perspectives* (Hanover, N.H.: University Press of New England, 2001), 15–45, 21, 36n37 and her unpublished analysis of the data compiled in Malcolm H. Stern, *First American Jewish Families: 600 Genealogies, 1654–1977* (Cincinnati: American Jewish Archives, 1978); Holly Snyder to Aviva Ben-Ur, email correspondence, August 27, 2013.

31. *Weeklysche Surinaamsche Courant* 20 (November 14, 1793): 6.

32. See, for example, NAN, NPIGS, inv. nr. 2, December 26, 1782, June 13, 1784, September 29, 1786; NAN, SONA, inv. nr. 7, will of Abraham Rephael Arrias, May 22, 1720, p. 50; inv. nr. 8, will of Joshua Hiskiahu Arias, November 5, 1728, p. 141; inv. nr. 11, will of Benjamin Henriques Granado [*sic*], February 19, 1732, p. 57; inv. nr. 13, will of Issac, son of Moses da Costa, 1725, p. 245; inv. nr. 44, will of David Raphael Robles de Medina and Ribca Robles de Medina, November 19, 1780, 252; inv. nr. 73, will of Samuel Henriques Moron, January 20, 1794, p. 59b.

33. Ben-Ur and Frankel, *Remnant Stones: The Jewish Cemeteries of Suriname*, 295 (epitaph 52); NAN, SONA, inv. nr. 82, will of Rachel de Miranda, April 4, 1803, will nr. 34.

34. NAN, SONA, inv. nr. 234, inventory of Roza Mendes Meza, Paramaribo, November 13 and 14, 1771, pp. 439–47, 441.

35. NAN, Archief West Indie Surinam, nr. 411, Gouvernements Journaal, August 10, 1759.

36. Ibid., February 29, 1756.

37. Teenstra, *De Landbouw in de Colonie Suriname*, 2:155.

38. Sidnie Ann White, "Esther: A Feminine Model for Jewish Diaspora," in Peggy L. Day, ed., *Gender and Difference in Ancient Israel* (Minneapolis: Fortress Press, 1989), 173 (for the appeal of the story to diasporic Jews).

39. Nell Painter, *Sojourner Truth: A Life, a Symbol* (New York: W. W. Norton, 1997), 135–36 (reference to Truth) and 318nn5–6 (reference to Truth's peers). I thank Joyce Berkman for this reference.

40. Ibid., 134.

41. Ben-Ur with Frankel, *Remnant Stones: The Jewish Cemeteries and Synagogues of Suriname*, 63–64.

42. NAN, NPIGS, inv. nr. 423, p. 15.

43. Ibid., inv. nr. 1, September 17, 1771, March 24, 1772; NAN, SONA, inv. nr. 788, inventory of slaves left by Ribca Mendes Vais, Jodensavanne, November 27, 1780, pp. 133–38, 134; Wilfred S. Samuel, *A Review of the Jewish Colonists in Barbados in the Year 1680* (London: Purnell & Sons, Ltd., 1936), 34, 61; NAN, SONA, inv. nr. 782, inventory and appraisal of Mahanaim Plantation on the Suriname River, November 29 and 30, 1758; NAN, SONA, inv. nr. 781, Inventario & avaluasaõ dos escravos pretenesendo ao boedel dos bems deixados por Selomoh Pereyra, savannah, May 3, 1756, pp. 204–8, 206; NAN, SONA, inv. nr. 783, inventory of slaves on the Quamabo plantation, owned by the late Sarah de la Parra, per order of David de Jah. B(?) d'Meza as Executor, January 25, 1762, will nr. 1 (note: the pagination begins anew several times in this book); inv. nr. 81, inventory of the Coffee Ground Tranquilité on the Suriname River, between the plantations of Mordehai Mendes Quiros and the heirs of Carillho [*sic*], April 30, 1762; NAN, Records of the Jurators of Suriname, inventory and appraisal of the ground lying outside of Paramaribo belonging to Raphael de Britto, May 15, 1763, fols. 47–49, as cited in Schorsch, *Jews and Blacks in the Early Modern World*, 317n (I am unable to locate this record as cited; it does not correspond to the indicated folios or to the Britto inventory in NAN, SONA, inv. nr. 215, August 1763, fols. 83–115; slaves listed on fols. 85–86); "New Advertisement, Two Joe Reward," *St. Thomas Gazette*, July 8, 1813, p. 1.

44. When racial classification does not appear in relation to slaves named Purim, it can be inferred by reference to a slave in the same sentence who is designated as *mulat*.

45. For Easter: Margaret Peckham Motes, *Blacks Found in the Deeds of Laurens & Newberry Counties, South Carolina: 1785–1827* (Baltimore: Clearfield, 2002), 3, 10, 15–16, 51, 67, 74–75, 94, 125; Mary Kemp Davis, "'What Happened in This Place?': In Search of the Female Slave in Nat Turner's Slave Insurrection," in Kenneth S. Greenberg, ed., *Nat Turner: A Slave Rebellion in History and Memory* (Oxford: Oxford University Press, 2004), 162–78, 162, 165, 167, 171; Federal Writers' Project, *North Carolina Slave Narratives* (Bedford, Mass.: Applewood Books, 2006), 2. For Christmas: Philip Morgan, *Slave Counterpoint: Black Culture in the Eighteenth-Century Chesapeake and Lowcountry* (Chapel Hill: University of North Carolina Press, 1998), 287; John Hope Franklin and Loren Schweniger, *Runaway Slaves: Rebels on the Plantation* (Oxford: Oxford University Press, 1999), 287; Gretchen Long, *Doctoring Freedom: The Politics of African American Medical Care in Slavery and Emancipation* (Chapel Hill: University of North Carolina Press, 2012), 54 (in fiction).

46. NAN, NPIGS, inv. nr. 493, Stukken betreffende de boedel van wijlen Samuel Abenacar, p. 1 (Vasty, a *moleca* who worked on the Wayamoe plantation in 1743); NAN, SONA, inv. nr. 788, will of Abraham Mendes Vais and Ribca Nones Forte, Jodensavanne, April 29, 1766 (manumission of "moleque named Harbona, son of our negress Amba"), 7–14, 12; NAN, SONA, inv. nr. 935, will and inventory of Ribca de Meza, widow of Joseph de Abraham de la Parra, February 13, 1783, December 21, 1794, January 5, 1795, pp. 1–19, 19; NAN, SONA, inv. nr. 41, will of Samuel Henriques Moron, January 9, 1777 (infant named Harbona), 8–10, 8; NAN, NPIGS, inv. nr. 11, May 12, 1825 (head carpenter named Haman).

47. Albert Montefiore Hyamson, *The Sephardim of England: A History of the Spanish and Portuguese Jewish Community, 1492–1951* (London: Methuen, 1951), 79 (reference to Isaac Purim, an Ashkenazi employed as *samas* in London's Saarei HaSamaim congregation in the late seventeenth century); TNAUK, "Naturalisation Index to Names, Naturalisation, Year ended 31st December, 1978, Oaths of Allegiance Registered at the Home Office (Certificates granted by the Secretary of State for the Home Department)," HO/409/30, p. 74 (David Purim, born in Israel and naturalized in Blackpool in 1978).

48. Vincent Carretta, *Equiano the African: Biography of a Self-Made Man* (Athens: University of Georgia Press, 2005), 41.

49. Mishna *Shekalim* 1:1 specifies that "all public needs" are carried out on Purim. *Mo'ed Katan* 80a understands the piercing of a slave with an awl (to indicate lifelong submission) as one of these needs. Cited in Jonathan R. Ziskind, trans. and ed., *John Selden on Jewish Marriage Law: The Uxor Hebraica* (Leiden: E. J. Brill, 1991), 361–62.

50. NAN, SONA, inv. nr. 788, inventory of slaves left by Ribca Mendes Vais, Jodensavanne, November 27, 1780, pp. 133–38, 134.

51. NAN, NPIGS, inv. nr. 1, September 17, 1771 (coinciding with 9 Tisry, the eve of Yom Kippur). The sentence reads "as insolencias de seu Negro Purim de haver masacrado ao Negro da sedaka, tendo cuidado q nao fizasem ruido os Negros, em qto estivesem na Esnoga." No punishment is mentioned.

52. Ibid., March 24, 1772.

53. Ibid., October 8, 1772.

54. NAN, SONA, inv. nr. 788, inventory of slaves left by Ribca Mendes Vais, Jodensavanne, November 27, 1780, pp. 133–38, 133 (died November 21, 1780) and 128–29 (executor Jeosua M. Arrias).

55. The key texts Portuguese Jews may have drawn from to connect the two holidays are the ancient *Midrash Yalkut Shimoni, Mishlei* 9, and *Tikkunei Zohar, Tikkun* 21, 57b. The former source names Purim and Yom Kippur as the two Jewish holidays that will never be nullified with the coming of the Messiah; the latter states that in messianic days Yom Kippur will resemble Purim in many ways as a day of rejoicing and material pleasures.

56. NAN, NPIGS, inv. nr. 6, September 21, 1817.

57. Julie-Marthe Cohen, "Ceremonial Objects in Early Seventeenth-Century Amsterdam: Three Inventories of Bet Israel Dates 1619, 1620, and 1635," *Images* 2 (2009): 172–216, 182, 193, 200, 210, 212.

58. Alex van Stipriaan, " 'Een verre verwijderd trommelen . . .': Ontwikkeling van Afro-Surinaamse muziek en dans in de slavernij," in Ton Bevers, Antoon Van den Braembussche, and Berend Jan Langenberg, eds., *De Kunstwereld: Produktie, distributie en receptie in de wereld van kunst en cultuur* (Hilversum: Verloren, 1993), 143–73, 145. I use the term "ethnic" advisedly, with the concern that this Western concept not be inappropriately imposed.

59. John Mbiti, *African Religions and Philosophy* (London: Heinemann, 1969), 118–19; Richard D. E. Burton, "Names and Naming in Afro-Caribbean Cultures," *New West India Guide* 73: 1 and 2 (1999): 35–58; Benjamin Edward Pierce, "Kinship and Residence Among the Urban Nengre of Surinam: A Re-Evaluation of Concepts and Theories of the Afro-American Family" (Ph.D. diss., Tulane University, 1971), 239.

60. NAN, NPIGS, inv. nr. 2, January 1, 1782 (*matando hua cabra*).

61. Ritual sacrifice of goats was a Calabar custom. Antera Duke calls it to "make doctor." See Stephen D. Behrendt, A. J. H. Latham, and David Northrup, eds., *The Diary of Antera*

Duke, an Eighteenth-Century African Slave Trader (New York: Oxford University Press, 2010), 151. For the practice in late seventeenth-century Angola as sacrifice for ancestors, see Sweet, *Recreating Africa*, 193.

62. Philip J. Havik, "Walking the Tightrope: Female Agency, Religious Practice, and the Portuguese Inquisition on the Upper Guinea Coast (Seventeenth Century)," in Caroline A. Williams, ed., *Bridging the Early Modern Atlantic World: People, Products, and Practices on the Move* (Surrey, England: Ashgate, 2009), 173–91, 178.

63. NAN, NPIGS, inv. nr. 2, January 1, 1782.

64. NAN, SONA, inv. nr. 788, will of Ribca Mendes Vays, née Nunes Fortes, Jodensavanne, September 27, 1780, nr. 78, pp. 77–78 (manumits "her mulate girl named Assie," daughter of her "negress Fortuna"); will of Ribca Mendes Vays, née Nunes Fortes, Jodensavanne, September 27, 1780, nr. 79, pp. 81–82 (manumits "her mulatto boy named Moses, son of her negress named Roselina"); will of Ribca Mendes Vays, Jodensavanne, November 24 and 27, 1780, pp. 125–38 (manumits Chozinja, "creole sewer and knitter"); will of Abraham Mendes Vais and Ribca Nones Forte, Jodensavanne, April 29, 1766, pp. 7–14 (manumission of "moleque named Harbona, son of our negress Amba"); inv. nr. 788, will of Ribca Mendes Vays, née Nunes Forte, Jodensavanne, December 21, 1779, pp. 31–32 (manumits "her negress Chosinja, daughter of her negress Isabeliña").

65. Frederick Douglass, *Narrative of the Life of Frederick Douglass: An American Slave* (New York: Random House, 2007), 87; J. Stewart, *A View of the Past and Present State of the Island of Jamaica, with Remarks on the Moral and Physical Condition of the Slaves, and on the Abolition of Slavery in the Colonies* (Edinburgh: Oliver & Boyd, 1823), 270–71 (for Jamaica).

66. Schiltkamp and De Smidt, *Placaten, ordonnantiën, en andere wetten, uitgevaardigd in Suriname*, 1:219–20 (May 8, 1698).

67. Ibid., 280 (August 25 [18 Elul], 1711).

68. Ibid., 348 (October 12, 1722), 409 (May 1, 1733), 484 (May 9, 1741; *baljaaren*).

69. Jill Salmons, "Mammy Wata," *African Arts* 10: 3 (April 1977): 8–15, and for notes: 87.

70. Scholars and contemporaries disagree on the origin of the word *baljaaren* and the related *banya* and *bandya*. The most common views point to provenance among Portuguese Jews or in what is today Angola. Alex van Stipriaan, "Muzikale Creolisering: De ontwikkeling van Afro-Surinaamse Muziek tijdens de slavernij," *Oso* 19: 1 (2000): 8–37, 34; Trudi Martinus-Guda, *Drie eeuwen Banya: De geschiedenis van een Surinaamse slavendans* (Paramaribo: Minov-Directoraat Cultuur, 2005), 40, 44, 46–47. The word is sometimes spelled *baljaren*.

71. NAN, NPIGS, inv. nr. 6, September 21, 1817.

72. Judah Cohen, *Through the Sands of Time: A History of the Jewish Community of St. Thomas, U.S. Virgin Islands* (Hanover, N.H.: Brandeis University Press, 2004); Josette Capriles Goldish, *Once Jews: Stories of Caribbean Sephardim* (Princeton, N.J.: Markus Wiener Publishers, 2009); Herskovits, "On the Provenience of the Portuguese in Saramacca Tongo," 550; Melville J. Herskovits and Frances S. Herskovits, *Surinam Folk-lore* (New York: Columbia University Press, 1936), 42n5 ("influence which the Jews of the colony have had on this Negro culture"); Egon Wolff and Frieda Wolff, *Judeus, Judaizantes e seus Escravos* (Rio de Janeiro: Instituto Histórico e Geográfico Brasileiro, 1987), 18–19.

73. Fernando Ortiz y Fernández (trans. Harriet de Onís), *Cuban Counterpoint: Tobacco and Sugar* (New York: Alfred Knopf, 1947); Kathleen Deagan, "Transculturation and Spanish American Ethnogenesis: The Archaeological Legacy of the Quincentenary," in James G. Cusick, ed., *Studies in Culture Contact: Interaction, Culture Change, and Archaeology* (Carbondale: Southern Illinois University Press, 1998), 23–43, 29.

74. Deuteronomy 25:17–19; Horowitz, *Reckless Rites*, 213, 252, 255.

75. Horowitz, *Reckless Rites*, 213, 252, 255; cf. *Midrash Bereshit Rabba* 49.

76. Coincidentally, this was the same Meza who ten years later would catch the slave Purim slaughtering a goat.

77. NAN, NPIGS, inv. nr. 1, April 16, 1772 ("Jos. Hm Pintto").

78. Ibid., inv. nr. 4, March 16, 1808.

79. Ibid., June 21, 1808.

80. Ibid., inv. nr. 1, February 26, 1777 (coinciding with 19 Adar).

81. Ibid., inv. nr. 3, March 11, 1797.

82. Ibid., inv. nr. 10, March 14, 1819.

83. Ibid., inv. nr. 12, February 7, 1826.

84. See Ben-Ur, "Atlantic Jewish History" and "The Absorption of Outsiders in London's Portuguese Jewish Community," in Federica Francesconi, Stanley Mirvis, and Brian Smollett, eds., *From Catalonia to the Caribbean: The Sephardic Orbit from Medieval to Modern Times: Essays in Honor of Jane S. Gerber* (Leiden: Brill, 2018), 255–78, 275–77.

85. Yosef Kaplan, "The Portuguese Community in Amsterdam in the Seventeenth Century," *Proceedings of the Israel Academy of Sciences and Humanities* 7: 6 (1986): 161–81, 181 (in Hebrew). See also the depiction of children pounding with hammers and rocks in the Portuguese synagogue in "Ceremonies de la Feste de Sorts" (Purim ceremonies in the synagogue at Amsterdam, engraving, Amsterdam, 1731), as reproduced in *Purim: The Face and the Mask*, 74.

86. Kaplan, "The Portuguese Community in Amsterdam," 181; Kaplan does not cite the original text of the ordinance.

87. Hyamson, *The Sephardim of England*, 19.

88. Moses Gaster, *History of the Ancient Synagogue of the Spanish and Portuguese Jews* (1901), 58 (year unspecified; I infer the approximate year from the previous paragraphs).

89. Chr. W. M. Schunck, "Michael Joannes Alexius Schabel S.J. 'Notitia de Coraçao, Bonaye, Oruba,' 1705 and 'Diurnum' (1707–1708)," *Archivum Historicum Societatis Iesu* 66 (1997): 89–162.

90. Schiltkamp and De Smidt, *Placaten, ordonnantiën, en andere wetten, uitgevaardigd in Suriname*, 1:280 (plakaat 244, "Plakaat. Verbod aan Slaven om op Zondag te Trommelen, Te Dansen of uit te Gaan," August 25, 1711), 280.

91. For a similar argument relating to beards, see Cohen, *Jews in Another Environment*, 156. However, Cohen was operating under the erroneous assumption that prior to the 1770s the majority of Suriname's Jewish population lived in Jodensavanne.

92. NAN, Oud Archief Suriname, Gouvernementssecretarie, inv. nr. 9, March 16, 1770.

93. Ben-Ur with Frankel, *Remnant Stones: The Jewish Cemeteries and Synagogues of Suriname*, 13–14.

94. NAN, NPIGS, inv. nr. 11, March 1, 1821.

95. Schiltkamp and De Smidt, *Placaten, ordonnantiën, en andere wetten, uitgevaardigd in Suriname*, 2:883–84 (plakaat 757, "Notifikatie, Maatregelen tegen uitspattingen op Feestdagen," May 24, 1775, Paramaribo). The ordinance refers to 's Heeren straaten, probably synonymous with Heerenstraat.

96. Ibid.

97. Horowitz, *Reckless Rites*, 16, 87, 158, 214, 223, 261; Tavim, "Purim in Cochin," 13–17.

98. NAN, NPIGS, inv. nr. 3, March 13, 1792.

99. Nassy, *Essai historique*, part 2, 25–26; Lampe, *Mission or Submission?*, 32.

100. NAN, NPIGS, inv. nr. 2, July 17, 1789; inv. nr. 538 II, letter from Rabbi Chumaceiro to Surinamese regents, Amsterdam, April 26, 1802 and inv. nr. 36, Prospectus of a college for children at the Savana, p. 8; *Beschryving van de Plechtigheden nevens de Lofdichten en Gebeden, uitgesproken op het eerste Jubelfeest van de Synagogue der Portugeesche Joodsche Gemeente op de Savane in de Colonie Suriname, genaamd Zegen en Vrede* (Amsterdam: Hendrik Wilem and Cornelis Dronsberg, 1785), 15.

101. NAN, NPIGS, inv. nr. 3, February 22, 1793.

102. See Chapters 4 and 5. Ben-Ur, "Peripheral Inclusion," 185–210 and "A Matriarchal Matter: Slavery, Conversion, and Upward Mobility in Colonial Suriname," in Richard L. Kagan and Philip D. Morgan, eds., *Atlantic Diasporas: Jews, Conversos, and Crypto-Jews in the Age of Mercantilism, 1500–1800* (Baltimore: Johns Hopkins University Press, 2009), 152–69, 270–79.

103. TNAUK, CO 178/4, Précis of letters to Secretary of State, July 18, 1799–August 24, 1805, August, 23, 1799.

104. TNAUK, CO 278/4, journal of Lieutenant General Trigge, Paramaribo, August 29 and 31, September 11, and November 14–15, 1799 (unpaginated).

105. Schalkwijk, *The Colonial State in the Caribbean*, 249 (figure 5.2; calculation based on months in office).

106. *Weeklysche Surinaamsche Courant* 20 (November 14, 1793): 6.

107. NAN, NPIGS, inv. nr. 3, March 13, 1799.

108. The ordinance does not appear in the Plakaatboek but is summarized in NAN, NPIGS, inv. nr. 3, February 27, 1800. It may have been a private letter addressed to the Portuguese Jewish regents.

109. Ibid., inv. nr. 4, March 27, 1807.

110. Nahma Sandrow, *Vagabond Stars: A World History of Yiddish Theater* (Syracuse, N.Y.: Syracuse University Press, 1996 [1977]), 18.

111. Karwan Fatah-Black, "Slaves and Sailors on Suriname's Rivers," *Itinerario* 36: 3 (2012): 61–82, 62–63.

112. Wim Klooster, "Marteling, Muiterij en Beeldenstorm: Militair Geweld in de Nederlandse Atlantische Wereld, 1624–1654," in Victor Enthoven, Henk den Heijer, and Han Jordaan, eds., *Geweld in de West: Een militaire geschiedenis van de Nederlandse Atlantische wereld, 1600–1800* (Leiden: Brill, 2013), 313–43, 330–31.

113. TNAUK, CO 178/4, journal of Lieutenant General Trigge, Paramaribo, February 4, 1800 (unpaginated).

114. NAN, NPIGS, inv. nr. 2, July 10, 1782; inv. nr. 3, June 29, 1792; and especially inv. nr 4, June 24, 1806; inv. nr. 5, June 29, 1813.

115. Fatah-Black, "Slaves and Sailors on Suriname's Rivers," 61.

116. NAN, NPIGS, inv. nr. 7, June 1, 1768.

117. Ibid., inv. nr. 3, September 26, 1796. Portuguese Jewish funerals began with the ritual circumvolution of the corpse in the "death house," where the person had expired.

118. Ibid., inv. nr. 1, October 15, 1778, October 5, 1774, October 14, 1776, October 22, 1777; NAN, Oud Archief Suriname, Raad van Politie, inv. nr. 210, Register van plakkaten, ordonnantiën, resoluties, notulen, 1669, p. 18.

119. Snyder, "A Sense of Place," 99 and "Customs of an Unruly Race," 154 (for Jamaica); J. Hartog, *The Jews and St. Eustatius: The Eighteenth Century Jewish Congregation Honen Dalim and Description of the Old Cemetery* (St. Maarten: Theodor Maxwell Pandt in cooperation with Winward Islands Bank, 1976), 10 (for Curaçao); NAN, Oud Archief Suriname, Raad van Politie, inv. nr. 210, Register van plakkaten, ordonnantiën, resoluties, notulen, 1669, p. 18 (for Suriname).

120. NAN, SONA, inv. nr. 939, Minuut-akten, gepasseerd voor de jurator Isaac C. de Barrios, inventory of David Haim del Monte, December 24, 1824, nrs. 21 and 22; Ben-Ur and Frankel, *Remnant Stones: The Jewish Cemeteries of Suriname*, 458 (epitaph 656).

121. Jessica Roitman, "Creating Confusion in the Colonies: Jews, Citizenship, and the Dutch and British Atlantics," *Itinerario* 36: 2 (August 2012): 55–90, 71, 74.

122. See, for example, the case of Joseph Lopes discussed in NAN, NPIGS, inv. nr. 3, February 6, 1791.

123. Daniel Mendoza, *Memoirs of the Life of Daniel Mendoza* (London: self-published, 1816 [written in 1808]), 12–15.

124. Bodian, *Hebrews of the Portuguese Nation*, 62.

125. LMA/4521/A/01/01/004, ascamot, 5492 [1731/1792], bylaw 43.

126. Swetschinski, *Reluctant Cosmopolitans*, 219.

127. NAN, NPIGS, inv. nr. 1, October 8, 1772.

128. Sullivan, *The Punishment of Crime in Colonial New York*, 238.

129. Yosef Kaplan, "Bom Judesmo: The Western Sephardic Diaspora," in David Biale, ed., *Cultures of the Jews: A New History* (New York: Schocken Books, 2002), 652–55, 655 and "Gente Política: The Portuguese Jews of Amsterdam vis-à-vis Dutch Society," in Chaya Brasz and Yosef Kaplan, eds., *Dutch Jews as Perceived by Themselves and by Others: Proceedings of the Eighth International Symposium on the History of the Jews in the Netherlands* (Leiden: Brill, 2001), 21–40.

130. Kaplan, "Bom Judesmo," 652–55 and "Gente Política."

131. Alexander Salonthay van Salontha, *Précis de deux Lettres avec une Reflexion generale sur l'état present de la colonie de Surinam* (Nimmegue: I. Van Campen, [1778]), 5.

132. NAN, NPIGS, inv. nr. 1, June 12, 1780; inv. nr. 5, June 29, 1813; inv. nr. 324, Libro de Insinuacoems, October 6, 1739 (Indian slave Florinda belonging to Rebecca, wife of Abraham Haim Cohen Nassy); Vrij, "Bosheren en konkelaars" (for visits of Maroons and Indians to Paramaribo).

133. NAN, NPIGS, inv. nr. 3, July 21, 1791.

134. Ibid., inv. nr. 4, December 5, 1808.

135. Ibid., October 12, 1802.

136. Ibid., inv. nr. 545, Inventaris van goederen toebehoorende aan de Heer Ah. J. da Costa aan 't comptoir der Gemeente ter bewaaren op de 4 July 1820.

137. James Robertson, whom I thank for his remark, suggests that skimpy costumes were simply a matter of convenience in a colony where material goods were scarce.

138. TNAUK, CO 278/1, "Memorandum of Suriname," June 6, 1800, pp. 51–55, 52. In the original, the word appears as "considerd."

139. For an interpretation that foregrounds the Afro-Caribbean nature of carnival and other leisurely gatherings among slaves in colonial and modern New Orleans, see Joseph Roache, "Carnival and Law in New Orleans," *Drama Review* 37: 3 (Autumn 1993): 42–75, 46.

On the African strains of carnival, see Rosita M. Sands, "Carnival Celebrations in Africa and the New World: Jankanoo and the Black Indians of Mardi Gras," *Black Music Research Journal* 11: 1 (Spring 1991): 75–92 and Judith Bettelheim and John Wallace Nunley, *Caribbean Festival Arts: Each and Every Bit of Difference* (St. Louis: Saint Louis Art Museum and Seattle: University of Washington Press, 1988).

140. Some scholars argue that contemporary Maroon dance and song are accurate reflections of slave festivities of the seventeenth through nineteenth century. See, for example, Sally Price and Richard Price, *Afro-American Arts of the Suriname Rain Forest* (Los Angeles: Museum of Cultural History/University of California, 1980), 170 and Martinus-Guda, *Drie eeuwen Banya*, 155–56.

141. On the link between legal interdiction and carnival, see Roache, "Carnival and Law in New Orleans."

142. Robert Wyndham Nicholls, *The Jumbies' Playing Ground: Old World Influence on Afro-Creole Masquerades in the Eastern Caribbean* (Jackson: University Press of Mississippi, 2012), 16.

143. See, for example, H. Liverpool, "Origins of Rituals and Customs in the Trinidad Carnival: African or European?" *Drama Review* 42: 3 (1998): 24–37; Jeroen Dewulf, "Pinkster: An Atlantic Creole Festival in a Dutch-American Context," *Journal of American Folklore* 126: 501 (Summer 2013): 245–71, 254.

144. Nicholls, *The Jumbies' Playing Ground*, 16.

145. For indigenous rituals, including marriage, death, and initiation rites, in Senegambia linked to community-wide dances and masquerades, see Peter Mark, "Art, Ritual, and Folklore: Dance and Cultural Identity Among the Peoples of the Casamance," *Cahiers D'Études Africaines* 136: 34/4 (1994): 563–84. For a reference to masquerading during Christmas in Jamaica, see Edward Long, *The history of Jamaica, or general survey of the ancient and modern state of that island: with reflections on its situations, settlements, inhabitants, climate, products, commerce, laws, and government* (London: Frank Cass & Co. Ltd., 1970 [1774]), 424.

146. These ideas are from Esiaba Irobi, "What They Came With: Carnival and the Persistence of African Performance Aesthetics in the Diaspora," *Journal of Black Studies* 37: 6 (July 2007): 896–913.

147. The regents complained that "there are stupid people [alternative reading: whites] with such vulgar ideas that they encourage slaves to dance and to create a racket while solemnizing their funerals" (*ha broncos* [alternative reading: *brancos*] *de tao triviais ideas q se ponem a festejar aos negros & a contribuhir com algararas em solemniçao de suas funeralias*). NAN, NPIGS, inv. nr. 1, February 21, 1780.

148. Ibid., and April 23, 1780.

149. *Surinaamsche almanak voor het jaar 1820*, v; *Surinaamsche almanak voor het jaar 1821*, v; *Surinaamsche almanak voor het jaar 1828*, xi; *Surinaamsche almanac voor het jaar 1833*, xiii; *Suriname: Jaarboekje voor het jaar 1856* (Den Haag: L. J. Verhoeven, 1856), ii; *Suriname: Jaarboekje voor het jaar 1857*, ii.

150. NAN, NPIGS, inv. nr. 12, February 7, 1826.

151. Ibid.

152. Similarly, beginning in the mid-eighteenth century, enslaved and free blacks developed a Pinkster Day in New York and New Jersey, coinciding with Pentecost. Pinkster Day, like its parallel Negro Election Day in New England, involved ritual role reversals, merrymaking, music, song, and dance. Berlin, *Many Thousands Gone*, 191; Dewulf, "Pinkster."

153. Schorsch, *Jews and Blacks in the Early Modern World*, 261.

154. NAN, NPIGS, inv. nr. 7, October 10, 1753; inv. nr. 2, June 17, 1789; Schorsch, *Jews and Blacks in the Early Modern World*, 262.

155. Schorsch, *Jews and Blacks in the Early Modern World*, 262.

156. On the negotiated length of *banyas*, from several days to up to a week, see Martinus-Guda, *Drie eeuwen banya*, 51, 158, and Alex van Stipriaan, "Community or No Unity, That's the Question!: A Tale of Two Slave Plantations, 1828," keynote address, "Beyond the 'Slave Community' and 'Resistance' Paradigms: Alternative Approaches to the Social Lives of Bondpeople in the Atlantic World," Leiden University, March 2017.

157. Tobias Green, "Equal Partners?: Proselytising by Africans and Jews in the 17th Century Atlantic Diaspora," *Melilah* 5 (2008): 1–21, 4.

158. See p. 185.

159. Slaves composed 61.3 percent of Curaçao's population in 1789. Wim Klooster, *Illicit Riches: Dutch Trade in the Caribbean, 1648–1795* (Leiden: KITLV, 1998), 61.

160. See, for example, Christoph Daxelmüller, "Organizational Forms of Popular Jewish Culture," in R. Po-Chia Hsia and Hartmut Lehmann, eds., *In and out of the Ghetto: Jewish-Gentile Relations in Late Medieval and Early Modern Germany* (Cambridge: Cambridge University Press, 2002), 29–48, esp. 40; James Houk, "The Role of the Kabbalah in the Afro-American Religious Complex in Trinidad," *Caribbean Quarterly* 39: 3/4 (September/December 1993): 42–55.

161. See, for example, Patrick Manning, "The Problem of Interactions in World History," *American Historical Review* 101: 3 (1996): 771–83, 779.

162. Kimberly Arkin, "Deconstruction Without Destruction: Reimagining Jewish Studies at the Crossroads of Anthropology and History," review of Ra'anan S. Boustan, Oren Kosansky, and Marina Rustow, eds., *Jewish Studies at the Crossroads of Anthropology and History: Authority, Diaspora, Tradition* (Philadelphia: University of Pennsylvania Press, 2011), H-Judaic, August 18, 2011.

163. Stephanie M. H. Camp, *Closer to Freedom: Enslaved Women and Everyday Resistance in the Plantation South* (Chapel Hill: University of North Carolina Press, 2004), 16.

164. Ibid., 65.

165. Ibid., 69 and 76 (for these terms).

Chapter 7

1. NAN, NPIGS, inv. nr. 12, July 7, 1825; Teenstra, *De Landbouw in de Colonie Suriname*, 2:137.

2. NAN, Ministerie van Kolonien, inv. nr. 3336, Gouvernements-Journaal van Suriname, pp. 140–42, 141. Suriname's Ashkenazi community received the news on July 13, 1825. AJA, MS-581, Box X-424a, folder 2.

3. Van Stipriaan, "An Unusual Parallel," 90.

4. NAN, NPIGS, inv. nr. 12, August 30, 1825. I was unable to locate the decree in the *Curaçaosche Courant*, possibly because it was overshadowed by the government's unification of the island's Reformed Protestant and Lutheran churches around the same time. See the issues from April 23, April 30, May 7, and May 14, 1825. The communal minutes from the island's Portuguese Jewish community for the year 1825 have not survived.

5. Wolbers, *Geschiedenis van Suriname*, 624, 830.

6. Vink, *Creole Jews*, 88. Laura Leibman and Sam May ("Making Jews," 1) also state, without attribution, that Surinamese Jews resented the elimination of their privileges.

7. Leibman and May, "Making Jews," 6; Gad J. Heuman, *Between Black and White: Race, Politics, and the Free Coloreds in Jamaica, 1792–1865* (Westport, Conn.: Greenwood Press, 1981), 73; Kriz, "Belisario's 'Kingston Cries,'" 163–78, 163, 167; Snyder, "'Customs of an Unruly Race,'" 151–62, 154–55, 159, 161n50.

8. The term was borrowed from a raging debate that year concerning the political parity of Catholics. Jacob Katz, "The Term Jewish Emancipation: Its Origin and Historical Impact," in Alexander Altmann, ed., *Studies in Nineteenth-Century Jewish Intellectual History* (Cambridge, Mass.: Harvard University Press, 1964), 1–25.

9. Baron, *A Social and Religious History of the Jews* (1937), 2:227; Simon Rabinovitch, *Jewish Rights, National Rites: Nationalism and Autonomy in Late Imperial Revolutionary Russia* (Stanford, Calif.: Stanford University Press, 2014), 28.

10. However, Simon Rabinovitz, with Austria, Prussia, France, and Poland in mind, argues that rescinding "inconvenient corporate privileges" was the government's foremost goal. See Rabinovitch, *Jewish Rights, National Rites*, 28.

11. Baron, *A Social and Religious History of the Jews* (1937), 2:164.

12. Paula Hyman, "Emancipation," in Arthur A. Cohen and Paul Mendes-Flohr, eds., *Contemporary Jewish Religious Thought: Original Essays on Critical Concepts, Movements, and Beliefs* (New York: Scribner, 1987),165–70, 166; Henri Grégoire, *Essai sur la regeneration physique, morale et politique des Juifs* (Metz: Claude Lamort, 1789); M. Zalkind-Hourwitz, *Apologie des Juifs: En réponse à la question: Est-il des moyens de rendre les Juifs plus heureux et plus utiles en France?* (Paris: Chez Gattey, 1789).

13. Baron, *A Social and Religious History of the Jews* (1937), 2:229 and "Ghetto and Emancipation: Shall We Revise the Traditional View?" *Menorah Journal* 14: 6 (June 1928): 515–26, 521n†.

14. Josue Jéhouda (trans. Eva Jackson), *The Five Stages of Jewish Emancipation* (South Brunswick, N.J.: Thomas Yoseloff, 1966), 32.

15. Leibman and May, "Making Jews" (on the Vestry Bill debate in Barbados from 1819 to 1820); Holly Snyder, "Rules, Rights and Redemption: The Negotiation of Jewish Status in British Atlantic Port Towns, 1740–1831," *Jewish History* 20 (2006): 147–70; Kriz, "Belisario's 'Kingston Cries'"; Snyder, "'Customs of an Unruly Race'"; Heuman, *Between Black and White*, 74; Samuel J. Hurwitz and Edith Hurwitz, "The New World Sets an Example for the Old: The Jews of Jamaica and Political Rights, 1661–1831," *American Jewish Historical Quarterly* 55: 1 (1965): 37–56; Vink, *Creole Jews*, 11, 78, 81–82, 84–86, 91, 193, 201, 262; Wolbers, *Geschiedenis van Suriname*, 624, 830; Van Stipriaan, "An Unusual Parallel," 90; Cohen, *Jews in Another Environment*, 116, 144–45.

16. Major works include Jacob Katz, *Emancipation and Assimilation: Studies in Modern Jewish History* (Farnborough: Gregg, 1972), *Out of the Ghetto: The Social Background of Jewish Emancipation, 1770–1870* (Cambridge, Mass.: Harvard University Press, 1973), and *Jewish Emancipation and Self-Emancipation* (Philadelphia: Jewish Publication Society, 1986); Michael A. Meyer, *The Origins of the Modern Jew: Jewish Identity and European Culture in Germany, 1749–1824* (Detroit: Wayne State University Press, 1967); Malino, *The Sephardic Jews of Bordeaux*; Naomi W. Cohen, *Encounter with Emancipation: The German Jews in the United States, 1830–1914* (Philadelphia: Jewish Publication Society of America, 1984); Jay R. Berkovitz, *The*

Shaping of Jewish Identity in Nineteenth-Century France (Detroit: Wayne State University Press, 1989); Paula E. Hyman, *The Emancipation of the Jews of Alsace: Acculturation and Tradition in the Nineteenth Century* (New Haven, Conn.: Yale University Press, 1991); Michman, *The History of Dutch Jewry During the Emancipation Period*; Michael Laurence Miller, *Rabbis and Revolution: The Jews of Moravia in the Age of Emancipation* (Stanford, Calif.: Stanford University Press, 2011); Paolo L. Bernardini and Diego Lucci, *The Jews, Instructions for Use: Four Eighteenth-Century Projects for the Emancipation of European Jews* (Boston: Academic Studies Press, 2012); Constantin Sonkwé Tayim, *Narrative der Emanzipation: Autobiographische Identitätsentwürfe deutschsprachiger Juden aus der Emanzipationszeit* (Berlin: De Gruyter, 2013); Geoffrey Alderman, *British Jewry Since Emancipation* (Buckingham: University of Buckingham Press, 2014); and Pierre Birnbaum, *Paths of Emancipation: Jews, States, and Citizenship* (Princeton, N.J.: Princeton University Press, 2014).

17. For the emergence of the process in Canada and the United States, see Godfrey and Godfrey, *Search out the Land* and Sorkin, "Is American Jewry Exceptional?"

18. Herbert Friedenwald, "Barbados," in Isidore Singer, ed., *Jewish Encyclopedia*, 12 vols. (New York: Funk and Wagnalls, 1901), 2:523–35, 524; "West Indies-Toleration Laws," *Parliamentary Papers, House of Commons, Accounts and Papers Relating to Colonies*, 18 vols. (Session 6, December 1831–16 August 1832), 4:7. The latter source is irregularly paginated.

19. Toleration Laws, Jamaica, in *Parliamentary Papers, House of Commons, Accounts and Papers Relating to Colonies*, 4:1–2.

20. Ibid., 4:9; Robert H. Schomburgk, *The History of Barbados: Comprising a Geographical and Statistical Description of the Island* (London: Longman, Brown, Green and Longmans, 1848), 97; Snyder, " 'Customs of an Unruly Race,' " 159, 161n50.

21. Joseph Jacobs, "Acts of Parliament Relating to the Jews of England," in *Jewish Encyclopedia*, 1:172–73 (for Britain); Snyder, " 'Customs of an Unruly Race,' " 161n50 (for Jamaica); John Garner, *The Franchise and Politics in British North America, 1755–1867* (Toronto: University of Toronto Press, 1969), 142 (for Canada).

22. Rosemarijn Hoefte and Jean Jacques Vrij, "Free Black and Colored Women in Early-Nineteenth-Century Paramaribo, Suriname," in David Barry Gaspar and Darlene Clark Hine, eds., *Beyond Bondage: Free Women of Color in the Americas* (Urbana: University of Illinois Press, 2004), 152; Cohen, *Jews in Another Environment*, 153, 173, 179.

23. Goslinga, *The Dutch in the Caribbean and in the Guianas*, 364; Natalie Zemon Davis, "Creole Languages and Their Uses: The Example of Colonial Suriname," *Historical Research* 82: 216 (May 2009): 278.

24. Teenstra, *De negerslaven in de colonie Suriname*, 45. The reference is to *negers* who would remark in Sranan Tongo, "Toe Bákkra lange wan Joe."

25. See 48, 50. See also the discussion on Jewish homeownership in Paramaribo in 1772 in Cohen, *Jews in Another Environment*, 80–81.

26. Neslo, *Een ongekende elite.*

27. Vink, *Creole Jews*, 153; NAN, NPIGS, inv. nr. 2, December 26, 1784, pp. 166–68.

28. Vink, *Creole Jews*, 138.

29. Ibid., 190–92.

30. TNAUK, CO 278/1, "Memorandum of Suriname," June 6, 1800, pp. 51–55, 52.

31. For a reference to this population's interrelation with the law, see W. E. H. Winkels, comp., *Publicatien en Verordeningen Betrekkelijk Suriname, Antrieur aan het jaar 1816* (Paramaribo: W. E. H. Winkels, 1816?), June 18, 1808 (*blanken van 't gemeen volk*).

32. Henry Bolingbroke, *A voyage to the Demerary, containing a statistical account of the settlements there, and those on the Essequebo, the Berbice, and other contiguous rivers of Guyana* (London: Richard Phillips, 1807), 371. See also Goslinga, *The Dutch in the Caribbean and in the Guianas*, 364, and for Jamaica, Kriz, "Belisario's 'Kingston Cries,'" 167.

33. A. J. A. Quintus Bosz, "De Weg tot de Invoering van de Nieuwe Wetgeving in 1869 en de Overgang van het Oude naar het Nieuwe Burgerlijk Recht," in *Een eeuw Surinaamse codificatie: Gedenkboek (1869–1 Mei-1969)* (Paramaribo: Surinaamse Juristen Vereniging, 1969), 7–25, 8–9.

34. *Een eeuw Surinaamse codificatie: Gedenkboek (1869–1 Mei-1969)* (Paramaribo: Surinaamse Juristen Vereniging, 1969), 3 (for quotes); Bosz, "De Weg tot de Invoering," 8–9.

35. *Een eeuw Surinaamse codificatie*, 3. The collection of placards published in 1973 in two volumes (Schiltkamp and De Smidt, *Plakaten, ordonnantiën en andere wetten, uitgevaardigd in Suriname*) is incomplete. For example, a 1731 law prohibiting marriages to anyone who had not resided in the colony for at least eighteen months does not appear in the compilation. Cohen, "Patterns of Marriage," 98n10.

36. No date for this incident is given. The presiding government could have been Pinson Bonham (November 8, 1811–February 27, 1816), Willem Benjamin van Panhuys (February 27, 1816–July 18, 1816), or Cornelis Reinhard Vaillant (July 1816–April 1, 1822).

37. NAN, NPIGS, inv. nr. 6, August 28, 1817 (Governor Vaillant's approval is dated August 22, 1817); inv. nr. 10, September 71, 1819; Sonnenberg-Stern, *Emancipation and Poverty*, 140–42.

38. NAN, NPIGS, inv. nr. 12, July 4, 1827.

39. Ibid., September 5, 1827.

40. Ibid., December 30, 1827.

41. Ibid., inv. nr. 6, June 1, 1818.

42. Ibid., August 24, 1818. The minutes taker refers to "article 24," but this does not correspond in content with the *Regeerings-reglement van Suriname* of 1816. I therefore infer that the reference was to article 134 of the 1814 Batavian constitution, which deals with the dignity of all religious groups. Only the year of this incident is given; the presiding governor could have been Pinson Bonham, Willem Benjamin van Panhuys, or Cornelis Reinhard Vaillant.

43. NAN, NPIGS, inv. nr. 6, August 24, 1818. Compare the ideological discrimination of municipal authorities in the Batavian Republic, who continued to refer to the "Jewish Nation." Michman, *The History of Dutch Jewry During the Emancipation Period*, 33.

44. NAN, NPIGS, inv. nr. 5, December 23, 1816. The communal minutes identify the petitioners as Jacob Zadok Soesman, M. A. Polak, then in Suriname, and A. Pardo Cardozo, in Europe. According to Wieke Vink (*Creole Jews*, 79n21), the intervening Jews in Amsterdam were Abraham Mendes de Leon, M. J. Meyer, and M. Carel Asser.

45. NAN, NPIGS, inv. nr. 5, December 23, 1816.

46. Van Stipriaan, *Surinaams contrast*, 297–98.

47. NAN, NPIGS, inv. nr. 25, Mem. das promesas que prometerao os Sres nomeados abaixo, 5450 [1689–90]. Van Stipriaan, *Surinaams contrast*, 297 (for Solomon de la Parra as the largest planter in the colony); Marten Schalkwijk, "De Plantocracie in Suriname Anno 1830," *Oso* 10: 2 (1991): 147–65, 149 (for C. L. Weissenbruch as the contemporaneous richest planter in the colony).

48. Van Stipriaan, "An Unusual Parallel," 90.

49. J. J. M. Ramakers, "Parallel Processes? The Emancipation of Jews and Catholics in the Netherlands, 1795/96–1848," *Studia Rosenthaliana* 30: 1 (1996): 33–40, 34–36, 38–39.

50. Sonnenberg-Stern, *Emancipation and Poverty*, 70, 81.

51. Vink, *Creole Jews*, 91–92.

52. Ibid., 92; Ramakers, "Parallel Processes?" 37.

53. NAN, NPIGS, inv. nr. 12, September 24, 1826, April 4, 1827.

54. Michman, *The History of Dutch Jewry During the Period of Emancipation*, 33n29.

55. AJA, MS-581, Box X-416, folder 4; NANA, SONA, passim. Some Jewish merchants in Suriname did correspond in Yiddish. See, for example, TNAUK, HCA 30/376.

56. Nassy, *Essai historique*, part 1, 83, 85; Isaac da Costa, *Noble Families Among the Sephardic Jews* (London: Oxford University Press, 1936), 100 ("especially since the close of the eighteenth century, they [the 'German Jews' in Suriname] have risen to be upon the same level with their brethren in civilization and esteem"). Costa's book consists of essays published in the 1850s.

57. Vink, *Creole Jews*, 54.

58. NAN, NPIGS, inv. nr. 7, September 6, 1757; inv. nr. 1, August 12, 1778.

59. NAN, NPIGS, inv. nr. 101 (1754), treatise 26, article 5; AJA, MS-581, Box X-416, folder 4, Escamoth of Instellinge gedaan, ende genoomen door de geregters van K. K. Askenazems, September 6, 1772, p. 15.

60. Cohen, "Patterns of Marriage," 93.

61. NAN, NPIGS, inv. nr. 508.

62. Vink, *Creole Jews*, 54.

63. NAN, NPIGS, inv. nr. 2, December 26, 1784, pp. 166–68.

64. His birthday, June 4, coincided with the second day of Sebuoth in 1805 (7 Sivan 5565).

65. NAN, NPIGS, inv. nr. 4, May 28, 1805.

66. Ibid., inv. nr. 10, March 14, 1819; UBLBC, "Ontwerp tot een Beschryving van Surinaamen," transcript of manuscript dating between 1739 and 1748, 3 (reference to "Jooden & Smousen").

67. NAN, NPIGS, inv. nr. 1, October 13, 1776.

68. Ibid., inv. nr. 4, January 21, 1805, December 6, 1808, September 17, 1811.

69. The controversy is discussed in NAN, NPIGS, inv. nr. 5, August 19, 1812, January 8, 1816, January 14, 1816; inv. nr. 6, April 29, 1817, May 11, 1817, May 16, 1817, June 9, 1817, June 29, 1817, July 24, 1817, September 2, 1818.

70. My assumption that Surinamese Jews followed oral tradition is based on the fact that the minutes never refer to cantillated printed Bibles but do reference Hebrew grammar books.

71. NAN, NPIGS, inv. nr. 6, April 28, 1817, May 11, 1817 (*milerang en nooit milehel*), June 9, 1817. Previous controversy over pronunciation was slight and grammatical concerns were dismissed over the sanctity of established custom. See, for example, the quickly resolved case about the proper accentuation of an unidentifiable Hebrew word transliterated as *vayanab*. NAN, NPIGS, inv. nr. 4, May 31, 1805.

72. NAN, NPIGS, inv. nr. 6, April 29, 1817 (response to letter of August 23, 1816). See Leviticus 1:2 (*bené Israel*); Deuteronomy 7:13 (*perí-vitneha*); Joshua 23:14 (*davár ehad*). The phrases in quotes are as they appear in the minutes.

73. NAN, NPIGS, inv. nr. 6, April 9, 1817, April 29, 1817. Louzada's dismissal from Sedek VeSalom in 1817 was ostensibly over another issue, but it was likely exacerbated by his "incorrect" Torah reading in 1819 (NAN, NPIGS, inv. nr. 5, August 19, 1812). Mesquita was fired from Beraha VeSalom over pronouncing the word "from Jerusalem" as *meyerusalaim* instead of *mirusalaim*. NAN, NPIGS, inv. nr. 6, July 24, 1817.

74. "Sichah bein Yachin Uvein Bo'az," *Hameasef* 8 (Iyar 5569 [1809]): 217–30; Ismar Schorsch, "The Myth of Sephardic Supremacy," *Leo Baeck Institute Year Book* 34: 1 (January 1989): 47–66, 53–54; Chaim Rabin, "The Revival of the Hebrew Language," *Ariel* 25 (Winter 1969): 25–34, 26; Moshe Pelli, "The Revival of Hebrew Began in Haskalah: 'Hame'asef', First Hebrew Periodical, as a Vehicle for the Rejuvenation of the Language," *Leshonenu La'am* 50: 2 (January–March 1999): 59–75 (in Hebrew); Sara Feinstein, *Sunshine, Blossoms and Blood: H. N. Bialik in His Time, a Literary Biography* (Lanham, Md.: University Press of America, 2005).

75. NAN, NPIGS, inv. nr. 6, April 29, 1817.

76. Hebrew ignorance was common among Portuguese Jews, including, of course, the *parnassim*. See, for example, NAN, NPIGS, inv. nr. 1, July 8, 1777 (for Suriname) and Malino, *The Sephardic Jews of Bordeaux*, 58 (for Bordeaux). Portuguese rabbis (i.e., teachers) and *hahamim* were of course the exception.

77. NAN, NPIGS, inv. nr. 6, May 27, 1817, September 9, 1817 (for *mitsva*), June 9, 1817, January 23, 1818 (for *tsdaka*), June 14, 1814 (for *halitsa*), July 24, 1817 (for *tishabeab*). Syllabic emphasis is not recorded.

78. Emmanuel and Emmanuel, *History of the Jews of the Netherlands Antilles*, 1:306; Goldstein, *My World as a Jew*, 1:311 (as understood in mid-twentieth-century Curaçao).

79. Emmanuel and Emmanuel, *History of the Jews of the Netherlands Antilles*, 1:306; Marten Douwes Teenstra, *De Nederlandsche West-Indische Eilanden* (Amsterdam: C. G. Sulpke, 1836), 1:91 (*sprak zekere comma niet goed uit*).

80. AJA, MS-505, Box No. 1675, folder 10, resolution of Governor P. Bonham, December 8, 1813.

81. Vink, *Creole Jews*, 203.

82. NAN, NPIGS, inv. nr. 12, August 27, 1828.

83. Ibid., August 19, 1827.

84. Vink, *Creole Jews*, 83 (for his birthplace, age, and year of immigration).

85. NAN, NPIGS, inv. nr. 12, August 20, 1827.

86. Ibid., August 19, 1827.

87. Ibid., August 20, 1827.

88. Ibid.

89. Ibid., September 3, 1826.

90. Ibid., October 2, 1827, December 30, 1827.

91. Vink, *Creole Jews*, 78 (without attribution).

92. Ibid.

93. NAN, NPIGS, inv. nr. 5, December 19, 1816; Vink, *Creole Jews*, 79.

94. NAN, NPIGS, inv. nr. 5, December 19, 1816.

95. Ibid.

96. Vink, *Creole Jews*, 80.

97. Ibid., 77.

98. NAN, NPIGS, inv. nr. 4, September 9, 1804, December 11, 1804.

99. See, for example, ibid., December 15, 1807.

100. NAN, NPIGS, inv. nr. 11, November 20, 1822.

101. Ibid., November 27, 1822.

102. Ibid., February 16, 1823.

103. Vink, Creole Jews, 78.

104. NAN, NPIGS, inv. nr. 7, July 7, 1825.

105. Ibid., inv. nr. 12, July 14, 1825, July 17, 1825, August 30, 1825; J. A. Schiltkamp, "Jewish Jurators in Surinam," in Cohen, ed., The Jewish Nation in Surinam, 57–63.

106. NAN, NPIGS, inv. nr. 12, November 27, 1825.

107. Ibid., February 7, 1825.

108. Ramakers, "Parallel Processes?" 39 (for the Netherlands).

109. NAN, NPIGS, inv. nr. 12, July 7 and July 14, 1825; Van Stipriaan, Surinaams contrast, 297–98 (on Parra).

110. NAN, NPIGS, inv. nr. 12, July 7, 1825.

111. Ibid., September 24, 1826.

112. Ibid., February 7, 1826. For a parallel situation in the fatherland, see Sonnenberg-Stern, Emancipation and Poverty, 51ff.

113. Vink, Creole Jews, 95.

114. NAN, NPIGS, inv. nr. 6, April 11 and 16, 1817.

115. The only earlier conversion case to my knowledge is that of Emanuel Vieira, a Reformed Protestant minister and planter of the Cottica and Pirica rivers. Born to Sara Orobio de Castro, a Jew who was living in Amsterdam in 1730, and Joseph Vieyra, Emanuel Vieira married Catharina Bremart, with whom he raised six Dutch Reformed Protestant children. NAN, SONA, inv. nr. 10, will of Emanuel Vieyra and Catharina Vieira, born Bremaart, June 13, 1730, pp. 133–35; inv. nr. 27, will of Emanuel Vieira and Catharina Bremaart, December 17, 1756, pp. 694–700; inv. nr. 29, will of widow Catharina Bremart [sic], p. 249; Wolbers, Geschiedenis van Suriname, 846. Egbert van Emden, discussed earlier, converted to Christianity in 1847. NAN, NPIGS, inv. nr. 542, October 31, 1892.

116. See NAN, NPIGS, inv. nr. 417, April 2, 1820, p. 33; inv. nr. 10, October 31, 1819. Purdy's husband had converted to Christianity in New York before their departure to Suriname. On Purdy, the granddaughter of a Methodist minister from New York, see Ralph G. Bennett, "The Case of the Part-Time Jew: A Unique Incident in Nineteenth-Century America," American Jewish Archives 46: 1 (1994): 38–61.

117. The concept of "narrative of ascent," originally applied to the genre of autobiography, is from Robert B. Stepto, From Behind the Veil: A Study of Afro-American Narrative (Urbana: University of Illinois Press, 1991 [1979]), 164.

118. Schiltkamp and De Smidt, Plakaten, ordonnantiën en andere wetten, uitgevaardigd in Suriname, 2:879 (#752, February 28, 1775).

119. Ibid., 726 (#597 February 4, 1761). The word appears as balliaren.

120. Teenstra, De negerslaven in de colonie Suriname, 47.

121. Hoefte, "Free Blacks and Coloureds," 117.

122. NAN, NPIGS, inv. nr. 437, Reglement van de gebroederschap 1778, [p. 4].

123. Ben-Ur, "Peripheral Inclusion," 197; NAN, NPIGS, inv. nr. 11, November 20, 1820, p. 13.

124. Vink, *Creole Jews*, 93.

125. NAN, NPIGS, inv. nr. 12, August 30, 1825.

126. Ibid., September 8, 1825.

127. Ibid., September 11 and 12, 1825.

128. Ibid., September 23, 1825.

129. Ibid., January 19, 1826.

130. John Bailey, *The Lost German Slave Girl: The Extraordinary True Story of Sally Miller and Her Fight for Freedom in Old New Orleans* (New York: Atlantic Monthly Press, 2005), 257.

131. Karen Y. Morrison, "Creating an Alternative Kinship: Slavery, Freedom, and Nineteenth-Century Afro-Cuban Hijos Naturales," *Journal of Social History* 41: 1 (Fall 2007): 55–80, 56.

132. Ibid., 60.

133. NAN, NPIGS, inv. nr. 6, June 17, 1818.

134. Kappler, *Zes Jaren in Suriname*, 90 (his observation from the 1850s is also applicable to earlier decades).

135. "Verhaal van een Togtje in Suriname," 183.

136. NAN, NPIGS, inv. nr. 8, June 24, 1783.

137. Ibid., inv. nr. 6, June 17 and 23, 1818.

138. Ibid., December 10, 1818.

139. Ibid., inv. nr. 2, December 31, 1787.

140. Ibid., inv. nr. 11, report by commissioners of Portuguese Jewish community, S(?). J. Bueno de Mesquita, Salomon de la Parra, and Isaac Abendanon, February 16, 1824.

141. Kappler, *Zes Jaren in Suriname*, 90 (for the reference to income-producing cows).

142. NAN, NPIGS, inv. nr. 2, 14 Tisry 5545 [September 29, 1784].

143. Ibid., inv. nr. 6, June 23, 1818.

144. Ibid., inv. nr. 12, November 26, 1828.

145. *Surinaamsche almanak voor het jaar 1820*, 23; *Surinaamsche almanak voor het jaar 1821*, 27.

146. Nassy, *Essai historique*, part 2, 55.

147. *Surinaamsche almanak voor het jaar 1821*, 27; "Verhaal van een Togtje in Suriname," 183.

148. NAN, Microfilms Brieven J. H. Lance, John Henry Lance to Elizabeth Lance, June 6, 1823, p. 125.

149. NAN, NPIGS, inv. nr. 11, December 2, 1821, p. 161.

150. Ibid., inv. nr. 160, entry 45 (scan 52).

151. Ibid., entry 55 (scan 61).

152. Ibid., inv. nr. 481, unaddressed letter by A. B. Bibaz, dated Paramaribo, August 28, 1838.

153. Kappler, *Zes Jaren in Suriname*, 90.

154. RBGK, DC/69/128, F. W. Hostmann to William J. Hooker, October 8, 1842, [p. 1]. The phrase appears as "brick build synagogue."

155. Roos, "Jodesavane of Joodsch Dorp," 392–93, 393.

156. Nassy, *Essai historique*, part 2, 51.

157. NAN, NPIGS, inv. nr. 141, inventory dated August 7, 1827.

158. "Beschrijving van de Joden-Savanah," 287.

159. NAN, NPIGS, inv. nr. 141, inventory dated Jodensavanne, December 12, 1848.

160. *Suriname: Jaarboekje voor het jaar 1856* (The Hague: L. J. Verhoeven, 1856), lix; *Almanak voor de Nederlandsche West-Indische Bezittingen, en de kust van Guinea. Jaargang 1861* (The Hague: De Gebroeders van Cleef, 1860), 52.

161. *Surinaamsche almanak voor het jaar 1821*, 27.

162. "Verhaal van een Togtje in Suriname," 183.

163. David Nassy, *Lettre politico-theologico-morale sur les juifs* (Paramaribo: A. Soulage Jr., 1798), 124.

164. Teenstra, *De negerslaven in de colonie Suriname*, 50.

165. NAN, inv. nr. 539, Lyst der inwoonen die op de Joode Savana woondende, benewens de gemacipeerde die in huur zijnde, zo als dezelve zich bevinden in Primo January 1867.

166. Ibid.; NAN, inv. nr. 539, Op gaaven der Inwooners die op de Joode Savana Woonende, January 10, 1868.

167. NAN, inv. nr. 539, Lyst der Inwooners op de Joode Savana. The census is undated but judging from the names of the census taker and emancipated residents probably also dates to the late 1860s.

168. Winkels, *Publicatien en Verordeningen Betrekkelijk Suriname*, May 23, 1808, unpaginated.

169. NAN, NPIGS, inv. nr. 545, Inventaris van goederen toebehoorende aan de Heer Ah. J. da Costa aan 't comptoir der Gemeente ter bewaaren op de 4 July 1820. His name in this document is spelled "Aaron."

170. See, for example, Philip John Crosskey Dark, *Bush Negro Art: An African Art in the Americas* (London: A. Tiranti, 1954). For remarkably similar wood engravings in West Africa, see Robert Sutherland Rattray, *Religion and Art in Ashanti* (Oxford: Clarendon Press, 1979), illustrations between 272 and 273.

171. Teenstra, *De Landbouw in de Colonie Suriname*, 2:136.

172. Sonnenberg-Stern, *Emancipation and Poverty*, 140–42.

173. Cohen, *Jews in Another Environment*, 145.

174. Goslinga, *The Dutch in the Caribbean and in Surinam*, 712.

175. AJA, MS-505, Box No. 1676, folder 16, decree of Governor Pinson Bonham, May 26, 1814.

Conclusion

1. Edmund S. Morgan, *American Slavery, American Freedom: The Ordeal of Colonial Virginia* (New York: W. W. Norton, 1975).

2. James Ron, *Frontiers and Ghettos: State Violence in Serbia and Israel* (Berkeley: University of California Press, 2003).

3. Mikkel Thorup, *An Intellectual History of Terror: War, Violence and the State* (London: Routledge, 2010), 62.

4. Schalkwijk, *The Colonial State in the Caribbean*, 222.

5. See, for example, Al-Qattan, "Dhimmis in the Muslim Court," 429–44. For contested authority within other Jewish diasporic communities, see Ray, "Contested Community," 11–25.

6. Jack P. Greene, *Negotiated Authorities: Essays in Colonial Political and Constitutional History* (Charlottesville: University Press of Virginia, 1994), 1–24; Roitman, "'A Flock of Wolves Instead of Sheep'" (for Curaçao).

7. Ray, "Contested Community," 16.

8. Flora Cassen, "The Sausage in the Jews' Pantry: Food and Jewish-Christian Relations in Renaissance Italy," in Hasia R. Diner and Simone Cinotto, eds., *Global Jewish Foodways* (Lincoln: University of Nebraska Press, 2018), 28; Shona N. Jackson, *Creole Indigeneity: Between Myth and Nation in the Caribbean* (Minneapolis: University of Minnesota Press, 2012).

9. Wolbers, *Geschiedenis van Suriname*, 442.

10. Marcus, *The Colonial American Jew*, 1:102.

INDEX

ACKNOWLEDGMENTS
_____

The research carried out for this book is the result of visits to twenty archival, rare book, and manuscript repositories located in six countries on three continents, in addition to my earlier on-site research on the four oldest Jewish cemeteries of Suriname and Jodensavanne's Creole cemetery, carried out from 1998 to 2002. I am deeply grateful to the generations of professionals and community members who safeguarded these and other archival depositories and have made them accessible.

I would like to acknowledge the following institutions, which have supported my travel, research, and writing since I commenced this project in 2008: the American Jewish Archives Jacob Rader Marcus Center; the American Jewish Historical Society; Duke University (including the Duke University Center for Jewish Studies and the Duke University Libraries); Hadassah–Brandeis Institute; the Memorial Foundation for Jewish Culture; Netherlands Institute for Advanced Studies in the Humanities and Social Sciences; the National Endowment for the Humanities Summer Seminar for College Instructors: "Roots: African Dimensions of the History and Cultures of the Americas (Through the Trans-Atlantic Slave Trade)," directed by Joseph C. Miller; the American Council of Learned Societies for an ACLS/SSRC/NEH International and Area Studies Fellowship; and the National Endowment for the Humanities (award ID number FA-58162–15). Any views, findings, conclusions, or recommendations expressed in this publication do not necessarily reflect those of the National Endowment for the Humanities. A publication subvention was provided by the Office of the Vice Chancellor for Research and Engagement, University of Massachusetts Amherst. Over the years the university also provided multiple research, microfilm, and salary supplementation grants through its Center for Teaching, College of Humanities and Fine Arts, and Office of the Provost. The university's Interlibrary Loan and Document Delivery fulfilled a steady stream of source requests, always promptly and cordially. Chapter 6 is a revised version of "Purim in the Public Eye: Leisure, Violence, and Cultural Convergence in the Dutch Atlantic," *Jewish Social Studies* 20: 1 (Fall 2014): 32–76, and is published with permission of the journal and Indiana University Press.

I am grateful to the following colleagues and communal leaders: Chaim Adelman, Adriana Van Alen-Koenraadt, Cátia Antunes, Daniel Chard, Julie-Marthe Cohen, the late Ena Dankmeijer-Maduro, Natalie Zemon Davis, Philip Dikland, Aaron Fogleman, Stephen Fokké, Rachel Frankel, Jane S. Gerber, Jane Gomes-Casseres, Ron Gomes-Casseres, Esther van Haaren-Hart, Norma Baumel Joseph, Marjoleine Kars, Wim Klooster, the late Joseph C. Miller, Gert Oostindie, Mark Ponte, James C. Robertson, Guido Robles, Jessica Vance Roitman, Jonathan L. Roses, Lorraine E. Roses, Jonathan D. Sarna, Gary Schiff, Marlou Schrover, Susan Shapiro, Harrold Sijlbing, Michael Studemund-Halévi, Wieke Vink, Jean Jacques Vrij, James E. Young, and Gary Zola.

I am obliged to thank the two originally anonymous reviewers of the manuscript, who turned out to be Trevor Burnard and Karwan Fatah-Black, for their comments and corrections. In addition, there are a number of individuals at the University of Pennsylvania Press I would like to recognize: Zoe Kovacs and Erica Ginsburg for their editorial work; cartographer Paul Dangel for the custom-designed maps; and Robert Lockhart and Peter Cooper Mancall for their interest in my work and for their patience.